THE AGE OF GLOBAL POWER:
THE UNITED STATES SINCE 1939

AMERICAN REPUBLIC SERIES

EDITED BY DON E. FEHRENBACHER

THE AGE OF GLOBAL POWER: THE UNITED STATES SINCE 1939

NORMAN A. GRAEBNER
University of Virginia

John Wiley & Sons

NEW YORK ● CHICHESTER ● BRISBANE ● TORONTO

Library of Congress Cataloging in Publication Data:

Graebner, Norman A.
The age of global power.

(American Republic series)
Bibliography: p.
Includes index.
1. United States—Foreign relations—1945-   2. United States—Foreign
relations—1933-1945.   3. United States—History—1945-   4.
United States—History—1933-1945.   I. Title.

E744.G68   973.9   78-12294
ISBN 0-471-32082-X

Printed in the United States of America

10 9 8 7 6 5 4 3 2 1

To Emily

Editor's Preface

"Is contemporary history real history?" H. Stuart Hughes
asked and answered this question in an essay published fifteen
years ago.* It has often been argued that the very recent past is
not a fit subject for professional historians because many of the
documents are unavailable, because one's perspective is too
short, and because a person writing about events in his or her
own time cannot achieve a proper degree of detachment. Yet
there was more complete documentation of the Watergate affair
within five years of its occurrence than there can ever be for
most historical events. As for perspective, it is not an unmixed
blessing; hindsight tends both to clarify and to distort the
meaning of the past. And even if one were to accept the
questionable view that the quality of historical writing depends
preeminently on its freedom from bias, there is no guarantee
that objectivity will increase with the passage of time. In any
case, as Hughes remarks, contemporary history is bound to be
written by *somebody* because of the great popular interest in it,
and professional historians are probably better suited than most
other persons to overcome the disadvantages inherent in the
enterprise.

American history since 1939 is often very difficult to separate
from the history of the rest of the world. In *The Age of Global
Power,* Norman A. Graebner's primary theme is the sudden
emergence and lengthening ordeal of the United States as a
superpower, but he also gives due attention to four decades of
domestic history from the wartime presidency of Franklin
Roosevelt to the early years of the Carter administration. His
book is an unusual achievement in the ordering and
compressing of an enormous amount of historical information
into a brief and readable narrative that is frequently illuminated

*H. Stuart Hughes, *History as Art and As Science: Twin Vistas on the Past* (New York, 1964), pp. 89-107.

with critical comment. It is one of the volumes in the Wiley "American Republic Series," a joint effort at exploring the meaning of the past to the present.

Don E. Fehrenbacher

Preface

Both diplomatically and economically Pearl Harbor propelled the United States into an era of unprecedented power and influence. For most Americans in December 1941, that future was not apparent. Nothing in the nation's experience of the 1930s presaged the destruction of its established relationships with the external world. Together the isolationism and utopian internationalism that guided American thought and action seemed to assure the country's peace and commerce with a minimum of military obligation. Yet even before Pearl Harbor, as this book's opening chapter demonstrates, analysts observed that a war that eliminated Germany from the core of world politics would elevate Russia in the global order of power and thereby damage the European balance irreparably. Similarly, some noted, a war in the Pacific would uproot Europe's Asian empires and bring American power permanently into the western Pacific, if not into Southeast Asia. During four years of war the Allies resolved the immediate challenge of the Axis; predictably, they destroyed the European-centered international system. Through three centuries Britain, as the manager of Europe's power balance, had successfully countered every aspirant to monopoly on the continent. If Russia's advance to proponderance in Europe had merely followed a British retreat, the United States might have remained a third party, free to define its interests amid the changing structure of imperial power . But the Soviet Union, moving into a vast, war-created power vacuum, threatened the traditional distribution of power so fundamentally that the United States and its western Allies responded with the determination to counter the spread of Soviet influence in Europe and elsewhere.

America's postwar effort to preserve what it could of the Versailles Treaty's essential provisions—its Eastern European settlement and its affirmation of Western leadership in world affairs—quickly cast the country into its new role of global power. In part the motivation in American expansion was economic, in part strategic. The nation's immediate postwar endeavor, with foundations well laid in wartime conferences, sought to encourage postwar economic development with currency stabilization and the extension of trade and investment through international agencies such as the International Monetary Fund, the World Bank, and the General Agreement on Trade and Tariffs. These international instruments received reinforcement from the Truman Doctrine, the Marshall Plan, the Technical Assistance Program, and a variety of regional and bilateral economic arrangements. Despite the American responsibility for financing and managing much of the world's postwar reconstruction, the effort in no measure exceeded the interests and capabilities of the United States. In the process the new agreements brought Germany, Japan, and England into the American system. The free-trade empire culminated in the Trade Expansion Act of 1962 and the subsequent rounds of tariff reductions. The most conspicuous elements in the expansion of American trade and investment were the United States-based multinational corporations.

Unfortunately the nation's global defense strategy proved to be far more costly and troublesome, ultimately exceeding both the interests and the capabilities of the United States. Before midcentury Americans agreed overwhelmingly that Russia endangered Western security, but they could never agree on the precise nature of the threat. Soviet totalitarianism, repression, and ideological crusading were neither proof of Russian expansionism nor necessarily a workable guide for Western policies. As early as the Truman Doctrine in 1947, American leaders ceased to define the Soviet challenge solely in terms of Russian power and defiance of Western principles in Europe's reconstruction; more and more they designated the enemy as Communist expansion, a term that generated fear by emphasizing Soviet ideology, but one that clouded understanding. The Communist-led civil war in Indochina and the Communist victory in China, added to the assumption of a Sino-Soviet complex across Eurasia, prompted successive Washington administrations to extend American power into the East Asian and Middle Eastern periphery of Russia and China. Behind the continued military expansion were direct Communist threats to Turkey, Iran, Taiwan, and the Chinese offshore islands; the apparent association of revolutionary states such as North Korea and North Vietnam with Russia and China; and, finally, the general breakdown of authority in much of Asia and Africa that, to official Washington, seemed uniquely exploitable by Communist agents. The ease whereby the United States gained its early postwar objectives created the illusion that its new global posture reflected a permanent arrangement of power in the world. What contributed to the illusion of effective power was the wartime destruction of the European and Japanese imperial structures, which had established the boundaries of traditional U.S. influence. Facing few restraints, the country moved beyond its natural limits.

It required no more than a war in Vietnam to break the ascendancy of the three controlling elements in the expansion of the American role—the imperial presidency, the military and bureaucratic directorship of the country's global defenses, and the scientific, economic, and political elite, whose support and expertise were essential to the imperial effort. The price of that war in death and destruction, in fueling inflation, and in undermining the government's credibility outran every calculation of national interest. The new Nixon-Kissinger strategy, recognizing the limits of American power, interest, and genuine intent, reversed the earlier concentration on the periphery and sought instead to improve the Great Power relationships. The diplomatic recovery of China eliminated anticommunism as the foundation of policy. By the 1970s the world had returned to its historical pluralism in power and purpose. Political divisions, competing goals, and economic restrictions weakened the unity of the trading nations. Conflicting nationalisms and traditional ambitions terminated whatever unity existed in the Communist world. The lesser states of Asia and Africa moved in directions that had no relationship to ideology or the Cold War. Through a long generation of unprecedented international stability, the American people discovered that the long pursuit of the lost world of Versailles was both futile and unnecessary. The search for détente was largely an attempt to achieve a more reasonable balance between the costs and the benefits of a global strategy. Whatever its limited success, détente expressed an American conviction that the political and military revolution wrought by Hitler's defeat had become a permanent feature of international life.

Domestically, World War II demonstrated the ease whereby heavy federal spending and deficit financing could eliminate the remaining vestiges of the Great Depression and create almost four decades of soaring prosperity—at least for most Americans. This volume attempts to isolate the factors that underlay the prosperity; to describe the many-faceted nature of the country's economic growth—the application of science and technology, the mixed economy, the momentum in business and educational expansion, and the effective use of fiscal and monetary devices; and to explain why the increase in production and consumption eventually took its toll in inflation and a sinking dollar. Measured by income statistics, the country's economic record was astonishing. Never had so many citizens reached a state of affluence. Even those of average income who could scarcely pay their bills lived in better houses and apartments, ate a wider variety of food, and had access to more time-saving appliances and gadgets than had their far less numerous counterparts in previous generations. Despite the steady postwar inflation, median family income (in 1968 dollars) rose from $4200 in 1947 to over $7400 in 1968. Those with incomes below $3000 a year dropped from 34 percent in 1947 to 19 percent in 1968, while those with incomes above $10,000 a year increased from 9 percent in 1947 to 33 percent in 1968.

Somehow the country's unprecedented prosperity failed to touch the traditional inequalities in economic status. The share of income received by American families at different levels of income changed imperceptibly. The lowest fifth received 4 percent of the total money income in both 1947 and 1968. Throughout that 20-year period, the bottom 40 percent received 15 percent of the total personal and family income; the top 20 percent received almost half of the total in both 1947 and 1968. Family status greatly determined educational attainment, occupation, income, and housing. The degree of economic inequality among brothers and sisters was considerably less than that among Americans generally. Gifts and bequests, on the average, accounted for half or more of the net worth of wealthy men and for almost all of the net worth of wealthy women. The persistent inequality of wealth in the United States rested on the power of the rich to transfer their accumulations from generation to generation. The billions spent on welfare and other forms of transfer payments merely permitted the poor to hold their own in the scramble for the fortunes that the country produced.

Inflation, the pervading economic problem of the 1970s, was made in Vietnam, the product of the Johnson administration's decision to fight the war without paying for it. What sustained the inflation thereafter was the growth of public and private indebtedness in the United States, encouraged by the fiscal and monetary policies of the federal government, and the noncompetitive character of the country's major producers. This permitted them to pass all of their costs and inefficiencies to consumers in the form of higher prices. The personal indebtedness that nurtured the inflationary economy reached $1.4 trillion in 1978. The critical payments deficits after 1975 were continuing evidence of the disinclination of the American people to live within their international means, particularly in terms of energy consumption, and the decline of the country's competitive position. The rush for gold, driving the price in mid-1978 to over $200 an ounce, while the value of the dollar dropped below 200 Japanese yen, reflected the parlous state of the American economy, the lack of economic discipline in the United States, and the erosion of worldwide confidence in the ability of the country to control its inflation.

Another domestic concern of this book is the ebb and flow of political power in the United States from the presidency of Franklin D. Roosevelt to that of Jimmy Carter. More important, the book recognizes and seeks to account for the gradual decline of governmental performance in the postwar era. It places emphasis on the presidential elections that seemed to matter in establishing the direction of national life—those of 1948, 1952, 1960, 1968, and 1976. Actually, the election of new personalities, the formation of new administrations, had little effect on the nation's experience, because the voting public had little influence on the basic decisions of government. American society was managed by an establishment of governmental, business, labor, military, and media leaders that determined the country's political and economic decisions. Its credit-induced prosperity contributed much to the welfare of the middle and upper classes, but relatively little to the cities and the poor. Newspapers and magazines confronted the evidences of trouble in America without equivocation. Yet throughout the postwar era, the country continued to tolerate highly visible levels of crime and domestic insecurity, racial tension and unemployment, poverty and even hunger, ghettos and slums, pollution and urban decay, use of hard drugs, public and private corruption, inequitable taxes and waste, and inflation and soft currency. Successive administrations, it seemed, had simply given up on the domestic front.

Analysts noted that the public that elected the President and Congress possessed no agency for determining governmental behavior. Whatever control earlier presidents exerted over Congress in behalf of the public rested mainly on party discipline. But the burgeoning complexity of postwar America eliminated whatever public consensus and party cohesion still remained. Having lost faith in the beneficence of federal programs, Americans—even the intellectuals—could no longer agree on the proper approach to civil rights; to questions of equal housing, equal neighborhoods, or equal access to income and employment; to solutions for poverty, unemployment, inflation, and a myriad of other economic and social disabilities. Political behavior simply reflected the Balkanization of American society. With the shifting emphasis of the media from the important to the interesting, politicians conducted polls about their images and resisted identification with issues that, at best, would command only minority support. What mattered in winning was not the voting records of members of Congress, but their style. Were they friendly, energetic, and accessible? Did they answer their mail and fill the requests of their constituents? Against such considerations party labels and political philosophy receded into insignificance. Owing little to parties and presidents for their success, members of Congress achieved a degree of independence that rendered the President more subject to challenge than at any time in the present century.

Congressional freedom from White House and party restraints encouraged the proliferation of lobbying activities in Washington. So vulnerable was Congress to lobby pressure that more than 500 corporations operated lobbies in the nation's capital. About 1500 national trade and professional associations established headquarters in Washington, where they could influence legislation that concerned them. Senator Abraham Ribicoff, chairman of the Government Affairs Commitee, observed in mid-1978 that "lobbying has reached a new dimension and is more effective than ever in history. It has become a big computerized operation in which the Congress and the public are being bombarded by single-issue groups." In legislative measures that disposed of more than $500 billion a year, a single clause, noted one lobbyist, could be worth 100 lifetime salaries. Lobbyists generally sought to identify the special interests of their clients with the national good. In dispensing information around Washington, they did, on occasion, serve the public by informing members of Congress of the possible consequences of contemplated action, but their essential concerns remained private. Against the power and resources of congressional lobbies the unorganized public, badly divided on every major issue and lacking the means for political expression, had no chance. One Carter legislative aide complained, "It's practically impossible to put together a coalition for something anymore." The perennial inflation of the world's most powerful economy, added to the declining value of the dollar in foreign exchange markets, measured the difficulties of government in serving the public interest. Such disabilities of government, the consequence of conflicting interests in American society, did not exceed the possibilities of leadership to direct the nation toward a greater unity of purpose.

In the preparation of this book I have accumulated the customary number of obligations to others. My wife and family shared the burden of the effort by forgoing mobility and travel during almost two years of weekends and vacation periods. Again I have benefited from the cooperation and helpfulness of many librarians. My students through the years have compelled me to re-examine my conclusions on all questions of recent U.S. foreign relations. Wayne Anderson and his associates at John Wiley & Sons have been patient and encouraging. I appreciate especially the publisher's decision to allow me to exceed the length originally established for volumes in the American Republic Series. The past 40 years have added immeasurably to the complexity of the country's experience. Don E. Fehrenbacher, the series editor, has improved the book with his perceptive notations on style. Finally, I am much indebted to Gary W. Reichard of Ohio State University, who read the first complete draft of this book at the request of the publisher. His numerous suggestions, most pointing to significant omissions, had a major influence on the book's eventual inclusions. For the volume's multiplicity of facts and judgments I alone assume responsibility.

Charlottesville, Virginia   *Norman A. Graebner*
August 1978

Contents

THE AGE OF GLOBAL POWER:
THE UNITED STATES SINCE 1939

Chapter I

The Challenges of Global War

EUROPE ADRIFT

Shortly before three on the morning of September 1, 1939, Ambassador William C. Bullitt's call from Paris reached President Franklin D. Roosevelt. "Tony Biddle has just got through from Warsaw, Mr. President," the ambassador explained. "Several German divisions are deep in Polish territory, and fighting is heavy. Tony said there were reports of bombers all over the city. Then he was cut off. . . . " Roosevelt responded in a mood of resignation. "Well, Bill, it's come at last." Bullitt's disquieting report caught few in Washington by surprise. Europe had been moving inextricably toward war since the Munich crisis of September 1938, when Adolf Hitler made clear his determination to tear up the Versailles provisions for Eastern Europe, by force if necessary. Czechoslovakia, deserted by the Western powers, had fallen without a struggle in March 1939. Poland's resistance to Germany's subsequent demands could not save that country, but it compelled Hitler, if he would impose his will on Warsaw, to employ force openly and thereby court the risk of a wider conflict. The British and French declarations of war is early September 1939 set the stage for the second global struggle in a generation.

Hitler's overt aggression confronted the United States with its greatest external challenge of the century. However, the country

1

entered the crisis of 1939 with neither a body of tradition nor a definable public consensus to guide it. Scarcely a generation earlier —in the Great War of 1914-1918—the United States, England, and France defeated Germany to create the European order that Hitler now threatened with destruction. That order of power, embodied in the Versailles Treaty of 1919, reflected in large measure the decisive American contribution to the Allied victory. Nothing less than the continued presence of American power in Europe would guarantee that continent's postwar stability, because President Woodrow Wilson failed at Versailles to create a reliable substitute for force in international affairs. Indeed, Allied leaders at the conference placed less faith for a peaceful future in Wilson's effort to institutionalize the peace through democratic and judicial procedures than in the remarkable capacity of the United States to wage total war. For France and Britain especially what mattered was not the League of Nations, but a perpetual U.S. commitment to the territorial and military provisions of the Versailles Treaty itself. Neither Europe nor the United States had escaped its historic concern for the European balance of power. Thus sound American policy, in the future as in the past, would define and protect a wide variety of specific historical and geographic interests abroad in competition with nations that would pursue traditional interests of their own by whatever means they believed effective.

Unfortunately, Wilson's concepts and personality so dominated the American scene that they drove the nation's policies toward the very extremes against which recent experience had warned. Isolationism—one powerful reaction to both the country's wartime involvement and the conviction that the prodigious effort had achieved little—denied the importance to American security of political and military events outside the Western Hemisphere. Isolationists never denied that U.S. economic interests were global; they assumed simply that such interests need not involve the country in war. For them the real danger to peace lay in political or military commitments that might circumscribe the nation's freedom of action. Postwar internationalism, as embodied in the Wilsonian purpose of protecting all peoples from the irrational and oppressive use of power, was as oblivious to political reality as was isolationism. Both denied that the United States need be concerned with any specific political or military configuration in Europe or Asia. If isolationists preached that affairs outside the hemisphere were strategically inconsequential, internationalists insisted not only that they mattered, but also that the United States, in its role as world leader, could not renounce its responsibilities for world order. In practice, however, the internationalists of the 1920s proposed to control world affairs, not with diplomacy or force, but by confronting aggressors with a combination of international law, signed agreements, and world opinion. Every program fostered by American internationalists throughout the 1920s—membership in the League of Nations and the World Court, the resort to arbitration and conciliation, collective security, naval limitation, or the outlawry of war—was a further effort to institutionalize the peace and a denial of the need for any precise definition of either the ends or the means of national policy. In the hands of the internationalists, the concept of peace and peaceful change became the bulwark of the established order.

Together American isolationists and internationalists, after 1920, decreed that the United States would withdraw all American forces from Europe and, following their final rejection of the Versailles Treaty, all responsibility for Europe's future. What sustained the Versailles structure after 1919 was the presence of British and French forces in Europe and the apparent willingness of all European governments to abide by the treaty's provisions. But England and France, the only real guarantors of the treaty, disagreed on every essential aspect of the postwar settlement: the role of Germany in European affairs, the levels of Allied military power required to sustain the Versailles impositions on Germany, and the necessary commitment to the independence and health of the new Slavic states of Eastern Europe—the keystone of the Versailles structure. The Allies had defeated Germany in 1918; they had not broken Germany's potential as Europe's leading military power. Russia, rendered momentarily chaotic by revolution, would soon, under Stalin's leadership, develop the productivity and the design to become a major world power. Long before Roosevelt entered the White House in March 1933, both Germany and Russia had made clear, in their mutual rejection of the Eastern European settlement, that they would tear the pivotal agreements reached at Versailles to shreds if they ever discovered the occasion for doing so. From the beginning, Europe's postwar stability lacked one essential element—a mutual interest in its perpetuation among the world's major powers.

Thus the peace of the 1920s rested essentially on the weakness of those nations whose governments had demonstrated their dissatisfaction with the Versailles settlement. Any collapse of the Western monopoly of power would witness the almost immediate return of force to international life. Within a decade after their priceless victory created the world of their choice, the great democracies, by refusing to defend their system with the same power that created it, had cast the international order adrift. Their faltering efforts of the 1930s would not rescue it. The reliance on moral sanctions would demonstrate again and again the hopelessness of any system that placed its preferences for peace on institutions such as the League of Nations or the World Court, on self-denying treaties such as the Kellogg-Briand Peace Act of 1928, or on world opinion. Roosevelt's easy victory of 1932 turned on domestic issues; not once did he challenge the assumptions and purposes that guided the Republican foreign policies of the 1920s.

ISOLATIONISM, INTERNATIONALISM, AND REVISIONISM

Hitler initiated his assault on the key military and territorial provisions of the Versailles Treaty in March 1935, when he successfully eliminated the Versailles restrictions on the German army and air force. With no country committed to the active defense of Europe's treaty arrangements, Hitler decreed that Germany would have universal military service and a peacetime army of 36 divisions, or approximately 550,000 men. On Sunday, March 17, German officials celebrated their Memorial Day with special ceremonies at the State Opera House. "Ostensibly," wrote journalist William L. Shirer, "this was a ceremony to honor Germany's war dead. It turned out to be a jubilant celebration of the death of Versailles and the rebirth of the conscript German army." One year later, in March 1936, German forces occupied the Rhineland in open defiance of the Versailles Treaty. Facing no response from

London, Paris, or Washington, Hitler now contemplated the total destruction of the Versailles order. If Germany wanted peace, Germany was no longer a peaceful country. Amid the growing crisis, congressional isolationists accepted primary responsibility for guarding the nation against costly European ventures.

Accepting the devil theory of war—that industrialists and financiers had pushed the United States into the Great War to protect their trade and investments—isolationists achieved their greatest triumph against the danger of another European involvement with the passage of the Neutrality Act of 1935. A year earlier Helmuth C. Engelbrecht, a journalist, gave these liberal isolationist charges special significance by publishing a book suggestively entitled *Merchants of Death*. The Senate responded by establishing a blue-ribbon investigating committee under the chairmanship of North Dakota's isolationist and anti-Wall Street Senator, Gerald P. Nye. Nye's committee, through long and careful interrogation, unveiled the effective lobbying, the sordid business practices, and the wartime profiteering of American industrialists. Nye did not prove that Wall Street bankers and munitions makers had single-handedly carried the country into war or had influenced Wilson more than had the German submarine. But in the atmosphere of 1935 such distinctions were lost on millions of Americans whose conviction that the United States could avoid European wars compelled them to attribute Wilson's decision to the influence of wartime profiteers. The Nye Committee's report stressed the incompatibility between neutrality and uncontrolled wartime shipping and investment. Nye's conclusions read in part: "Loans to belligerents militate against neutrality, for when only one group of belligerents can purchase and transport commodities the loans act in favor of that belligerent. They are especially unneutral when used to convert this country into an auxiliary arsenal for that belligerent who happens to control the seas, for that arsenal then becomes the subject of the military strategy of the other belligerent."

Early in April 1935, Nye introduced a set of resolutions into the Senate that promised to keep the United States out of the next European war. An impartial arms embargo, with restrictions on wartime loans to belligerents, he believed, would eliminate those precise pressures that had undermined American neutrality in the days of Wilson. Congress passed the Neutrality Act in August, compelling the President, when he acknowledged a state of war, to ban the export of arms and credit to all belligerents and to warn Americans traveling on the vessels of warring nations that they did so at their own risk. Roosevelt signed the law despite his misgivings that it might, to the country's detriment, restrict presidential action in some future crisis. Neither the Congress nor the executive, he declared, could anticipate the behavior of foreign powers. But Roosevelt had no desire to challenge American isolationist sentiment. On October 2, 1935, at the San Diego Exposition, he promised the American people that whatever "happens in continents overseas, the United States of America shall and must remain, as long ago the Father of Our Country prayed it might remain, unentangled and free." Congress passed the second neutrality law in February 1936, again rejecting the President's request for a more flexible embargo.

As isolationism reached high tide, Congress moved to perfect the neutrality legislation. The earlier measures had avoided the issue of noncontraband trade in time of war—a trade that American shippers hoped to maintain despite its obvious defiance of American neutrality. Roosevelt, moreover, still favored a more flexible embargo program that would permit him to distinguish between aggressors and their victims. The Neutrality Act of May 1937, partially mandatory and partially discriminatory, gave the President greater freedom in determining the outflow of American goods to belligerents. The established prohibitions on the export of arms, ammunition, or implements of war to any belligerent and the purchase, sale, or exchange of bonds and other securities of any nation named in a presidential proclamation of neutrality still held. But the prohibitions against the solicitation of funds in the United States did not apply to medical aid, food, or clothing to relieve human suffering when the soliciting agent was not itself a belligerent. The 1937 law again banned American trade on belligerent passenger and merchant vessels. The President could, at his discretion, remove belligerent submarines and armed merchant vessels from the ports and territorial waters of the United States. Finally, the new act embodied the right of discretion toward belligerents by permitting the sale of arms to nations at war (ostensibly the Western democracies) on a *cash-and-carry* arrangement. Congress had apparently discovered a formula that would guarantee both commercial profits and the avoidance of war. The cash-and-carry provision expired in the summer of 1939 when Congress failed to renew it.

What separated Americans in their response to the Nazi challenge was not their desire to avoid war, but their varying perceptions of the price that peace would require. Isolationists, in general, could discover no effective defense of American interests in international law, neutral rights, or the treaty structure; they assumed that peace would require its price in diminished trade and a changing international order. Many agreed that Versailles had imposed unfair restrictions on Germany; the democracies, therefore, could serve their interests more effectively through treaty revision than through moral sanctions against Germany, which would save neither the treaty nor the peace. Nye insisted that the American people would not "consciously endorse a war which had no other object than to maintain the particular status quo which was established at Versailles." Nye insisted that isolationists were realists who believed that U.S. policies should reflect "an honest measure of the gains and losses to us and to other peoples of each practical measure suggested." Convinced that the United States was safe from European attack, isolationists after 1935 voted overwhelmingly for all military appropriations in their desire to strengthen the country's hemispheric defenses. Such preparedness would keep order in the Western Hemisphere. There the country could flourish without regard to what happened in the outside world.

Internationalists who dominated the Roosevelt administration shared the Wilsonian belief that the breakdown of peace anywhere endangered the peace everywhere. For that reason they insisted that U.S. security required the diplomatic rejection of every assault on the world's treaty structure. Roosevelt and his Secretary of State, Cordell Hull, searched for a formula that would convey the administration's deep concern for Europe's stability but still permit the country to escape all responsibility for its preservation. Hull quickly perfected a uniquely American tactic for upholding the status quo (without any direct commitment to it) by urging aggressors to follow the treaty-abiding example of the United States.

Thus, when Hitler announced the German resumption of military conscription in March 1935, the Secretary informed a press conference: "Everybody knows that the United States has always believed that treaties must constitute the foundation on which any stable peace structure must rest. . . . I believe that the moral influence of the United States and its people must always encourage living up to treaties." Hull reminded the German ambassador late in March that Germany had an almost unprecedented opportunity to create conditions of peace and security in Europe by honoring its international agreements. Unfortunately, the fact that the United States abided by treaties that served its interests hardly provided a guide to those leaders who found their treaty arrangements restrictive or otherwise obnoxious.

At a secret strategy conference on November 5, 1937, Hitler unfolded his plans to incorporate all German-speaking people into the German Reich and thereby strike the crucial territorial provisions of the Versailles settlement. For three years German war production had outstripped that of France and England, giving Germany an immediate military and psychological advantage over the two democracies. Hitler assured his chief advisers that both London and Paris had written off Austria and Czechoslovakia. Ready to gamble Germany's future for high stakes, Hitler stripped his ministry and officer corps of their cautious elements and, by January 1938, was prepared to test the commitment of Britain, France, and the United States to the settlement that their power had wrought in 1918. Ambassador Hans Heinrich Dieckhoff informed Washington early in February that the personnel changes in the German Foreign Office would not affect German policy. But when Austrian Chancellor Kurt von Schuschnigg resisted Hitler's effort to annex Austria's German population through peaceful agreement, Hitler ordered an invasion, and on March 12, announced the absorption of Austria into the German Reich. Hull responded to the Austrian *anschluss* with a characteristic appeal to principle. "It is our profound conviction," he wrote, "that the most effective contribution which we, as a nation sincerely devoted to peace, can make . . . is to have this country respected throughout the world for integrity, justice, good-will, strength, and unswerving loyalty to principles."

Both Hitler's seizure of the Sudetenland following the Munich agreement of September 1938 and his annexation of Czechoslovakia in March 1939 disturbed Roosevelt deeply. Yet, even as the crisis became more profound, Roosevelt asked only that German behavior conform to the principle of peaceful change. In his famed Quarantine Speech of October 1937, the President condemned aggressors, not because they wanted what they did not have, but because they chose to employ force to achieve it. He reminded Hitler on April 14, 1939 that Germany, by rejecting American appeals that it settle its external disagreements through peaceful means, had placed Europe on the road to war. Time was running out. "Plainly," he wrote, "the world is moving toward the moment when the situation must end in catastrophe unless a more rational way of guiding events is found." Roosevelt, committed both the American noninvolvement and to the European status quo, could satisfy the requirements of U.S. policy only if he could bind German policy to American principles. American leaders assumed that in a rational environment the highest interests of nations would automatically converge on the question of peace. As Hull expressed it in 1936, "We conceive modern civilization to be incompatible with war." But if nations would avoid war, they had no choice but to accept the limits imposed on them by the world's treaty structure. It was logical, therefore, that Roosevelt and Hull would direct their major diplomatic effort toward the goal of impressing on all governments their obligations to honor their international agreements.

Tragically, the status quo that Hull and Roosevelt sought to preserve did not serve the interests of all countries equally. Hull's approach to the problem of conflict, designed to eliminate all but the most insignificant change in the Versailles order, served the interests of the United States quite as admirably as the destruction of that order would serve the interests of other, less satisfied, countries. Hull's rigid approach based world politics not on the rights conveyed by strength and efficiency, but on the rights of possession. This would-be utopia, like all those that become institutionalized, became the bulwark of an unchanging order. National leaders no less than students of international relations defined proper American policies not in terms of the world that existed, but in terms of the world that they thought *should* exist—one that could, through abstract principles, resolve the conflicting purposes between the satisfied and dissatisfied powers peacefully and without change. Charles A. Lindbergh noted the fundamental error in such behavior with considerable accuracy in a national radio address of September 1939: "Arbitrary boundaries can be maintained only by strength of arms. The Treaty of Versailles either had to be reversed as time passed, or England and France, to be successful, had to keep Germany weak by force. Neither policy was followed. . . . As a result, another war had begun."

EUROPEAN WAR AND THE DECLINE OF ISOLATIONISM

When the Nazis invaded Poland, Roosevelt informed Germany and the world that the United States would not remain emotionally isolated from the European war. On September 3, 1939, he addressed the American people: "This nation will remain a neutral nation, but I cannot ask that every American remain neutral in thought as well. . . . Even a neutral cannot be asked to close his mind or his conscience." At the same time the President assured American isolationists that as long as he had the power to prevent it, there would be "no blackout of peace in the United States." For Roosevelt German aggression comprised a mortal threat to both the nation's security and its way of life. Determined to prevent a Nazi conquest of Europe, Roosevelt would be guided relentlessly by the needs of those nations fighting Germany. It was, finally, Roosevelt's refusal to risk a British defeat that drove him toward an ever-increasing involvement in the European war. What varied after September 1939 was simply the demands that continued Allied resistance would inflict on U.S. leadership and resources. From the beginning the President placed the country's isolationist hopes on the altar of his preference for an Allied victory.

Before Roosevelt could aid those fighting Germany, he required the elimination of those restrictions on the sale of munitions imposed on him by the neutrality legislation. Isolationists that fall battled Roosevelt's move to open cash-and-carry arms trade with the belligerents, especially with England and France, because such trade would destroy their carefully built program to defend the country against a repetition of what occurred between 1914 and 1917 when President Wilson insisted on the right of American vessels, citizens, and war materiel to enter the European war zone. But they lost, because Roosevelt argued effectively that the increased flow of U.S. aid to England and France would be the best assurance against this country's involvement in the European conflict. "I give to you my deep and unalterable conviction, based on years of experience as a worker in the field of international peace," he assured Congress, "that by the repeal of the embargo the United States will more probably remain at peace than if the law remains as it stands today." Following six weeks of bitter debate and repeated warnings that open American support for England would terminate again with U.S. forces dying in Europe, Congress, with wide majorities, adopted the President's formula for victory and noninvolvement. As long as Hitler withheld his full power from western Europe, the deep contradictions in American policy were scarcely apparent.

For some months after the Nazi conquest of Poland the *Wehrmacht* remained inactive while the German military command prepared for a massive advance into western Europe. Suddenly, in April 1940, German forces struck Denmark and Norway. Then, on May 10, Hitler launched a dazzling *blitzkrieg* against Holland and Belgium, spearheaded by his magnificently equipped Panzer divisions. As Hitler now prepared to send his vaunted power into France, Benito Mussolini, leader of Fascist Italy, announced his intention to bring his country into the war on the side of Germany. Early in June six Panzer divisions invaded France through the Ardennes west of the famed Maginot Line of French fortifications, quickly reached the open plains of northern France, and rolled forward toward Paris at the rate of 60 miles a day. In part the French military collapse reflected the growing despair and decay within the French government itself, in part the traditionalism of the French army and the previous decision to send the prime French divisions into Belgium and Holland. France was on its knees when, on June 10, Mussolini entered the war. The French government declared Paris an open city and fled to the south. Amid the French disasters British Prime Minister Winston Churchill informed Roosevelt that a "declaration that the United States will if necessary enter the war might save France." If the United States failed to act, Britain would stand alone.

On June 10, 1940, the distraught President addressed the graduating class of the University of Virginia at Charlottesville. He threw down the gauntlet to the noninterventionists. "Some indeed still hold," he declared, "to the now somewhat obvious delusion that we . . . can safely permit the United States to become . . . a lone island in a world dominated by the philosophy of force. . . . Such an island represents to me and to the overwhelming majority of Americans . . . the helpless nightmare of a people without freedom; yes, the nightmare of a people lodged in prison, handcuffed, hungry, and fed through the bars from day to day by the contemptuous, unpitying masters of other continents." To those who opposed these forces, Roosevelt warned his detractors, the United States would extend its material resources, converting them into equipment and training equal to the emergency. Still the President could not commit the United States to action in Europe. On June 13 he reminded French Premier Paul Reynaud that he did not possess the power to save France. He would, he repeated, make available to Allied governments fighting Hitler what U.S. industry could produce—airplanes, artillery, and munitions—but no manpower, since Congress alone could declare war.

Despite England's heroic resistance during the summer and autumn of 1940, German's total dominance of western Europe made it clear that only greater American support would save Britain from a slow and painful collapse. Roosevelt was determined to sustain the British people by whatever action his presidential power permitted. In September Roosevelt, at Churchill's request, transferred 50 overage U.S. destroyers to England for long-term leases to British naval bases in Newfoundland, Bermuda, and the British West Indies. To encourage such interventionism, a group of prominent Americans, led by popular Republican editor William Allen White, organized, in April 1940, the Committee to Defend America by Aiding the Allies. Leading isolationists, Republican and Democratic, prepared for their final showdown with Roosevelt by organizing the America First Committee in September 1940. Eventually America First captured the support of isolationists generally, but it began as a conservative anti-New Deal movement, characterized in outlook by its chairman, General Robert E. Wood of Sears Roebuck,. The committee advocated a fortress America approach to war. It favored an impregnable Western Hemispheric defense that would permit the American people to ignore the progress of German arms. This program, committee spokesmen argued, would protect the United States from the dangers of totalitarianism both at home and abroad.

During 1940 Roosevelt and Churchill entered their wartime relationship as profound realists who understood both the possibilities and the limitations of their collaboration. In his desire to maximize U.S. aid to Britain, Churchill recognized the special restraints that isolationism imposed on the President. He wheedled and charmed Roosevelt into doing as much as possible for the British cause. Roosevelt extended his executive authority to the limit, convinced, with the Prime Minister, that a German victory would be disastrous for both democracies. He agreed fully with Churchill's observation of December 7, 1940, that "the defeat of the Nazi and Fascist tyranny is a matter of high consequence to the people of the United States and to the Western Hemisphere." Churchill pushed Roosevelt another giant step toward an open commitment to London's success when he warned the President in December that British expenditures for munitions in the United States far exceeded his country's exchange resources. Roosevelt responded to the challenge in January 1941 with his lend-lease proposal. The British, he assured Congress, did not need manpower, but they did require billions of dollars worth of weapons for defense. "We cannot, and we will not," he said, "tell them that they must surrender, merely because of present inability to pay for the weapons we know they must have." The ultimate passage of the "aid-to-Britain" bill was never in doubt, although it faced the stubborn opposition of the isolationists who saw in the proposal the further destruction of their effort to prevent direct U.S. involvement in the war. In March 1941, both houses of Congress passed the Lend-Lease Act overwhelmingly.

Thereafter Roosevelt undermined whatever effectiveness the isolationists retained by combining the growing U.S. commitment to British with public assurances that such aid would keep this nation out of war. Interventionists in the administration, especially

Secretary of War Henry L. Stimson and Secretary of the Navy
Frank Knox, believed that the President moved much too cau-
tiously. But Roosevelt refused to take the country to war against a
sharply divided public, especially since his congressional majorities
had comprised both interventionists and moderate noninterventionists who shared his desire for a British victory but who accepted
also at face value his promises to keep the country out of war. What
demonstrated the success of Roosevelt's appeal to the moderates—
and accounted for his ultimate refusal to oppose them—was the fact
that while the President carried every aid-short-of-war proposal
through Congress from September 1939 through the spring of
1941, usually with wide majorities, 80 percent of the American
people continued to oppose a declaration of war.

ENTER RUSSIA

Even as the success of Roosevelt's interventionist policies in
Congress demanded that he keep the country out of war, Hitler
revolutionized the long-term American relationship to the struggle
for Europe. On June 22, 1941, he sent his legions storming into
Russia on a front that stretched from the Baltic to the Black Sea.
Operation *Barbarossa*, designed to eliminate the Russian danger
with one lightning stroke, drove the Soviets into the anti-German
coalition. Germany and Russia, locked in the greatest and potentially most destructive military confrontation of all time, offered the
West two possibilities: Nazi domination of much of the Eurasian
continent or a new source of power to stem the Nazi tide. Indeed,
without the full military involvement of the USSR it was no longer
clear in 1941 how Britain, even with the support of the United
States, could restore Europe to its traditional balance. Yet successful Russian resistance, which alone assured an eventual German
collapse, presaged a troubled peace, because postwar leadership
would belong not only to the United States and Britain, but also
to the Soviet Union, the world's most pervasive dictatorship and
known enemy of the Versailles settlement.

This conclusion fell most heavily on the small coterie of Soviet
experts in the U.S. diplomatic service who, through two interwar

decades, had developed a profound distrust of the Russian government. DeWitt Clinton Poole, a State Department official, had advised against recognition of the "unconstitutional" Bolshevik regime in 1919 with what had already become the common assumption in Washington: "Their aim is world-wide revolution. . . . Their doctrines aim at the destruction of all governments as now constituted." Thereafter the Division of Russian Affairs in the State Department, having no diplomatic role, devoted itself to the accumulation and interpretation of whatever information drifted out of Bolshevik Russia. To observe Soviet behavior at close range, the State Department maintained a listening post at Riga, a port city in the tiny Baltic country of Latvia. When the Eastern European Division absorbed the Russian Division in 1924, it perpetuated the departmental concern over Russian intentions. Under the determined leadership of Robert F. Kelley, the division continued to turn out papers that warned against any normalization of relations with the Kremlin. Eventually four young officers became the core of expertise on Soviet matters—George F. Kennan, Charles E. Bohlen, Loy W. Henderson, and Elbridge Durbrow. All opposed recognition. Kennan later expressed his early convictions: "Never —neither then nor at any later date—did I consider the Soviet Union a fit ally or associate, actual or potential, for this country." Nothing in Russian history or psychology convinced Kennan that the United States could establish satisfactory relations with the Bolshevik leaders.

Roosevelt's recognition of the USSR in 1933 was scarcely reassuring to either the Riga alumni or those editors and politicians who had long distrusted the Bolshevik regime. William C. Bullitt, the first American ambassador to the Soviet Union, reached Moscow with the hope of establishing open and fruitful relations with the Soviet leadership. In time Bullitt discovered that he could settle none of the outstanding issues, such as Russia's wartime debts to the United States, and gradually became disenchanted at Soviet behavior. By 1936 he was happy to leave Moscow for the ambassadorship in Paris. Bullitt's departure reinforced the siege mentality of the American staff in Moscow. Having little work to perform outside the embassy, the beleaguered legation continued its endless studies, analyses, and debates on the meaning of the Soviet Union. So deep was the sense of harrassment created by Soviet rudeness, secrecy, and spying that Kennan once recommended from Moscow that the United States cease to maintain an ambassador there. The purges of the mid-1930s merely confirmed the American conviction that the Soviet regime was barbaric, untrustworthy, and undeserving of any respect. That many of the purged were friends and acquaintances of embassy officials gradually isolated the Americans almost completely from Russian society. "Personal friendship," wrote Kennan, "like some powerful curse, would spell ruin for those to whom it attached itself." To American officials in Moscow the totalitarianism of the Soviet state merely accentuated the dangers inherent in Soviet ideology. The USSR, they agreed, was dedicated to revolution and expansion, and because its ambitions were global, it endangered the United States as well as the countries around the Russian periphery.

For Russian specialists in the State Department the Soviet decision to sign the Nazi-Soviet Pact of August 1939, thereby freeing Hitler to attack the West, was a further demonstration of Soviet duplicity. Subsequent Soviet actions in attacking Finland, partitioning Poland, and annexing Bessarabia and the Baltic states (in fulfillment of the Nazi-Soviet Pact) seemed equally despicable. State Department axioms not only explained Russia's new expansionism in Europe but also suggested a proper course for the United States to follow. Ambassador Laurence Steinhardt, in Moscow, reminded Henderson in October 1940 that only a policy of "toughness" would impress the Kremlin. "Approaches by Britain or the United States," he warned, "must be interpreted here as signs of weakness and the best policy to pursue is one of aloofness, indicating strength. . . . As you know from your own experiences, the moment these people here get it into their heads that we are 'appeasing them, making up to them or need them', they immediately stop being cooperative. . . . My experience has been that they respond only to force and if force cannot be applied, then to straight oriental bartering or trading methods. . . . That, in my opinion, is the only language they understand and the only language productive of results." Henderson reminded Washington that the Russians were as expansive as the Germans; Hull, reflecting such fears, assured

State Department officials that he would sacrifice no principle to improve U.S. relations with the Soviet Union.

For American isolationists, Germany's invasion of Russia in June 1941 came as salvation. Those who regarded the dictatorships and policies of Germany and Russia equally reprehensible argued that the United States should permit the two giant protagonists to destroy each other, unaided. For some any European ally was preferable to the Soviet Union. Lindbergh, addressing an America First rally in July 1941, declared characteristically: "I would a hundred times rather see my country ally herself with England, or even with Germany with all her faults, than with the cruelty, the godlessness and the barbarism that exist in Soviet Russia." Former President Herbert Hoover warned the nation against taking up arms on the side of the Soviets. "The gargantuan jest of all history," he wrote, "would be if we should give aid to Stalin in the war. . . . The result would be to spread communism over the world."

Whatever the aversion to Russia both inside and outside the U.S. government, the Nazi invasion destroyed its relevance. What mattered to Roosevelt was not the moral quality of the Soviet system, but the capacity of the USSR to resist the Nazi assault. From the beginning Roosevelt, like Churchill, regarded Russia an ally. On June 24 the President informed the press, "Of course we are going to give all the aid we possibly can to Russia." Hitler, not Stalin, was the enemy, more dangerous because more powerful. Under Secretary of State Sumner Welles explained to the nation: "Any rallying of the forces opposing Hitler, from whatever sources these forces may spring, will hasten the eventual downfall of the present German leaders and will therefore redound to the benefit of our own defense. . . . This is the present issue which faces a realistic America." Much of the interventionist press favored the extension of lend-lease aid to Russia, as did White's Committee to Defend America. Roosevelt proceeded to direct the expanding American military production toward Russia and Britain alike, assuring Soviet Ambassador Ivan Oumansky that the administration's program would bring materiel in quantity to Russia by October. Ambassador Steinhardt's opposition to such aid, even in the crisis of 1941, gave Roosevelt little choice but to replace him. The President sent Harry Hopkins to Moscow; Hopkins' reports were encouraging. "The morale of the population is exceptionally good," he wrote late in July, "there is unbounded determination to win." Two months later W. Averell Harriman headed another special mission to determine Russia's precise needs. Thereafter American shipments reached Soviet ports in increasing volume, demonstrating Washington's new confidence not only in Russia's capacity to withstand the Nazi assault, but also in the Kremlin's good intentions. For the moment the United States asked nothing of Russia but victories on the Eastern Front.

Meanwhile Roosevelt responded to Germany's growing power on land and sea with both his private naval war in the Atlantic and a more determined attack on the extreme isolationists. In the late autumn of 1941 the President pressed the attorney general to initiate a judicial investigation of the America First Committee. Even as the isolationists denounced Roosevelt's interventionism and his verbal commitments to Nazism's destruction, their power continued to disintegrate. Still, it required the Japanese attack on Pearl Harbor on December 7, 1941 to blast the country's primary international concerns irretrievably into the Eastern Hemisphere with consequences then scarcely predictable. Despite its ferocity, the Great War of 1914 had not prevented the victors from recreating some semblance of Europe's traditional order. Britain and France regained their historic positions of leadership in European affairs; the empires of the victors emerged from the war intact. But whether the global war of attrition that began in 1939 would leave in its wake a Europe sufficiently stable to permit another U.S. retreat from it was not certain. Already Europe's challenge to wartime America seemed clear. Supported by needed Russian resistance, the United States and Britain might again achieve the total destruction of German power, but this time victory would require the uprooting of the historic European balance of power.

JAPAN: THE CHALLENGE TO UNDERSTANDING

Throughout the decade that separated the Manchurian crisis from the attack of Pearl Harbor, Japanese diplomacy sought to avoid war with the United States. After the absorption of Manchuria into the Japanese economy in 1932, Tokyo hoped to establish major Japanese influence in Chinese industry, again without provoking a war in the Pacific. Following the clash of Japanese and Chinese troops at the Marco Polo Bridge outside Peking, China, in July, 1937, the Japanese government accepted the price of a limited war to impose its will on China. But Japan soon found itself confronted by an uncompromising Chinese leadership. What had promised to be a brief, successful war on the Asian mainland became for Japan a long, exhausting struggle. Japanese officials discovered to their dismay that they could not reconcile their goal of altering the Far Eastern treaty structure to their country's advantage, largely at the expense of China, with Washington's determination to limit all change in the Far East, as elsewhere, to peaceful processes. What the United States expected of Japan Secretary Hull made clear in a statement that he released to the press on July 16, 1937. "We advocate," he said, "adjustment of problems in international relations by processes of peaceful negotiation and agreement. We advocate faithful observance of international agreements. Upholding the principle of the sanctity of treaties, we believe in modification of provisions of treaties . . . by orderly processes carried out in a spirit of mutual helpfulness and accommodation." Hull's principles, which denied the legitimacy of all change emanating from the use of force, gave Japan the simple choice of discarding its ambitions in the Far East or facing the persistent opposition of the United States.

For Washington the choices were equally narrow. Japan, engaged in a war to alter the political and economic status of East Asia, presented the United States with only two realistic alternatives: to accept a larger role for Japan in Far Eastern affairs or to fight Japan in its effort to prevent economic and administrative changes in China and elsewhere that defied its will. Japanese ambitions appeared more determined and expansive when, on November 3, 1938, Tokyo announced its program for a "New Order in East Asia." That day Premier Konoe Fumimaro explained Japanese purpose in a radio broadcast: "Japan desires to build up a stabilized Far East by cooperating with the Chinese people who have awakened to the need of self-determination as an Oriental race. . . . History shows that Japan, Manchukuo [Manchuria], and China are so related to each other that they must bind themselves closely together in a common mission for the establishment of peace and order in the Far East by displaying their own individuality. . . . Japan desires to establish a new peace fabric in the Far East on the basis of justice." Behind Japanese expansionism was a broad national conviction that Japan required and merited a new order in East Asia.

Japanese Foreign Minister Matsuoka Yosuke, faced with both an expensive war on the Chinese mainland and the status quo policies in Washington, observed bitterly that the "Western Powers had taught the Japanese the game of poker but . . . after acquiring most of the chips they pronounced the game immoral and took up contract bridge." Matsuoka noted that international law was in fact the law of the Western powers, because it served their interest in the status quo admirably. For Matsuoka Japan was the natural leader of East Asia and thus merited the right to reorganize portions of the Asian world. Finding no support for Japanese purpose in the capitals of western Europe, the Japanese Foreigh Minister, backed by Japan's military leadership, negotiated the troublesome Tripartite Pact with Germany and Italy in September 1940. At the same time the Japanese, to strengthen their position on the Asian mainland, moved into Indochina and Thailand. The United States responded to these advances with a burgeoning program of export restrictions that, by the end of 1940, included munitions, strategic raw materials, airplane parts, metal working machinery, aviation motor fuel, lubricants, and heavy melting iron and steel scrap.

Ambassador Joseph C. Grew, who reached Tokyo in 1932, urged Washington from the outset to consider Japan's needs and aspirations in defining its policies for the Far East. It seemed essential to him that the United States recognize in Japanese expansion a program of self-preservation. Japan, Grew noted, possessed only two realistic alternatives to solve its population problem: territorial or industrial growth. Any effort to restrain Japanese commerce, he warned, could only propel that country into a course of territorial expansion. Grew, unlike Hull, hesitated to condemn Japan for employing its superior efficiency to satisfy it internal needs, even at the expense of China. He once explained to Washington why Japan was becoming more and more hostile toward the United States: "It is true that the Japanese fighting forces consider the United States as their potential enemy . . . but that is because they think that the United States is standing in the path of the nation's natural expansion and is more apt to interfere with Japan's ambitions than are the European nations." Only a more compromising American posture, he believed, would permit Japanese moderates to maintain an official cordiality toward the United States and enable the Tokyo government to control Japan's military extremists. Late in 1940 Grew warned the President in a series of private letters that an economic boycott would drive Japan into open aggression, perhaps even into war with the United States. Determined to prevent a general confrontation in the Pacific, Grew argued for modification of the official hard-line approach to Japan.

Grew's appeals made no impression on the Roosevelt administration. Indeed, Washington's inflexibility keep pace with Japanese demands. Eventually Grew, to protect his credibility as a spokesman for U.S. policy, adopted a less compromising tone in Tokyo. But in his correspondence he continued to distinguish between America's short-term interest in avoiding war and its long-term interest in stabilizing the international politics of the Orient. At the same time Grew hoped that his tougher stance in Tokyo might encourage some modification in Japanese purpose by reminding Japanese officials that their perennial defiance of American principles might lead to a wider conflict in Asia. Grew failed both in Tokyo and in Washington. Unable to penetrate the secretiveness that surrounded Roosevelt and Hull, Grew eventually found himself entirely eliminated from a policymaking role. During the critical months of 1941, the ambassador admitted that the State Department no longer welcomed his opinions.

Ultimately it was the Chinese diplomatic corps that found favor in Washington. Still, the convergence of U.S. and Chinese purpose in the Far East came slowly. What determined American policy until 1940 was the intention, not to defend China, but to perpetuate the post-Versailles treaty structure. Only in the sense that Japanese expansion violated the Chinese treaty system, and thus allegedly endangered world stability, did it challenge this nation's general complacency toward matters relating to the Far East. Long after Washington comprehended the full magnitude and violence of the Japanese assault on China, it continued to reveal little direct concern for China's future. Reluctant to antagonize Tokyo unnecessarily, the U.S. government extended little aid and credit to China. It was only when the Tripartite Pact and the Japanese invasion of Southeast Asia linked Japan in the American mind with Axis aggression that the United States viewed China as an ally in the growing struggle against totalitarianism. As the program of anti-Japanese sanctions slowed trade with Japan in 1940, Washington stepped up its shipments of war material to China. No longer would China suffer the consequences of American neglect.

Nomura Kichisaburo, an admiral little versed in the art of diplomacy, arrived in Washington during February 1941 to conduct Tokyo's final effort to reach an agreement with the government of the United States. Nomura accepted the mission to Washington only with the assurance that his superiors in Tokyo genuinely desired a *rapprochement.* He had long denounced the Tripartite Pact and had challenged Foreign Minister Matsuoka's anti-American behavior at every turn. Historians as well as Nomura's own Japanese contemporaries have condemned his inaccurate and overly optimistic reporting. Whether this mattered in the ultimate breakdown of U.S.-Japanese relations that year is doubtful. What the Japanese wanted was clear: the freedom to negotiate an end to the Sino-Japanese war on the basis of Japan's superior power and efficiency. Such purpose had no chance against Hull's principles of peaceful change.

On April 16 Hull presented to Nomura the final American proposal for peace in the Far East: "(1) respect for the territorial integrity and the sovereignty of each and all nations; (2) support of the principle of non-interference in the internal affairs of other countries; (3) support of the principle of equality, including equality of commercial opportunity; (4) non-disturbance of the *status quo* in the Pacific except as the *status quo* may be altered by peaceful means." For Hull there could be no Japanese negotiation with China until Tokyo agreed to accept the limits imposed by the principle of peaceful change. This placed Japan in the unfortunate position of either fighting an endless war on the Asian mainland or terminating that war on Chinese terms. Neither Washington nor Tokyo wanted a war in the Pacific; yet both preferred war to the acceptance of the conditions that each sought to impose on the other. In the end Nomura's diplomacy had no chance against Tokyo's determined search for *lebensraum* in East Asia and Washington's total rejection of any change emanating from the use of force. Indeed, the historic conflict between the United States and Japan over China's future virtually eliminated diplomacy as a means of avoiding war.

Determined to compel a Japanese withdrawal from China and Southeast Asia even while avoiding war, Roosevelt, on July 25, 1941, issued an executive order freezing Japanese assets in the United States and thus effectively terminated all American commercial and financial relations with Japan. Both public officials and the press lauded the decision, assuring the President that his strong action would quickly bring the Tokyo government to terms. *The New Republic* predicted characteristically that the embargo would strangle Japanese industry and advance that country's moment of military collapse. The almost universal public assumption that Japan would capitulate before it would engage the United States in war was tragic. The confident President saw no need to attach any objectives, achievable through diplomacy alone, to his embargo. Even while he placed the Japanese economy in a state of crisis, Roosevelt gave Japan the simple choice between capitulation and an expanded conflict. When Premier Konoe, on August 8, requested a top-level conference with Roosevelt to stop the drift toward war, State Department officials advised the President to avoid all private talks. There could be no agreement, observed Far Eastern adviser Stanley Hornbeck, that would not defy American principles. Besides, wrote Hornbeck, a settlement with Japan was not an urgent matter. "We are not in great danger vis-a-vis Japan," he added, "and Japan . . . does not possess military capacity sufficient to warrant an attack by her upon the United States. . . ." Hornbeck, like the press, assumed that the Japanese would capitulate under the pressure of U.S. economic restrictions. He stood in the vanguard of Washington hard-liners who identified the American search for peace with the absolute rejection of compromise with Japan.

This almost universal assumption that this country could guarantee the peace in direct proportion to its diplomatic inflexibility proved to be disastrous. The Japanese had no intention of permitting the United States a cheap victory in the Far East. In late November, even as Hull rejected the final Japanese proposal and Hornbeck assured the administration that the Japanese would avoid war with the United States at all costs, Tokyo dispatched its task force to Pearl Harbor. In preventing compromise to the end, the Chinese had their way. They demanded nothing less than total victory for their cause and pursued that objective with an effective program of public relations. The support that the Chinese leaders sought in Washington came easily enough, and if the uncompromisable goals they pursued required, after November, a direct U.S. military involvement in the Pacific, then Pearl Harbor was indeed the final measure of their success. Still, their single-minded determination to snatch victory from defeat ended in further disaster, because they failed to recognize the military and political weakness of their own government and the limited Western interest in sustaining the purposes and even the existence of that government.

Official U.S. policy toward Japan promised the American people both peace in the Pacific and the triumph of their principles. Neither Roosevelt nor the press at large ever presented the real choices that confronted the nation: a drastic compromise with principle or an enervating and expensive struggle without end for a new stability in Asia. One who recognized both the tragic quality in Roosevelt's demands and the reasons for their immense popularity was William Henry Chamberlin, a leading critic of the President's interventionist policies. He wrote in *Harpers* in March 1942:

> Japan was confronted with the choice, made specifically clear in Mr. Hull's memorandum of November 26th, of withdrawing from China, of becoming progressively relatively weaker as the economic sanctions took effect, or of fighting. It is hard to see how anyone familiar with the character of the Japanese people and with the mentality of the military and naval groups that dominated Japanese policy could have escaped the conclusion that the third choice was the most probable.
>
> Yet even the most diehard isolationists had little, if anything, to say in criticism of Mr. Roosevelt's action in freezing Japanese assets and practically breaking off trade relations. Had this measure been put to a popular or Congressional vote it would almost certainly have been ratified by a large majority. This marked difference in attitude between war with Germany and war with Japan may well be explained largely by the general

belief that war with Japan would be a swift and easy process, involving only the Navy and Air Force, while war with Germany seemed to portend mass overseas armies and heavy casualty lists.

Some observant Americans doubted that the United States could escape the turmoil that a general war would unleash in the Orient. On May 31, 1940, Hornbeck warned the Department of State's Advisory Committee that a Japanese invasion of the Dutch East Indies would constitute an unacceptable diplomatic defeat for the United States. He argued that this country should prevent such an invasion by destroying the Japanese navy and breaking Japan's links with the southern Pacific. Hugh R. Wilson, the distinguished American diplomat, recorded Under Secretary Welles's reply.

> Mr. Welles stated that in no event would he advocate sending the American fleet to the East Indies. . . . As to rubber and tin, he declared that the former could be manufactured in a short space of time, . . . and the latter could be obtained in sufficient quantities from Bolivia. . . . I stated that I concurred with Mr. Welles both for the reason of defensive needs of this country and hemisphere and because the assumption of responsibility in that remote area meant in the event of victory a perpetual assumption of protection for spots in remote parts of the world, in other words, a replacement by the United States of the British Empire. I questioned whether our public was ready for such responsibility for a long duration in this era of growing national feeling and growing industrial resource. We are not confronting a period of the nineteenth century but are living in a century where industry and warlike power are growing in various portions of the world, thus making infinitely more difficult the maintenance of a far-flung empire.

Neither Tokyo nor Washington could escape responsibility for what went wrong. Japan had embarked on an aggressive war against China and should not have expected the United States, with its long tradition of paternalism toward China and its dedication to the world's peace structure, to accept readily the notion of an imposed settlement. Still, the American response scarcely served the cause of peace; the principles that it proclaimed, whatever their intrinsic merit, never demanded less than Japan's capitulation. The final Japanese note of December 7, 1941 explained why those who chose to interfere in Sino-Japanese affairs under the principles of self-determination and peaceful change had ultimately to pay a heavy price. "The American Government," ran the Japanese accusation, "advocates in the name of world peace those principles favorable to it and urges upon the Japanese Government the acceptance thereof. The peace of the world may be brought about only by discovering a mutually acceptable formula through recognition of the reality of the situation and mutual appreciation of one another's position."

For the United States the sudden and devastating Japanese attack on Pearl Harbor resolved the issue of war. Roosevelt responded to the attack—which he had done nothing to avoid—with confidence. He wrote to Churchill: "Today all of us are in the same boat with you and the people of the Empire and it is a ship which will not and cannot be sunk." Hitler backed Japan by declaring war on the United States four days later. Italy followed Germany's lead. Congressional isolationists, with one exception, approved the war against Japan. The congressional vote for war against Germany and Italy was unanimous. The long contest between isolationists and interventionists ended with a total victory for the latter. Thereafter isolationists remained silent or joined the other side. In their wartime assumptions and purposes Americans generally became indistinguishable. That minority of confirmed critics who insisted that Roosevelt, with greater determination and more astute diplomacy, could have avoided war were largely ignored.

As Roosevelt turned from the failures of peace to the challenges of war, he rejected only the means that he had employed, because they had proved ineffective. He did not discard the internationalist goals of a world order based on the principles of peaceful change and self-determination of peoples. Never did he acknowledge that such purposes had rendered war with Japan unavoidable. The United States, he said, would fight to defend the "principles of law and order and justice, against an effort of unprecedented ferocity to overthrow those principles. . . . " The country would at last "make good the right of nations and mankind to live in peace under conditions of security and justice." What the previous reliance on principle had failed to achieve, the United States would now gain through the unstinting application of force. Unfortunately, the achievement of such universal goals could be as elusive in war as in peace, while their pursuit could interpose American will, again at heavy cost, in the conflicts of other peoples wherever the nation's leadership chose to make the defiance of American principles a matter of national concern.

Chapter II

Total War and Limited Peace

TURN OF THE TIDE

Strategically the United States faced problems in 1942 unlike those of 1917. Japan, an associate power in 1917, was now an active enemy, expanding its conquests against little opposition on the Asian mainland and across the South Pacific. The immediate loss of Guam, the Philippines, and Wake was sobering. When the United States entered the European war in 1917, Germany faced a stable front in France and Italy that limited its access to the Atlantic Ocean. In 1942 there was no front in western Europe at all, and only the Russian success in turning back the initial German on-slaught at Moscow and Leningrad created a battlefront in the east. Few Americans were sanguine enough to believe that the Russians could withstand the Nazi assault indefinitely, much less smash the German war machine. Still the American people never doubted their ability to win the global struggle. The United States possessed an industrial base of high capacity that lay beyond the reach of invading armies, perhaps even assaults from the sky. It was clear, moreover, that the three allies—the United States, Britain, and Russia—commanded the human resources to fight a total war suc-cessfully. In the Declaration of the United Nations, signed on January 1, 1942, these three powers, joined by lesser enemies of the Axis, agreed to push the war to a successful military conclusion.

However, the quiet assurance of victory did not necessarily suggest how and where the Grand Alliance might bring its power to bear on the enemy with greatest efficiency. Before the outbreak of war in Europe, the Joint Planning Committee in Washington concluded that the United States, if it became involved in a two-front war, would conduct a defensive operation in the Pacific and employ its major effort to destroy the German *Wehrmacht.* British and American officials, at the Argentia Conference off Newfoundland in August 1941, accepted a basic strategy for Europe—a total naval blockade of the continent, the bombing of German targets from British bases, limited strikes around the periphery of Europe and, finally, a massive assault on Germany itself. Subsequently, however, British and American officers disagreed on the best means to carry out this basic strategy. Britain, with its small but seasoned army and powerful navy, favored immediate strikes along the boundaries of German power, especially in the Mediterranean. General George C. Marshall, U.S. Chief of Staff and the nation's leading wartime strategist, argued instead for a prolonged buildup of United States and British manpower and materiel in England for a cross-channel invasion of western Europe. Roosevelt proposed a second front for 1942. The British saw no possibility for a second front before 1943. But to bring the necessary Western power to bear against Germany in 1942, Churchill suggested Operation Torch, an invasion of North Africa to check the German drive into the eastern Mediterranean. Marshall opposed all Mediterranean operations, but Churchill, supported by Roosevelt, had his way.

When British and American forces finally executed Torch in November 1942, they faced a German army in North Africa that was overextended and weakened by its earlier successes. Hitler and Mussolini had inaugurated their drive through the Balkans and into North Africa in 1940. That year the Germans occupied Hungary and Rumania. The Italians failed to capture Greece but, in March 1941, the Germans brought Bulgaria and Yugoslavia under their control. During April Hitler's Panzer divisions invaded Greece, pushing the British and Greeks before them. Hitler followed the conquest of Greece with a spectacular airborne invasion of Crete that captured the island in May. Without hesitation the Germans decided to move on into North Africa, drive out the British already there, and gain control of the Suez. During the late spring of 1941 Edwin Rommel's famed *Afrika Korps* invaded Libya and drove the British out of Benghazi and eastward to Tobruk. For a year both sides prepared for the eventual showdown. Finally, in May 1942, Rommel launched his desert offensive, driving the British back to El Alamein, 70 miles west of Alexandria. As the British general, Bernard Law Montgomery, prepared his counteroffensive, he received a heavy shipment of U.S. equipment that gave him the edge in armor. His forces broke through Rommel's north flank in late October and forced the Germans into retreat. Churchill saw the importance of Montgomery's victory. "The Battle of El Alamein," he recalled, "was the turning point in British military fortunes during the World War. Up to Alamein we survived. After Alamein we conquered." By November 1942, Rommel was in full retreat across North Africa, losing Tobruk and Benghazi.

Now Rommel faced a challenge from the west—Operation Torch. During November, British and American forces, under General Dwight D. Eisenhower, landed in Morocco and Algeria, quickly neutralized the pro-German French officials in the region, and moved eastward to meet Rommel's retreating armies. Montgomery, after taking Tripoli in January 1943, closed in from the southeast and broke through the powerful German Mareth line near Gabès in March. Meanwhile British and American forces entered Tunisia from the west, captured Tunis and Bizerte, and then drove the fleeing Germans, now without Rommel, who had left, into the Cape Bon peninsula where, on May 13, they surrendered. That day Hitler lost 250,000 of his finest troops as prisoners of war.

Even more disastrous were the German losses on the Russian front. During the summer of 1942 the Nazi forces, facing little opposition, swept through the Crimea into the Caucasus Mountains and onward toward the Baku oil fields. During August 1942 other German divisions reached Stalingrad, key city on the Volga. Here, as at Moscow and Leningrad, the Russians refused to withdraw. For two months the battle raged, reducing the city to rubble. "Men died," recalled Russian General Georgi Zhukov, "but they did not retreat." Eventually Russian numbers and morale had their effect, forcing the Germans to retire. As the Germans prepared for a terrible winter on the Russian plains, Zhukov ordered a Russian counteroffensive that cut off 20 German divisions from supplies and reinforcements. Their surrender in January 1943 ended Hitler's drive toward the east. Stalingrad made Russia the dominant power on the continent and assured the steady collapse of Germany.

Despite Russian successes on the Eastern Front, Stalin pressed Roosevelt and Churchill for a major front in western Europe and chided them for their tardiness in entering the European war with a full-scale invasion. Conscious of Russia's essential contribution to the Allied cause, the two Western leaders met at Casablanca, Morocco, in January 1943 to plan the next step in the British-American effort. There Roosevelt and Churchill, to reassure Stalin and give the war an appealing and noble objective, announced the goal of "unconditional surrender." Marshall still preferred to concentrate Allied power in England for the cross-channel invasion of France (the strategy that Stalin approved), but the logic of the anticipated Allied victory in North Africa dictated a movement across the Mediterranean to Sicily, this to be followed by an invasion of Italy. Allied strategy, as it evolved in 1943, was a compromise between the American preference for the massing of Western power in England and the British preference for flanking operations in the Mediterranean. Not until the Quadrant Conference at Quebec in August 1943 did the British agree to the cross-channel attack, now designated as Overlord, to come in the late spring of 1944. At the Big Three conference at Teheran in November 1943, Stalin endorsed Overlord and promised a powerful Russian offensive to coincide with the establishment of a major second front in Europe. For Stalin, long critical of his tardy Western allies, the future at last promised relief.

Militarily the British-American compromise was a remarkable success. The Sicilian campaign ended quickly in a complete Allied victory. The progress through Italy, beginning with the Salerno beachhead, proved to be more difficult. It soon drove Italy out of the war, but Hitler pushed a powerful army into the Italian peninsula and thereby converted it into a major battleground. The hoarding of U.S. and British strength in England forced Allied troops in Italy to engage in prolonged heavy fighting, always against strategic odds. United States forces under General Mark W. Clark continued their northward advance, reaching Naples in October 1943. So telling had been the Allied successes of 1943 in Russia, North Africa, and the Mediterranean that even without the full commitment of British and American power in Europe, the tide of war had turned. Thereafter only a scientific miracle could have saved Germany.

MOBILIZATION FOR WAR

Behind the Allied victories in Africa and the Mediterranean and, to a lesser extent, on the Eastern Front was the almost total conversion of American manpower and industry to the requirements of war. The evolution of the United States into democracy's arsenal was at times slow, halting, and inefficient, but ultimately the organization of the country's human and physical resources for war was nothing less than phenomenal. As late as July 1939, the U.S. Army had only 174,000 enlisted men scattered through the country and a number of foreign posts. Even after September 1939, when war broke out in Europe, Congress resisted every executive attempt to increase the nation's land forces. As General Marshall reported later, "The fundamental obstacle at the time was the fact that the American people were unable to visualize the dangerous possibilities of the situation." Not until the *Wehrmacht* began to roll through western Europe in the spring of 1940 did Roosevelt successfully extract greatly increased appropriations for defense from a special session of Congress. With the fall of France, the President called the National Guard into service and, in September 1940, signed the nation's first peacetime selective service act. This permitted a projection of 1,400,000 in the nation's ground forces. By July 1941 the Army had reached that figure. As the danger of American involvement in both Europe and Asia mounted that year, the federal government created huge training centers, opened several officer candidate schools, and extended the length of service for draftees. When Pearl Harbor committed the nation directly to the defeat of the Axis, Congress provided for the expansion of the Army to approximately 7,700,000 by the end of 1943. Every month thereafter the draft boards sent new thousands to fill the ranks of the armed forces.

During World War II the Navy and Air Force, the latter an integral part of the Army, underwent comparable expansion. Even before the British and German experience demonstrated the importance of air power Roosevelt, in January 1939, had requested funds to increase plane production and flight training. The expansion came slowly, because the country lacked both facilities and equipment. By December 1941, the Air Force had completed 114 bases and was constructing several dozen more. During 1942 the United States trained thousands of pilots while American industry turned out new aircraft with astonishing rapidity. Meanwhile the Navy, always a popular branch of the service, kept pace in the development of manpower and equipment. Not until December 1942, when its personnel had reached 900,000, did the Navy resort to selective service. The Marine Corps, under the Navy Department, eventually expanded to almost a half million men.

Advances in weaponry and health care demanded special scientific knowledge. Roosevelt established the Office of Scientific Research and Development in 1941, with Dr. Vannevar Bush, president of the Carnegie Institution in Washington, as its head. The OSRD had two branches, one concerned with the physical sciences and involved directly in the defense effort, the other devoted to biological and medical science. By the end of 1942 the OSRD had negotiated more than 2000 contracts with 280 research institutions and universities; its expenditures had reached $100 million a year. To cooperate with the program, scientists moved freely from one institution to another. So severe was the program's security that journalists could report few of its achievements, yet among them were the new "wonder" drugs, important in the control of disease and infection, and improvements in rocketry, sighting devices, explosives, and even weaponry.

By far the most spectacular breakthrough in scientific knowledge for war use lay in the development of atomic energy. Behind this effort were the minds and the determination of five European-born scientists associated with Columbia and Princeton universities —Albert Einstein, Enrico Fermi, Leo Szilard, Eugene P. Wigner, and Niels Bohr. Their studies of uranium fission paralleled similar studies in Europe and convinced them that Germany could, in time, develop a superweapon that would permit that nation to dominate the world. Wigner and Szilard prevailed on Einstein, the country's most renowned scientist, to inform Roosevelt by letter of the current discoveries in the study of uranium, both in Europe and America. Einstein's letter, dated August 2, 1939, warned the President of secret German studies and outlined steps whereby the U.S. government might accelerate uranium research in this country. Roosevelt turned the matter over to a special committee that recommended action. With limited federal support, Arthur H. Compton and Fermi set off a chain reaction at the University of Chicago in December 1942. To translate the knowledge acquired that day into a usable atomic weapon demanded the full economic support of the U.S. government. In May 1943, all government work on atomic energy was fused in the new Manhattan Project. To develop both fissionable material and a bomb design, the government established three centers of activity: Oak Ridge, Tennessee; Hanford, Washington; and Los Alamos, New Mexico. At the New Mexico site a group of scientists, led by J. Robert Oppenheimer of the University of California at Berkeley, developed the bomb itself. When, in July 1945, the first bomb was ready for testing at White Sands, New Mexico, the U.S. government had spent $2 billion in its research and development.

American industry, compelled to retool and expand to satisfy the requirements of total war, created a miracle of production. Before Pearl Harbor Roosevelt had established a series of defense councils to oversee the distribution of war materials to the nation's basic war industries. In January 1942, the President created the War Production Board under Donald Nelson, a vice-president of Sears, Roebuck, and Company. The Board had six major divisions: production, labor, materials, purchases, industrial operations, and civilian supply. The Board had the power to force the acceptance of controls, requisition private property, allocate raw materials, and stop production of nonessential goods. Before Pearl Harbor the country had achieved partial conversion to meet the needs of Lend-Lease; now the WPB quickly converted the economy to total war. By May 1942, it had stopped the manufacture of hundreds of civilian products requiring iron and steel. It permitted the assembling of 220,000 automobiles in 1942; two years later it reduced that number to 610.

On January 6, 1942, the President announced what he expected of American industry: 60,000 planes and 45,000 tanks in 1942, 125,000 planes and 75,000 tanks in 1943, plus millions of tons of shipping and large quantities of guns, ammunition, and other military equipment. To the amazement of industrialists, the country produced 47,000 planes in 1942. One year later aircraft production reached 86,000; in 1944 it climbed to 96,000. One American official observed that "planes were flying out of Uncle Sam's star-spangled costume like a plague of moths." Under the pressure of war American industry produced more steel than all other nations combined. During the war years shipbuilders created merchant vessels with a total tonnage of over 50 million. Henry J. Kaiser's shipyards eventually turned out 10,000-ton Liberty ships in two weeks. The gross national output of goods and services (GNP) was less than $100 billion in 1940; five years later it approached $200 billion. In 1944 the United States produced twice as much war material as Japan and Germany combined.

Japan's advance into Malaya and the Dutch East Indies in 1942 reduced the nation's supply of rubber. Scientists had perfected the process of making synthetic rubber from petroleum but, under the assumption that crude rubber would remain plentiful, the oil industry had refused to manufacture the more expensive substitute. The country's annual synthetic rubber capacity in 1941 stood at 40,000 tons. To meet the need for additional rubber, the government encouraged the public to turn in old tires and other rubber products for reprocessing. Soon it contemplated gasoline rationing to reduce the wear on automobile tires but, since rationing threatened the welfare of the oil-producing states, Roosevelt and congressional Democrats decided to postpone the decision until after the November 1942 elections. To avoid direct responsibility for any unpopular decision, Roosevelt appointed a blue-ribbon nonpartisan committee, headed by Bernard Baruch, to study the rubber shortage. With the approval of the committee, Roosevelt imposed gasoline rationing in December 1942. This reduced the consumption of gasoline, but did not create the necessary rubber supply. Late in 1942 the President appointed William Jeffers, president of the Union Pacific Railroad, as Rubber Director. Jeffers organized his program for manufacturing synthetic rubber around members of the rubber industry. Eventually the government spent $700 million on 51 plants that it leased to rubber companies under arrangements that assured high production and adequate profits. By 1944 the nation's output of synthetic rubber reached 800,000 tons annually, or almost 90 percent of all the rubber used in the country.

This revolution in production transformed the nation's industrial centers into cauldrons of activity. War contracts shaped the nation's future. Large industries such as the automotive, household appliance, and radio turned to the manufacture of tanks, jeeps, trucks, and guns. New war plants, financed by government and private enterprise alike, grew as giant increments to established corporate holdings. By March 1942, the government had completed more than 300 new factory projects across the country. One Ford bomber plant covered 100 acres. Supported by federal funding, San Diego, Los Angeles, and Seattle became major workshops for war. This industrial expansion set off the largest internal migration in the country's history. Five million Americans left farms to join the war effort in the cities. Altogether, between Pearl Harbor and the spring of 1945, 15,000,000 Americans moved to new surroundings. Middle River, north of Baltimore, the site of a Glenn Martin bomber plant, was a village of 2500 in 1941. By March 1942, the community had 40,000 workers in a bomber plant that covered 73 acres. Housing could not keep pace with such rapid change. Migrants to the major centers of war production lived in tenements, garages, shacks, tents, and trailers as they awaited the construction of new houses. Women joined the migration into the factories, working on production lines and filling the administrative facilities of most large corporations. During the war 7,500,000 Americans earned incomes for the first time.

WARTIME FINANCE AND PROSPERITY

Washington underwrote the wartime economy through deficit financing. Theoretically the government could have collected sufficient taxes to pay for its purchases of industrial goods even while it waged the war. For reasons of politics and morale it chose to limit the tax burden and pushed the costs of war to the postwar generation through borrowing. In 1941 the federal government financed the $13 billion that it spent with $7 billion in taxes and $6 billion in increased indebtedness. Three years later the annual expenditure reached $95 billion, of which over $51 billion was borrowed. During 1945—the last year of the war—the federal government spent $98 billion, but collected only $44 billion in taxes, adding $54 billion to the national debt. The country paid scarcely half of its war costs from current income. In 1941 the national debt stood at $43 billion; in 1945 it approached $260 billion. In part this growing deficit reflected the sale of war bonds, in part the customary process whereby the Treasury sold government securities to the Federal Reserve banks, which paid for them by increasing the Treasury's deposit account. Those who received the Treasury checks deposited them in commercial banks and thereby increased the reserves against which such banks could make new loans. Thus the federal government, by selling securities to the Federal Reserve, enlarged the nation's money supply and its demand for goods and services.

Federal purchases, financed largely by credit, exerted additional inflationary pressures on the nation's price structure. Recognizing the need to hold prices stable against the rising demand created by credit, Roosevelt established the Office of Price Administration (OPA) in April 1941. Not until the passage of the Emergency Price Control Act of January 1942 did OPA have the statutory authority to control inflation. Even then OPA remained ineffective. As prices continued to rise, Roosevelt warned Congress that unless it acted he would use his authority to stabilize prices. The President requested additional taxes to reduce the purchasing power of the millions whose competitive buying pushed prices upward. Congress refused to vote them, convinced that the public did not care to pay a greater portion of the war's costs to control inflation. Finally, on April 8, 1943, the President issued his Hold-the-Line Order, which directed the Price Administrator to place ceiling prices on all items that affected the cost of living and refuse further increases except those required by law. This action proved to be effective. The attempts of government to control inflation did not always work smoothly, but they were successful enough to sustain the war effort.

None benefited more from federal wartime financing than did the nation's largest industrial corporations with whom the government did its direct contracting. Under Secretary of War Robert P. Patterson once explained that war orders "had to be placed with companies best equipped to handle them with speed. . . . We had to take industrial America as we found it." Washington discovered that it was easier and more efficient to place a large order with one company, ultimately without competitive bids, than to distribute contracts among a variety of smaller, competing companies. The nation's 100 largest firms controlled about seven-eighths of the country's military output and about four-fifths of all its prime war contracts. As late as 1940, 2,750,000 small companies conducted about a third of the nation's business, some in manufacturing but most in retailing and service. After Pearl Harbor the physical output of small plants continued at the prewar level, despite the demise of thousands that were unable to convert to war production. But the role of the survivors changed; most of them made the bits and pieces for the large corporations. The Kleenex Company, for example, turned to the manufacture of gun mounts. One large corporation placed over $100 million in subcontracts in 1941. It was the vast increase in subcontracting after Pearl Harbor that kept thousands of small industries in operation. Cost-plus contracts, which guaranteed profits to large and small businesses alike, could be lucrative. Congress followed the proliferation of agencies and contracts carefully. As early as 1941 the Senate established its War Investigating Committee, headed by Senator Harry S. Truman of Missouri, to check defense contracts and examine other phases of the war effort, including the behavior of labor in war industries. To curtail profits, the government often renegotiated contracts after production itself determined the actual costs of manufacturing. Still, as Under Secretary Patterson phrased it early in 1943, "If inordinate profits were reaped by a few under a $22,000,000,000 war program [in World War I], what will be the consequences under $240,000,000,000 of current appropriations and authorizations?" By 1942 industrial profits exceeded those of the boom years of the 1920s.

Farmers experienced the most rapid rise in income of any group in the country. Increases in agricultural productivity from heavier mechanization, consolidations of farming units, greater crop diversification, favorable weather conditions, higher prices, and the dramatic use of commercial fertilizers more than balanced the wartime movement of more than one-sixth of the farm population off the land. Farm income increased from $6.5 billion in 1940 to almost $17 billion in 1945. Farmers bought land, paid off mortgages, and put aside savings. Still farm income increased more rapidly than that of urban laborers only because the average farmer started at a much lower level. With all their wartime gains, farmers still earned only half as much as factory employees.

Wartime prosperity pushed American labor up the economic ladder, creating a large lower middle class of urban blue- and white-collar workers who, often for the first time in their lives, managed to escape underemployment, if not poverty. Payrolls more than doubled between 1939 and 1944, moving well above $100 billion a year. However, labor's high wages did not necessarily reflect increased wage rates. The large increase in the number of employees alone accounted for one-third of the rise in payrolls. Some of the increase resulted from the movement of laborers from low-paying to high-paying plants and industries. Finally, increases in labor income reflected longer working hours and special compensation for overtime. Actually, for laborers generally, hourly wage rates moved upward between 15 and 20 percent while the cost of living index rose about 25 percent. It was not strange that labor favored price controls. To offset the rising living costs the War Labor Board, organized in January 1942, permitted steelworkers a 15 percent raise in May to offset the cost-of-living increases after January 1941. This agreement, known as the "Little Steel" formula, established the pattern for other war industries. The increasing disparity between prices and wages produced mounting discontent in labor ranks and set off numerous strikes in 1943.

What limited the nation's sympathy for labor's demands was the widespread recognition that countless citizens did not benefit in any manner from the wartime prosperity. Salaried, largely white-collar incomes did not keep pace with those of the highly unionized industrial workers. Teachers, ministers, clerks, salespeople, and government employees often received no advances in income at all. A Senate subcommittee estimated that 20 million Americans fell into this category. Even worse off were those of low fixed incomes, such as pensioners and dependents of military personnel. The wartime prosperity did not eliminate the country's large-scale poverty. Many who found employment continued to live in decaying slums. The war did nothing for tenant and migrant farmers in the South. Most were unsuited for steady jobs in industry and depended on the protection of the federal government. With the decline of the Farm Security Administration and the growing demands of war, these farmers faced reduced mobility and standards of living, if not unemployment. Unable to protect themselves, they again came under the control of large agricultural producers.

Undoubtedly the war's most pervading economic innovation lay in the federal promotion of industrial expansion. Economic goals that the New Deal failed to achieve in its eight years, the war, with its massive infusions of public purchasing and credit, reached and exceeded. War had become an effective device to generate jobs and prosperity. Conscious of the past and unable to see the future, many Americans feared that victory would end the greatest boom they had ever known. They had grown accustomed to the temporary and feared transition to the permanent. Every federal contract cancellation after 1944 sent shudders through the economy. What would happen to the country's prosperity when it ceased to make tanks, guns, and ammunition was not clear. Yet, as the *Saturday Evening Post* editorialized on July 1, 1944, the government was "not obligated to provide a perpetual war in order to keep people working at jobs that no longer need to be done." If Americans could not experience a wartime economy indefinitely, they would not soon forget the wartime lesson that massive deficits could overcome the usual impediments to economic growth.

Beyond its contribution to the nation's prosperity, the war reinforced the trends toward the concentration of governmental and economic power in American society. Roosevelt's struggle for national security, conducted always to achieve the most rapid victory possible with the least loss of American life, placed the burden of national policy on the country's industry and science no less than on its military establishment. Thus the new emergency state solidified the power of the federal executive, the large corporations, and the military in national life. The wartime experience, in establishing a strong common interest among these elements in enhancing the nation's security, laid the foundation for what became the scientific-military-industrial complex. In 1944 Charles E. Wilson, president of General Electric, proposed a "permanent war economy" in which the military and business, acting together, would buttress both the postwar economy and the state of American preparedness. The new army would emerge from the war as the country's most powerful pressure group, as well as the source of much of its leadership. For many economists and businessmen the same cooperation between government and industry that created the war economy would provide the motive power for private enterprise in the postwar era. The infusion of government purchasing and credit would prevent both the wild fluctuations of the past and the recurrence of economic disasters at home and abroad. The American economy had outgrown its prewar limitations.

SOCIETY IN WARTIME

Having again escaped an enemy invasion or any serious assault on their safety, the American people fought the war free of the restraints that might have compelled a more severe sharing of the war's burdens. Americans overwhelmingly believed in the war and enthusiastically entered upon the task of winning it. Never before had the country been so united in spirit and purpose. With millions in the armed forces, other millions at home—not only those in defense production—chose to aid the war effort by joining a variety of volunteer agencies. The movement to the colors was scarcely a rush, but countless civilians ultimately made their special contributions. Some 600,000 airplane spotters scanned the skies, looking for the enemy aircraft that never came. Another 670,000 assumed their duties as air raid wardens; 80,000 joined the Civil Air Patrol. Communities staged their trial blackouts, first-aiders stood by to save lives, blood donors reminded others of the negligible price in time and discomfort for giving blood, and women by the thousands gathered to make bandages. Advertisements encouraged people to obey the restrictions on consumption and to fight inflation by curtailing their purchases. Four brief lines summed up the wartime mood:

Use it up,
Wear it out,
Make it do
Or do without.

But the country was not without its black marketing, its individual and group selfishness. Many never shared any sense of crisis; they took their profits and jammed the bars, night clubs, and theaters in pursuit of pleasure and relaxation. Despite the mounting casualty lists and the genuine sacrifices that did occur, the tempo of life changed little. Most Americans went about their tasks, worked long hours, and accepted their defeats and triumphs with little show of emotion.

Civil libertarians who recalled the widespread repression of dissenters during the Great War against Germany were troubled by the approach of another global conflict. However, the repressive policies of the earlier war did not reoccur. Radicals—normally war's most vociferous critics—supported the country's efforts with enthusiasm; Hitler, spokesman of the extreme right on the political spectrum, had become the special enemy of radicals and Communists everywhere. Earl Browder, head of the American Communist party, condemned the war critics and joined the American Legion in the battle for universal military training. Germany's drive toward the east brought the support of the Slavic minorities. Russians and Eastern Europeans residing in the United States expressed their American nationalism in prowar parades and town meetings. Such expressions of patriotism emanating from both national and ideological minorities received strong confirmation in the pro-Soviet declarations of American officials, writers, and businessmen. *Life* magazine noted that the Soviet secret police, like the Federal Bureau of Investigation, often required vigorous methods in "tracking down traitors." Wartime books on Russia emphasized Soviet achievement as well as the magnitude of the Russian war effort.

Assured of the nation's overwhelming support, the Roosevelt administration adopted a relaxed attitude toward freedom of expression. It refused to prosecute cases under the Smith Act of 1940, the first peacetime sedition law since 1798. Conscientious objectors faced a generally tolerant government in Washington. Some ultimately compromised their convictions and entered the combat forces, but most accepted service as noncombatants. Those who refused to wear uniforms worked in civilian service camps, clearing forests, building roads and trails, fighting fires, or digging irrigation ditches. The minority that refused to register for the draft, many of them Jehovah's Witnesses, went to jail. Although the government made no serious effort to silence its critics on the right, it did establish loyalty tests for public employees. In July 1942 the Attorney General brought a group of right-wing, allegedly pro-German critics to trial, but failed to secure any convictions. In large measure the government as well as the nation's citizens escaped the antiforeignism and antiradicalism that guided their behavior toward dissenters during World War I.

America's two-front war, coming as it did from a series of dramatic assaults on the world's peace structure, required no public rationalization, but the government needed some informational agency to counter the right-wing and isolationist criticism of its conduct of the war. Through the cooperation of the Catholic Archbishop of Detroit, the administration managed to terminate the publication of Father Charles E. Coughlin's highly anti-Semitic and inflammatory publication, *Social Justice.* But the *Chicago Tribune* sustained an unrelenting attack on the war and those allegedly responsible for it. It accused the administration of sacrificing U.S. interests to "the foreign princelings who have infested the eastern seabord and the capital." Archibald MacLeish's Office of Facts and Figures, established early in the war, had little authority to coordinate the government's effort at public information. Finally, to combat the antiadministration press, the President, in June 1942, established the Office of War Information (OWI), headed by Elmer Davis, the popular radio news commentator. Davis explained the task of OWI. "Our job at home," he declared, "is to give the American people the fullest possible understanding of what this war is about. . . . [I]t is the job of OWI not only to tell the American people how the war is going but where it is going and where it came from." By 1943 the annual budget of OWI had reached $25 million. The Office employed over 4000 writers, linguists, publicists, radio figures, and artists. It used the press, radio, movies, and every mechanism for dispensing information and conducting psychological warfare.

German, Italian, and Japanese minorities in the United States experienced wartime gains or losses in accordance with their political influence. German-Americans had lost their ethnicity. Having among their numbers many of the country's leading industrialists and highest ranking military officers, they faced no trouble from professional patriots. Italian-Americans, also numerous, had become full participants in the American system. But, after Pearl Harbor, Japanese-Americans, residing largely on the West Coast and numbering a mere 110,000, faced deportation to concentration camps as potential saboteurs.

What rendered Japanese-Americans especially vulnerable to anti-Japanese hysteria was their employment in domestic service and vegetable farming, not government and industry, and their easy separation from the general public by race. General John DeWitt, who headed the Western Defense Command, argued effectively that racial ties were stronger than nationality. "The Japanese race is an enemy race," he warned. "To conclude otherwise is to expect that children born of white parents on Japanese soil sever all racial affinity and become loyal Japanese subjects, ready to fight and, if necessary, to die for Japan in a war against the nation of their parents." Some officials argued, furthermore, that no method of partial segregation could separate loyal from disloyal Japanese-Americans; only the confinement of all Japanese would guarantee the nation's internal security. Earl Warren, California's attorney general, explained the need for a total Japanese evacuation. "A wave of organized sabotage in California accompanied by an actual air raid or even by a prolonged black-out," he predicted, "could not only be more destructive of life and property but could result in retarding the entire war effort of this nation far more than the treacherous bombing of Pearl Harbor. . . . To assume that the enemy has not planned fifth column activities for us in a wave of sabotage is simply to live in a fool's paradise."

Not one Japanese resident was ever found guilty of sabotage. Yet, by June 1942, all of them, whether aliens or citizens, had been routed from their West Coast communities; most were forced to spend the remaining war years in desert encampments. Eventually the War Relocation Authority created 10 camps in seven western states. Every effort to release the Japanese-Americans faced a storm of opposition. "You know," advised one Democratic Senator from Washington, "a Jap would be an awfully good dog right up to the point that he can pull something. . . . They might be able to go out some place and blow up maybe Coulee Dam or Bonneville, or maybe some large munitions plant." During 1943 thousands of Japanese-Americans were allowed it accept employment in the East and Midwest, to attend college, or to enlist. By 1944 Roosevelt admitted that the Japanese-Americans were no threat to the American war effort, but so pervading was the anti-Japanese sentiment from Los Angeles to Washington that not until January 1945 did he permit the Japanese-Americans to leave the relocation centers. Meanwhile the U.S. Supreme Court, in a series of notable decisions, upheld the government's evacuation program as a legitimate wartime security measure. During their long confinement many Japanese-Americans suffered privation, neglect, and even brutality, yet some had become so distrustful of the public that they had no desire to escape the protection of the camps. Eventually half the Japanese-Americans returned to the West Coast; there they found their property confiscated and their jobs preempted. Altogether these citizens and residents suffered property losses in excess of $350 million.

What the war would contribute to the progress of black Americans was not immediately apparent. As late as 1940 one black described life in America: "We are still deprived of proper education, robbed of our vote and ruled by lynch law in the South. In the North we are discriminated against in business: forced to live in ghettos like Harlem, through housing restrictions and prejudice. We are 'undesirable' socially. We can take no pride in our armed forces. . . . We can become no more than flunkies in the army and kitchen boys in the navy." Still, from the beginning, blacks supported the war. They shared the deep American opposition to Hitler and his racial policies. Nothing less than victory, they agreed, would enable the struggle for equality to continue. The black press lauded the war effort without restraint under the assumption that the war experience would improve the status of blacks in American society. Its editors warned the nation that blacks were not entering the struggle against Hitler to perpetuate their condition of poverty, starvation, and humiliation.

Blacks who detected the unique opportunity provided by a war emergency to improve their status organized a movement to stage a protest march in Washington during the summer of 1941. A. Philip Randolph of the Brotherhood of Sleeping Car Porters planned the march in response to the discrimination against blacks in the defense industries and the armed services. Randolph believed a mass demonstration was necessary to "shake up white America." The demands that Randolph presented to Roosevelt were, with one exception, improvements for blacks that the President himself could grant. What alone required congressional action was Randolph's request that bargaining rights under the Wagner Labor Act be denied to unions that barred black membership. Roosevelt opposed the march and warned Randolph that a black demonstration in wartime would stir up racial hatreds and hamper progress toward racial equality. The bargain that prompted Randolph to call off the march compelled the President to issue an executive order that ended discrimination in hiring practices among all agencies and companies engaged in defense production. In addition, the President created the Fair Employment Practices Committee (FEPC) to investigate complaints and enforce the ruling. Randolph kept his movement intact. He continued to denounce Jim Crow laws and urged blacks to defy them.

Randolph's crusade could not survive the movement of blacks into the war industries but, in 1942, pacifists organized the Congress of Racial Equality (CORE) to bring to the American scene the nonviolent techniques that Gandhi had used effectively to undermine the British position in India. Attacking segregation in all its forms, CORE used sit-ins to desegregate theaters and restaurants in several cities outside the South. But the more influential organizations were the long-established National Association for the Advancement of Colored People (NAACP) and the Urban League, which still anticipated progress through political action, court decisions, education, and white support. Oswald Garrison Villard advised his fellow NAACP leaders to "refrain from any acts which will unduly arouse or antagonize white people." Government decrees, he warned, would not eliminate prejudice or white supremacy. As blacks stepped up their demands for racial equality, Southern congressmen and editors accused them of threatening the harmony of the South. They reminded Roosevelt that except for the Democratic party in the South he would not be in the White House. In Congress the Southerners focused their hostility on the FEPC, which they accused of fomenting racial discord. To protect the committee, all of its wartime chairmen insisted that the committee was designed less to eradicate discrimination than to make reasonable progress in the nation's employment practices. In many cases employers and unions simply defied the committee's orders. Congress crippled the FEPC with a drastic budget cut in the summer of 1945 and arranged for its dissolution within a year.

Nowhere in the country was segregation as complete as in the armed forces, where blacks served in separate units under white officers and generally performed menial tasks. Officials justified this practice by insisting that blacks were ineffective in combat, were racially inferior, and required white leadership. Moreover, as General Marshall observed in 1941, the Army dared not cripple morale by ignoring "the special relationships between negroes and whites which have been established by the American people through custom and habit." Despite such strong segregationist traditions, blacks entered the armed services in large numbers. Only 10 percent of the population, they comprised 16 percent of the Army enlistments. The special attractiveness of military pay for low-income blacks could not deny their widespread acceptance of the American cause. In the armed forces, however, they faced established segregation practices. They received assignments to segregated units, theaters, clubs, and recreation and transportation facilities. The draft increased the number of blacks in the armed forces to 700,000 by the fall of 1944. By that time conditions had improved. Blacks in the Navy had advanced to technical positions and received assignments to integrated crews. Blacks in the Army had received special training; some had gone abroad in combat units. But desegregation on Europe's battlefields never went beyond the assignment of black platoons to white companies.

Black gains, if real, had been limited, leaving a chasm between the dream and the reality of racial equality. The contributions of blacks to the nation's war effort, added to the country's official commitment to freedom for the victims of aggression, rendered the near absence of civil rights among blacks in the United States more and more intolerable. In communities around the military camps blacks found family housing unattainable. Those in war work experienced little improvement in their living conditions. Between 1940 and 1943 Detroit's wartime boom brought a half million people, including 60,000 blacks, to that city. Many white and black families lived in crowded, substandard housing. The competition for jobs and housing increased racial tensions until, one Sunday evening in June 1943, they exploded into violence. Rioting engulfed the black ghetto. When the police lost control, the governor sent in 6000 soldiers to disperse the crowds. Altogether the race riot took 34 lives, 25 of them black. During the rioting Detroit police killed 17 blacks, but no whites. Prejudice was still the normal condition. In August 1943 thousands of New York blacks took to the streets of Harlem, looting and destroying property. The disturbance, quieted by teams of black and white policemen, was less a race riot than an expression of resentment against the frustrations of ghetto life. But a new day was dawning. The Supreme Court had extended voting rights through its decision in *Smith* v. *Allwright* (1944), which outlawed white primaries. The war provided black leaders the opportunity to improve their organization and infused them with renewed hope and determination. Increasingly militant, they recognized the power of protest, agitation, and mass action in their effort to eliminate their unequal status.

WARTIME POLITICS AND THE ELECTION OF 1944

Managing the war was a Democratic responsibility, since that party controlled both Congress and the presidency. By conducting the war in a bipartisan manner, with Republicans holding many key positions in his administration, Roosevelt sought to maintain a truce in American politics. By mid-1942 the country appeared to be more united than at any time since the early months of the New Deal. The main lines of the President's international and domestic policies faced no opposition worthy of the name. Roosevelt's political

enemies seemed demoralized by the apparent unanimity of opinion, which demanded a successful prosecution of the war; Republican spokesmen agreed that Congress could not run it. Few prewar
isolationists favored a postwar return to isolationism which might
again consign Europe to the instability of the interwar period. Still
the Republicans distrusted the New Dealers in the Roosevelt administration. These holdovers were determined, warned Senator
Robert A. Taft of Ohio, "to make the country over under the cover
of war if they can."

Such traditional Republican opposition to Roosevelt's liberal
policies found unanticipated support in the country's conservative
revival. Wartime economic opportunities turned much of the populace to the right. Forgetting that it was the demands of government
on the American economy that created the new prosperity, many
of the well-employed reverted to the verities of the 1920s, which
taught that a self-reliant people could work out its destiny free of
governmental interference. One Democrat observed bitterly, "I'll
bet half the people who were on W.P.A. wouldn't admit that fact
if they were asked. Actually they think it was somebody else who
was starving back in 1933." Similarly, corporate executives, even
as their cost-plus contracts guaranteed ample profits and enhanced
their preponderant positions in the American economy, proclaimed
the virtues of free enterprise.

Republicans, conscious of their growing strength, made a
strong bid for victory in the midterm elections of 1942. Some
Republican candidates campaigned against Roosevelt, his policies,
and his leadership as if there were no war. Democrats responded
with appeals for national unity, charging that partisan criticism of
national policy would encourage the enemy. Edward J. Flynn, the
Democratic national chairman, reminded the country that "the
only beneficiaries of the Republican policy of criticism are in
Tokyo, . . . in Rome, in Berlin, and in other Axis centers." Such
Democratic tactics failed. Republicans gained heavily in the
November elections, adding 46 seats in the House and nine in the
Senate. The Republican upsurge sent several well-known conserva-
tives to Congress and defeated the noted progressive, Senator
George Norris of Nebraska. Only 28 million voted, 22 million less
than in 1940. Many industrial employees, working long hours and

often recently residents of other states, no less than members of the armed forces, found voting difficult, if not impossible.

When the new Congress met in January 1943, the conservatives, both Democratic and Republican, were ready to reassert their prerogatives. They established special committees to investigate the defense programs and the performance of executive agencies. Congressional conservatives led the final assault on Roosevelt's economic policies. During 1943 much of what remained of the New Deal disappeared. Under wartime conditions the work of its agencies became unnecessary. Conservatives managed at last to reverse the experience of 1933 when the reformers took command of Washington. This time the change was less dramatic, but it promised to be no less sweeping. Congress voted special legislation to prevent unions from seeking wage increases through strikes. To deal with a more and more independent Congress, the President pulled James F. Byrnes off the Supreme Court bench and appointed him as his personal liaison. In 1944 the Senate created its own bipartisan Postwar Planning Committee as a warning to Roosevelt that it had no intention of carrying out his sweeping "Economic Bill of Rights," outlined in his message of January 1944. One administration measure faced no conservative opposition. In June 1944 Congress passed the Servicemen's Readjustment Act, or the "G. I. Bill of Rights," designed to ease the anticipated return of millions of soldiers to civilian life with loans for houses, businesses, hospitals, and other facilities, and generous educational benefits.

So pronounced had been the country's reversion to conservatism by mid-1944 that many Democrats wondered whether the President's mandate still held. Several Republicans pursued their party's nomination in what promised to be a Republican year. Wendell Willkie, who had done well as the Republican candidate in 1940, wanted another nomination, but the Republican managers of the Midwest regarded him as too liberal and moved early to stop his candidacy. Wilkie entrusted his chances to the Wisconsin primary, where he received a scant 16 percent of the vote. This display of conservative Republican solidarity terminated Willkie's effort without aiding the cause of Governor John W. Bricker of Ohio. By 1944 the Republican front-runner was Governor Thomas E. Dewey of New York who, as district attorney, had made a national reputation as a fighter of organized crime. In July the Republican convention at Chicago gave Dewey the nomination on the first ballot with one dissenting vote. The convention selected Bricker for the vice-presidency. The Republican platform upheld Roosevelt's war policies and the New Deal reforms, but it attacked the President for poor administration.

Roosevelt's nomination for a fourth term was scarcely in doubt, but Southern conservatives demanded that the President replace Vice-President Henry A. Wallace, still an ardent New Dealer, with a less liberal candidate. James F. Byrnes, the South's choice, was anathema to labor and the blacks. Roosevelt required a candidate who was equally acceptable to all factions of the party. Flynn explained the President's decision: "Truman was the only one who fitted. . . . He just dropped into the slot." Truman was popular among congressional conservatives and labor leaders, and his support of the administration made him acceptable to the White House. Dewey based his hopes for a successful race against Roosevelt on the rebirth of conservatism and the widespread distrust of governmental power. But he, with his party, accepted the social and economic advances of the New Deal and the basic thrust of Roosevelt's war policies. Dewey's failure to stake out an independent position on the important issues erased much of his political support among Democrats and independents and compelled him ultimately to engage in a personal attack on Roosevelt—his age, his health, and his alleged harboring of Communists in government. The Communist issue dominated much of the Republican campaigning.

Roosevelt opened his short, masterful campaign before the Teamster's Union on September 23. Warming to his labor audience, Roosevelt turned his full ridicule on Dewey and the Republicans. "These Republican leaders," he said, "have not been content with attacks on me, or my wife, or on my sons. No, not content with that, they now include my little dog, Fala. Well, of course, I don't resent attacks, and my family doesn't resent attacks, but Fala *does* resent them." Roosevelt's remarks so enraged Dewey that he spent the remainder of the campaign in a meaningless vilification of the President. Meanwhile Roosevelt championed the New Deal and the cause of labor, relying more on labor leaders than on Democratic regulars and conservatives to carry the election. Even *The*

New Republic revealed little enthusiasm for the President. "The aging Roosevelt Cabinet doesn't fill us with our old enthusiasm and zip," it editorialized on October 23. "But after looking over the field, we find nowhere else to go." Dewey had faced no issue forthrightly. "Any time you want to find him," the editorial complained, "he's right out in the middle of a Gallup poll." In November Roosevelt carried 36 states with 432 electoral votes, leaving 99 for Dewey. But Roosevelt received only 53.4 percent of the popular vote, a margin of 3.6 million votes. Roosevelt captured the cities overwhelmingly for the fourth time; the farmers of the Midwest continued their drift back to Republican ranks. The Democrats increased their congressional margins, giving them sure control of the federal government as the war entered its final months.

VICTORY IN EUROPE

Early in 1944 the British and American military effort concentrated on the forthcoming invasion of the European continent. Already the German positions were collapsing on both the Mediterranean and Eastern fronts. During June the American Fifth Army occupied Rome and continued to drive the German forces from the Italian peninsula. Strengthened by Lend-Lease aid pouring into Russia through Iran, the Red Armies sustained their counteroffensive against the German invaders. By May 1944, they had recaptured Kiev, had freed Leningrad and Moscow from the German siege, and had regained Odessa and Sevastopol on the Black Sea. During June the Russians opened their summer offensive along an 800-mile front to the south of Leningrad. Meanwhile, during April and May, strategic air bombing of German targets from British bases reached their peak of intensity. Supported by the long-range P-51B Mustang fighters, U.S. bombers, formerly limited in their range by German fighter craft, now inaugurated a succession of high-altitude daytime runs over industrial and transportation targets in the heart of Germany. But, in June 1944, the bombing stopped momentarily while British and American aircraft were readied for the cross-channel invasion.

General Eisenhower reached England in January 1944 to take

command of the Allied Expeditionary Forces. A sudden Channel storm on June 5 forced a delay but, at dawn on the following morning, after months of tedious preparation, the Allied forces struck the mainland in the largest amphibious operation in history. The initial landing along the Cotentin Peninsula involved 176,000 men, 4000 landing craft, 600 warships, and 11,000 aircraft. The Allied vanguard reached the beach through a heavy surf. German reserves could not enter the battle with sufficient speed and numbers to be effective. Before the end of June, American troops had reached Cherbourg. General Omar Bradley's First Army, along with Montgomery's British Second, fought their way southward through Normandy against continued German resistance. By July, when British and American forces entered Caen and St. Lo, Eisenhower had dispatched 1 million men to the mainland. Thereafter Allied power and mobility, aided by the arrival of thousands of trucks and tanks, were so overwhelming that the Germans could never stabilize the lines of battle. During August the U.S. Seventh Army, under General Alexander M. Patch, landed on the southern French coast and advanced rapidly northward through the Rhone Valley. On August 25 American troops entered Paris. Hitler's final, desperate order that Paris be destroyed was ignored. After four years of Nazi occupation, Paris presented a scene of wild jubilation. General Charles de Gaulle took command of the French nation and committed what remained of France's resources to the Allied effort.

Following the liberation of Paris, British, American, and Canadian forces pressed onward toward Germany through France, Belgium, Luxembourg, and Holland. During October the U.S. First Army punctured the Siegfried Line and entered Aachen. In November General George Patton pushed his Third Army eastward to Metz and Strasbourg. The speed of the American advance weakened the allied center, encouraging Hitler to believe that a powerful German counteroffensive in the Ardennes Forest could compel a general Allied retreat. Suddenly in mid-December the German command drove 24 divisions against the overextended American forces on a 40-mile front. In this Battle of the Bulge the Germans advanced 50 miles to the Meuse. At Bastogne they surrounded the American defenders, but failed to gain a capitulation. General Eisenhower quickly sent the American First and Third from the south and Montgomery's British forces from the north to the relief of Bastogne. During January the Germans grudgingly gave up their gains in what had been, for the United States, the most costly battle of the war—8000 dead and 48,000 wounded.

To prevent the movement of German troops to the Eastern Front, the United States and Britain maintained a steady bombing of key transportation centers in eastern Germany. There, at Dresden, in February 1945, occurred the most devastating air raid of the European war. British bombers dropped incendiary bombs in such numbers that they created a fire-storm that burned out six square miles and killed an estimated 135,000 residents of the crowded city. Even Churchill questioned the wisdom and morality of such air attacks, commenting in March 1945 that "the destruction of Dresden remains a serious query against the conduct of Allied bombing." After February Allied bombers rained destruction on German cities and industrial complexes with increasing efficiency. However, it is not clear that Allied strategic bombing, despite the destruction it produced, played a major role in the German defeat. Bombing rendered almost 8 million Germans homeless and deprived another 12 million of utilities for some period of time. Despite the apparent effectiveness of the bombing effort, strategic bombing surveys conducted by Allied personnel concluded that, until 1945, the German people continued to maintain German war production at a high level. When morale finally collapsed in the spring of 1945, it resulted less from the air raids than from the defeat of the German armies along both the Western and the Eastern fronts.

Throughout the spring of 1945 the Allied victories became more routine. During February British forces crossed Holland to reach the German border. The U.S. Third Army entered the Ruhr Valley and reached the Rhine at Dusseldorf. Expecting to meet stiff resistance at the Rhine, the Americans, on March 7, captured the Remagen bridge before the Germans could destroy it. Pouring across the bridge, U. S. soldiers established a strong bridgehead on the right bank. During April American forces enveloped the Ruhr and captured over 300,000 Germans. Now the British and American armies had most of Germany open to them. Instead of pushing toward Berlin, however, Eisenhower preferred to capture Bavaria

to the south and move eastward toward Austria and Czechoslovakia. Anticipating no trouble with the Russians over Berlin, he
hoped to avoid further military disaster by keeping his units and
communications intact. Patton's Third Army crossed Bavaria and
entered Czechoslovakia, but stopped short of Prague. Meanwhile
the Russians, late in 1944, had crossed East Prussia, had captured
Belgrade, Budapest, and Warsaw and, by early 1945, had reached
the Oder River. In mid-April they launched their final assault on
Berlin, entering the city on April 24 to begin their deliberate
reduction of the historic German capital. Other Russian units, pushing westward across Czechoslovakia and Germany, entered Prague
and joined the American forces on the Elbe at Torgau. On May 1,
the German provisional government announced Hitler's death.
Berlin fell on the following day, and on May 7 Field Marshal Alfred
Jodl, at Reims, signed the documents of unconditional surrender.
On May 8—VE Day—the people of the Allied and occupied countries celebrated the end of the European war.

ADVANCE ACROSS THE PACIFIC

When the United States turned its attention to the Pacific in
mid-1942, it faced the task of destroying a Japanese Empire that
extended thousands of miles from China to the Solomon Islands off
Australia. Still, that vast imperial structure was far less formidable
than Hitler's expanded dominion, because Japan lacked the natural
and manpower resources of Germany. By expanding over such an
extensive area, the Japanese had scattered their forces so thinly that
American units, having again established control of the sea, could
either destroy or bypass the isolated Japanese garrisons without the
need of great numbers. The Japanese could never break communications between the United States and Australia. In China, moreover, Japan still faced the presence of Chiang Kai-shek's armies.
Given time, the United States could build its striking power in the
Pacific to the point where it could slowly and efficiently dismantle
the entire Japanese Empire. Even before the nation was actually
prepared for operations in the Pacific, U. S. naval forces, during

May and June 1942, stopped the Japanese offensive in two remarkable naval battles, the Coral Sea and Midway.

Marines inaugurated the American counteroffensive in the Pacific with landings at Tulagi and Guadalcanal during August 1942. At Guadalcanal the Japanese resisted fiercely, and not until early 1943 did American forces gain complete control of the southern Solomons. Meanwhile U. S. commanders in the Pacific disagreed on the basic strategy that the nation should pursue. General Douglas MacArthur, with headquarters in Australia, favored a sweep through the Bismarcks to the Philippine Sea, ending with the capture of the Philippine Islands. Admiral Chester W. Nimitz of the Pacific fleet argued for an advance through the central Pacific toward Japan itself. Somewhere along the route the U. S. fleet would meet and destroy the Japanese navy. General H. H. Arnold, commander of the U.S. Air Force, anticipated the capture of the Marianas from which the new long-range B-29's would bomb the Japanese home islands. In Washington the Joint Chiefs of Staff perfected a strategy that included American advances through both the southwest and the central Pacific.

MacArthur began his successful assault on the Bismarcks barrier in January 1943. After gaining the central Solomons, the Americans established an airfield at Empress Augusta Bay, Bougainville, from which they could strike Rabaul, 235 miles away. Meanwhile other American forces swept around New Guinea and bypassed the strongest Japanese positions, now rendered useless by U. S. control of the seas. By February 1944, MacArthur's forces had skirted Rabaul and had established the huge base of Manus in the Admiralties. The next target was Hollandia on the coast of Dutch New Guinea. Here Generals Walter Krueger and Robert Eichelberger established the headquarters of their Sixth and Eighth armies. At the same time MacArthur transferred his headquarters from Brisbane to Hollandia. In one year U. S. forces, with effective Australian support, had moved 1300 miles through Japanese-held territory and had cut off 135,000 Japanese troops, totally isolated from the areas of conflict.

Admiral Nimitz began his campaign across the central Pacific in November 1943, with an assault on Makin Island in the Gilberts. Bypassing several Japanese bases, the fleet entered the Marshalls, captured Kwajalein in a costly battle, and occupied Eniwetok Atoll. Next the fleet passed Truk and moved into the Marianas. There, on June 20, 1944, it faced the Japanese squadron and drove it back to the Philippines. During June and July marines captured Saipan and Tinian after overcoming stiff resistance. Other U. S. forces occupied Guam and, by November 1944, U. S. aircraft had commenced the bombing of Japanese cities from bases in the Marianas.

During the early winter of 1944-1945 MacArthur achieved another of his goals—the successful invasion of the Philippines. In mid-October 1944, perhaps the greatest armada of all time gathered off the coast of Leyte. What remained of the Japanese battle fleet came out to meet it. In the Second Battle of the Philippine Sea (October 23-25), the Japanese fought well but had no chance. It required a month of heavy fighting to capture Leyte. Samar fell easily. The armada moved through the islands to Mindoro from where, in January 1945, the Americans began the assault of Luzon. A month later units of the Sixth Army entered Manila. During March U. S. forces cleared the Japanese out of the other islands of the Philippine archipelago. Only in northern Luzon the Japanese continued to hold out. Meanwhile, on the Asian mainland the war against Japan met with equal, if less spectacular, success. Early in the war the Japanese had cut the overland routes from Burma into China, forcing the United States to supply the Chinese armies by flying the Hump from India into southern China. This effort permitted Chiang Kai-shek, despite his declining fortunes in China and almost scandalous refusal to engage the Japanese, to remain in the war and occupy tens of thousands of Japanese troops. During March 1945, British forces in India captured Burma. During April and May the Japanese hold on the Asian mainland collapsed everywhere, including Indochina.

Between February and April 1945, U. S. Navy and Marine units pushed into the Bonins. The capture of Iwo Jima, after what was to that time the hardest battle of the Pacific war, gave the United States an air base close enough to Japan to provide fighter escort for bombers stationed on Guam and Saipan. Then, on April 1, Army and Marine forces, supported by an intense naval bombardment, reached the west coast of Okinawa in the Ryukyus. In what proved to be the fiercest struggle of the entire war, made so by Japanese soldiers holed up at the south end of the island and by Japanese Baka planes, carrying a ton of explosives and guided by suicide pilots, the United States finally pushed the Japanese back to their home islands. American bombers, facing little opposition, conducted almost daily runs over Japanese targets. In the Philippines MacArthur's command busily prepared two invasions of Japan—Olympia to strike southern Kyushu in the autumn of 1945, and Coronet to invade the Tokyo plain in the spring of 1946. Still the Japanese refused to ask for terms.

THE TROUBLED ALLIANCE

Unfortunately this vast display of American power, aimed at the total destruction of Germany and Japan, had long ceased to contribute much to world stability. That power had been unleashed so remorselessly under the assumption that these two enemy nations, as aggressors, would continue to be the major, if not sole, sources of instability in world politics. Thus their defeat, if complete, would inaugurate a new era of international stability in which the Wilsonian principles of peaceful change and self-determination would triumph at last. As early as August 1941—four months before Pearl Harbor—Roosevelt and Churchill proclaimed that vision in the form of the Atlantic Charter. After denying that their two countries desired any political advantages from the war, they attempted to universalize their self-denial by expressing their desire "to see no territorial changes that [did] not accord with the freely expressed wishes of the people concerned. . . ." Undoubtedly the Atlantic Charter had no initial purpose other than that of giving encouragement to the peoples under Nazi domination. Beyond that it sought to identify the Allied cause with a return to the relative peace and security of the Versailles system. As a practical program, however, the Atlantic Charter could have no continuing influence beyond the reach of British and American power. Stalin made it clear that he had no interest in a postwar settlement for Eastern and Central Europe that conformed to the principles of self-determination.

Stalin's reasons were obvious, and he made no effort to conceal them. Slavic Europe had been the high road of Nazi invasion, offering almost no resistance to Hitler's eastward advance. Second, invading German armies had twice in one long generation exacted an exorbitant price of the Russian people for their military weakness. This time the Russians, if victorious, would never compromise their determination to limit German power and ambition and to assure themselves pro-Soviet governments along Russia's western periphery. Perhaps Russian diplomats, under the pressure to conform, might sign the Atlantic Charter, but Russia's historic problems and goals would not be curtailed by adherence to principle. Indeed, Stalin, during the summer of 1941, announced his intention to retain all territories granted to Russia by the Nazi-Soviet Pact of August 1939. When Roosevelt's personal emissary, Harry Hopkins, visited London in July 1941 on the matter of aid to Russia, the Soviet government, he recalled, "appeared to be more anxious to discuss future frontiers and spheres of influence than to negotiate for military supplies." In September the Soviet ambassador to Britain, during ceremonies in London, accepted for the Kremlin the principles of the Atlantic Charter, but even then defined self-determination according to Soviet practice. The Polish government in exile, then residing in London, caught the significance of the Russian proviso, and from that moment on warned Washington that on this country's adherence to the Atlantic Charter hinged the future of a free Poland.

Even before Pearl Harbor the Soviet rejection of the principle of self-determination for Eastern Europe confronted Roosevelt and Secretary of State Cordell Hull with a cruel dilemma. The United States could not accept the known purposes of a needed ally, even partially, without compromising the principle of self-determination. Yet to deny Soviet demands for political and territorial gains would endanger the alliance, and with it the possibility of victory over the Axis. Hull solved the immediate dilemma by insisting that the Allies *postpone* all territorial decisions until the end of the war. On December 4, 1941, three days before Pearl Harbor, the London government informed Washington that the Kremlin questioned Western sincerity and that Anthony Eden, the British Foreign Minister, would shortly depart for Moscow to reassure the Soviets of Western support. Immediately Hull warned the British against any secret accords that might defy the principle of self-determination. United States postwar policies, he wrote, "have been determined in the Atlantic Charter which today represents the attitudes not only of the United States but also of Great Britain and of the Soviet Union." Unfortunately, the decision to postpone all territorial arrangements promised no victories for principle when the fighting stopped. To defeat Germany the United States had no choice but to encourage the USSR to invade and occupy those regions of Slavic Europe to which even the Russia of the Czars had traditionally aspired. Stalin's minimum objectives, presented to Eden during his Moscow visit of December 1941, would expand rather than contract with the subsequent triumphs of the Red Army.

For Stalin, Russian security in the postwar world required a system of spheres of influence whereby the great powers would dominate those regions where they had special economic or security interests. As long as Stalin required a second front, he kept his demands for a Soviet sphere of influence muffled. At the Moscow Conference of Foreign Ministers, which met in October 1943, he accepted the American-inspired Four-Power Declaration, carefully phrased to reaffirm the principles of the Atlantic Charter. At the Teheran Conference several weeks later, when Churchill posed the question of Russia's territorial interests, Stalin replied simply, "There is no need to speak at the present time about any Soviet desires, but when the time comes we will speak." Russian armies, early in 1944, crossed the borders of Slavic Europe; immediately Stalin made clear the Kremlin's determination to deal with that region on its own terms. During February 1944, Hull confided to Ambassador W. Averell Harriman in Moscow: "Matters are rapidly approaching the point where the Soviet Government will have to choose between the development and extension of the foundation of international cooperation as the guiding principle of the postwar world as against the continuation of a unilateral and arbitrary method of dealing with its special problems even though these problems are admittedly of more direct interest to the Soviet Union than to other great powers."

United States leaders, in contrast to Stalin, clung to the universalist view that postwar peace demanded the recognition by all nations of their common interest in trade, self-determination, and the rule of law. To that end Roosevelt and Hull, with the full backing of Congress, took the lead in preparing the charter of a postwar United Nations Organization. Hull especially pinned his hopes for the triumph of America's principles on the formation of such a league. Upon his return from Moscow in October 1943, he declared that the four-power declaration on postwar security eliminated any "need for spheres of influence, for alliances, for balance of power, or any other of the special arrangements through which, in the unhappy past, the nations strove to safeguard their security or to promote their interests." What held the President to postponement as the one available escape from unwanted political and territorial compromises was the combined pressures of the Eastern European governments in exile, military advisers motivated by the singleminded purpose of defeating the Axis powers with a still-united alliance, Hull's determination to hold the administration to its principles, and his own self-assurance that he could in time remove the conflict in purpose among Allied leaders through personal diplomacy. As the Russians continued their advance across the Balkan states during 1944, Churchill believed it imperative that the Western Allies negotiate with the Kremlin on spheres of influence that would retain some Western presence in areas about to fall to the Soviet Union. Churchill traveled to Moscow in October and reached an agreement on spheres with Stalin, one, Churchill hoped, that would keep at least Greece out of Soviet hands. Hull opposed the arrangement. "I was not and am not," he wrote, "a believer in the idea of balance of power or spheres of influence. During the First World War I had made an intensive study of the system of spheres of influence and balance of power, and I was grounded to the taproots in their iniquitous consequences."

Hull and Roosevelt were not alone in their determination to uphold the universalist approach to peace. Official Washington overwhelmingly opposed any agreements that defied the principle of self-determination. Whatever the popularity of such an approach to postwar reconstruction, it could only lead to eventual embarrassment and disillusionment. It promised free governments to peoples who would soon be under the control of Red armies. The more complete the Allied conquest of Germany, the more complete would be that Soviet control, the more thorough the destruction of the vital balance of power. If Roosevelt and Hull prepared any program to follow Germany's defeat with hard bargaining over the Soviet future in Eastern Europe, they never revealed it. In anchoring their purpose firmly to the principles of the Atlantic Charter, they failed to define either the means required to compel a Russian acceptance of such principles or the price required to prepare the peoples of Eastern Europe and the United States for the ultimate failure of those principles. Such neglect could terminate in one of two possible situations. Either the West would accept a settlement that it had been taught to regard as immoral, or the Russian people, having suffered such profound destruction at the hands of the Nazi invaders, would feel betrayed by Western leadership. From this simple alternative, both carrying heavy political penalties, there was no escape.

At Yalta, in February 1945, the Big Three—Roosevelt, Churchill, and Stalin—succeeded again in burying their disagreements in broad declarations of purpose that conformed to the principle of self-determination. Early in January 1945, a Moscow broadcast announced that the Soviet Union would recognize the Communist-led Lublin Committee as the provisional government of Poland. At Yalta Roosevelt and Churchill argued for a free Poland. Churchill warned Stalin that for Britain a free Poland was a matter of honor. Europe in 1939 had gone to war to save Poland from Hitler and would not now willingly see that country pass under the control of another power. "It was not only a question of honor for Russia," Stalin replied, "but one of life and death." Throughout history Poland had been the corridor for attack on Russia. Still the Russians, facing two more months of stiff German resistance, shrank from the responsibility of openly defying Western intentions toward liberated Europe. Stalin, in lieu of a settlement, agreed to the Declaration on Poland, which promised free elections based on universal suffrage and the secret ballot. Churchill and Roosevelt readily accepted the Curzon line as Poland's eastern boundary. This line, defined originally by the British during World War I, would convey the eastern third of interwar Poland to Russia. At least in principle the Yalta Conference appeared to be united. Stalin accepted the agreement prepared by the European Advisory

Commission on the tripartite occupation of Germany and Roosevelt's appeal that France be guaranteed a zone of occupation, provided that it be carved from the British and American Zones. But the key issues of German reparations and Western access to Berlin, a city well inside the Russian zone, the Big Three ignored. Again the wartime policy of postponing decisions on all fundamental European issues triumphed.

Yalta made clear Stalin's determination to deal with Slavic Europe on his own terms. It demonstrated with equal clarity that the Western Allies had no interests in Eastern Europe worth a direct confrontation with Soviet power and purpose. On other fronts, where Soviet interests were less compelling, Roosevelt achieved more promising agreements. Stalin renewed his promise, first made in Moscow in October 1943, to enter the Pacific war three months after the final victory in Europe. In exchange, Stalin received the northern Japanese islands, including the southern half of Sakhalin and the Kuriles, and a free hand in Manchuria and Outer Mongolia. At Yalta, moreover, Roosevelt secured a Soviet endorsement of his approach to postwar peace. Stalin accepted Soviet membership in the forthcoming United Nations Organization. To the President this appeared as a final measure of his success in breaking Soviet isolationism and assigning that country a leading and responsible role in world affairs. On March 1, 1945, Roosevelt assured Congress that the Yalta Conference had indeed found a common ground for peace. "It spells," he said, "the end of the system of unilateral action and exclusive alliance and spheres of influence and balances of power and all the other expedients which have been tried for centuries—and have failed. We propose to substitute for all these a universal organization in which all peace-loving nations will finally have a chance to join."

Roosevelt's public optimism, shared by key members of his administration, reflected neither the Yalta Agreements nor the realities of Eastern European politics. Stalin, it was already clear, would not give up his control of East-Central Europe in deference to principles that neither the United States nor Britain would enforce. Nor was it certain that Roosevelt, at Yalta or earlier, could have prevented the subsequent establishment of Communist-led puppet regimes throughout the regions occupied by the Red Army.

At Yalta Roosevelt and Churchill, confronted with the actuality of Russian power in Slavic Europe, had sought to prevent a permanent Soviet hegemony with the only means of influence available to them—extracting from Stalin the promise of self-determination. Yalta did not establish Soviet control of Slavic Europe; it simply demonstrated the absence of Western will to prevent it. At no time, in 1945 or later, would the United States make any effort to drive the Soviet forces out of East-Central Europe. Early in April 1945 Roosevelt, informed of the Kremlin's program of systematic repression in Eastern Europe, cabled his concern to Stalin. On the morning of his death—April 12— the President warned Churchill that Stalin's actions demanded a firm response. But Roosevelt, having refused through more than three years of war to acknowledge publicly Stalin's determination and power to create a Soviet sphere of influence in Eastern Europe, was not prepared to face the Soviet challenge when wartime strategies for victory could no longer keep the Kremlin's intentions from view. Already it was clear to some thoughtful Americans that the problems of peace would be far more intellectually and emotionally demanding than those of war.

Chapter III

Harry Truman and the Rise of American Globalism

END OF THE GRAND ALLIANCE

When Harry S Truman took the presidential oath on April 12, 1945, the American people, conscious of the burgeoning problems of peace at home and abroad, doubted generally that the new President possessed the capacity to handle them. Roosevelt had been a towering figure in the White House; to comparatively few was Truman, even as Vice-President, more than a name, and how could an unknown manage the country in such a critical time? David E. Lilienthal, chairman of the Tennessee Valley Authority, noted in his diary: "Complete unbelief. . . . Then a sick, hapless feeling. Then consternation at the thought of that Throttlebottom, Truman. 'The country and the world doesn't deserve to be left this way. . . . ' " Truman's background offered little assurance of a successful presidency. He was still a Missouri farmer when, at the age of 34, he entered the army and fought in France as a captain of field artillery. After the war he opened a haberdashery shop in Kansas City. When it failed in 1921, he moved into politics through the support to Tom Pendergast's Kansas City political machine. He held elective office as administrator of Jackson County until 1934, when he won election to the U. S. Senate. He was reelected in

1940. By 1945 Truman's political career had spanned more than two decades. It had not, in the public's estimation, elevated him above the Washington crowd, but it had taught him much about political power and its limits.

For many in Congress and the cabinet, Truman's qualities seemed substantial enough. His Senate colleagues knew something of his competence. Senator Arthur H. Vandenberg of Michigan responded to Truman's elevation with the following diary notation: "The gravest question-mark in every American heart is Truman. Can he swing the job? Despite his limited capacities, I think he can." Unfortunately, Roosevelt, despite his declining health, had made no effort to familiarize Truman with the problems before the country. Thus Truman came face to face with the responsibilities of national leadership without adequate preparation. But even such obstacles, some predicted, would not prevent him from asserting his authority over the executive branch. Indeed, Truman's behavior in office soon established his reputation for courage and directness. On May 2, Under Secretary of State Joseph C. Grew described a conversation with the new President: "When I saw him today I had fourteen problems to take up with him and got through them in less than fifteen minutes with a clear directive on every one of them. You can imagine what a joy it is to deal with a man like that." Similarly, Secretary of Commerce Henry A. Wallace, while questioning the President's knowledge, lauded his manner. "Truman's decisiveness is admirable," he recorded in his diary on May 4.

Truman could not avoid the consequences of Roosevelt's wartime refusal to come to terms with Russian ambitions in Europe. At Yalta, Roosevelt recommitted the United States publicly to a Europe reconstructed on the principle of self-determination. Much of Europe and America took that pledge seriously. Yet, in the spring of 1945, the Western powers could no longer guarantee even limited self-determination to the Slavic peoples. Less than a month after Truman entered the presidency, Soviet forces captured Berlin to end the European war and extend the vast region under their control into the heart of Europe. As the Kremlin continued to organize Eastern Europe in accordance with its own political, economic, and security interests, the United States had either to retreat from its promises or demonstrate the will to achieve the triumph of its principles. American leaders could neither discover an honorable retreat nor move forward on the latter course. The first alternative demanded too high a political price; the second was too dangerous militarily. Avoiding the hard choice between recognizing the Soviet sphere or undoing it by force, the Truman administration, in possession of superior economic and military power, assumed that it could compel the Soviets to accept its design for Europe's postwar reconstruction without threats or any genuine show of force.

In April, Ambassador W. Averell Harriman returned from Moscow to inform Truman that the Soviets were breaking the Yalta agreements. These called for Big-Three collaboration in holding "free and unfettered elections" in the regions occupied by Russian forces. Harriman warned the President that Stalin, unless stopped, would exploit the devastation and economic dislocation of western Europe to impose Russian influence there as well. Others in Washington shared Harriman's fears. Under Secretary of State Joseph C. Grew predicted that victory would merely transfer the danger of totalitarian aggression from Germany and Japan to Russia. With its stranglehold on the Slavic states, he noted, "Russia's power will steadily increase and she will in the not distant future be in a favorable position to expand her control, step by step, throughout Europe." Such anti-Soviet views quickly pervaded the cabinet, the State Department, the Joint Chiefs of Staff, the Congress, and even Washington society. Mrs. Joseph Grew responded to a dinner observation that Russia might join the war against Japan with the remark, "Well, in that case we must now begin to think about strengthening Japan." Diplomats in the field ceased to curtail their denunciations of Soviet repression and thereby reaffirmed the notion that the United States should neither condone nor accept Soviet control of Eastern Europe diplomatically.

For Truman, it was far easier to recognize the Soviet dilemma than to formulate an adequate response to it. In Washington the illusion of power was sufficiently strong to sustain a show of resistance to Soviet behavior. Secretary of the Navy James V. Forrestal, at a cabinet meeting on April 23, argued that Soviet policy in Poland was "not an isolated incident but was one of a pattern of unilateral actions of the part of Russia, that they had taken similar positions vis-a-vis Bulgaria, Rumania, Turkey, Greece, and that we might as well meet the issue now as later." Truman, anticipating a meeting with Soviet Foreign Minister V. M. Molotov, told the cabinet that "if the Russians did not wish to join us [at the United Nations Conference in San Francisco] they could go to hell." When Molotov arrived, the President informed him that the United States was becoming tired of waiting for the Soviet Union to carry out its agreements on freely elected governments for Eastern Europe. Molotov complained that no one had ever talked to him like that before. Eventually, the President dismissed Molotov with the request that the Foreign Minister transmit his views to Stalin. Unfortunately, such displays of toughness did not comprise an effective policy for Eastern Europe.

As Western and Soviet purpose toward Slavic Europe moved beyond the point of reconciliation, Truman, both to discover Soviet intention and to issue a warning to the Soviets, dispatched Harry Hopkins to Moscow to confer with Stalin on the question of Poland's future. Hopkins reminded Stalin that the American people took a deep interest in Poland and regarded that nation's political condition symbolic of the status of U.S.-Russian relations. Stalin informed Hopkins, as he had Roosevelt, that a friendly Poland was vital to Russian security. Perhaps better than Hopkins' recorded conversations with Stalin, Ambassador Harriman's personal report of May explained Stalin's concern for Poland: "I am afraid that Stalin does not and never will fully understand our interest in a free Poland as a matter of principle. The Russian Premier is a realist in all of his actions, and it is hard for him to appreciate our faith in abstract principles. It is difficult for him to understand why we should want to interfere with Soviet policy in a country like Poland which he considers so important to Russia's security unless we have some ulterior motive."

In London, Winston Churchill searched for some diplomatic advantage that would permit the West to negotiate realistically with the Kremlim over the future of Europe. When it appeared that Truman would withdraw U.S. advance units to the agreed-on American zone of occupation, Churchill wired the President on May 12: "Surely it is vital now to come to an understanding with Russia, or see where we are with her, before weakening our armies mortally or retiring to the zones of occupation." Columnist Walter Lippmann voiced the same impatience with the tendency toward drift. He asserted on May 8 that Europe was indeed divided into two exclusive spheres of influence, one dominated by the United States and the other by the USSR. "No nation, however strong," he wrote, "has universal world power which reaches everywhere. The realm in which each state has the determining influence is limited by geography and circumstance. Beyond that realm it is possible to bargain and persuade but not compel, and no foreign policy is well conducted which does not recognize these invincible realities." Truman refused either to recognize the Soviet sphere or to exert diplomatic pressure on Stalin. Clearly, the administration had no policy for Eastern Europe at all.

Those Americans who had no interest in power politics looked to the deliberations in San Francisco where, from late April until June 1945, spokesmen of the victorious nations succeeded in framing the United Nations Charter. For some Americans, the United Nations was a welcome substitute for power politics. Actually, it created a convenient location where the delegates of its member nations could debate and discuss; it did not do more. The UN did not establish a new international order and thus wielded no authority that transcended the will of individual nations. What counted were the foreign policies of the major powers, represented in the Security Council. The UN charter placed major authority in the Council under the assumption that world politics still hinged on the will of the strong, and that the United States and Russia, acting in unison, would dominate the Security Council and place their preponderant power behind the Council's decisions. The Charter assumed big-power unity; without it the veto power would destroy the effectiveness of the Council completely. From the outset, therefore, the disagreements that characterized postwar Soviet-American relations prevented any unity within the Security Council. This forced the UN, if it would act at all, to place leadership in the Secretary-General and the General Assembly, where the entire membership conducted its annual business, largely by the majority vote. As the Grand Alliance slowly collapsed under the pressure of postwar issues, the UN emerged as a major Cold War battleground.

Facing the dual challenge of negotiating a settlement for

Europe and bringing peace to the Far East, the Big Three met at Potsdam from July 17 to August 2, 1945. There, on July 26, Truman and Churchill issued the Potsdam Declaration on Japan, demanding immediate surrender unless the Japanese wished to see their homeland devastated. The new Premier, Baron Kantaro Suzuki, favored peace, but the Japanese Army forced him to reject the ultimatum. Still, the days of war were numbered. In mid-July, at Alamagordo, New Mexico, American scientists detonated the first atomic bomb. Informed that this weapon was now available for use against Japan, Truman decided that its employment would save both American and Japanese lives by bringing the war to an immediate end. On August 6, the United States, with British concurrence, dropped an atomic bomb on the Japanese city of Hiroshima, killing almost 80,000 people and exposing countless others to fire and radioactivity. Two days later Russia, fulfilling its promise, declared war on Japan and quickly brought its forces into Manchuria. On August 9, an American bomber dropped a second atomic bomb over Nagasaki. Suzuki, supported by the Japanese Emperor, now agreed to accept the Potsdam Declaration provided that the Emperor could maintain his throne. After imposing restrictions on the Emperor's power and influence, Truman agreed. On August 15— VJ Day—the Pacific war ended.

Meanwhile, at Potsdam the Grand Alliance continued to disintegrate over the questions of Germany and Eastern Europe. Stalin gave Truman and Churchill (the latter replaced on July 28 by the new Prime Minister, Clement Atlee) the choice of accepting the new Soviet posture in East-Central Europe or of perpetuating the process of postponement which, in peacetime, would subject the world to a new set of tensions. Stalin sought guarantees against the resurrection of German military power, largely through heavy reparations. Ultimately, he wanted Western recognition of the new Soviet sphere of influence. At Postdam, the Big Three agreed to demilitarize, de-Nazify, and democratize Germany. Beyond that, they agreed on very little. Lord Alanbrooke, Chief of the British Staff, noted in his diary, "One fact that stands out more clearly than others is that nothing is ever settled." In the absence of any genuine negotiation, power and position alone mattered. Truman and Attlee might object, but they could not influence the Soviet decision to organize Germany's eastern zone politically or to strip it of its industrial resources. In the Potsdam agreement, the Western leaders even permitted the Soviets to take industrial equipment, not required for the peacetime German economy, from the British and American zones as well. Having accepted in practice, if not in principle, the existence of spheres of influence, the Big Three established a Council of Foreign Ministers to preside over the continued postponement of all major substantive issues.

For some Americans, the atomic bomb offered the final assurance that the United States could manage Europe's reconstruction in accordance with its own principles. If the bomb worked, Truman remarked shortly before the Potsdam Conference, "I'll certainly have a hammer on those boys [the Russians]." In September, Secretary of War Henry L. Stimson observed that James F. Byrnes, the new Secretary of State, would go to the London Foreign Ministers Conference with the atomic bomb in his hip pocket. At London, Molotov admitted on one occasion that Byrnes had two advantages over him—eloquence and the atomic bomb. But Byrnes never resorted to atomic diplomacy—the threat of atomic destruction unless the Russians met specific American demands. The Soviets understood clearly that the United States could never establish any interest in Eastern Europe equivalent to the cost of another war. The bomb remained a factor in the stabilization of a divided Europe, nothing more.

For Eastern Europe the die was cast. In London, Byrnes attempted to reassure Molotov that the United States recognized Russia's security interests in Eastern Europe and wanted Russia to have friendly governments along its western borders. Molotov replied simply that any governments of Eastern Europe that resulted from free elections would be anti-Soviet; therefore, free elections would endanger Russian security. Still unwilling to accept the reality of a divided Europe, Byrnes traveled to Moscow in December 1945 in search of an agreement with Stalin. In Moscow, Byrnes compromised his earlier position by recognizing the Communist-led regimes of Rumania and Bulgaria. Stalin agreed, in exchange, to send delegates to a general peace conference. These agreements measured the limits of effective diplomacy. Byrnes' recognition of the satellite states in no way affected the consolidation of Soviet power within the region under Red Army control. Still, so vociferous had become the demand of some Americans that the United States fulfill its promise of self-determination that the President found Byrnes' decisions embarrassing and dated his break with the Secretary from that conference.

By 1946, diplomacy had reached a dead end, caught on issues rendered insoluble by the Russian occupation and predominant interest in East-Central Europe. Unable to accept the Soviet sphere or to reduce it without war, the United States continued to coexist with what it could not change. What minimized the danger of this drift in policy was the actuality of a static, divided Europe. Soviet power had already resolved all specific territorial and political questions under conditions quite tolerable to Washington. American officials never entertained any policy designed to turn the Russians out of Eastern Europe; thus, the American preference for self-determination was never a real threat to Russian interests. The Paris Conference of Foreign Ministers in the spring of 1946, and those that followed, produced neither proposals of compromise nor threats of reprisal. To break this deadlock, Secretary of Commerce Wallace, speaking at Madison Square Garden on September 12, 1946, warned the country that a policy of toughness would settle nothing in Europe; the United States, therefore, could better serve the cause of peace by agreeing to a division of Europe into spheres of influence. Wallace's speech so antagonized Byrnes and other members of the administration that the President called for his resignation. National leaders perferred to behave as if the United States still had choices other than recognition or postponement.

Meanwhile, Big-Three disagreements over Germany became more profound. In Berlin, the Allied Control Council sought to determine how much industrial equipment the Russians could remove from the Western zones without destroying the capacity of the German people to subsist without external assistance. The Russians insisted that Germany required little industry; the British, who again wanted to see Germany prosper, disagreed. The Americans eventually sided with the British. Finally, in early June 1946, General Lucius D. Clay, the American deputy military governor for Germany, ordered a halt to all further reparations shipments from the American zone. The United States and Britain already faced the problem in financing heavy imports into their zones to prevent economic hardship. By mid-1946, the ultimate solution for the German problem was clear. If a united Germany, economically powerful, would again threaten European security, the Allies had no choice but to keep Germany an economic slum or divide it, placing the Russian zone in the economy of Eastern Europe and linking the three Western zones to western Europe. Speaking at Stuttgart, Germany, in September 1946, Secretary Byrnes announced that the three Western occupying powers would proceed to merge their zones into a single economic unit. Creating a strong, united West Germany now became the essence of Western policy.

FROM TRUMAN DOCTRINE TO MARSHALL PLAN

Unfortunately, the Soviet problem could not remain a simple disagreement over principle. Russian power, added to Soviet repression in Eastern Europe, had convinced key officials in Washington as early as 1945 that the USSR was an expansive force with ambitions that included western Europe and more. The continued display of Soviet diplomatic intransigence after Potsdam merely confirmed such conclusions. What had been a noncooperative wartime ally now became, for many Americans, a hostile, ideological enemy. During January 1946, Forrestal confided his new fears of the Soviet Union to his diary: "Our task is . . . complicated by the fact that we are trying to preserve a world in which a capitalistic-democratic method can continue, whereas if the Russian adherence to truly Marxian dialectics continues, their interest lies in a collapse of this system." Stalin's widely monitored speech of February 9 confirmed Forrestal's distrust. By praising the wartime achievements of Russian communism, Stalin seemed to imply that genuine peace and prosperity required a Communist-led worldwide economic order. Supreme Court Justice William O. Douglas termed Stalin's speech "the Declaration of World War III." Amid such mounting fears, the State Department called on George F. Kennan, then Chargé d'Affaires in Moscow, to produce an analysis of Soviet behavior. Kennan warned Washington in a telegraphic message of February 22, 1946: "We have here a force committed fanatically to the belief that with the United States there can be no permanent modus vivendi, that it is desirable and necessary that the internal harmony of our society be disrupted, our traditional way of life be destroyed, and international authority of our state broken, if Soviet power is to be secure." Kennan's views reinforced the suppositions of a widening spectrum of American opinion that the Soviet Union, with its ideological imperatives, endangered American institutions no less than American security.

It was only a matter of time before the policies of the United States would reflect these mounting fears. Whether the Kremlin had designs on regions beyond its immediate control was never certain but, as the conflict deepened, Soviet words and behavior suggested and aggressive intent. If the USSR, in denying the principle of self-determination in East-Central Europe, had broken one set of wartime promises, of what value were Kremlin assurances on other questions? Having reestablished the Cominform in 1947, Soviet officials proclaimed the superiority of Communist dogma and predicted confidently its ultimate triumph. The obvious control that the USSR wielded over Eastern Europe made that nation appear especially ruthless and formidable. Except for the American monopoly of atomic weapons, the Soviet Union enjoyed a vast superiority in available military power.

As 1947 dawned, the western European economies were on the verge of total collapse. So completely had Britain and the other nations relied on American production that their expenditures of credits and other monetary resources in the United States had driven them to the edge of bankruptcy. Western Europe had been so debilitated by war that it seemed powerless to protect itself. Any direct Soviet thrust would set off an unwanted war, but Soviet preponderance in Slavic Europe, the presence of large and seemingly ascendant Communist parties in France and Italy, and the general weakness of western Europe itself seemed to expose it to possible Soviet probing.

Suddenly, the United States faced the unanticipated task of saving non-Communist Europe. But the initial U.S. commitment to European rehabilitation came in response to a specific challenge. Greece, in 1947, was in the throes of a Communist-led revolution; Turkey, militarily weak and lying at Russia's borders, appeared vulnerable to Soviet encroachment. In February the British informed Washington that they could no longer sustain their historic commitment to eastern Mediterranean stability. The President, with the overwhelming concurrence of his advisers, presented his Truman Doctrine to Congress in March 1947. His address committed the United States to "support free peoples who are resisting attempted subjugation by armed minorities or by outside pressures." The President requested $400 million in economic and military aid for Greece and Turkey; beyond these two countries, the Truman Doctrine was a vague and indeterminant promise to support governments under Communist attack. To its critics, the policy appeared so general that it had no visible limits. Congress avoided the issue of the doctrine's meaning. By May, after a long and vigorous debate that revealed the continuing presence of isolationism toward Europe, the measure had passed both houses of Congress and had become the official policy of the United States.

This commitment to economic aid, with its assurance of immediate success, led logically to the Marshall Plan. Still, the program recommended by Secretary of State George C. Marshall at Harvard University in June 1947, differed in purpose and tone from the Truman Doctrine. The new program committed the United States not to a crusade against communism, but to the economic rehabilitation of Europe. Marshall made it a multilateral program by placing the responsibility for economic planning on the European countries themselves. The Secretary pointedly refrained from voicing any universal purpose. "Our policy," he declared, "is directed not against country or doctrine, but against hunger, poverty, desperation, and chaos." Indeed, Marshall invited the Soviet Union and its Slavic satellites to enter the program. Despite this intent, the Marshall Plan, because of Soviet behavior, evolved into a primarily Western endeavor. Molotov arrived at the Paris organizational meeting in July with more than 80 economic advisers. Suddenly the Kremlin recalled the Soviet delegation and denounced the program as an American plot to gain control of the entire European economy. The Soviets responded to this perceived danger by completing the monolithic structure of their Eastern European hegemony.

Kennan faced the immediate issue of European instability in

his noted article, "The Sources of Soviet Conduct," written under the pseudonym "X" in the July 1947 issue of *Foreign Affairs*. Stalin, Kennan observed, would continue to dominate Eastern Europe; every display of political freedom would convince him that only through rigid control could he guarantee pro-Soviet governments along Russia's western periphery. Kennan warned as well that the West could not escape a lengthy struggle with the USSR. Both its concept of history, which predicted a breakdown of capitalism, and its apparent opportunities in Europe offered the Kremlin too many possibilities for additional gains. Thus Kennan recommended, as the basis of American policy, "a long-term, patient but firm and vigilant containment of Russian expansive tendencies." Kennan anticipated the time when containment would bring world politics "to the point where we could discuss effectively with the Russians the dangers and drawbacks this status quo involved, and to arrange with them for its peaceful replacement by a better and sounder one." Meanwhile, Kennan hoped, the United States would conduct its relationships with civility. "It is important to note," he added, "that such a policy [of containment] has nothing to do with outward histrionics: with threats of blustering or superfluous gestures of outward 'toughness.'"

Lippmann argued that containment, in extending U.S. commitments to regions that the nation would not defend, would compel it to expend its "energies and . . . substance upon . . . dubious and unnatural allies on the perimeter of the Soviet Union." Lippmann believed that Washington had overestimated the Soviet danger; this would save containment from disaster. Because Soviet ambitions were unknown, the successes of containment would remain elusive and defy accurate measurement. But the nation's effort to encourage world economic recovery soon experienced dramatic gains. Through international agencies such as the International Monetary Fund, the World Bank, and the General Agreement on Trade and Tariffs, the United States and its European partners achieved both a desired stabilization of currency and the necessary expansion of trade and investment. Despite the American responsibility for financing and managing much of this postwar reconstruction, the effort in no measure exceeded the capabilities of the United States. The limited objectives of international stabilization and economic expansion marked the perimeters of basic American interests and thus, in large measure, the limits of successful national action. The Marshall Plan itself, pouring billions of American dollars into western European nations with the necessary leadership, experience, and traditions to use the aid effectively, wrought such economic triumphs that, by midcentury, the recipient countries had regained or surpassed their productivity of prewar years.

POSTWAR ADJUSTMENT AT HOME

World War II broke the last restraints on the growth of the American economy. What the small budgets, the limited public expenditures and credit expansion of the interwar years could not achieve, the almost inexhaustible power of the federal government to purchase goods and create credit accomplished during the war years. The result was an economic explosion that made the U.S. economy of the 1930s appear small by comparison. Despite the economic dangers in converting the booming wartime economy to peacetime uses, the American people seemed prepared to extend the wartime prosperity into the postwar era. Returning soldiers, no less than millions of others who had engaged in war production, emerged from the war with unprecedented savings. These savings stood at almost $145 billion in 1945, an amount far higher than the national income of 1939. Those who possessed them were determined to acquire the new houses, automobiles, household appliances, and other amenities that measured comfort, convenience, and success in a consumer society.

One contributor to the *Saturday Evening Post* of May 5, 1945, expressed the chief goal of many who anticipated the return of civilian production—the end of car coddling.

> That little crate of mine has had the tenderness, mixed with alarm and apprehension, devoted in normal times only to invalid children and expectant wives. I watch every expression on those dear dials, hunt the soft-looking parts of every road, and every time those delicate casings run over anything harder than a cigar butt, I wince. I look at the tires as anxiously as a man opens the report on a chest X ray. I listen to the motor as nervously as a hypochondriac listens to a new skip in his heartbeat. I have given more thought to that neurotic battery alone than a man ought

to have to give the whole subject of automobiles in a lifetime. Well, it will be like springtime after winter to have this involuntary infatuation over with.

For years, the American automobile industry, extending ample credit, had sold what cars it chose to produce. The automobile offered not only privacy, convenience, and status, but also freedom to travel and explore. It was not strange that countless Americans in 1945 were anxious to exchange their savings for new automobiles.

Population increases, added to the availability of credit, spurred the demand for new housing. In 1945, a federal survey concluded that the country required 12.6 million new housing units. That year over 2.5 million couples still lived with relatives. The Federal Housing Administration and the Veterans Administration encouraged home building by covering almost the entire purchase price of inexpensive houses and extending the time for repayment to 30 years. The resulting market for small houses enabled builders to mass-produce them, to create vast suburbs of identical dwellings, and to sell them at competitive prices to eager purchasers. In Levittown, east of New York City, Abraham Levitt and his sons erected as many as 400 houses a week.

Unfortunately, many problems of reconversion required government action, and few knew what economic policies the President would advocate. Truman claimed to be a New Dealer; in the Senate he had supported Roosevelt's measures with remarkable consistency. In a major address of September 6, 1945, he promised to continue Roosevelt's liberal program and prevent a postwar conservative reaction such as the one that followed World War I. He asked for higher minimum wages, full employment legislation, unemployment compensation, a law to make permanent the wartime Fair Employment Practices Committee, and the continuation of the New Deal farm programs. He recommended slum clearance, limited tax reductions, assistance to small business, and the conservation of natural resources. Finally, he asked for an economic bill of rights that would include access to a job, a decent home, adequate medical care, a good education, and protection against the economic problems of old age, sickness, and unemployment. But Truman's America was conservative, consumer-minded, and divided. Businessmen clamored for the elimination of wartime price and production controls, assuring the country that nothing would stimulate production as effectively as increased prices. Liberals warned that price increases would outstrip production, magnify profit margins, and send the country into a depression. With both political parties avoiding such divisive issues, the President could supply no sense of direction. One Democratic Senator complained bitterly: "I used to visit F.D.R. perhaps once or twice a month. He would encourage me and give me ideas. I don't think I realized how much I depended on him until he died. A few weeks later I went to the White House to talk things over with Harry Truman. He didn't know what I was talking about."

To guarantee full employment, the administration prepared a program of federal spending to ease the transition to a peacetime economy. As a compromise, Congress passed the Employment Act of February 1946, which established the President's Council of Economic Advisers and committed the federal government to the use of "all its plans, functions, and resources [to] promote maximum employment, production, and purchasing power." Having failed to prevent the abolition of the Fair Employment Practices Committee, or to secure a public housing program, Truman took up the issue of price controls. By mid-1946, the National Association of Manufacturers, most industrial and commercial trade associations, the National Association of Real Estate Boards, and several labor unions had combined their efforts to repeal the Office of Price Administration (OPA). The bill to extend the agency's life beyond June 30, 1946, suffered from crippling amendments. When Congress passed the measure with all its infirmities, Truman responded with a resounding veto message. Congress, he warned, could let OPA die and face the wrath of the voters, or it could frame a strong price control bill and face the wrath of the big industries. Congress passed another weak measure on July 25 that reestablished rent and some price controls for another year. Inflation was already out of control, and there was little that the administration could do to halt it. During November, the President placed the burden of inflation on his Republican opponents by removing all controls except those on rents, sugar, and rice. Prices shot up over 30 percent in 1946.

As the economy, lacking direction, moved toward inflation and higher profits, labor demanded a greater share of the prosperity. Similar contentions of industrial profiteering had set off massive strikes during the war. Beginning in late 1945, the nation experienced another round of strikes in the automobile, steel, electrical, and mining industries. On August 18, 1945, Walter P. Reuther wrote to General Motors president, Charles E. Wilson, of his desire for a 30 percent wage increase without any increase in prices: 'We oppose the special interest, pressure-group approach of 'Let's get ours—and the public be damned.' . . . Our proposal for maintaining high labor income without any increase in prices is imperative if we are to achieve an economy of Full Production, Full Employment, and Full Distribution and Consumption." The economy, Reuther argued, could not tolerate the high profit margins of 1929. Even with the wage increases, he continued, General Motors' profits would be far above prewar levels. Wilson responded with the warning that wage increases would be added to prices and would thereby reduce instead of increase the market for automobiles. He offered a 10 percent wage increase. General Motors employees left their jobs on November 21, 1945, and captured the headlines until March 13, 1946. Throughout the long strike, union leaders continued to base their arguments, not only on the immediate needs of the workers, but also on the contribution of high wages to a sounder economy. The settlement included wage increases of 18½ percent, plus a wage-equalization fund to compensate union members for their failure to achieve a better wage agreement. Price increases for automobiles kept pace with the added labor costs.

In May 1946, the federal government broke a major strike in the bituminous coal industry with a court injunction against John L. Lewis's United Mine Workers. When a federal court fined the union $3.5 million (later reduced to $700,000), Lewis sent his miners back to work. Truman had established the principle that the public interest exceeded the private interest even in labor disputes, but this alone did not satisfy the conservative leadership in Congress. During the spring of 1946, Representative Francis Case of South Dakota introduced a bill that provided for a 60-day cooling-off period in labor-management disputes, possible suits against unions for breach of contract, and the out-lawing of secondary boycotts. Truman, angered by union behavior, supported the measure. But when big labor condemned the bill, the President killed it with a veto.

In November 1946 the Republican party, having promised the public both price reduction and business expansion through greater economic freedom, won control of Congress for the first time in 16 years. Republicans campaigned as well on the issues of tax relief, especially for business, and lowered federal expenditures. The economy drive was appealing; it was also ineffective. The new congressional majority soon discovered that Truman had reduced the budget almost to the minimum required by the ongoing costs of the war. Some Republicans, in their new crusade against labor, hoped to ban union shops and end all industrywide bargaining, but they settled for the Taft-Hartley Act. The Eightieth Congress passed this measure in June 1947, over the President's veto. The Taft-Hartley Act—which labor leaders termed a "slave-labor law" —restored to industry the right to determine its own hiring policies. It reduced labor's freedom to engage in political activities, to strike against the public interest, or to strike at all before the termination of a 60-day cooling-off period. Labor's basic gains of New Deal days, especially the right of collective bargaining, were not touched by the Taft-Hartley Act.

By 1947 production had reached an all-time high. So brisk was the demand for goods that the economy had created 60 million jobs. That year the gross national product of $225 billion surpassed even the highest of the war years. Never had American economic power appeared so dominant. Harold J. Laski, the British writer, wrote from London in November:

> America bestrides the world like a collossus; neither Rome at the height of its power nor Great Britain in the period of its economic supremacy enjoyed an influence so direct, so profound, or so pervasive. It has half the wealth of the world today in its hands, it has rather more than half of the world's productive capacity, and it exports more than twice as much as it imports. Today literally hundreds of millions of Europeans and Asiatics know that both the quality and the rhythm of their lives depend upon decisions made in Washington. On the wisdom of those decisions hangs the fate of the next generation.

What sustained the prosperity was not alone high wages and relatively full employment, heavy business investment, exports, and construction. By 1947, as the wartime savings of average Americans vanished, much of the needed purchasing power rested on borrowing. Personal indebtedness rose from $32.7 billion in 1944 to $45 billion in 1947. Much of the rising debt took the form of mortgages, but consumer credit reached $10 billion.

Despite the high production that threatened to saturate certain markets, prices continued to rise. By January 1948, prices were almost 50 percent higher than they had been 18 months earlier. Why business refused to adjust prices downward, even where they had become unreasonable, was obvious enough. Reduced prices did not guarantee a larger total market; other sellers would follow the trend and thus maintain the established market distribution. Most American industry, moreover, was semimonopolistic and thus under no market compulsion. The industrial giants that dominated the country's basic manufacturing exerted much of the price leadership. Asked why he did not cut prices, one textile manufacturer explained, "Demand is so high we'd probably be alone if we were to pioneer a price-cutting drive. And the public wouldn't benefit anyway. Intermediate processors and retailers would grab the profit; they'd mark up our goods to the level of our competitors." The chief concern of business was profit, not full employment. Corporations netted four times as much in 1947 as they had in the 1936-1939 period. With production outstripping income by some $40 billion a year, some economists predicted a recession unless higher wages or lower prices increased the country's purchasing power. By 1948 inflation had become the country's major public issue.

THE ELECTION OF 1948 AND THE FAIR DEAL

Republican victories in 1946 promised even greater triumphs in the presidential contest of 1948. Truman's record in domestic affairs was scarcely reassuring; many Democratic leaders doubted that he could have won a national election on his own. In no way did he fit the stereotype of the successful national politician. Among top Democrats were many who expected less of the Missourian than a distinguished record in the White House, and Truman's failure in managing Congress seemed to prove the supposition that the task of leading the nation exceeded his capacity. Truman seemed unable to maintain even a semblance of party unity. His speeches, often well prepared, were rendered uninspiring by a flat delivery. Everywhere across the country Truman's popularity was on the decline. The President brought men of distinction into his cabinet, but otherwise his close associates appeared to be cronies and second-level politicians. With time, the press seized on Truman's personal idiosyncrasies, his associations, his displays of temper, and his failures as party chief to diminish his stature even further.

Truman's failures in matters of reform alienated much of the country's liberal leadership. Indeed, so marked had been the decline of New Deal liberalism that by 1947 two new organizations attempted to stop the retreat. One, the Progressive Citizens of America (PCA), opposed the inflexibility and anti-Communism that controlled U.S. policies toward Russia; it favored a revival of Roosevelt's New Deal. Those who promoted international conflicts (big business and the military), PCA spokesmen observed, also opposed reform. Only the destruction of their power would permit the nation to adopt new approaches in its foreign and domestic policies. Late in 1947, Henry A. Wallace announced that he would run for the presidency on the PCA's third-party ticket. Organized in January 1947, the Americans for Democratic Action (ADA) comprised middle-of-the-road liberals who sought to counter the political trends in America toward both the right and the left. The ADA, actively anti-Communist, served notice that the middle ground of social democracy was still alive. This powerful element in the Democratic Party favored moderate New Deal policies at home; in matters of foreign affairs it generally lauded the policies of the Truman administration. But many of its leaders had no interest in a Truman nomination in 1948.

Opposed to the ADA was the powerful conservative coalition in Congress, which included a large number of Democrats. This coalition had dominated the Eightieth Congress. Conservative Democrats exerted pressure on Truman from the right, warning him against the adoption of a liberal domestic program. In Wallace's candidacy, Truman faced a clear party split on the left. By 1948, he faced a Southern revolt as well. Convinced that America's world role would no longer permit discrimination in matters of race and that the blacks, pouring into the Northern cities, were turning to the Republican party, the President established a Committee on Civil Rights. When Truman endorsed its conclusions, expressed forcefully in the volume, *To Secure These Rights,* Southern states' rights leaders warned the President that they were prepared to organize a third-party movement in the South.

As the election approached, Democratic prospects brightened. Truman's programs toward Greece, Turkey, and western Europe had already brought some measurable successes and promised even greater ones in the future. The American interest in European stability was obvious enough. Reflecting a broad, national consensus, the administration's European policies appeared to all but a handful of Americans as the best available. What embarrassed the President, however, was the well-publicized crusade of the House Un-American Activities Committee to uncover Communist influence in many areas of American political and intellectual life. By running loyalty checks on government employees, the administration managed to keep the Communist issue out of national politics. The President's loyalty program antagonized only that minority of civil libertarians who predicted that it would turn up few, if any, spies, but would drive many vigorous, self-confident, and capable people from public service. Prosperity continued to keep up with inflation, giving the American people, despite rising prices, a broad sense of well-being.

When the National Democratic Convention met at Philadelphia in July 1948, Truman's many opponents, on both the right and the left, could not agree on a single candidate. Ultimately they had no choice but to accept his nomination. The convention offered the vice-presidential nomination to Senator Alben W. Barkley of Kentucky. The ADA managed to secure a progressive platform that promised the expansion of the New Deal and civil rights to blacks. The platform also endorsed the fundamentally anti-Soviet policy of the Truman administration. Truman appeared before the convention in a white flannel suit to deliver a fiery acceptance speech that scourged the Republican record. Yet his nomination held no assurance of victory and sent the two extremes into open revolt. In the North, Wallace challenged the Democratic Party with a platform endorsing a move toward socialism, increased racial desegregation, and greater cooperation with the Soviet Union. Southern "Dixiecrats" organized their States' Rights Democratic party, nominated Governor J. Strom Thurmond of South Carolina for the presidency, and presented a platform opposing civil rights and defending state authority against the further extension of federal power.

Facing a badly divided and generally demoralized Democratic party, the Republicans entered the 1948 contest supremely confident of victory. Their remarkable show of unity accentuated the contrast between the Republican and Democratic organizations. Convinced that any Republican could win, the party leaders embarked on a methodical search for a candidate. Conservatives liked Senator Robert A. Taft of Ohio; the more progressive element preferred former Governor Harold E. Stassen of Minnesota. But the party's core of managers quickly agreed that Thomas E. Dewey, the nominee of 1944, was the best candidate available. For the vice-presidency they named the popular Governor Earl Warren of California. Dewey, with his known interest in world affairs and a still remarkable record as Governor of New York, appeared a sure winner against a man less formidable than Roosevelt. In the subsequent campaign, the Republican party offered little at variance with the major Democratic policies of the past. It agreed to continue, but more efficiently, the established New Deal measures; it endorsed the basic Truman policies toward Europe. Believing that their strength lay in unity, the Republicans again avoided all the controversial issues of the day. What Republican campaigning could not achieve in reducing the normal Democratic majority, the Northern and Southern rebellions from Democratic ranks would accomplish. The polls seemed to assure a Republican victory, and as Truman's chances appeared to decline, much of the Democratic Party's central leadership denied Truman their open support.

Still Truman would not be denied another term in the White House that easily. Revealing an astonishing confidence and determination, he almost single-handedly took up the Democratic cause, discovered the weaknesses in the Republican position, and slowly turned sure defeat into victory. Truman centered his attack on the Eightieth Republican-controlled "do-nothing" Congress. Whereas that Congress had underwritten the President's foreign policies overwhelmingly, it had been, Truman now reminded the nation, exceedingly reluctant to pass farm and antiinflationary legislation. When Republicans, to counter the Democratic challenge, promised inflationary controls and other economic reforms, Truman called a special session of the Eightieth Congress in the late summer of 1948 and presented to it a body of antiinflationary and social legislation. Predictably, Congress rejected the President's program. Truman traveled 31,000 miles on his whistle-stop tours, hammering the Republican conservatism and inconsistency with telling effect. He made 356 speeches, averaging 10 per working day. As he warmed to his theme of condemning the Republicans for Congress's failure to pass progressive legislation, the crowds responded with the campaign's dominant cry, "Give 'em hell, Harry!" As Election Day approached, Truman denounced the polls, which favored Dewey, as part of a design to keep voters at home on November 2 by convincing them that their votes would make no difference.

Truman's victory was complete. His popular vote of 24 million topped Dewey's by over 2 million, giving him 303 electoral votes to Dewey's 189 and Thurmond's 38 (South Carolina, Alabama, Mississippi, and Louisiana). Pollsters and Republicans were mystified, but they had forgotten that the Democratic party was still the normal majority party in the United States. Wallace's popular vote of 1,156,000 was almost identical to that of Thurmond, but scattered as it was through the more populous North, it won him no electoral votes. Dewey ran strong in the Northeast, whereas Truman carried the important Midwest and the Pacific coast. Behind Truman's victory was not only his own vigorous campaigning, but also the popular identification of prosperity and an apparently successful foreign policy with the Democratic Party. Truman's hard line against Russia preempted the foreign policy issue from the Republicans, while it permitted him to retain the support of anti-Communist liberals. Republican leaders, realizing more than ever before that the nation's established domestic and foreign policies belonged to the Democratic party, were determined to find either new issues or a new candidate. Within four years they would find both.

Confident that he had the support of the nation, Truman proposed to Congress, in his January 1949 message, a broad extension of federal policy known as the "Fair Deal." Many attributed Truman's victory and the Democratic control of both houses of Congress to an upsurge of liberalism that would change the direction of national policy. Yet there were signs by early 1949 that the new Congress would differ only in degree from the Republican-controlled Eightieth Congress. The narrow balance of power in the federal government between the executive and Congress, Republicans and Democrats, conservatives and liberals, prevented any major legislative innovation. Every decided move provoked a countering move that kept national policy almost precisely where it had been. Prosperity ruled out any public demands for reform. As the country recovered from the recession of 1949, Leon H. Keyserling, chairman of the President's Council of Economic Advisers, assured the country that its prosperity would be continuous, with business expansion and federal expenditures, added to price stability, creating the demand necessary to achieve full employment.

Despite the limited public concern, the Fair Deal scored some notable victories. Congress increased minimum wages from 40 to 75 cents per hour; it extended Social Security to 10 million more citizens; it continued and strengthened several key New Deal agencies; it provided for some slum clearance and low-cost housing; it extended immigration quotas to encompass 400,000 additional European refugees. But Truman could not secure repeal of the Taft-Hartley Act or alter the farm program to eliminate the piling up of huge surpluses. To control both farm prices and overproduction, Secretary of Agriculture Charles F. Brannan recommended high support prices for basic commodities and market prices for perishable commodities. The government, under his proposal, would compensate farmers for the difference between market prices and what, to the Department of Agriculture, were fair prices. Congress believed the program to be too expensive and rejected it. On matters of civil rights, federal health insurance, and federal aid to education, the administration achieved nothing. To further racial equality, the President asked Congress to reestablish the Fair Employment Practices Committee, to pass legislation against lynching and poll taxes, and to underwrite the major recommendations of his Commission on Civil Rights. Southern Democrats managed to defeat the administration's entire civil rights program. Acting through an executive order, Truman proceeded to end segregation in the armed forces and federal agencies. Facing little organized opposition, the American Medical Association lobbied Truman's health insurance plan to death. Similarly, the President's proposals for federal aid to education fell before the assault of those who insisted that any federal program extend aid to private and parochial as well as to public schools. By November 1950, the President had lost control of public sentiment so completely that the Republican party overcame most of the Democratic gains of 1948 in both Congress and the states.

Meanwhile, Truman attempted to curtail the search for evidence of Communist influence in American life; such activity questioned the capacity of the administration and the Democratic party to protect the nation's security. In some measure the fear-laden phraseology that dominated official foreign policy statements reinforced the suspicion that communism was an internal and an external threat. The House Un-American Activities Committee, with its hearings around the country, kept the Communist issue in the headlines. The timely charge that Alger Hiss, a State Department official, had given documents to Soviet agents sounded the alarm in 1949 that subversion had indeed penetrated the highest levels of government. To his detractors Hiss's conviction for perjury instead of treason in January 1950 did not disprove the contention that he had been guilty of a treasonable conspiracy. One month later, Dr. Klaus Fuchs, a German-born scientist who had represented Britain on the team that developed the atomic bomb, admitted that he had given atomic secrets to the Russians. Fuchs, in his confession, implicated several Americans, among them Julius and Ethel Rosenberg, who were tried and convicted of treason in 1951. Both were executed two years later. For many Americans these revelations accounted for the alleged failure of the United States to halt the expansion of communism and convinced congressional leaders that the country required more effective laws against subversion. Congress passed the McCarran Internal Security Act of September 1950 over the President's veto. This measure compelled all Communist and Communist-front organizations to register with the Justice Department. The McCarran-Walter Immigration Act of 1952, also passed over a presidential veto, maintained the quota system of 1924 with some minor concessions to Asians. The pervading assumption, encouraged by the President's vetoes, that the administration was soft on communism gave the Republican party another enticing issue as it contemplated the task of recapturing control of the federal government in 1952.

CONTAINMENT IN EUROPE

Two events of 1948 suggested that the Soviet Union would exploit any opportunity to strengthen its position in Europe, even with resort to force. During February a Communist coup toppled the neutral Czechoslovakian government of Edward Benes. The political conditions in Czechoslovakia were unique; the Communist leadership, already strong, required only a minor shake-up in the cabinet to gain control of the government. But American officials, ignoring the fact that Czechoslovakia's situation was singularly precarious, interpreted the coup as merely the first of a series of Soviet efforts to expand through Communist seizures of power. Then, in June, the USSR, in an effort to prevent the organization of Germany's three western zones into a West German state, blockaded the Western access routes to West Berlin, a Western community well within the Soviet zone. Britain and the United States, choosing to avoid a showdown on the ground, responded with the famed Berlin airlift, which supplied the beleaguered city so effectively over its three assigned air corridors that Stalin, early in 1949, ended the blockade and permitted the subsequent creation of the West German Republic. The Kremlin countered this Western triumph, the defection of Yugoslavia from the Soviet bloc, and the final victory of antiguerrilla forces in Greece by establishing the East German Democratic Republic. The political division of Germany was now complete.

Western Europeans, believing themselves threatened for the

first time by Soviet military power, looked to their defenses. In the Brussels Pact of March 1948, Britain, France, and the Benelux countries signed a 50-year defense alliance against Soviet aggression; they then sought military aid in Washington. President Truman reacted favorably to Europe's request and quickly assumed the lead in the creation of the North Atlantic Treaty Organization. Congress, responding to growing public apprehension, endorsed the President's views by passing the Vandenberg Resolution of June 1948 by a vote of 64 to 4, thus preparing the country for its first defense treaty since 1800. Twelve nations signed the pact amid special ceremonies in Washington in April 1949. The Senate approved the treaty in July by a vote of 82 to 13. Behind NATO's military shield, which consisted chiefly of U.S. air-atomic power, the western European economies continued to expand. Moscow responded by exploding its own atomic device and planning its own military alliance—the Warsaw Pact.

To Dean G. Acheson, Secretary of State from 1949 until 1953, fell the task of managing Europe's defense effort. In dominating the evolution of American Cold War policy, Acheson gave expression to a national consensus that, by 1949, viewed the USSR as an immediate threat to Western security. Thus Acheson's major contribution lay less in his perception of danger—which all elements in American society seemingly shared—than in his role as director of the nation's foreign policy establishment. In command of his office, assured of presidential support, Acheson touched most policies with a sure hand, instilling confidence in the soundness of his suppositions. Acheson and his close advisers seldom paused to reexamine their assumptions or to entertain the possibility that they were wrong. George Kennan was the only State Department official who challenged the Acheson consensus directly. He left the State Department in 1950, never to return.

What muted Acheson's potential critics was the Munich analogy. For Acheson, Hitler's aggression in the 1930s was a simple measure of Western military weakness. Never again would the United States become trapped in a war because it was unprepared. Acheson based his quest for greater strength and unity in NATO on the assumption that the USSR remained an expansive force bent on world domination—a danger not only to western Europe but ultimately to the United States and its way of life. To Acheson, the USSR was an elemental force of nature, not unlike a mighty river, that counterforce might keep within its banks but could not stop. In its persistent drive to expand, believed Acheson, the Soviet leadership would never approach any negotiation with a sense of fairness or reciprocity. As early as the Senate hearings on the Truman Doctrine in April 1947, Acheson denied that direct negotiations with the Kremlin would resolve any existing Cold War issues. "I do not think," he said, "that is the way our problems are going to be worked out with the Russians. I think they will have to be worked out over a long period of time and by always indicating to the Russians that we are quite aware of what our own interests are and that we are quite firm about them and quite prepared to take necessary action. Then I think solutions will become possible." Acheson's notions regarding power and diplomacy, always supported by the Munich analogy, won overwhelming support both in Washington and in the capitals of western Europe.

Western power, it seemed, had eliminated the need for compromise. Confronted with inflexible will over West Berlin, the Soviets had retreated. Following the show of Western unity at the Paris Foreign Ministers Conference in May 1949, Acheson announced that the West had gained the initiative in Europe. "[T]hese conferences from now on," he informed the press on June 23, "seem to me to be like the steam gauge on a boiler. . . . They indicate the pressure which has been built up. They indicate the various gains and losses in positions which have taken place between the meetings, and I think that the recording of this Conference is that the position of the West has grown greatly in strength, and that the position of the Soviet Union in regard to the struggle for the soul of Europe has changed from the offensive to the defensive." Settlements, when they came, would simply record the corroding effect of Western power on the ambitions and designs of the Communist bloc. Negotiation recorded facts; it did not create them.

The minority of Americans and Europeans who doubted that NATO, whatever its military effort, would have its way in Europe without war questioned the Western buildup of power. The immediate goal of Western policy was security; the ultimate goal could be only a negotiated settlement or war. Yet it was clear that Washington was determined to avoid both alternatives under the assumption of a gradual Soviet retreat. This compelled Acheson to rationalize his preoccupation with power as a temporary condition preparatory to an eventual resolution of the Cold War largely on Western terms. To give the nation's defense policies a needed sense of direction, especially after the President's decision to proceed with the development of the hydrogen bomb, Acheson developed the promising concept of negotiation from strength. He first developed this theme in a press conference of February 8, 1950.

> What we have . . . observed over the last few years is that the Soviet Government is highly realistic and we have seen time after time that it can adjust itself to facts where facts exist. We have also seen that agreements reached with the Soviet Government are useful when those agreements register facts. . . . So it has been our basic policy to build situations which will extend the area of possible agreement; that is to create strength instead of weakness which exists in many quarters. . . . Those are ways in which in various parts of the world we are trying to extend the area of possible agreement with the Soviet Union by creating situations so strong they can be recognized, and out of them can grow agreement.

Acheson's concept of negotiation from strength meant, in practice, no negotiation at all. Strength adequate to alter Soviet purpose would render negotiation unnecessary. Until Western advantage was sufficient to produce precisely that result, Acheson preferred that the West avoid any settlements. That this policy would merely reaffirm the divisions of Europe and Germany mattered little to security-minded peoples bound together in a full-blown defensive alliance. If U.S. purpose in Europe was that of stabilizing a divided continent—beyond which no policy would be effective anyway—the United States had achieved its goal as early as 1950. In September, the foreign ministers of the United States, Britain, and France agreed to terminate their state of war with West Germany and freed that country to build its own army and conduct its own diplomacy in the interest of increasing Western power. In December, the NATO Council invited General Dwight D. Eisenhower, then president of Columbia University, to become Supreme Commander in Europe. The popular general, the Council hoped, would transform NATO into a powerful defense organization.

Successful containment in a divided Europe would scarcely further the cause of either self-determination within the Slavic states or German unity, but it would provide an escape from the dilemma of coming to terms with the political realities of Europe. For leaders on both sides of the Atlantic, the emerging status of postwar Europe was supremely satisfactory. Whereas western Europeans quickly achieved economic expansion under conditions of political freedom, the United States assumed primary responsibility for their defense against both Russia and Germany. This eliminated for London, Paris, and Rome the need to formulate any genuine policies toward either power. If Europeans after midcentury shared neither the fears nor the long-range goal of self-determination that drove American policy, they could bask in their prosperity while they coexisted in reasonable security with the Soviet hegemony, which they dared not recognize.

GLOBAL CONTAINMENT: CHINA, INDOCHINA, AND KOREA

United States policies in Europe did not presage a resolution of the Soviet problem but, after midcentury, they assured a high degree of stability, prosperity, and security. The nation's response to Asia's postwar upheaval produced policies far more demanding, divisive, and unsatisfactory. Yet only in time would Washington's miscalculations in the Far East exact their full price. In 1945 Asia scarcely seemed a challenge at all. Throughout the twentieth century, Japan had been the major, if not exclusive, threat to a stable and peaceful Orient. But Japanese power had disintegrated in the Pacific war; after September 1945, that country existed under the direct control of U.S. occupation forces. Eventually the American occupation would subject every aspect of Japanese economic and political life to the severest scrutiny and control. Under the direction of General Douglas MacArthur, Supreme Commander of the Allied Powers, occupation authorities methodically assaulted every source of nationalistic indoctrination and centralized authority to create Japan's new climate of intellectual and political freedom. Japan's new constitution of 1946 limited Japan's military forces to levels required by internal security. As the United States perfected its occupation, it effectively barred Russia from a major presence in the northern Pacific. Japan, under American tutelage, embarked on a successful course of political democracy and economic expansion. With American purpose triumphant in Japan, the Far East, despite the dramatic changes occurring elsewhere, posed no visible threats to Western security.

Unfortunately, the occupation of Japan, successful as it was, did not assure a stable Orient at all. Japanese expansionism was not the only danger to Western interests in the Far East. Asian nationalism was another. Long before the present century, East and Southeast Asia, with the exception of China and Thailand, had become the exclusive domain of the Western imperial nations. Through the imposition of unequal treaties, moreover, the major powers had reduced China to a colonial status. It was this massive and almost unchallenged Western dominance that gave the Orient its internal stability and guaranteed political and economic arrangements that served the West admirably. After the Versailles Conference of 1919, this Western hegemony more and more faced the opposition of native elites, often trained in Western universities, who resented the social and political inferiority that foreign white rule imposed on them. They were determined to transfer power to themselves, hopefully without altering the fundamental social and economic structure of Asia. Most nationalists anchored their independence movements to Western notions of self-determination, but a significant minority—which included China's Mao Tse-tung and Indochina's Ho Chi Minh—found their intellectual authority in Marxism and its virulent opposition to colonialism. Whether Marxist or not, all Asian leaders shared the common goal of independence from foreign rule. Mao Tse-tung, for example, sought to direct the force of a Communist-led, cohesive China against the unequal treaties and to build China into a modern, independent nation. Nowhere had Asian nationalists, whatever their ideological preferences, achieved any notable triumphs before Pearl Harbor.

What gave Asian nationalism its first promise of success was the collapse of the Western imperial structures before the Japanese assault of 1942. As their power receded in 1944 and 1945, the Japanese adopted two distinct courses of action to assure Asia's postwar independence: they elevated key Asian leaders to positions of authority within the Japanese imperial structure from which the latter could perfect their revolutionary organizations; and they assigned arms to native forces to enable them to resist any Europeans who chose to return. Confronted after 1945 with determined native opposition, the imperial structures began to disintegrate. Britain, exhausted by war, granted independence to India, Pakistan, Burma, and Ceylon. The Dutch, facing resistance in both Indonesia and the United Nations, eventually capitulated. In Indochina, the French, with British support, regained control of Saigon, while Ho Chi Minh, now in complete command of the Indochinese independence movement, quickly established his authority in the north. With neither Ho nor the French willing to accept a divided country, the contest for Indochina degenerated by 1946 into a bitter civil war in which the French had little chance of success.

Both the Roosevelt and Truman administrations favored the movement toward self-determination in the Far East. Still they refused, because of their concern for cooperation in Europe, to oppose the French in Indochina. Charles de Gaulle, in the spring of 1945, issued a simple but effective warning that any French dissatisfaction with U.S. policy in Southeast Asia might result in the loss of France itself to Russian influence. Thereafter, the State Department split internally on what became one of the most critical American decisions of the decade. The Far Eastern division, arguing for self-determination, regarded Ho as an effective and legitimate spokesman for Indochinese nationalism. The European division, led by Acheson, insisted that the Cold War would be won or lost in Europe and that French support for U.S. policy there was crucial. Still, the ultimate danger in the decision to support French colonialism lay not in its defiance of self-determination, but in its assumption that Ho, as a Marxist, was the agent of the Kremlin and thus a threat, not to French purpose in Indochina, but to the peace and stability of all Southeast Asia. As Acheson explained in a cable of May 1949: "Question whether Ho as much nationalist as Commie is irrelevant. All Stalinists in colonial areas are nationalists. With achievement nat(ionalist) aims (independence) their objective necessarily becomes subordination state to commie purposes. . . . " This assumption of a Soviet threat to Southeast Asia, more than the Truman Doctrine, laid the foundation for the globalization of American foreign policy.

American officials and writers warned the French that they would never defeat Ho unless they separated him from the main thrust of Indochinese nationalism by promising independence and supporting a native leader capable of bidding successfully against Ho for the support of the anti-colonial revolution. Ultimately, the French, in the Elysee Agreements of March 1949, promised independence to Indochina and named Bao Dai, the former king of Annam, as spokesman for the new state of Vietnam. Thereafter, Washington maintained the illusion that its continuing support for France rested on the need to prevent Soviet expansion into Southeast Asia. When, in January 1950, Moscow recognized Ho's Democratic Republic of Vietnam, Acheson declared that such recognition revealed Ho "in his true color as the mortal enemy of national independence in Indochina." When, in May 1950, Acheson negotiated an agreement in Paris whereby France and the governments of Indochina together would carry the responsibility for Indochinese security, the rationale for U.S. aid was clear. "The United States Government," declared Acheson, "convinced that neither national independence nor democratic evolution exist in any area dominated by Soviet imperialism, considers the situation to be such as to warrant its according economic aid and military equipment to the Associated States of Indochina and to France in order to assist them in restoring stability and permitting these states to pursue their peaceful and democratic development."

Events in China, where the regime of Chiang Kai-shek was slowly disintegrating under the pressure of Mao Tse-tung's Communist forces, reinforced the trend toward globalism. The United States, in December 1941, had gone to war against Japan rather than accept any compromise that infringed on China's territorial or administrative integrity. During the war, however, it became clear that the Chinese Nationalists at Chungking, weakened by incompetence and a lack of morale, would not, once the Japanese had departed, compete for power successfully against Mao's highly disciplined Communists to the north. Convinced that only a coalition government would preserve some authority for Chiang, the Truman administration, through the special mission of General George

C. Marshall, sought throughout 1946 to negotiate a compromise between the two competing forces. When Marshall, after months of failure, returned to the United States in January 1947 to assume his duties as Secretary of State, the Chinese civil war broke out again. Secretary Marshall, now convinced that Chiang alone could save himself through massive political, economic, and military reforms, attempted to exert pressure on the Chinese leader by limiting U.S. aid. The Secretary opposed any direct American involvement in the Chinese conflict, warning those who demanded action that no less than 1 million American soldiers and $1 billion could save the Nationalists. Unable to desert Chiang out of deference to his many friends in the United States, yet unwilling to pay the price of saving him, the Truman administration sent moderate quantities of aid, far less than Congress had appropriated, and awaited the ultimate Nationalist collapse.

Chiang's gradual withdrawl to Formosa in 1949 compelled Washington to explain the American failure to keep the Chinese leader in power, because Chiang had countless friends and supporters in the United States. In August 1949 the State Department issued the famed China White Paper, a lengthy document that attempted to prove that the Chinese revolution was an indigenous uprising beyond U.S. control. At the same time, the China White Paper sought to minimize the danger of the Chinese revolution to American security and warned the country against any effort to limit change in Asia through the use of military power. Such notions of limited Soviet power and influence in China could not withstand the pressures of the ensuing China debate. With Chiang's fall, critics charged that it was inconceivable that a nation as powerful as the United States could not have saved Chiang and thereby prevented Mao's astonishing victory for international communism in Asia. Republican spokesmen insisted that a moderate aid program would have been sufficient.

Even as Chiang went into exile, his allies in Congress, led by Senator William F. Knowland of California and Congressman Walter Judd of Minnesota, demanded nonrecognition of the new Peking regime and the resumption of aid to the Nationalists on Formosa. Such aid, ran their prediction, would not only protect that regime from further assault, but also would permit the pro-Chiang

forces along China's periphery to undermine the mainland government. Such a counterrevolutionary program had failed in Russia 30
years earlier; it had even less chance in China, where fewer enemies
of the regime would welcome Chiang's return. If the Nationalists
could not retain control of the mainland with $3 billion in Ameri-
can aid when they still had an army of 3 million men, it was not clear
how any level of military and economic aid would enable them to
return to power. If Communist behavior, especially toward Americans in China, was inexcusable, that behavior would not improve
as the result of nonrecognition. Nor would nonrecognition undermine Mao's government and thereby ease Chiang's return to the
mainland.

To sustain their support of the exiled Chiang, his defenders in
Congress and the press required a rationale that would explain the
Nationalist collapse by demonstrating the failure, not of that
regime, but of the government in Washington. It was left for Senator Joseph R. McCarthy of Wisconsin to supply the needed rationale. McCarthy, troubled by his declining political fortunes,
suddenly recognized the full potential of the Communist issue that
the House Un-American Activities Committee had publicized
thoroughly during the previous three years. McCarthy attributed
Mao's victory not to the energy unleashed by Asian revolution, but
simply to Communist subversion in the conduct of American foreign relations. What else, he asked, could explain disasters of such
magnitude? At Wheeling, West Virginia, early in February 1950,
McCarthy opened his assault on American policy by charging, without any evidence, that the State Department was "thoroughly infested" with Communists. If the United States had failed to subdue
the Chinese revolution, he argued, the reason lay not in China but
in the State Department. Subversives in Washington, who had
denied Chiang the necessary aid to save him, were responsible for
his exile; their removal from power would prepare the way for
Chiang's return to the mainland. Much of the Republican party
moved into line behind the Wisconsin Senator; he had transformed
the support of Chiang into an inexpensive, yet promising, crusade
to undo the Chinese revolution. However, such intentions had no
future in policy formulation. The Chinese Communists were responsible for their own success; and because the Chinese revolution

could be reversed only at the price of war, a counterrevolutionary policy toward China would never have meaning except as an issue in American politics.

Until 1949 American defense planning contemplated no more than the stabilization of Europe. But with the collapse of Nationalist China in December, Asia assumed a strategic importance. If the Soviet Union dictated the behavior of the Communist world, as a minority of Americans had long insisted, it could use its Asian satellites to probe elsewhere in South and Southeast Asia. In November, Foreign Service Officer Karl Lott Rankin warned from Hong Kong: "Now that communist control of China proper is all but assured, it may be taken for granted that efforts will be redoubled to place communist regimes in power elsewhere in Asia. . . . Supported by communist dynamism, China might well be able to dominate not only Indochina, Siam, and Burma, but eventually the Philippines, Indonesia, Pakistan and India itself." Whatever the official perceptions of danger, Acheson, in his noted Washington Press Club speech of January 1950, not only warned the country against any effort to suppress revolution with military power, but also limited the American defense perimeter to the island chain along the eastern coast of Asia, including Japan and Formosa, but excluding South Korea. The decision, approved by the Joint Chiefs of Staff, to avoid a military commitment to the Asian mainland assumed the absence of any direct threat to American security in the Far East.

Thereafter the search for a clear definition of the Asian problem continued. During April 1950, the National Security Council submitted its report on United States Objectives and Programs for National Security, known by its serial number, NSC-68. This document, unlike Acheson's January speech, emphasized not the indigenous character of the revolutionary pressures, which threatened Asia's stability, but the force of Soviet imperialism, which sought to encompass revolutionary Asia within the Soviet sphere. It concluded that the USSR, "unlike previous aspirants to hegemony, is animated by a new fanatic faith, antithetical to our own, and seeks to impose its absolute authority over the rest of the world. . . . To that end Soviet efforts are now directed toward the domination of the Eurasian land mass." NSC-68 warned that "the Communist success in China, taken with the politico-economic situation in the rest of South and South-East Asia, provides a springboard for a further incursion in this troubled area." Such official references to Soviet expansionism again made clear Washington's failure to define the relationship between nationalism and communism as two forces for change in a turbulent Asia. Yet Asian communism could not be both a fundamentally nationalist movement, seeking independence and a new order in Asia, and an international conspiracy, directed by Moscow, in search of nations to conquer and add to the Communist bloc. Governing a nation and serving an international cause were not compatible enterprises.

Under what circumstances the United States would consign forces to a war in Asia was not clear. The burgeoning assumption of a global, Kremlin-based threat to Asia rendered noninvolvement in the event of another Communist-led assault more and more difficult, if not totally illogical. The test came with remarkable suddenness on June 25, 1950, when the U.S. Ambassador in Seoul, South Korea, informed Washington that the Communist-led forces of North Korea had invaded the country. The Soviet Union had trained and financed the North Korean forces, and Stalin undoubtedly acceded to the invasion, but the decision belonged to Kim Il Sung, the North Korean leader. Truman and his advisers, however, had conditioned themselves to see Soviet predominance in any assault on the non-Communist world. On June 27, the President explained his decision to dispatch American forces to Korea. "If we let Korea down," he warned, "the Soviet will keep right on going and swallow up one piece of Asia after another. We had to make a stand some time, or else let all Asia go by the board. If we were to let Asia go, the Near East would collapse and no telling what would happen to Europe." That day the State Department cabled U.S. embassies throughout the world: "Possible that Korea is the only first of a series of coordinated actions on part of Soviet. Maintain utmost vigilance and report immediately any positive or negative information." Much of Congress and the press accepted the administration's judgment that Stalin threatened Asia with endless disasters. The Security Council, with the USSR absent, voted unanimously on June 27 to support the American decision to fight. The resolution recommended only that the UN aid South Korea in restoring peace to the peninsula.

Encouraged by early American success in Korea, many Washington officials pressed the administration for an invasion of North Korea and the forceful reunification of the peninsula. Those who warned that such an advance would expose American forces to mass counterattack and place the United States at a disadvantage faced the opposition of Acheson, who argued that the Soviet Union, not China, had a direct interest in the Korean War, and that neither would intervene. It would be madness, Acheson declared on September 10, for China to enter the war merely to protect the interests of the Kremlin. By October, General MacArthur's forces had regained all South Korean territory. On October 7, the General Assembly, again pressed by Washington, accepted the unification of an independence Korea as its goal and instructed MacArthur to carry out that purpose. MacArthur pushed into North Korea against little resistance and, by November, had neared the Yalu River. Many in Washington knew that success would be neither cheap nor sudden, but they refrained from relaying their doubts to the President. Few cared to argue the questions of strategy and purpose when Truman had assured the country a compelling victory.

MacArthur fell into the trap. During November, large numbers of Chinese crossed the Yalu and put the U.N. forces to flight. Washington was terrified. If the Kremlin possessed the influence to drive China into a war against its own interests, what indeed was the limit of its power? The White House warned in December that if the new attack succeeded, the nation "can expect it to spread through Asia and Europe to this hemisphere. We are fighting in Korea for our own national security and survival." Korea perfected the notion of Chinese subservience to a Moscow-dominated international communism. Truman reminded the American people in his State of the Union message of January 8, 1951: "Our men are fighting . . . because they know, as we do, that the aggression in Korea is part of the attempt of the Russian communist dictatorship to take over the world, step by step." In its new war the administration faced a deep intellectual dilemma. Its rhetoric of global danger, repeated often and without restraint, demanded no less than a victory over Soviet expansionism. At the same time, the administration had no interest in a general war against China, much less against the USSR. This created a chasm between the argument for victory in Korea and the actual military policies that the government intended to pursue. When MacArthur managed to stabilize the battle lines at the South Korean border, the administration decided to stalemate the war and seek a truce. MacArthur publicly defied the President's decision and advocated the military victory that the alleged global nature of the war seemed to require. Truman, on April 11, 1951, relieved the general of his command.

Under the impact of the Korean War and the fears it generated, Truman and Acheson globalized the country's containment policies and prepared Congress for the creation of the force levels essential to the strategy of NSC-68. In August 1950, Congress appropriated over $12 billion for additional military expenses in Europe and Asia and authorized the expansion of the armed forces. In his budget message of 1951, the President declared that military aid had become a permanent element in the American defense program. During 1952, military assistance to Asia began to exceed that earmarked for Europe. In South Korea, the United States supported one of the world's largest non-Communist armies at a cost of almost $1 billion per year. In Indochina, where the French insisted that they also were containing international communism, the United States eventually underwrote 80 percent of the financial expenditure of Paris's military effort. During 1951, the United States, for the first time, extended its formal alliance system into the Far East. That year John Foster Dulles, as special ambassador, negotiated a treaty with Japan designed to encourage that nation's economic growth and thereby its evolution into a strong, dependable ally. At the same time the United States negotiated a number of mutual defense treaties with the Philippines, Australia, and New Zealand. The Senate approved these pacts overwhelmingly during the spring of 1952. In these pacts, Dulles reminded Washington, the United States undertook no obligation except to consult in the event of aggression. Whatever the magnitude of the danger, the defense against it would remain limited.

1952: THE REPUBLICAN TRIUMPH

Long before the summer of 1952, the Republican party prepared to exploit the Democratic administration's embarrassments both at home and abroad. No longer after midcentury could the Democratic party, in the public mind, escape the notion that it had permitted Communists and communist sympathizers too much influence in national decisions, and that it was responsible for the nation's troubles in China and Korea. Truman's second administration, moreover, had been guilty of favoritism, which reflected adversely on the President's judgment. Newspapers made much of five-percenters, mink coats, and deep freezes. The revelations of conflict of interest in the Bureau of Internal Revenue had saddled the administration with charges of corruption. (Senator Karl E. Mundt applied the formula $K_1 C_2$ to the issues of Korea, communism, and corruption.)

Those determined to rebuild Republican power on Democratic failures in Asia especially—largely the Midwestern Old Guard in the Senate—found their ideal candidate in Senator Robert A. Taft of Ohio. Taft had succeeded Arthur H. Vandenberg of Michigan as the party's chief spokesman in the Senate. Vandenberg, as chairman of the Senate Foreign Relations Committee in the Republican-controlled Eightieth Congress, had taken major responsibility for the bipartisanship of the critical years from 1947 to 1949. His close cooperation with the Truman administration assured the national consensus that underwrote the basic policy decisions for Europe. Conscious of the limited and unsatisfactory choices that confronted the United States in China, Vandenberg refused to criticize the disintegration of American policy toward the Nationalist government publicly. Unlike Vandenberg, who died in April 1951, Taft emerged primarily as a critic of both the European and Asian policies of the Truman years. Taft, joined by Herbert Hoover and other traditional isolationists, opposed containment in Europe as an overextension of American power. Convinced that Truman and Acheson exaggerated the Soviet danger, Taft voted against the North Atlantic Treaty. Taft denounced the entire spectrum of Truman decisions for the Far East; he eagerly embraced McCarthy's charges of subversion in the Truman administration.

By binding their party to the issues of China and Korea, Midwestern Republicans believed that they could sidetrack the nomination of the popular General Dwight D. Eisenhower, the choice of the more liberal and coastal wing of the party. An Eisenhower nomination, the Taftites warned their fellow Republicans, would deny the party the use of its best issues, inasmuch as Eisenhower had been a willing partner to all the Truman policies as Chief of Staff and head of NATO. Yet so obvious was Eisenhower's public appeal that the Taft group could not prevent his nomination on the first ballot. Eisenhower had a high military reputation, and in 1952 such a reputation carried special merit. Eisenhower was born in Denison, Texas, in 1890, but had grown up in Abilene, Kansas. He played football at West Point until he injured a knee. After graduation he entered active service and advanced during the interwar years through a series of staff assignments. His organizational ability carried him to his position as Supreme Commander in Europe in 1944 and 1945. For vice-president, the Republicans selected young Richard M. Nixon, who had built a useful anti-Communist reputation in his attacks on Truman's Asian policies.

To bridge the foreign policy gap between Eisenhower and the Taft wing, John Foster Dulles, the noted Republican foreign policy expert, created a foreign policy plank for the Republican platform that ignored Eisenhower's previous refusal to attack Democratic policies and repeated every accusation of purposeful failure that had been leveled at the Truman administration since early 1950. The Democratic leadership, the platform charged, had deliberately denied Chiang Kai-Shek the support he needed and had invited the Korean War by refusing to maintain an effective deterrent. To cement party unity even further, Eisenhower, as the campaign progressed, adopted the foreign policy views of Taft and McCarthy. By September, in speech after speech, he charged the Truman administration with softness toward communism and failure to win the Korean War in accordance with MacArthur's recommendations. Finally, in Detroit on October 25, Eisenhower promised that if he were elected, he would go to Korea in search of a formula to terminate the war.

Obviously the Democratic party entered the 1952 campaign burdened with the dual challenge of defending a thoroughly discredited foreign policy record and defeating the most popular candidate of the century. To make matters worse, the charges of corruption and subversion were undermining Democratic morale. Truman announced in March that he planned to retire at the end of the term. In the resulting scramble for the nomination, Northern Democrats succeeded in drafting Governor Adlai Stevenson of Illinois, a Chicago lawyer with a long record of public service under Roosevelt and Truman. Hesitant to the end, Stevenson accepted the nomination with a convention speech that charmed millions and convinced party leaders that the campaign was not hopeless after all. Stevenson's speeches, which sought out the issues for realistic discussion, captured the imagination of the nation's intellectuals perhaps even more than Roosevelt had done. He defended both containment in Europe and the Korean War in Asia as the necessary price for discouraging further aggression. Above all, he condemned those who promised easy victories in Europe and Asia. But against Eisenhower's popularity he ultimately had little chance.

Both the excitement of the campaign and the unusual attractiveness of both candidates brought a record turnout to the polls in November. Eisenhower received 33,800,000 votes to Stevenson's 27,300,000. Even in defeat, Stevenson's returns exceeded those of Truman in 1948. The Republicans scored heavily on the three issues of Korea, communism, and corruption but, throughout the campaign, the Korean War remained the dominant issue. Yet the polls offered no alternative to the limited war policies of the Truman administration. Whereas Americans generally opposed the war, they rejected equally the only genuine choices available to them: a withdrawal of American troops or an escalation of the fighting in pursuit of victory. This confusion of mind, aggravated by excessive language, crystallized the country's frustration. Korea demonstrated that wars in Asia, where the nation's interests were unclear, could demand an exorbitant emotional and military price of the American public. More than the issues, however, it was the personality of General Eisenhower that carried the Republican party to victory. Nothing demonstrated this more forcefully than the contrast between Eisenhower's easy victory and the Republican failure to secure more than a scant majority in Congress. For even their narrow victory the Republicans paid a price. The central

question in any election is not whether effective campaigning se-
cures votes, but whether it leaves the victor free to develop policies
that reflect reality. Whatever his personal convictions, Eisenhower
had promised the nation more than he could achieve. Thus as
President, he would pursue goals in Europe and Asia that exceeded
the nation's interests and the possibilities for successful action. In
November 1952, that mattered little. The American people had
elected a leader, allegedly above politics, whose inauguration, they
hoped, would usher in a new era of national relaxation from internal and external strife.

Chapter IV

Consolidation: The Eisenhower Years

BUSINESSMEN IN POWER

For the nation's dominant business elite Dwight D. Eisenhower's inauguration in January 1953 heralded the return of businessmen to power over the policies and destinies of the Republic. Dominating the administration were leading representatives of the managerial class—the highly paid executives hired to manage the great industrial and commercial enterprises of the country. This class had thrown its corporate power behind Eisenhower in 1952; now it provided two-thirds of the new President's appointments to cabinet and key administrative posts. Eisenhower's first cabinet reputedly contained "eight millionaires and a plumber." The plumber was Labor Secretary Martin Durkin, head of the plumbers and steamfitters union of the American Federation of Labor. Cabinet spokesmen interpreted the Republican victory as a clarion call for a conservative revolution. To Sinclair Weeks, the new Secretary of Commerce, the election "gave a clear mandate to slam on the brakes and move forward in a different direction." For 20 years, he observed, the federal government had been wrecking the American free enterprise system. Douglas McKay, the new Secretary of the Interior, expressed the same outlook. "We're here in the saddle as an administration representing business and industry," he said. The new Republican leadership, added Secretary of Agricul-

ture Ezra Taft Benson, would "turn America back from an era of
. . . give-away Government programs that were steadily and surely
undermining the moral and spiritual values of our people." Not
since the flush days of Herbert Hoover had Americans in high
office enunciated such economic principles.

There was nothing strange in this determination to transform
the Eisenhower victory into a thoroughgoing conservative political
revolution. Major segments of any coalition will interpret a party
triumph as a vindication of their special preferences and, for traditional Republicans, a national victory at the polls was synonymous
with a victory for American business. Earlier, many Old Guard
Republicans had questioned Eisenhower's economic orthodoxy.
The New York Herald Tribune had published the general's personal
"creed" before his nomination. There he avowed a fundamental
economic conservatism, warning that too much federal intervention would turn "the American dream into an American nightmare." But Eisenhower had not publicized such views, and his
initial supporters had not offered him to the country as the expo-
nent of any specific economic faith. Indeed, Republican campaigning had avoided any open clash with established Democratic
dogma. Eisenhower's top-level appointments were the first clear
revelation of his genuine Republicanism.

As business men filled policymaking posts down to the third
and fourth echelons of government, analysts noted that many Eisenhower appointees had spent their careers fighting the bureaus and
agencies to which they were assigned. Shortly after taking office,
Commerce Secretary Weeks removed Dr. Allen Astin from his
position as head of the Bureau of Standards because he seemed
unmindful of business interests. So vociferous was the public outcry
that Weeks quickly restored Astin to his position. Former congressman Parke M. Banta of Missouri, counsel for Mrs. Olveta Culp
Hobby's new Health, Education, and Welfare Department, voted
in the Eightieth Congress to remove 750,000 people from the
Social Security rolls. Former congressman Albert Cole of Kansas,
head of the Housing Administration, once remarked in Congress
that the idea for public housing "came from the Kremlin." Two of
McKay's top Interior assistants had long voiced their opposition to
federal public land policy. It was never clear to Washington observ-

ers how such men could administer federal programs that they had long rejected.

From its inception the Eisenhower administration faced charges of political favoritism and profiteering. During 1954 the evidence of actual wrongdoing became a source of embarrassment for the President. One notable case concerned Harold E. Talbott, Secretary of the Air Force, who had retained his partnership in the New York engineering firm of Paul B. Mulligan and Company. In testimony before the Senate Permanent Investigations Subcommittee, Talbott admitted that he had sought business for Mulligan and, during his two years in the Pentagon, had received over $130,000 in profits from the Mulligan company. Obviously Eisenhower had appointed many to high office who displayed less than adequate concern for their new responsibilities, but never did the President decry publicly the wrongdoing in his administration. The gifts that he received, especially for his Gettysburg farm, totaled an estimated $300,000 in value. In his defense the President insisted that none of these gifts had any selfish motive behind them.

Eisenhower's record at the administrative level delighted much of conservative America. The introduction of top business managers into government, the President declared, "is proving its worth daily in greater efficiency and lower costs." The San Francisco *Call Bulletin* rejoiced on May 1, 1953, that "Golfer Ike is out of the socialist rough and back on the American fairway." Whatever the preferences of the new leadership, however, it could not ignore the twin legacies of the past—the New Deal and the Cold War. Republican leaders might speak the language of free enterprise but, in the essential areas of national action, they could deviate little from the Roosevelt-Truman tradition. Secretary of the Treasury George M. Humphrey could neither disassemble the budget nor halt the continued inflation. Secretary Benson could not return the farmers to free enterprise. Benson insisted that federal price supports encouraged farmers to overproduce. This, he complained, drove down farm prices and compelled the government to intervene with heavy subsidies. But Benson's program of flexible price supports did not stop the accumulation of huge surpluses. Eventually he would hand out far more in agricultural subsidies than any of his Democratic predecessors. Necessity took its toll of Republican ambitions. Never was a national leadership forced to operate so completely outside its established philosophy. With its deep allegiance to American business, however, the administration refused to modify or restate its new-Hooverian beliefs. It talked the language of Main Street, but Main Street did not control the electorate. This, in essence, underlay the Republican dilemma.

THE REPUBLICAN DILEMMA

Eisenhower's election in 1952 was a demonstration of his personal popularity, little more. That his personality would become the dominant fact of American politics in the 1950s was apparent even before his nomination. His widely publicized and genuine personal charm, added to an illustrious military reputation at a time when such a reputation had some relevance to the needs of the country, made his selection by the Republican convention equivalent to his election to the White House. Except for the Korean War, the campaign was devoid of issues that mattered. Many supported Eisenhower to escape the troubles of the past. Thomas L. Stokes, the noted columnist, later recalled the mood of November 1952.

> Our people were plagued with frustrations of all sorts. . . . The Second World War, with all its bloodshed and sacrifice, had been followed by the "cold war" with its constant tensions, and then the Korean War—all identified with the Democrats. The people were aching for a "deliverer," and it was very natural that they should give a thundering welcome to a hero whose name was a household word.

Eisenhower seemed to offer an independent leadership above the strife of party; this expectation brought millions of stay-at-homes to the polls to produce his landslide victory. Eisenhower's increasing partisanship in the late stages of the campaign created major defections among newsmen and intellectuals, but it never lessened his appeal among the masses. The election returns, moreover, demonstrated not the strength, but the weakness of the Republican party. Never did an American President enter office so easily without carrying a workable majority into Congress with him. The Republican party in 1953 controlled exactly 48 of 96 seats in the Senate. Independent Wayne Morse of Oregon voted with the Republicans on organization, thus giving them a nominal majority. The Republican majority in the House was almost equally nonexistent. With few exceptions, the Republicans who returned to the Senate ran far behind Eisenhower. Thus the challenge to the Republican party was clear. How could the party convert millions of voters who trusted the President but not his party to a state of genuine Republicanism? Many Democrats and independents who voted for Eisenhower resented and distrusted the business administration in Washington. If the Republican high command had any intention of building a majority party on Republican economic dogma, its task was prodigious. Philip L. Graham, publisher of *The Washington Post*, defined the challenge to the Republican Party in a speech at the University of Chicago.

> You cannot keep a Tory government in office simply by saying, "It is less wasteful." The challenge to conservatives in America—and that means largely the challenge to American business—that challenge is to show that there can be conservative social programs. Business must demonstrate that all the twenty years of objections and wails and yells over things such as housing, health, and social security programs, were objections to methods, management, and procedure. And if this conservative party is going to be honest, then it is going to come up with a truly sound, wellrun, conservative social program—one that will affect the people, one that will do something for their betterment.

In essence, the Republican party, with its heavy obligations to American business, needed to prove to millions of Eisenhower voters that its economic policies, whatever their nature, were operating in the broad interest of the American people. But the times did not call for action on the domestic front vigorous enough to solidify the Republican gains. What remained in the Republican arsenal were the alleged failures in the Truman foreign policy that the Republicans had exploited with some success in the 1952 campaign. Senatory Taft admitted that additional GOP victories would not be won by efficiency, honesty, and frugality in government alone. Writing for *Look* magazine in April 1953, he recommended a more promising course. "The particular job to be done," he advised his fellow Republicans, "is to publicise constantly the contrasts between the present administration and the Truman administration. . . . In one way or another, there must be presented to the people the failures in the conduct of the Korean War itself—the lack of ammunition, the mishandling of prisoners, armistice negotiations which enabled the Chinese Communists to build up a tremendously strong force and remedy all their deficiencies, and the outrageous dismissal of MacArthur because he thought that the only purpose of war was victory."

For the Taft Republicans in Congress, foreign policy had become the pawn in a conservative revolution. Attributing past failures in Europe and Asia not only to subversion but also to New Dealism and Fair Dealism, they would delve into everything from alleged treason and corruption to the decisions of the Korean War. This was a dead-end strategy; the partisan effort would never demonstrate the truth of the charges or create a more successful body of foreign policy. Any insistence that the country should have achieved more under Roosevelt and Truman would merely separate the ends from the means of policy until nothing but words remained. Of more immediate significance, this Republican program for party building assigned Senator McCarthy a major role in party strategy; McCarthy's crusade against Communists in government was designed to strip the Truman administration and, with it, the Democratic Party, of every claim to respectability and patriotism.

Conscious of McCarthy's widespread support in Congress and elsewhere, the President ordered his advisers to avoid any confrontation with the Wisconsin senator. When McCarthy launched his crusade against the Voice of America and the Overseas Books Program and then negotiated an agreement with Greek shipowners, Secretary of State John Foster Dulles received McCarthy at the State Department and assured him that he was acting in the nation's best interest. In exchange for administrative silence, McCarthy agreed to attack nothing that occurred after January 20, 1953. Freed of all restraints from Congress and the administration, McCarthy went to new extremes in his pursuit of subversives in government. So prompt were the State Department's reversals of policy on the Overseas Books Program, which resulted from McCarthy's charges, that William S. White of *The New York Times* observed in February 1953: "No greater series of victories by a

Congressional body over a senior Executive Department in so short a time is recalled here."

To further his campaign against the Overseas Books Program, McCarthy sent his subcommittee staff counsel, Roy Cohn, and an unpaid subcommittee consultant, G. David Schine, on a whirlwind trip through western Europe to uncover subversion in the overseas libraries. McCarthy, meanwhile, charged that the program had been sabotaged by appalling infiltration. The State Department asked for several resignations and ordered librarians to remove all books and other material by Communists and fellow travellers. On June 14 Eisenhower told a Dartmouth audience: "Don't join the book burners. Don't think that you are going to conceal faults by concealing evidence that they ever existed. Don't be afraid to go in your library and read every book as long as any document does not offend your own ideas of decency. That should be the only censorship." Three days later Eisenhower met the press; under sharp questioning he admitted that he had ordered no change in policy and really knew little about the matter.

With Executive Order 10450 the Eisenhower administration sought to fulfill the campaign pledge of ridding the government of security risks. It appointed Scott McLeod, a close friend of McCarthy, to administer the order. McLeod soon discovered that he could, without difficulty, remove old Acheson associates under the new order, because it enumerated about 70 characteristics for which a government employee could be termed a security risk. Under the new security system the administration became involved in the "numbers game." As hundreds left the federal service, Washington officials never made clear the number of actual subversives it found in the government. McLeod demurred when questioned: "I don't think that people are concerned with any breakdown. They don't care if they are drunks, perverts, or Communists—they just want us to get rid of them." In February 1954 McLeod told a Lincoln Day rally in Worland, Wyoming: "In the twenty years from 1933-1953, traitors had free run in high places and low. It is not for me to tell you why—it is up to those who permitted it to tell you why. . . . I wish they would stop squealing 'smear' and stand up like men and offer an explanation if they can. . . ." In its first seven months Executive Order 10450 produced somewhat less than 200 removals from the State Department. In June 1954 Under Secretary Walter Bedell Smith testified that the review had not uncovered one Communist in the State Department. The entire security system did not turn up a single traitor, spy, or subversive whom the government was willing to indict.

Meanwhile the attacks on the Democratic past became more sweeping. Thomas E. Dewey entered the fray by telling a Hartford audience that for the remainder of their lives they must associate the words "Truman and Democrat [with] diplomatic failures, military failures, death and tragedy." Even members of the administration took up the theme of Democratic treason. Finding no defense of their loyalty in the White House, some Democratic congressmen warned the President that unless he silenced his fellow Republicans they would no longer support his legislative program. Actually, Democratic leaders never forced the President to pay that political price for the support they gave him in Congress. The foreign aid bill of 1953, for example, passed an almost equally divided House with 160 Democratic and 119 Republican votes. On critical matters of foreign affairs the Democratic party carried the administration's program. These Democratic votes, for which Eisenhower paid nothing, permitted him to coexist peacefully with all elements of his party.

Eventually McCarthy destroyed himself without much help from the President. In January 1954 the Senator came upon the case of Major Irving Peress, an Army dentist accused of Communist activities. When Peress, in a confrontation with McCarthy's subcommittee, invoked the Fifth Amendment, the Senator demanded a court-martial. Instead, the Army granted Peress an honorable discharge. Following a hearing with the commandant at Camp Kilmer, General Ralph Zwicker, McCarthy publicly accused Zwicker of "coddling Communists" and demanded that he be relieved of his command. Secretary of the Army Robert Stevens entered the controversy by ordering Zwicker not to appear before McCarthy again. Meanwhile the White House avoided any involvement. At a private luncheon with McCarthy, made public by the Senators who arranged it, Stevens retreated from his previous stand and agreed to give McCarthy the names of all those responsible for Peress's discharge. So adverse was the reaction to this capitulation that it forced the administration's hand. The White House press secretary arranged for Stevens to read an approved statement to the press: "I shall never accede to the abuse of Army personnel. . . . I shall never accede to their being browbeaten and humiliated." Returning from a vacation at Palm Springs, Eisenhower praised Zwicker for his courage and loyalty.

What inaugurated the Senate investigation of the Army-McCarthy dispute was the Army's decision to give each member of McCarthy's subcommittee a copy of a report that charged McCarthy and Cohn with resort to threats to secure a military commission for Cohn's friend, Private Schine. McCarthy's own Permanent Investigations Subcommittee assumed the necessary investigative role to resolve the charges, with Senator Karl E. Mundt of South Dakota acting as chairman. The hearings opened on April 22, 1954, with full television coverage. From the beginning they presented a drama of rare quality, with a remarkable assortment of characters headed by McCarthy and Boston attorney Joseph Welch, counsel for the Army. Through 36 days of hearings, McCarthy, under Welch's prodding, revealed the hollowness of his crusade against Communists in government. When McCarthy, as in the past, claimed to have evidence to support his charges, Welch suggested that he reveal it promptly for the safety of the country. From such exposure McCarthy could not retreat. At the end, the Senator's prestige had dwindled so badly that even the Senate, in December, voted to condemn him for conduct unbecoming a senator. Republicans, noting McCarthy's continuing strength in the polls, split evenly on the issue. After the Senate action McCarthy had no power to challenge the President or any other citizen.

THE NEW LOOK IN FOREIGN POLICY

Long before Eisenhower entered the White House, the nation's foreign policy elites had formulated two distinct approaches to the challenge of Soviet power and ideology. One group, among them leading public officials, viewed the European situation as one in flux, with the Soviets, having taken possession of Slavic Europe, determined to extend their influence, if not their military power, over portions of western Europe. Soviet power, allegedly in control of China and the Communist-led forces of Indochina, had converted these traditionally friendly and nonaggressive regions into enemies of peace and stability in Asia. To meet this global challenge centering, by definition, in the Kremlin, the United States sustained its commitment both to NATO and to the anti-Communist elements in China, Indochina, and Korea. American officials and those who supported them were determined to accept no change in world politics that flowed from the Soviet victory over Germany or from the triumph of Mao Tse-tung in China. The greater their perceptions of danger, the greater was their insistence that the United States eliminate Soviet control from Eastern Europe and the Peking regime from China. For official Washington the achievement of such purposes presented no problem. Successful containment, they predicted, would aggravate the inconsistencies within the Communist world and assure an ultimate victory without war.

Those who questioned this official view of the Cold War—largely members of the academic community—argued that Europe, if divided, was stable, and that the Soviet intention was less to conquer western Europe than to legitimize the Russian hegemony in Eastern Europe. Such assumptions dictated two realistic courses of action for the United States and its allies in Europe: the maintenance of NATO at a reduced level of military expenditure, and the ultimate diplomatic recognition of the military-political division of Europe as the best settlement available without another war. The critics of official American policy in Asia argued that the power that propelled both Mao Tse-tung and Ho Chi Minh into positions of leadership and established their goals was not a monolithic communism that centered in the Kremlin, but a radical, indigenous nationalism that sought above all the creation of two successful, thoroughly independent nations in East Asia. Since the Peking regime, they warned, rested on the foundation of a massive, internal revolution, not the power and influences of the USSR, it would survive any American effort to return Chiang Kai-shek to power over the mainland. Similarly, this minority argued, the United States would be no more successful in resisting Ho Chi Minh in his crusade to free Indochina of French rule and unite its people into one independent nation. Thus the United States had no realistic alternative to that of coming to terms with Asia's Communist leaders.

Dulles no less than Acheson believed that the United States possessed the moral and physical resources to secure an ultimate victory over the USSR without war. But Dulles shared these suppositions with less patience. He represented the bourgeoning conviction that the United States could, without danger, speed up the process of Soviet disintegration. In his article, "A Policy of Boldness," published in *Life* on May 19, 1952, he asserted that the country's *moral* resources could topple the Soviet imperial structure. The time had come to move beyond containment, to develop a *dynamic* foreign policy that would express the nation's moral purpose. United States policy, he wrote, must stop consigning millions to slavery under Communist domination; it must seek their *liberation*. In the Republican platform of 1952 Dulles promised a program that would "mark the end of the negative, futile, and immoral policy of 'containment' which abandons countless human beings to a despotism and Godless terrorism which in turn enables the rulers to forge the captives into a weapon of our destruction." The new concept of liberation demanded, as its initial step, that the United States shun any settlement that would recognize Soviet control of alien people. Eisenhower embraced the Dulles formula for liberation during his campaign for the presidency.

Eisenhower accepted the Truman consensus on the need for an adequate national defense, but he was determined as well to fullfill his campaign pledge of budget reduction. As early as February 1953, Eisenhower stated his purpose: "Our problem is to achieve military strength within the limits of durable strain upon our economy." In May he spoke of a budget cut of $8 billion to achieve his goal "of creating a situation of maximum strength within economic capabilities." A healthy and functioning economy, he said, was inseparable from true defense. Under the direction of industrialists Charles E. Wilson and Roger Kyes of General Motors, Secretary and Deputy Secretary of Defense, the administration proceeded to reduce the military budget, distributing savings somewhat evenly among the Army, Navy, and Air Force. In January 1954 the President gave the "New Look" in military policy precise meaning when he declared that the nation's defense would emphasize air-atomic power, permitting the country to wield maximum destructive force at minimum cost. Thus the New Look spelled out the administration's effort to fulfill its promise of tax reduction without endangering the country's security. Military experts warned that the concentration on weapons of massive destruction would narrow the American response, in the event of aggression, either to inaction or to nuclear war. The President upheld the new emphasis simply by placing his personal prestige and military reputation behind his basic military decisions. In the absence of any direct military challenge, the precise nature of the American defense structure mattered little.

Secretary of State Dulles soon elevated the military New Look into a broad strategic concept that assured superior national performance at reduced costs and risks of war. On January 12, 1954, the Secretary informed the New York Council on Foreign Relations that the United States would rely less on conventional forces than on its "great capacity to retaliate, instantly, by means and places of our own choosing." This new strategy would eliminate future Koreas; no national government would engage in aggression knowing that its urban centers might be reduced to rubble. But Dulles promised more. The achievement of world stability through the constant threat of massive disaster, he assured the nation, would permit time and the human desire for freedom to work its destruction on the Communist enemy. "If we persist in the course I outline," he promised, "we shall confront dictatorship with a task that is, in the long run, beyond its strength. . . . If the dictators persist in their present course, then it is they who will be limited to superficial successes, while their foundations crumble under the tread of their iron boots. . . . " Not since the 1920s had an administration promised the American people so much for so little. It was not clear even then how the mere threat of retaliation would sustain the peace in areas where American interests were too limited to risk the danger of nuclear war.

Unfortunately, the Secretary's attachment to the goal of liberation, like all broad objectives based on principle, either meant nothing or it meant war. Time would demonstrate that it meant nothing and that the Eisenhower administration, like that of Truman, would emphasize containment. In February 1953 Dulles visited six western European countries and Great Britain to urge their governments to perfect the organization of the European defense structure. At issue was French ratification of the European Defense Community, which included German forces. Dulles warned Paris that further delay would compel Washington to undertake an "agonizing reappraisal" of its European policies. In April the French government delivered a resounding defeat to Dulles' efforts and left the West searching for some formula to tie German power to an intergrated European defense. British Prime Minister Anthony Eden entered the crisis by committing four British divisions to the continent and placing curbs on Germany that were satisfactory to the French. In London in September 1954, Dulles accepted the French demands. Germany now received full independence and membership in NATO. This completed the West's basic defense structure. The Soviets responded to this Western display of unity by establishing, in the Warsaw Pact of May 1955, a binding alliance of their own. Containment thereafter would reinforce the divisions of Europe; it would not do more.

For many scientists, writers, and statesmen, this perennial reliance on power, to the exclusion of any genuine search for accommodation, was both unpromising and dangerous. With the development of hydrogen weapons, war had ceased to be a rational alternative to peace. Shortly before his death, Albert Einstein, whose theories first exposed the secrets of atomic energy, wrote these poignant words: "Our world faces a crisis yet unperceived by those possessing the power to make great decisions for good or evil. The unleashed power of the atom has changed everything save our modes of thinking, and thus we drift toward unparalled catastrophe." During 1955 the mounting fear of nuclear war propelled both Russia and the United States toward a summit meeting. Soviet policy that spring revealed a new flexibility; in April and May, after a decade of obstruction, the Russians negotiated a peace settlement for Austria. Eisenhower responded to the pressures for a meeting with reluctance; the administration's commitment to liberation ruled out any territorial or political agreements with the Kremlin. Still, he joined British, French, and Russian leaders in completing the plans for a Big-Four summit conference to convene in Geneva on July 18.

Those who acclaimed the Geneva Conference as the beginning of a new day in Soviet-American relationship misinterpreted its meaning. The summit was not designed to settle the Cold War; it was called to reassure a world appalled by the spectre of nuclear war. In Geneva Eisenhower assumed the lead in easing tensions. "The United States will never take part in an aggressive war," he told Russian Premier Nikolai Bulganin; the Soviet leader replied, "We believe that statement." Such exchanges created the so-called "spirit of Geneva." What gave the conference its lasting significance was the agreement between the two great powers that under conditions of nuclear stalemate they would settle future differences by means other than war. On the substantive issues that divided Europe the conference made no progress. Dulles, in the months following Geneva, continued to condemn the Soviets for denying self-determination to Eastern Europe and blocking the reunification of Germany through free elections. American inaction during the Hungarian revolt of October 1956 demonstrated how completely Dulles' preachments on liberation were divorced from American power and intent; the United States had no interests in East-Central Europe worth the price of a direct Soviet-American confrontation.

EISENHOWER, DULLES, AND THE FAR EAST

Republican dogma, deeply shared by Secretary Dulles, demanded nothing less than the return of Chiang Kai-sek to power over the Chinese mainland. To avoid any criticism of his possible failure to achieve this goal, Dulles virtually turned over the control of China policy to Chiang's leading proponents in Washington— Admiral Arthur W. Radford, Chairman of the Joint Chiefs of Staff; Walter S. Robertson, Assistant Secretary of State for Far Eastern Affairs; and Senator William F. Knowland of California. These men, joined by Dulles and dozens of others in Congress, the administration, and the press, sustained an attitude of uncompromising hostility toward the Peking regime, a task rendered simple by the obvious contempt in which China's leadership held the United States. Outside government Chiang's organized support centered in the powerful Committee of One Million. Whatever its power over both public sentiment and official policy, the China bloc could never return Chiang to the mainland, because the triumph of such purpose would require a general war in East Asia.

Eisenhower had no interest in any military adventures in China, but he assured his potential critics that his administration's anti-Peking crusade would ultimately succeed. Nonrecognition of the Peking regime, backed by words of unending defiance, sustained the hope of Chiang's return and enabled the administration to avoid the hard necessity of formulating a policy for China at all. Nothing revealed the emptiness of the Eisenhower effort as did the "unleashing" of Chiang Kai-shek in February 1953, when the President, in a gesture of reversing Truman's Korean War order to defend Formosa, announced that the U.S. Seventh Fleet would no longer protect the mainland. Lauded by Chiang's friends in the United States as the beginning of a new policy, the "unleashing" had no effect on the Far East whatever. Thereafter U.S. policy toward China settled down to the perennial recognition of the Republic of China on Formosa as the legitimate government of China, alone deserving representation in the United Nations. This posture demanded nothing of the United States beyond military and economic aid for the Nationalist regime and the perennial promise of the Peking regime's destruction. What permitted such behavior was simply the absence of any Chinese threat to American security.

Eisenhower entered the White House determined to end the war in Korea. Already it was clear that any effort to effect a political change in that country would entail a cost far in excess of any possible gains. What prevented an agreement, despite the military stalemate, was the prisoner of war issue. So crowded were the UN prisoner-of-war camps that Koje Island alone had 130,000 North Koreans and 20,000 Chinese. When these prisoners discovered that the Panmunjom negotiations, which began in 1951, might produce a truce, thousands of Chinese at Koje announced that they would commit suicide rather than return to China. For Moscow and Peking such behavior was nothing less than treason. United States officials, hopeful of ending the war, found this development embarrassing. To return the prisoners to China by force would condemn them to execution. Stalin's death in March 1953 eased the way for greater Soviet cooperation. Late that month, the Communist leaders agreed to the exchange of sick and wounded prisoners. Soon the Chinese and North Koreans accepted the principle of voluntary repatriation and suggested that all prisoners who rejected repatriation be turned over to a neutral commission. Finally, on July 27, the negotiators signed a truce. Ultimately 20,000 North Korean and Chinese prisoners, as well as about two dozen Americans, refused to return to their homes. For the United States the war had cost $22 billion and 140,000 casualties. The nation had discovered again that wars on the Asian mainland could be expensive and indecisive. Events in Southeast Asia soon demonstrated that Washington had not learned that lesson.

What underlay U.S. policy in the Orient after 1949 was the official view that every Communist-led assault on the status quo, whether in China, Korea, Indochina, or elsewhere, emanated from the Kremlin as the center of the international Communist conspiracy. What made this threat of Soviet expansion into Asia appear so acute was the theory, accepted at face value in Washington, that Marxism was antithetical to national sovereignty, and that communism, unless contained, would eventually undermine all national entities in Asia and create one vast community under Soviet domination. It was this assumption—that Soviet imperialism was the real danger in Asia—that prompted the Truman administration to underwrite the French defense of Indochina against the revolutionary forces of Ho Chi Minh. Eisenhower and Dulles shared this perception of the Communist threat to Southeast Asia.

By early 1954, the French position in Indochina, despite $2 billion of U.S. aid, was on the verge of collapse. Convinced that the issue in this struggle was no less than Communist mastery of Asia, Dulles declared before the Overseas Press Club in New York on March 29, 1954: "Under the conditions of today the imposition on Southeast Asia of the political system of Communist Russia and its Chinese Communist ally, by whatever means, would be a grave threat to the whole free world community. The United States feels that that possibility should not be passively accepted, but should be met by united action." Eisenhower, in a press conference, described as *falling dominoes* the process whereby country after country, as if responding to pressure from some central source, would follow one another into the Communist camp. The French, now fighting the cause of containment in Southeast Asia, could not be permitted to lose. During March and April, successive declarations by Dulles, Eisenhower, Nixon, and Radford suggested that the United States would enter the war, if necessary, to assure the needed victory. But the British refusal to act, added to French weariness, isolated Washington diplomatically and prevented the "united action" that Dulles sought. Short of effective involvement in the war, the United States could not prevent the final collapse of the French defenses at Dienbienphu. The Geneva Accords of July 1954 divided Indochina into the three independent states of Laos, Cambodia, and Vietnam, with Vietnam temporarily divided at the seventeenth parallel. Eisenhower and Dulles regarded the Geneva settlement a disaster. The United States refused to sign, because the Geneva conference granted Ho Chi Minh control of North Vietnam and promised a national election no later than 1956.

Ho had achieved a nation of his own. To queries about the effect of the Geneva agreement on the domino theory, Dulles informed a press conference in July 1954 that the theory no longer applied. The United States, he said, had negotiated a new alliance for Southeast Asia that removed the possibility of further Communist gains. This new pact, signed in Manila in September, established the Southeast Asia Treaty Organization (SEATO), consisting of eight nations with a common interest in defending the status quo established at Geneva. Three of these nations were Asian—the Philippines, Thailand, and Pakistan. Two were the South Pacific democracies of Australia and New Zealand. The remaining three were Britain, France, and the United States. The new organization established its headquarters in Bangkok. In Manila Secretary Dulles warned the delegates that the United States, having worldwide military obligations, would fight no more conventional wars in Asia. It would grant logistical, naval, and air support to allied armies on Asian soil, but if this failed to halt a Communist-led aggression—the only kind that Dulles would recognize—the United States would defend the status quo with massive retaliation. What value this alliance system would have in repelling attack was not clear; the Asian nations possessed only conventional weapons, and Dulles had warned that the United States would not fight another land war. In approving the Southeast Asia Treaty, moreover, the Senate acknowledged no American responsibility except that of consulting in the event of aggression. SEATO was scarcely prepared to function.

Still Dulles, without restraint, committed the United States to the defense of South Vietnam's new anti-Communist government in Saigon. In Geneva in the summer of 1954, even as the French prepared to extricate themselves from Vietnam, neither American nor French officials recognized the victorious revolutionaries of the north as the legitimate spokesmen for the independent, but temporarily divided, Vietnam. Instead, they assigned legitimacy to the Vietnamese losers who had supported the French—largely the Catholic minority in control of the Saigon government. This arrangement promised success only as long as the United States could build sufficient military and political effectiveness in South Vietnam to offset the known power of Ho Chi Minh's forces, which had inflicted 175,000 casualties on the French, including 92,000 dead. Undaunted, the United States proceeded to support the Saigon regime with military and economic aid and identified its interest in a stable Orient with the political success of that regime. From its inception the U.S. commitment to South Vietnam and its leader, Ngo Dinh Diem, carried the seeds of disaster.

PROSPERITY WITHOUT END

Eisenhower's approach to federal economic policy reflected the orthodox views of the businessmen in his administration. The economy would return to normal, argued Secretary of the Treasury Humphrey, when production caught up with demand. To stimulate production, Humphrey favored a rapid lifting of all remaining wage and price controls. Early in February 1953, less than three weeks after his inauguration, Eisenhower ended all wage and some price controls. The consumer price index rose only slightly more than a point during the succeeding 12 months. But Humphrey's effort to counter the anticipated inflationary pressures with a billion-dollar issue of long-term Treasury bonds severely restricted the money supply and broke the Eisenhower bubble. By November 1953, the economy was slipping into a recession. Liberal economists such as Senator Paul Douglas of Illinois warned that only greater federal spending would prevent a serious depression; spokesmen for the administration insisted that the situation was self-correcting. The lapsing of both the excess profits tax and the Korean emergency tax in December 1953, together with reductions in numerous excise taxes, increased the public's capacity to spend and stopped the downward trend. By the spring of 1954 the recession had passed. When another recession struck in late 1957, Eisenhower and his economic advisers adopted a similar course. At heart a proponent of sound money, Eisenhower had no interest in governmental interference and again assumed, with some accuracy, that the economy would recover as it did in 1954.

Economists viewed the economy of the 1950s with optimism. Overwhelmingly they found the assurance of prosperity in a sustained consumer demand resulting from the rapid increase in the population and the demand for new houses, schools, streets, roads, hospitals, and water and sewage systems. Population growth, moreover, would limit savings and compel people to extend their credit and use their full capacity to buy. What added to these demand factors was the production of new, attractive goods, new marketing techniques, the expansion of industrial research, the creation of new, large industries, the foreign demand for American goods, and the resultant guarantee of continued, high-level business activity. If the private sector failed to provide the necessary markets, the federal government could still prevent a slump with whacking tax reductions made possible by the high postwar plateau of federal expenditures. Thus, any adjustment to a fully peacetime economy, predicted Harvard's Sumner H. Slichter, would not be damaging. He concluded his optimistic judgment in the June 1954 issue of *The Atlantic* with this observation:

> The real significance of industrial research is that, for the first time in the history of private enterprise, business is able within wide limits to control the demand for goods. It cannot do this without limit or on extremely short notice, but its ability to develop new and better goods is now so well established that it can set production and employment goals five or so years ahead and expect, by the method of discovering and developing new

products and new methods of production, to achieve those goals. Hence, fears that demand cannot be expected to expand rapidly enough to provide sufficient jobs are out of date. They reflect lack of familiarity with the new control of demand that technology has given to industry. This new control over the long-run trend of demand enables us to view the economic future in a new light—not with a mixture of hope and fear because anything might happen, but with quiet confidence that the demand for goods can be made to grow as rapidly as our capacity to produce goods.

Older values of self-reliance and thrift had no chance against the almost universal rush to enter the greatest consumer buying spree in the nation's history. Much of the consumption reflected buying power instead of need. Countless well-paid citizens devoted their energies to advertising, packaging, designing, and merchandising products of marginal importance. What troubled some analysts was the role of credit in the rising public consumption. Consumer credit became indispensable after midcentury because expensive items, such as automobiles and appliances, became primary elements in the American standard of living. What sustained the credit-consumer economy essentially was the willingness of the public to bet on the continuity of jobs. Some writers warned against the danger that consumer credit, if not restrained, would rise more rapidly than disposable income, and that dealers, especially in automobiles, would offer wildly unsound credit terms to sustain sales. Fortunately, the Eisenhower prosperity brought no day of reckoning for the nation's expanding credit structure.

Already the impact of the postwar economic expansion was clear. In 1939 only 4 million Americans out of 130 million paid taxes on incomes above $2000 a year; in 1960 over 25 million out of 180 million Americans declared incomes above $5000. In 1939 only 200,000 persons declared more than $10,000, and 42,500, more than $25,000. By 1960 more than 5.2 million declared incomes of $10,000, and more than a half million, over $25,000. If inflation discounted these gains, the advance in the general standard of living was prodigious. Still, the prosperity did not alleviate the nagging problem of unemployment. The jobless continued to exceed 3 million. For businessmen and economists alike the answer lay in growth that would, in time, generate the required demand for full and continuous employment. Roger Blough, board chairman of United States Steel, expressed the gospel well: "From a dollar and cents point of view it is quite obvious that over a period of years even those who find themselves at the short end of inequality have more to gain from faster growth than from any conceivable income redistribution."

Even as the national income continued to rise, the portion of the nation's wealth that went into public services declined. Secretary Humphrey warned against larger federal expenditures. "I don't think," he said, "that you can spend yourself rich." Aided by the Korean truce, the administration managed to reduce the federal budget from $58 billion in 1953 to $47.5 billion in 1954 and $45 billion in each of the following two years. Thereafter federal appropriations again moved upward, but never rapidly enough to unleash another inflationary spiral. The Eisenhower experience demonstrated the power of government to control inflation through fiscal restraint. Public expenditures totaled less than a fifth of the gross national product, and of this the bulk went into national defense and a variety of traditional activities; scarcely 3 percent of the GNP went into public services. Democratic critics condemned the decisions of government that gave more respect to private purchases of steaks, television, alcohol, gasoline, comic books, and golf than to public expenditures for education, parks, hospitals, medical schools, sanitation, police protection, and flood control. Republican conservatism, they complained, curtailed economic growth and perpetuated high levels of unemployment unnecessarily. Some argued that the United States, with its $400-billion economy, could afford a national debt in excess of the $275-billion national debt ceiling imposed by Congress. They regarded inflation a lesser evil than economic stagnation. Despite the fiscal conservatism of the Eisenhower years, federal spending for goods and services, with military outlays alone reaching $42 billion by 1960, was a primary element in the decade's unprecedented prosperity.

EISENHOWER'S POPULAR LEADERSHIP

Republican reverses in November 1953 demonstrated the party's failure to discover a satisfactory approach to the voting public.

Republican chairman Leonard W. Hall admitted, "There is no question about it—as of today we are in trouble politically." To moderate Republicans there was an answer. The party essentially required a restatement of its philosophy that would form an appealing compromise between the Republican dogma of the 1920s and the New Deal. Jacob K. Javits of New York suggested that moderate Republicanism could meet the challenge. "Republican progressives," he wrote in *The New York Times Magazine* of November 15, 1953,

> subscribe whole-heartedly to the principle of individual freedom and to the idea of an economic system of competitive, private enterprise functioning with government help and cooperation rather than under government domination. But they also hold that belief in free enterprise does not eliminate a wide area of activities in which government can and should provide the individual's welfare by providing him with greater opportunities for social improvement than he could otherwise obtain.

Eisenhower embraced the new formula, convinced of its political appeal. In his message of January 1954, he warned the business community that he expected it to meet the basic requirements of an expanding economy; government would face the issues of welfare, social security, health, education, and housing. "Banishing of destitution and cushioning the shock of personal disaster on the individual," he said, "are proper concerns of all levels of government, including the federal government." One Democratic Senator complained, "We're being sandbagged with our own weapons." Actually, Eisenhower remained a conservative; he never planned to submit a broad social program to Congress.

Despite Eisenhower's generally good record in the 1953-1954 session, all signs in the summer of 1954 pointed to a Democratic resurgence. Under pressure from party leaders, the President made a major campaign trip to Colorado, the Pacific Northwest, and Los Angeles. Eisenhower captured the headlines, but Nixon carried the burden of the campaign. The Vice-President traveled 26,000 miles, visited 95 cities, and delivered over 200 speeches. Again he painted the Democratic party with the Communist brush. He exploited McLeod's "numbers game" by declaring that the Eisenhower administration had kicked "Communists and fellow travelers and security risks out of the government . . . by the thousands." He warned the nation that if a left-wing crowd of Democrats again dominated Congress, "the security risks which have been fired by the Eisenhower administration will all be hired back." Eisenhower, unlike Nixon, focused on the economy and other issues before the nation. The Democratic victory in November was not overwhelming, but it returned that party to firm control over both houses of Congress. Yet the new Congress was no less inclined to follow the Eisenhower lead than the previous one.

To attribute some permanent political significance to Eisenhower's leadership, Republican writers such as Arthur Larson, author of *A Republican Looks at His Party* (1956), accepted the challenge of giving the Eisenhower consensus, embodied in the President's broad public support, the stature of a philosophy that was neither old Republicanism nor New Dealism. They insisted that Eisenhower had become the architect and embodiment of a coherent political movement that had an entity of its own and that would continue after him. In their judgment the new Republicanism reflected the President's vision of the general good that the country could best achieve with moderation in everything. The President applied terms such as "moderate progressivism" and "progressive moderation" to his program. Essentially the new consensus represented the Republican conservatism that had made its necessary bargain with the New Deal. As such it embraced the political realities of the times; it was not a new philosophy of government. The new Republicanism expressed the preferences of a people who had reached a new plateau of affluence and, for the moment, asked nothing of government except the protection of their economic gains. It acknowledged federal responsibility for the public's welfare. But it accepted only the New Dealism that it could not eliminate without committing political suicide.

Actually, the country had long been moving toward the Eisenhower equilibrium. Moderates had taken control of both political parties. This movement toward the center resulted from a mood of complacency and the conviction that enough had been done by previous administrations. At the new center stood the conservative Democrats who, after 1954, managed the affairs of Congress. Many Southern and some Northern Democrats were closer in economic

philosophy to Eisenhower than to Truman. With them at the center
of political power were the Eisenhower Republicans of 1952,
largely moderates of the Northeast. In October 1956 Paul Hoffman, viewing this moderate center as a permanent phenomenon,
declared that Eisenhower had done more to reshape American
politics than had any party leader in 50 years. The new consensus
left little room for the extremes in national political affairs. But the
new center would last only as long as the nation's prosperity. Any
serious break in the economy or other major crisis would again
send politicians and the public scurrying to the edges of the political
spectrum in search of answers and action.

Eisenhower was no party builder. His concept of the presidency was humble, even deferential, when compared to that of
successful presidents of the past. He viewed his role as that of a
presiding officer who exhorted and proposed, but who refused to
enforce party discipline. "I would rather try to persuade a man to
go along," he once observed, "because once I have persuaded him,
he will stick. If I scare him, he will stay just as long as he is scared
and then he is gone." Eisenhower was by training and habit a man
of action, not of ideas. For that reason he sought to avoid arguments
over principles and organized his White House staff to keep intellectual conflict within the administration to a minimum. As President he seldom read newspapers, preferring to secure his
information through briefings by the Pentagon, the State Department, and his White House advisers. Occasionally he conferred
with Republican leaders in formal meetings, with White House
aides sitting in, but generally he had no interest in outside sources
of information. He often argued that details merely impeded decisions. Eisenhower viewed his administrative machine as partially a
military staff, partially a board of directors. The cohesion and loyalty of the White House team was apparently a controlling factor
in his willingness to run for a second term. "It's taken four years
to get this outfit into top working shape," he told a friend. "It
would be a shame to wash it out just as they are reaching their peak
efficiency."

Eisenhower combined his official duties with periods of hunt-
ing, golfing, and bridge. He frequently sought relaxation away
from Washington, usually at his Gettysburg farm or at the Augusta

National Golf Club. Occasionally he took a vacation in the West or New England. He once explained to a Washington press conference that recreation was essential to maintain the fitness necessary to meet the demands of the presidency. Presidents generally had sought relief from the burdens of office. To Eisenhower's critics it was simply a matter of balance, and many believed that too often golf took precedence over matters of state. Edward P. Morgan of ABC quipped characteristically on one newscast: "President Eisenhower had hoped to helicopter to Gettysburg to cast his ballot today but found his schedule too tight. At the last minute, however, he did manage to squeeze in a round of golf."

Whatever the nature of Eisenhower's leadership, his personality remained the dominant reality in presidential politics. What mattered was not the intellectual content of his statements, but the sincerity and warmth that he communicated to the public. But even as he became more confident in his presidential role, he continued to place his leadership in the service of drift, providing, in the words of Richard H. Rovere, "the spectacle, novel in the history of the Presidency, of a man strenuously in motion yet doing essentially nothing—traveling all the time yet going nowhere." At issue was not the President's decisiveness, but the decisions themselves. Despite the energy behind them, Eisenhower's words still suggested that the country faced no problems that good intentions would not cure. He did not call the American people to any high purpose; he acknowledged few problems, human or environmental, whose eradication required any special effort or sacrifice. British writer D. W. Brogan once described the Eisenhower administration as "the most elaborate, unchallenged, sponsored campaign of political tranquillizing to which any people, outside the totalitarian countries, has been exposed."

On September 24, 1955, while in Denver, the President suffered a heart attack, diagnosed quickly as a coronary thrombosis. After months of good care, he concluded by January 1956 that his heart attack would not disqualify him physically from a second term. Shortly thereafter he announced that he would again seek the Republican nomination. "The work that I set out four years ago to do," he explained, "has not yet reached the state of development and function that I had hoped could be accomplished within the period of a single term in this office." The Republican leadership, anticipating another victory, was overjoyed. Richard Nixon was scarcely an automatic choice for the vice-presidency. His brashness had antagonized Republicans; his partisanship had alienated Democrats and independents. Still, party managers convinced Eisenhower by April that Nixon's support among regular Republicans was so strong that any decision to drop him from the ticket would prove detrimental to his campaign. Thus the President accepted Nixon's announcement that he would join the ticket with a public display of personal satisfaction.

Eisenhower's position at the center of American political life emerged with dramatic clarity at the Republican national convention that met in San Francisco in August 1956. Eisenhower was the convention; he was the party. The President's mastery of the convention resulted, ironically, from the party's decline during the previous four years. Without an appealing record, the party had only Eisenhower to offer the American people. For millions the phrase "I Like Ike" summarized the only issue of the campaign. Again the Democratic convention, which met in Chicago in early August, nominated Adlai Stevenson. Despite his efforts to define a distinctive Democratic program that embodied his party's liberal heritage, Stevenson was even less successful than four years earlier in holding the Democratic majority coalition together. What contributed to Eisenhower's remarkable support were the Hungarian revolt and the Suez crisis, which occurred in late October and early November. Confronted with an international crisis, the public preferred to entrust the future to an experienced incumbent. Eisenhower's popular vote in November reached 35,500,000; his electoral vote climbed from 442 to 457. In a minor shuffle Eisenhower lost Missouri, but gained West Virginia, Kentucky, and Lousiana.

Sustaining the Eisenhower image did little for the Republican organization. The Democrats solidified their control of Congress. Republican leaders who sought to exploit the President's personality succeeded merely in assuring the American people that whatever happened, the President, not the party, would assume the burdens of leadership. This accounted for the strange dichotomy between the President's growing popularity and the persistent decline of Republican strength. Republican Governor Theodore R. McKeldin of Maryland reminded a Republican audience in February 1957 that the party "hasn't a thing the country wants" except Eisenhower. Nowhere had the Republican party succeeded in turning the President's image into any genuine political gains. If the country was prosperous, it had known prosperity for a decade under Democrats, and there was little in the Republican record to which the American people could attribute their continuing good fortune. Despite the Republican party's acceptance of New Deal reforms, it could not, in the public mind, discard its fundamental identification with big business and its ideological opposition to the very measures that it approved.

SECOND TERM

If Eisenhower exerted a minimum of political leadership during his first administration, he exerted even less during his second. The issues that confronted the nation were no less critical, but the President revealed no desire to pay the political and emotional price that any effective response would necessitate. On November 25, 1957, the President suffered a stroke and, although he recovered officially by the spring of 1958, his leadership remained spasmodic and inadequate. Eisenhower, moreover, was philosophically opposed to further federal intervention into the areas of education, civil rights, social service, and agriculture. True, the administration launched a massive program for highway construction to counter the 1957-1958 recession, but it seemed helpless in the face of continuing unemployment and declining farm income that resulted from the weakening effect of surpluses on agricultural prices. Generally the President responded to Democratic-inspired domestic programs, especially after the Democratic sweep of 1958, with vetoes and public denunciations of excess spending. With the support of a powerful conservative Republican-Democratic coalition in Congress, he was able to eliminate most programs for education, regional development, and social welfare. It was not strange that his relations with Congress became more and more strained.

Congressional conservatism took its toll of the labor movement. The perennial refusal of Congress to revise the Taft-Hartley Act, added to the expansion of state "right to work" laws, reflected the widespread conviction that labor had become too powerful and thus required stricter regulation. In 1957 a special Senate committee, headed by John L. McClellan of Arkansas, exposed shocking examples of bribery, graft, misuse of union funds, and affluent living among union officials. Labor leaders, under public scrutiny, moved quickly to put their own house in order. That year the AFL-CIO adopted six codes of ethical practices, suspended Dave Beck, head of the Teamster's Union, from his AFL-CIO vice-presidency for administrative malfeasance, and eventually expelled the Teamster's and other unions from the national organization. In September 1959 Congress moved to enforce higher standards of union behavior by passing the Landrum-Griffin Labor Law. This act extended legal protection to union members against the corruption of union officials. It also broadened the secondary boycott and picketing provisions of the Taft-Hartley Act. A further law of 1959 compelled unions to make a public accounting of their pension and welfare funds. These federal encroachments on labor-management relations provoked little public reaction, since the chief concerns of labor were job security and adequate wages. These required not independence from federal regulations, but a high degree of prosperity.

Meanwhile the civil rights issue confronted Eisenhower with an embarrassing, yet inescapable, challenge. American society, in its dealings with blacks, continued to hold out rewards or bar the way as it saw fit. Except for a handful of musicians, atheletes, scholars, businessmen, and professionals, the black population remained a largely dispossessed element in American life. Clearly the impediments to change were gargantuan. Eisenhower himself had long opposed desegregation by federal decree. But Earl Warren, his own appointee to the Chief Justiceship of the United States, soon challenged the tradition of local jurisdiction in matters of civil rights as had no previous public official in the nation's history. With its unanimous 1954 decision in *Brown* v. *Board of Education of Topeka,* the Warren court struck down the historic "separate but equal" doctrine for all public facilities, including schools. The decision faced violent resistance in the South and profound silence in the White House. Later Eisenhower remarked that Warren's appointment to the Court was "the worst mistake I ever made."

Ultimately the President could not escape the civil rights controversy that erupted in Little Rock, Arkansas, during September 1957. When that city's school board voted to permit nine black children to enter Central High School, Governor Orval E. Faubus, under extreme segregationist pressure, ordered the Arkansas National Guard to surround the school and prevent the children from entering. When the Justice Department issued an injunction to prevent the use of National Guardsmen, mobs closed in on the school. To prevent further trouble, police removed the children. Finally, late in September, Eisenhower ordered the Arkansas National Guard into federal service with instructions to disperse the crowd and protect the children's right to attend the school. Some Guardsmen remained on duty throughout the year. The President lent some support to the Civil Rights Act of 1957, but he did little to enforce Southern compliance with the federal judicial desegregation decrees or remind the American people that segregation had moral implications.

American assumptions of technological and military leadership received a rude shock in early October 1957, when the Russians launched their first earth satellite, Sputnik I, a vehicle weighing 184 pounds. Only a month later, Russia's powerful propellants launched a second satellite, which weighed over 1000 pounds. Actually, American space technology was only a step behind and, in January 1958, the United States successfully orbited a small space vehicle of its own, Explorer I. But burgeoning fear that the United States was falling behind the Russians in scientific knowledge spurred a return to basic education in the schools, a move long advocated by educational reformers. In 1958 the administration secured passage of the National Defense Education Act (NDEA), which broadened educational opportunities in areas deemed essential for national defense. Eisenhower had no desire to commit the United States to a massive space effort, but he responded favorably to pressures for an increase in the nation's military preparedness. Even then the President sustained sufficient confidence in the country's military might to resist much of the Pentagon's appeal for greater expenditures.

No less than other critics, Eisenhower questioned the Pentagon's postwar influence over defense decisions and the apparent willingness of Congress and the public to accept the military's judgment regarding the size and nature of an adequate defense structure. Military analyst Hanson W. Baldwin warned in *Harper's* as early as December 1947 that the excessive influence of the military in the decisions of government endangered the country's institutions. "Total war," he wrote, "means the direction of every phase of the national life to the end of military victory. And preparation for it in time of peace may mean—if the preparations are pushed to full effectiveness—the direction of every phase of national life toward the maintenance of military strength." Eisenhower repeated that theme in his farewell address, reminding the nation that military pressures threatened the balance between the need for national security and the broader considerations of domestic welfare. He warned specifically against the dangers of a growing military-industrial complex that dominated the business of defense:

> This conjunction of an immense military establishment and a large arms industry is new in American experience. The total influence—economic, political, even spiritual—is felt in every city, every state house, every office of the federal government. We recognize the imperative need for this development. Yet we must not fail to comprehend its grave implications. . . . Our toil, resources and livelihood are all involved; so is the very structure of our society. In the councils of government, we must guard against the acquisition of unwarranted influence, whether sought or unsought, by the military-industrial complex. The potential for the disastrous rise of misplaced power exists and will persist. We must never let the weight of this combination endanger our liberties or democratic processes. We should take nothing for granted. . . .

IN LIEU OF DIPLOMACY

Throughout the late 1950s the Eisenhower administration continued to confront every Soviet or Chinese action, or suspected action, with a combination of diplomatic inflexibility, alliances, economic and military aid, threats of retaliation, or congressional resolutions—depending on the degree of danger. But the official assumption of a sharply divided bipolar world no longer had much relation to reality. That became clear when Dulles' move to eliminate Soviet influence from the Middle East terminated, instead, in a serious Western confrontation with Arab nationalism. The misadventure began when the Secretary responded to Egyptian leader Gamal Abdel Nasser's recognition of mainland China and his acceptance of Soviet aid for Egypt's massive Aswan Dam by announcing, in July 1956, that the United States would no longer participate in the Aswan project. Nasser struck back by nationalizing the Suez Canal Company, owned largely by British and French investors. Canal tolls, he said, would build the dam. Nasser's action raised no issues in U. S.-Soviet relations, since nowhere in the Middle East was communism a genuine political force. But Nasser's seizure of the Suez Canal aggravated the traditional animosity between Egypt and the former colonial powers. Having no interests at Suez comparable to those of Britain and France, Dulles played for time. Nasser rejected every American proposal, including the concept of a User's Club. Convinced at last that Washington had no plan of action beyond the repeated request for patience, the Israelis, late in October, overran Egypt's Sinai Peninsula to terminate Egyptian raids into Israeli territory. When Nasser refused to clear the approaches to the Suez Canal, British and French forces, on November 5, seized the canal and occupied Port Said. Washington now turned on its allies and led the successful maneuver in the UN General Assembly to condemn British and French action and force both countries to capitulate.

Having destroyed what remained of British power and prestige in the Middle East, the United States now assumed the burden of maintaining Middle Eastern stability and, with it, the obligation to defend the interests of Israel. Nasser's Pan-Arabism threatened not only Israel but also several pro-Western Arab regimes. Soviet policy had not created the Suez crisis; still, by late 1956 Nasser had managed to bring the United States and the USSR into conflict in the Middle East, not by transforming his Pan-Arabism into a pro-Soviet movement, but by importing arms and technicians from Russia. What permitted the growing Soviet presence in Egypt was not Nasser's ideological preferences, but his fear of Israel. How the Soviets, through the mere sale of arms, could endanger Arab sovereignty or infiltrate the Middle East was not clear. But Eisenhower's Washington, ignoring the Kremlin's limited and nonideological role in Middle Eastern affairs, attributed regional instability to Russia's manipulation of Arab nationalism. Dulles warned the Senate Foreign Relations Committee that the Middle East was in imminent danger of falling to international communism. To meet that danger, Congress, in March 1957, adopted the so-called Eisenhower Doctrine, which declared, in part: "The United States regards as vital to the national interest and world peace the preservation of the independence and integrity of the nations of the Middle East. To this end . . . the United States is prepared to use armed force to assist any such nation or group of nations requesting assistance against armed aggression from any country controlled by international communism. . . . " Shortly thereafter Eisenhower dispatched former congressman James P. Richards to the Middle East to carry out the aid policies outlined in the Joint Resolution.

Senate critics such as Wayne Morse of Oregon and J. William Fulbright of Arkansas denied that the Soviet Union endangered the independence of any Middle Eastern country. But the administration's success in identifying Pan-Arabism and Soviet arms with the ultimate loss of Middle Eastern independence encouraged every resistance to change. On February 1, 1958, Syria and Egypt announced their union as the United Arab Republic. Several days later State Department officer William M. Rountree assured the Senate Foreign Relations Committee that the USSR had not converted any Middle Eastern country into a satellite, but it had, through deception, "succeeded in exploiting the mistaken belief of some of those countries that they can deal closely with the Soviet Union without risking subversion and ultimate loss of independence." During the summer of 1958 Eisenhower dispatched troops to Lebanon to save the regime of President Camille Chamoun. At the same time the British dropped a regiment of paratroops into Jordan to protect the regime of King Hussein. The operations saved two pro-Western governments from their Arab opponents; in neither case were the pressures for change Soviet inspired. For Washington officials that mattered little. Denying the primary force of nationalism in middle Eastern politics, they insisted that only pro-Western governments, whatever the basis of their support, could guarantee regional independence from Soviet encroachment.

This identification of Communist-led revolution with Soviet

imperialism dominated official American views toward China, although during the late 1950s China replaced Russia, in Washington's view, as the dominant threat to Asian stability—the major partner in the Asian Communist monolith. In his noted San Francisco speech of June 1957, Dulles reminded his audience that China "fought the United Nations in Korea; it supported the Communist war in Indochina; it took Tibet by force. It fomented the Communist Huk rebellion in the Philippines and the Communists' insurrection in Malaya." Still China, to American officials, had not achieved full independence from the Kremlin; the achievement of Chinese independence would have destroyed the major rationale for nonrecognition—that the government of China was Russian and not Chinese. Nonrecognition still carried the burden of both the containment and the eventual liberation of the mainland. Recognition, Dulles warned an Australian audience in March 1957, would "strengthen and encourage influences hostile to us and our allies and further imperil lands whose independence is related to our own peace and security." Beyond containment, nonrecognition assured China's eventual liberation. As Dulles declared in San Francisco, "We can confidently assume that international communism's rule of strict conformity is, in China, as elsewhere, a passing and not a perpetual phase. We owe it to ourselves, our allies, and the Chinese people to do all we can to contribute to that passing." Unlike other countries suffering under Communist tyranny, observed Ambassador Karl Lott Rankin in Taipei, China had its Taiwan as "a bastion and rallying point where hope is being kept alive and preparations made for a better future." One day, predicted Rankin, Taiwan might prove to be the Achilles heel of communism in Asia. What disturbed both Rankin and the Chinese on Taiwan was the realization that beyond nonrecognition, the means for liberation were nonexistent.

In Indochina the power to guarantee the ultimate retreat of communism remained equally elusive. Having supplanted the French as the sole guarantor of the post-Geneva peace in Southeast Asia, the Eisenhower administration placed its faith for the future on Ngo Dinh Diem's success both in creating a stable government for South Vietnam and in resisting any accommodation with Hanoi, the capital of Ho's state of North Vietnam. After 1954 the Saigon regime carried the chief burden of containment in Southeast Asia. Dulles had no desire to commit the United States to another ground war in Asia and SEATO soon proved to be totally ineffective. Thus Washington had no choice but to heap aid and praise on the South Vietnamese leader. During Diem's official visit to Washington in May 1957, President Eisenhower lauded him at the airport for bringing to his task of organizing his country "the greatest of courage, the greatest of statesmanship. . . . " When Diem departed from Washington on May 11, the two presidents issued a joint communiqué that "looked forward to the end of the unhappy division of the Vietnamese people and confirmed the determination of the two governments to work together to seek suitable means to bring about the peaceful unification of Viet-Nam in freedom."

Somehow such statements had little relationship to reality. After 1956 Diem's regime took on many features of a police state as it drove its opponents into exile or jail. As Diem's control of the countryside began to disintegrate under the dual pressure of subversion and infiltration, Communist-led revolutionaries, with a well-organized campaign of terror, kidnapped or assassinated Saigon- appointed local officials and replaced them with village chiefs sympathetic to their cause. In 1960, when North Vietnamese infiltration had scarcely begun, the Saigon government controlled only somewhat more than half the country. Diem's miracle in Vietnam had turned out to be a triumph in public relations, nothing more. Despite the evidence of failure, President Eisenhower continued his official praise of Diem in a letter to the Vietnamese leader, dated October 26, 1960, commemorating the fifth anniversary of the founding of the Republic of Vietnam. Vietnam's capacity to defend itself from Communist aggression, Eisenhower observed, had "grown immeasurably since its successful struggle to become an independent Republic." Forgetting that Ho Chi Minh, not Diem, had led the fight for Indochinese independence, Eisenhower continued:

> . . . I sense how deeply the Vietnamese value their country's independence and strength and I know how well you used your boldness when you led your countrymen in winning it. I also know that your determination has been a vital factor in guarding that independence while steadily advancing the economic development of your country. I am confident that

these same qualities of determination and boldness will meet the renewed threat as well as the needs and desires of your countrymen for further progress on all fronts.

Actually, American policy in Indochina was entering a period of major crisis. In December, southern guerrilla leaders formed the National Liberation Front (NLF) to impose a state of civil war on South Vietnam. Whatever Eisenhower's ultimate intention in Southeast Asia, his often repeated reference to falling dominoes, which assumed the existence of a global threat, denied the United States any easy retreat from its commitment to Saigon.

For Washington the Soviet challenge outside Europe lay in revolution and change; within Europe it lay in the continent's perennial stability. If the Kremlin enjoyed a stable relationship with Eastern Europe, it still desired Western recognition of the Russian hegemony. Backed by the diplomatic advantage that their lead in space provided, the Soviets throughout 1958 pressed the Western Big-Three powers for another summit conference on disarmament and peaceful coexistence. To publicize his personal concern, Soviet leader Nikita Khrushchev initiated an exchange of public letters with the Western heads of state. Unable to secure the desired Western response, Khrushchev, in November 1958, announced that within six months he would sign a peace treaty with East Germany and terminate all Allied rights in West Berlin unless the Western powers agreed to make West Berlin a free city. Dulles had no interest in fighting for Berlin, but German Chancellor Conrad Adenauer would not compromise. Eisenhower managed finally to push the issues of Berlin and Germany to the Big-Four Geneva Conference, which opened on May 11, 1959. There, both sides, unable to reach a settlement, agreed again that the status quo in Germany was far more advantageous to all than any effort to change it through war. As in every previous crisis, Washington chose to coexist with the European arrangements that flowed from the Soviet victories of 1944 and 1945. But never would it recognize those arrangements diplomatically.

In time Khrushchev managed to negotiate a summit conference to convene in Paris during May 1960. Shortly before the meeting date arrived, the Soviets announced that on May 1 they had shot down an American plane over Russian territory. Washington described the aircraft as a weather plane that had strayed off course. The Russians then informed the world that the plane, a high-altitude photoreconnaissance craft, had crashed 1200 miles inside Soviet territory. The pilot, Francis Gary Powers, admitted that he was on a spy mission, flying from Pakistan to Norway. Khrushchev accused the United States of aggression and demanded a formal apology. The embarrassed Eisenhower admitted the existence of the U-2 reconnaissance flights, but insisted that U. S. security required them. Receiving no apology, Khrushchev employed the U-2 incident to terminate the Paris meeting. He demanded the cancellation of Eisenhower's scheduled visit to Russia, thereby terminating all Soviet efforts to negotiate with the Eisenhower administration. It mattered little. Neither nation was prepared to compromise any of its established objectives. But the Cold War issues in Europe no longer carried their former significance. The areas of conflict had become too stabilized.

Fortunately, the East-West quarrels in Europe focused on issues or regions where either the West or the USSR had the predominant interest and strategic advantage. This enabled the Cold War rivals to escape every crisis without a direct confrontation. Meanwhile, Dulles's proclaimed goal of liberation, exceeding both the power and the genuine intent of the United States, prevented the settlement of every major Cold War issue in Europe and reduced American territorial and political objectives on the continent to expressions of sentiment, since none of them had any chance of attainment. As political scientist Hans J. Morgenthau wrote in December 1956: "When we heard spokesmen for the government propound the legal and moral platitudes which had passed for foreign policy in the interwar period, we thought that this was the way in which the government—as all governments must—tried to make the stark facts of foreign policy palatable to the people. . . . We were mistaken. Those platitudes *are* the foreign policy of the United States." If Dulles settled nothing, he also gave nothing away. The result of his tenure as Secretary of State was a stalemate that, in time, undermined the seriousness of his revisionist goals. This erosion did not necessarily damage the economic or security interest of the United States; those interests never required the triumph of self-determination in Europe.

If the prevailing conditions in Europe, Asia, and the Middle East assured the continued frustration of American purpose, they presaged no greater successes for the USSR. Whereas Russia revealed both the capacity and the will to maintain its hegemony across East-Central Europe, Soviet gains even there remained elusive. In Europe as elsewhere nationalism set the limits to Russian influence. The Kremlin required enormous effort to contain the pressures exerted against its rule by German and Slavic nationalism. What held the Soviet bloc together was the power of the Red Army. It had long been apparent that the USSR could not transform, through ideology or repression, those areas under its control into the unitary society that its Communist dogma demanded. Not one square foot of Slavic Europe could the Soviets integrate emotionally or spiritually into the Soviet empire. China challenged the unity of the Communist bloc even more than did the European satellites. Indeed, China, despite American assumptions of Soviet influence in Peking, had never entered the Soviet hegemony at all. During the late 1950s China embarked on a career of open defiance of Soviet leadership in the Communist world.

Elsewhere in Asia the fundamental impulses of nationalism, if encouraged by the Kremlin, were never the creation of Soviet will. The very nationalist pressures that contributed to revolution and change placed insuperable barriers against external influence. The Soviets gained nothing militarily and little politically in the continuing revolutions that swept the Afro-Asian world. Nations are not in the habit of giving themselves away. The Soviet-controlled monolith was largely a creation of American rhetoric. That perception of danger proved to be costly. Whereas the Soviets transported no troops outside their direct sphere of influence, the United States spent tens of billions in economic and military aid and maintained dozens of military establishments throughout Europe and Asia. This gigantic effort supported a worldwide alliance system that nowhere was prepared to deal with revolution and insurgency or to deter, except with nuclear weapons, direct Russian or Chinese aggression. What sustained world stability was the powerful and

continuing assertion of sovereign will by all nations, the nuclear
balance, global economic interdependence, and the overriding interest of the superpowers in the existing international order.

   After Dulles's death in 1959, the nation's foreign policy, like
its domestic politics, became subjected more directly to the Eisenhower personality. To further the country's interests abroad, the
President embarked on a series of public tours to Europe, Asia, and
Latin America. These state visits gave him the opportunity to demonstrate his good will before the world. Unfortunately, there was
always a marked contrast between the cheers of the crowds and the
lack of diplomatic progress in the chancelleries; the visit of a digni-
tary to another land has no function other than to please and excite
the people who swarm along the thoroughfares. Writers, editors,
and even members of Congress warned the President, after the
collapse of the Paris summit, not to run the risk of a trip around the
fringes of the Communist world in the Far East. While the President waited in the Philippines, anti-American riots compelled him
to cancel his trip to Tokyo. Eisenhower responded to his disappointment with an air of injured innocence. For the decline of
American prestige in Japan he blamed the Communists, not the
challenge to Japanese neutralism posed by American missiles. He
identified world peace with his personal diplomacy, repeating that
conviction after his return from the Orient in July 1960: "No
consideration of personal fatigue or inconvenience, no threat or
argument would deter me from once again setting out on a course
that has meant much for our country, for her friends, and for the
cause of freedom—and peace with justice in the world." Always the
sacrifice was to the person; he asked no sacrifice of the nation in the
form of added strength or reduced ambitions.

1960: NIXON VERSUS KENNEDY

   With Eisenhower's second term approaching its end, the
Democratic party entered the 1960 campaign with a clear advantage over its opponents. The President's successive victories in the
1950s had produced few permanent gains for the Republican party.
In the 1958 congressional elections Democrats won a lopsided

majority of 281 to 153 in the House and 62 to 34 in the Senate. The Republicans, despite their control of the White House, failed to build any program, distinct from that of the Democratic party, that could command majority approval. In 1960 any Democratic nominee would enter the campaign for the White House with a preponderance of between 7 and 8 million more registered Democrats than Republicans. To win, it seemed, he had merely to conduct a campaign around the traditional economic and social issues that underwrote the strength of the old Democratic coalition of labor, the minorities, the intellectuals, and the South. For Democrats the charge that Eisenhower's conservatism had permitted a "missile gap" to develop created another exploitable issue.

Even with its advantage the Democratic party entered the 1960 campaign in its usual state of disarray. Among its avowed contestants for the nomination at convention time were Senators John F. Kennedy of Massachusetts, Lyndon B. Johnson of Texas, Stuart Symington of Missouri, and Adlai Stevenson, the still-popular nominee of 1952 and 1956. Kennedy's campaign for the nomination had begun soon after the Democratic convention of 1956, where Senator Estes Kefauver edged him out of the vice-presidential nomination. When Kennedy formally announced his candidacy early in 1960, he was clearly far out in front with not only pledged support but also a tireless, enthusiastic, young, and efficient organization headed by his brother, Robert. Kennedy had three additional assets—his personal attractiveness, the Kennedy fortune, and a long experience in national politics. After graduation from Harvard he entered the Navy in World War II. When a Japanese destroyer sliced through his PT boat in the Solomon Islands in 1943, he saved the survivors of his crew by leading them to a small island. He won election to Congress in 1946 and, during his six years in the House, generally supported Truman's liberal program. He defeated Henry Cabot Lodge in the Massachusetts Senate race of 1952. In 1954 he underwent surgery; while recuperating he wrote his Pulitzer Prize-winning book, *Profiles in Courage*. After winning the 1960 primaries, Kennedy arrived at the Los Angeles convention confident of victory over his rivals. Johnson, with heavy support in the South and West, held out until the end. He obtained a sizable minority on the first ballot, which nominated Kennedy. To placate the South and secure a strong running mate, the Massachusetts Senator chose Johnson for the vice-presidency.

Throughout his second term as Vice-President, Richard M. Nixon had been moving toward an unchallengeable position of leadership among Republican presidential hopefuls. His office had brought him into high-level policy conferences and permitted him to represent the nation officially on tours to the Far East, Latin America, and Europe. By convention time in 1960, only Governor Nelson Rockefeller of New York could challenge his lead for the party's nomination. Before the Chicago convention opened in July, New York Republicans assured their popular governor that the party really favored Nixon. Following Rockefeller's withdrawal, the Republican party handed Nixon the nomination almost unanimously on the first ballot. Republican strategists at the convention inaugurated the pattern of campaigning that they would pursue until November. Congressman Walter Judd's keynote address recounted the alleged failures of the Democratic party in foreign affairs. Thomas E. Dewey, in a major convention address, pointed to the Vice-President's heavy responsiblity in shaping the Republican policies "which brought victory after victory for freedom in Iran, in Trieste, in Austria, in Guatemala, in Lebanon, in Jordan, in Laos, in West Berlin, yes, in Quemoy and Matsu and Formosa." Republican delegates left the emotion-laden convention enthusiastic and united.

Leading a minority party, Nixon focused his campaign on himself—his knowledge, his experience, and his long association with Eisenhower. "Don't just look at the [party] label—look behind the label," he said in Paterson, New Jersey. What mattered was the quality, not of the party, but of the national leadership. Even the President took up this theme in late October. He urged a Philadelphia audience to ignore the parties and study the candidates themselves. Only by rising above party as a potentially great leader of the nation, much as Eisenhower had done, had Nixon any hope of winning the necessary independent and wavering Democratic votes. Kennedy, backed by a normal majority coalition, attempted to turn the campaign into a contest between parties. In Sioux City, Iowa, he declared characteristically, "It is not a fight merely between Mr. Nixon and myself. We lead two parties, two forces, two sources of energy." In Florida, on October 19, Kennedy observed again that "the record of my party is not so bad that I have to deny it every four years." Kennedy campaigned hard in the North on the Democratic record of liberal legislation, while Johnson attempted to keep the South in line. Both candidates sought to expand the New Deal coalition by identifying the Democratic party with the new civil rights movement. Kennedy knew that he could not prevent some migration from Democratic ranks among Southern and Midwestern Protestants, but he hoped to offset his anti-Catholic losses by drawing back into the Democratic fold large blocs of Catholic voters who had strayed into the Eisenhower camp, largely on foreign policy issues.

Throughout the campaign both Nixon and Kennedy promised to sustain the uncompromising external positions of the past. They assured Eastern European nationality groups that they would never recognize the Soviet control of captive nations behind the Iron Curtain. Their competition for the crucial Eastern European ethnic vote reached its ultimate stage a few days before the election, when Nixon promised to carry the idea of freedom across the Iron Curtain by dispatching former presidents Hoover, Truman, and Eisenhower on a tour of the satellite countries. This final bid failed to carry the election. Kennedy's returns among urban Catholics ran as much as 25 percent above those of Stevenson in 1956. These votes made the difference; they helped the Senator to capture the large states, often by narrow margins, and thus achieve victory in the electoral college, 303 to 219. Elsewhere across the country Kennedy ran far behind the Democratic party. In the South he failed to carry four states. Kennedy's strength centered in those areas of traditional Democratic power, the urban East, the Midwest, and much of the South. With Kennedy's election the era of Eisenhower's presidency—which had scarcely been a Republican era at all—approached its end.

Chapter V

Affluence and the Social Order

INDUSTRIAL EXPANSION

By almost any standard the postwar American economy was a wonder of the modern world. Even before the 1960s the standard of living for most Americans had reached levels undreamed of before Pearl Harbor. The gross national product (GNP), or the total output of goods and services at current market prices, had reached $285 billion by 1950, but then rose rapidly to almost $400 billion by 1955, to over $500 billion by 1960, to $650 billion by 1965, and to almost $1 trillion by the end of the decade. If inflation reduced the significance of these figures, the country's economic growth was still remarkable. Large businesses reaped the predominant gains. After the mid-1960s, annual corporate profits after taxes soared to between $40 and $50 billion. General Motors, the nation's largest corporation, consistently netted over $1 billion a year. The rate of business investment reflected both the high level of corporate profits and the promise of rising demand. In 1963 business expenditures for new plant and equipment reached $40 billion; by the end of the decade such investments exceeded $75 billion each year. Despite the heavy accent on labor-saving machinery, the country's economy created millions of new jobs. The civilian labor force increased from about 60 million at midcentury to 78 million by the end of the 1960s. While automation reduced the percentage of blue-collar workers to far less than half the total, the expansion of service, financial, educational, and governmental occupations created new opportunities for mass employment.

Personal income kept pace with economic growth. By 1950 it reached $200 billion, then jumped to about $350 billion in 1960, and to somewhat over $600 billion in 1967. The advance in personal income for millions of citizens was astonishing. As late as 1960 only 14 percent of all American families received incomes as high as $10,000 a year; by 1967 over a third had reached that level, and median family income had approached $8000. The United States not only manufactured more goods than analysts once believed possible, but also distributed its industrial products more widely than ever before. Americans surpassed all others in the quest for comfort and convenience. Millions of them acquired new homes or inhabited attractive apartments laden with electrical appliances and expensive furnishings. Americans spent over $30 billion a year on new automobiles and additional billions on sports, both as spectators and as participants. By the mid-1960s they spent more than $40 billion a year on recreation, including domestic travel, and another $3 to $4 billion on foreign travel. For Americans generally the country's phenomenal economic growth and prosperity created one of history's golden ages.

What most clearly separated the postwar era from earlier periods in the nation's history, at least quantitatively, was the pace of scientific and technological change. By 1960 industry was spending $4 billion annually for research and development; this expenditure provided employment for almost 765,000 scientists and engineers. Both federal and industrial research programs relied heavily on the facilities of the large universities. The most significant technological advances emerged from the electronics revolution, particularly the development of the computer and the linkage of the new electronic devices with automated machinery. This permitted programming and continuous-flow production and record-keeping. The electronics industry, exploiting all forms of commercially useful research, created a flood of new products for the consumer market—electronic calculators, color television, and high-fidelity sound systems. New research produced dramatic advances as well in atomic energy, space exploration, oceanography, molecular biology, and the health sciences.

Another giant industry based on science and technology, the petrochemical industry, was largely a creation of the postwar era and thus a major contributor to the country's postwar economic expansion. Its products, made largely from crude oil and natural gas, comprised an enchanting catalog of useful materials—synthetic fibers, plastics, detergents, fertilizers, pesticides, and drugs. Because of its heavy investment in machinery, the petrochemical industry could operate efficiently and profitably only on a massive scale. Entering the market with low-priced yet attractive substitutes for cotton, wool, and leather, the industry, once established, became invincible in the market-place. By almost any measure—its rate of growth, its profitability, and the appeal of its products—the petrochemical industry was the most successful in postwar America. Its growth rate was twice that for manufacturing as a whole; its profits were correspondingly great.

Unfortunately, the petrochemical industry produced a variety of externalities that levied a heavy cost on society and even on the economy itself. Aside from the threat of many of its products to the nation's health, the petrochemical industry, in the production of fibers, consumed at least five times as much nonrenewable energy in the form of fuel as did the farmer to produce cotton, including the use of tractor fuel and fertilizer. The gap in energy use between the production of petrochemicals and that of leather and woolen goods was even greater. Two additional externalities of the petrochemical industry were the underemployment of labor and the overemployment of capital. Because of their heavy use of technology, the petroleum and chemical industries returned far less for capital investment than did American industries generally. At the same time, that technology created a labor productivity in these industries that far exceeded that of others. Indeed, the value added per man-hour of labor in the production of petrochemicals more than doubled the average for all manufacturing in the United States. The petrochemical industry, together with transportation and all production that depended on petroleum, represented 28 percent of the GNP; it employed only 2.7 percent of the labor force. The petrochemical industry, in relation to its capacity to consume energy and capital, employed few people. The industry was thus a major factor in the country's unemployment, its increasingly short supply of capital, and its depletion of energy.

At the core of the country's productivity were the giant corporations, more in command of the American economy than ever before. Corporations with assets in excess of $1 billion—fewer than 100 of them—comprised almost half the country's corporate wealth. These corporations actually represented a larger percentage of the nation's corporate assets than had the leading 200 corporations in 1945. Before the end of the 1960s, General Motors had 700,000 employees and 500 upper-level executives; Ford Motor Company and General Electric employed approximately 400,000 each. So concentrated was American corporate power that three or four firms dominated many of the major industries. Three companies produced 95 percent of all automobiles manufactured in the United States; three companies produced 90 percent of the country's aluminium. Four firms—Kellogg, General Mills, General Foods, and Quaker Oats—dominated the production of breakfast cereals. DuPont, Dow, and Monsanto led the country in the manufacture of petrochemicals. Mergers continued the trend toward bigness. The general absence of price competition among the giant corporations prompted occasional investigations of alleged price fixing. To hedge against shifting markets, many large corporations, most notably International Telephone and Telegraph (ITT), created conglomerates whereby they added firms engaged in totally unrelated activities. Never, it seemed, had corporate America been more influential or self-confident.

Perhaps the country's ultimate economic power lay in its mammoth international corporations with their extensive operations in foreign countries. Companies such as Proctor and Gamble, General Motors, Ford, International Telephone and Telegraph, International Business Machines (IBM), Exxon, Mobil, Texaco, Unilever, Chrysler, and Kodak employed as much as a third of their work forces in Europe and elsewhere. Some companies had plants in as many as 20 countries. Together the multinationals had investments of more than $100 billion in plant and equipment outside the

United States. Backed by sophisticated technology, these giants wielded immeasurable economic and political influence. By the 1960s they accounted for $450 billion in annual production, or 15 percent of the gross world product. The sales of American-controlled international corporations exceeded the combined GNP of England and France. The world sales of General Motors exceeded $28 billion a year and the GNP of Switzerland. Exxon's world sales of $18.7 billion were greater than the total production of both Denmark and Austria. Unlike the large corporations in the age of imperialism that invested abroad to exploit the poorer countries, the multinationals concentrated their investing and marketing in advanced economies with their superior purchasing power.

World commerce played a larger role in U.S. prosperity in the 1960s than ever before in the country's history—at least since colonial times. To establish the rules for fair international trade, the leading nations negotiated, in Geneva in 1947 and 1948, the General Agreement on Trade and Tariffs (GATT). This agreement removed all quotas on imports, except for nations that found it impossible to compete effectively in the world market. If, for some compelling reason, one country found it necessary to protect some domestic product, it compensated for any special restrictions by reducing its tariffs on other goods. Between 1948 and 1967 the trading nations negotiated six rounds of tariff reductions, the last being the famed Kennedy round. What provided the impetus for the Kennedy round, which began in 1964, was the 1962 U.S. Trade Expansion Act, designed especially to improve American trade relations with the Common Market countries of western Europe. The Kennedy round, concluded in May 1967, established thousands of additional tariff reductions to become effective over a five-year period. With all nations generally abiding by the rules, world trade doubled between 1959 and 1967. By the mid-1960s it reached $200 billion. In some measure the prosperity of the United States reflected the unprecedented productivity and purchasing power of Japan and the major trading nations of Europe. For the first time in history, international trade and investment had created a worldwide economic system in which every major country's decisions influenced some aspect of life elsewhere.

MOMENTUM

Behind the operation of the free market, determining in large measure the nature and quality of the nation's economic growth, was an industrial momentum that responded less to national need than to a carefully contrived consumer demand, previous investments, available technology, and anticipated profits. The television industry was gigantic in its operations and powerful in its effect on viewers. If portions of the public regarded television advertising as misleading, the public responded favorably enough to sustain the huge marketing budgets that underwrote the profitability of the advertising industry. Such expenditures measured dramatically the capacity of industry to generate wants. Large segments of the American economy expanded and flourished by creating a demand for goods and services that the public did not require—and often did not want. Consumers, declared Henry Ford II with some exaggeration, "don't think they are getting what they wanted when they buy a product—any product." To many of its critics industry appeared structured less to satisfy the requirements of human existence—to make life more attractive and satisfactory—than to turn out and sell more and more goods as a measure of economic progress.

After midcentury the momentum in automobile production, highway construction, large-scale agriculture, and university expansion characterized the continuing revolution in the American economy. The number of automobiles in the United States increased five times as rapidly as the population, reaching 1.4 cars per family during the 1960s. Automobiles kept getting larger, more powerful, and more expensive. In 1965, the Ford Galaxie, with its small engine, weighed approximately 3500 pounds, as did the Chevrolet Impala. Soon both automobiles, with more powerful engines, would gain 1000 pounds in weight, while Cadillacs and Lincolns would eventually exceed 5000 pounds. Nothing remained small, cheap, or simple for very long. Such changes in size did not serve any national (or even personal) requirement. They meant only that the automotive industry could manufacture, advertise, and sell larger automobiles at a greater profit than smaller ones.

However, the automobile industry, considering all its financial and productive triumphs, revealed little respect for genuine innovation or for its customers. The effort to create new models each year led to waste and avoidable imperfections in design.

Under the assumption that efficient power in the form of gasoline would remain cheap and plentiful, the public cooperated with the automobile industry in eliminating other forms of transportation—railroads, streetcars, and electrical interurban lines. To underwrite the shift to automobiles, the federal government spent $60 billion for a 42,000-mile interstate highway system, the largest single public work in history. In behalf of the automobile, cities buried themselves more and more under seas of concrete and asphalt. The center of Los Angeles was 60 percent roads and parking areas. The average car was on the road only two hours a day, but enough to fill the air with exhaust, clog the roads, sustain the mania for new cars, and strain the budgets of most families. Why the public purchased as many as 9 million automobiles each year was not clear. "There is no economic virtue—nor any other virtue," wrote Hans J. Morgenthau in 1960, "for a nation to produce more automobiles this year than last and more next year than this. Nor is there any virtue, except that of prestige, in the ability to buy a new automobile every year." The national reliance on the automobile was so complete that any threatened gasoline shortage could create a national energy crisis and push the price of fuel to unprecedented levels. Clearly the utopia promised by Detroit remained elusive. The country had committed itself so deeply to automotive transportation that the economy would never recover fully from its decline.

The technology that transformed the American economy to its heavy reliance on petroleum produced a revolution in American agriculture by unleashing the trend toward large-scale farming operations. Through much of its history the United States had regarded its many independent farmers as the backbone of its phenomenal agricultural production and the special guardians of its values. New Deal measures had attempted to keep a maximum number of citizens on the countryside, but nothing could protect the farming population from the impact of the large, complex, and efficient machinery that, by the 1960s, enabled individual operators, with little help, to handle as many as 1000 acres of prime agricultural land. Farmers, propelled by the need for ever-greater production to cover the mounting costs of machinery, gasoline, and fertilizer, faced the choice of assuming heavier debts to buy larger and more expensive machinery or of giving up. Eventually the capital requirements of a typical Iowa or Illinois farm exceeded what the average farmer could save in a lifetime. But thousands of farmers, seeing a profitable future in even such expensive operations, often accumulated debts of a half million dollars to buy additional land and machinery. Others in even larger numbers, unwilling or unable to follow the trend, sold or rented their land and left. The abandoned houses and decaying barns that dotted the countryside of the nation's richest agricultural regions stood as mute testimony to the erosion of the old family farms. The number of farms in the United States declined from 4 million in 1960 to 2.8 million in the mid-1970s. During that period the farm population dwindled from 15.6 to 8.9 million. Eventually, some predicted, no more than a half million farms would produce the nation's food.

Despite the skyrocketing productivity of those who responded to the new technology, the changes wrought by the momentum toward larger operations did not necessarily serve any national or human needs. For consumers there were no discernible benefits; the new efficiency did not reduce the price of food. The costs of production and marketing kept pace with farm income. Rising land prices encouraged both the growing agricultural indebtedness and the large-scale movement of outside money from insurance companies, urban investors, or land companies into farm ownership. This created an ever-wider separation between absentee landlords and those who tilled the soil. Even for the large, efficient producers the costs of operation eliminated sizable profits except under the most favorable market conditions. Unlike industrialists, farmers could not push the rising costs of land, labor, machinery, and fuel to food processors and consumers in the form of higher prices. The heavy borrowing required by the demand for fertilizer and more sophisticated machinery placed farmers and bankers in a vulnerable position; any marked decline in prices or production would create an emergency that would result either in bankruptcies or in new federal programs of expanded farm credit, higher price supports, or new production controls.

Motivated by the fear, unleashed by Sputnik, that the United States might become second-best in scientific and technological achievement, the nation began, in the late 1950s, to spend more on higher education than at any time in its own or the world's history. The expenditure, stimulated as well by the promises of endless employment for the educated in an expanding and more and more sophisticated economy, and by legislatures well attuned to public and institutional demands for ever-larger educational appropriations, soon had no visible limits. Higher education became one of the nation's leading growth factors. Caught in a momentum that responded to unprecedented public and private funding, many of the country's colleges and universities quickly doubled or trebled in size. By the mid-1960s the educational system had become frightfully expensive. The outlays for public education soared more than seven times as rapidly as enrollments. Whether the effort served any national requirement was never clear. University administrators seldom acknowledged any need for growth except that of qualifying for the available state and federal appropriations. John W. Oswald recalled the golden years of higher education—the first half ot the 1960s when he was president of the University of Kentucky—in these words:

> Funding from state and federal and private sources was never higher or more easily achieved. Following Sputnik, there had developed an appreciation of what research could accomplish—and of course the universities were doing a large part of that research. Never were there higher expectations for universities or more willingness on the part of the public to support these expectations.
>
> A president's job then was mostly to try to keep buildings going up fast enough and programs sound enough to stay even with the influx of students and monies. And there was an opportunity to do certain things quite different and new and important to universities.
>
> Looking back, I think perhaps we oversold the universities, but at the time we sincerely thought that we might be able to do for the cities and the urban crisis what we had done for agriculture.

Unfortunately, there was little relationship between expenditure and excellence. Much of the specialized university research, conducted at enormous cost to society, returned little useful knowledge to the community. Growth served the interests of the larger faculties, even more the huge educational bureaucracies. It created strong interlocking relationships among professors, college presidents, trustees, financial institutions, industry, and government. Academic entrepreneurs moved freely between campus, government, and business. Professors often created the engineering and electronics firms with which they were associated. Psychologists and professors of education established companies that sold educational materials, ran camps or schools for small children, established community-development programs, or prepared courses to improve the performance of businessmen. These activities of university professors and administrators contributed variously to the welfare of students. Franklin D. Murphy, the chancellor of the University of California, Los Angeles, agreed that the close relationship of universities to business and government created difficulties. "If you have your professors running around and consulting all over the place," he declared in a 1968 interview, "they are not around to talk to students. If you can keep it under control, . . . this is enormously valuable from my point of view. . . . [I]t does provide for the university professor the technique of guaranteeing to some degree that he will not be in an ivory tower and that he will be dealing in the teaching process with things that are germane and contemporary, not entirely theoretical."

Educational expansion converted scholars, scientists, intellectuals, and administrators into a new aristocracy. University salaries kept pace with the rise of the GNP, despite the difficulty of showing comparable increases in the productivity of institutions that had no clear measure of what they produced. It was enough for legislators and the public to believe that larger universities were good for students, for the economy, and for the nation. Few sought to define a university system that would produce the optimum number of well-educated graduates and permit the nation's institutions themselves to perform at a reasonably high level of competence and efficiency. New attitudes toward teaching were often reflected in lighter teaching loads. Widely supported university research did not necessarily provide superior educational opportunity for undergraduates. It established, instead, a disturbing conflict between the university's teaching and research functions as countless faculty members, especially at the major universities, shunned their obligations to undergraduate education. What aggravated this tendency was the decision of university administrators to reserve their special rewards for specialized education and research.

Undoubtedly the educational effort created a better informed public than at any time in history but, in overselling education as a personal and social panacea, colleges and universities brought far more students into higher education than could benefit from the experience or find positions upon graduation commensurate with their education and expectations. Many students who enrolled in such institutions had no genuine commitment to higher education. A disenchanted public would discover soon enough that the monetary and occupational promises of learning were exaggerated. The problems of cost from overexpansion and overstaffing and the ultimate need for contraction, which in time would plague college and university administrators, were predictable from the beginning; the expansion lacked direction and a sense of limits.

THE MIXED ECONOMY

During the 1960s the federal government became not merely the regulator of the economy, but its guarantor as well. The Employment Act of 1946 imposed on Washington the obligation to sustain maximum employment through fiscal and monetary devices. The successful pursuit of that goal demanded whatever governmental intervention a socially and politically acceptable level of economic growth required. The report of a prestigious Rockefeller study group, *Prospect for America,* concluded in 1958: "Public expenditures in support of growth are an essential part of our economy. Far from being a hindrance to progress, they provide the environment within which our economy moves forward." Even to many economists and businessmen the concept of the mixed economy had replaced that of laissez-faire; government, not private enterprise, now carried the responsibility for sustaining the country's employment and economic growth. Under Eisenhower the government created the new Department of Health, Education, and Welfare (HEW) with its ever-mounting budgets. Under Kennedy the notion of a mixed economy became more explicit as the federal government moved more freely into the nation's economic affairs. Behind the country's economic expansion of the 1960s were increasing federal expenditures for social welfare and national defense. During that decade federal, state, and local governments together accounted for 20 percent of all expenditures in the private sector of the economy.

Nowhere was the impact of federal decisions on the nation's economy more apparent than in the space and defense programs. After Russia's initial space triumphs of the 1950s, Washington determined to recapture and thereafter guarantee U.S. leadership in space technology as a symbolic Cold War triumph over the USSR. Senator Richard B. Russell of Georgia expressed the official conviction well: "Sputnik confronts America with a new and terrifying military danger and a disastrous blow to our prestige." The creation of the National Aeronautics and Space Administration (NASA) in 1958 committed Congress to the space program; thereafter the American space effort commanded huge congressional appropriations against no measurable resistance. President Eisenhower denied the existence of any military or security need for the program but, nevertheless, permitted the space budget to reach $1.25 billion by 1960. To resurrect the nation's prestige fully, President Kennedy launched what became a $20-billion space program to reach the moon by the end of the decade. As early as May 1961, Commander Alan B. Shepard, Jr., completed a 300-mile suborbital flight from Cape Canaveral, Florida, into the Atlantic. Thereafter, the American triumphs in space became increasingly spectacular. During February 1962, Lieutenant Colonel John G. Glenn circled the earth three times in a Mercury space capsule. Technologically, the achievements of the United States in space were astonishing, but many questioned the human value of the billions expended in the effort.

Similarly, federal expenditures for national defense mounted sharply during the Kennedy years. The President's disturbing and disillusioning confrontation with Soviet leader Nikita Khrushchev in Vienna in June 1961 resurrected fears of Soviet aggression in Europe. Moscow's decision to erect the Berlin Wall in August merely reaffirmed the new apprehension. Late in July Kennedy announced his intention to increase the nation's armed forces by stepping up the draft and mustering some reserve and National Guard units. To achieve these goals the President sought an increase of over $3 billion in the 1961 defense budget, bringing the total to $47.5 billion, by far the largest military budget since World War II. Early in August Congress voted the new defense budget overwhelmingly.

Thereafter the influence of the military became more pervasive than it had been under Eisenhower. In the name of national security spokesmen for national defense, despite the persistence of official peace, commanded almost a tenth of the gross national product, usually without congressional debate or the necessity of compromise. The weapons establishment possessed an essential advantage over Congress because of its access to highly specialized, generally secret information that permitted it to operate largely free of inspection and control. New weapons projects seemed to flow automatically from technological innovation; often new systems were built simply because they *could* be built. One Congressman admitted, "Pressure to spend more comes in part from the military and in part from industry selling new weapons, with the support of Congress which perceives of needs in the same light." Ultimately, what sustained Congress's perennial support of lavish defense budgets was its gloomy view of Soviet intentions with the concomitant assumption that power and the fear of destruction alone deterred the spirit of domination that allegedly guided the Kremlin. Only a national paranoia that encouraged few questions and thrived on exaggeration of external dangers could excuse the cost, profiteering, inefficiency, and waste in national preparedness. At issue was not the need for national defense, but the level of expenditures and efficiency required to maintain it. As long as military spokesmen argued successfully that defense preparations needed to reflect enemy capabilities, not enemy intentions, and that the United States itself was vulnerable to sudden attack, security would require an almost limitless application of money, effort, and technology.

This abdication of congressional authority made those who controlled the huge defense enterprise among the most influential men in the country. The $1.5 trillion military expenditure after midcentury cemented close working relationships among Pentagon officials, industrial suppliers, military-oriented congressmen, presidential assistants for defense, and all others who might benefit from the flow of such vast quantities of money. That expenditure underwrote the welfare of a variety of huge industries and a number of large personal fortunes. Defense spending brought special benefits to industrialists, scientists, engineers, and skilled laborers in several specific regions of the United States. It paid the salaries and pensions of 2.1 million men and women in the armed services and 1 million civilian employees. Industries directly involved in contracts for weaponry employed 1.7 million. Individuals who benefited indirectly from defense budgets numbered an additional 2.5 million. Thus the Pentagon was responsible ultimately for over 7 million jobs—a high percentage of the country's total labor force. Five large corporations—General Dynamics, Lockheed, Boeing, General Electric, and North American Aviation—controlled a quarter of the nation's defense budget. Military spending pushed the expansion of the Pacific Coast economy. Directly or indirectly it accounted for half of all employment in California (60 percent in the Los Angeles area), and almost half in Seattle, Washington, the home of Boeing aircraft. During the 1960s California became the wealthiest and most populous state in the Union, first in both agricultural and industrial production.

If the war economy, which soon approached $100 billion a year, underwrote the prosperity of millions of Americans, it threatened the private sector in two ways. First, it drained away much of the country's capital; defense expenditures were far greater than corporate investments in new plants and machinery. Second, defense contracts encouraged excessive employment and thus elevated inefficiency to a national purpose. Federal officials negotiated 90 percent of all defense contracts without competitive bidding and on a cost-plus arrangement. The lack of competition, the almost limitless funding, the guaranteed profits, and the resulting lack of efficiency produced cost overruns averaging more than $1 billion for each major weapons system. These overruns permitted the employment of almost double the administrative overload customary in American industry. Still, even for businessmen, economists, writers, and other citizens who condemned the waste of federal resources and the concentration of economic power in Washington, national defense expenditures remained a national necessity and thus a tolerable burden for the taxpaying public. The American people wanted their security and were willing to pay for it.

PROSPERITY AND THE NEW ECONOMICS

President John F. Kennedy inherited the third Eisenhower recession. In February 1961, unemployment stood at 7 percent, the highest level since the Great Depression. That year the economy recovered completely with sharp increases in business investments and industrial production and a resurgence in consumer buying. During 1962 the economy moved toward new records on all fronts, with business recording unprecedented sales. Still, economic analysts believed that the economy lacked zip; unemployment continued at 5.5 percent and the stock market was exceedingly ragged. During June 1962, Wall Street suffered one of the most disastrous selling sprees in its history. Kennedy, having promised in his campaign to "get the country moving again," now listened to those who advocated bolder action. In 1963 he presented a budget to Congress with a deliberately planned deficit. Federal programs such as mass transit, public housing, environmental restoration, or public works might have increased the country's purchasing power, but Kennedy found it more feasible politically to create the desired lift by pressing a reluctant Congress for a $11 billion tax cut instead of expensive social legislation. Indeed, Kennedy placed the full power of his office less behind his domestic program than behind policies designed to impress the Russians— larger commitments of money and manpower to Vietnam, increased military spending, and the mobilization of American science and industry to win the race to the moon.

As Kennedy's economists predicted, the tax cut, adopted early in 1964 after Kennedy's death, created much of the demand that underlay the subsequent economic expansion. To sustain the new prosperity, the federal government reduced taxes further in 1965, sweeping way a host of wartime nuisance taxes. Unemployment declined rapidly from 5.5 percent to 3 percent. The genuine increase in industrial production during the Kennedy years, aided in some degree by Kennedy's policy of holding business and labor to voluntary price and wage guidelines—an approach that became known as "jawboning"—limited the inflationary pressure, exerted by growing demand, to about 1 percent annually. Even more important in restraining prices was the general fiscal moderation of the Kennedy years, reflected in the limited growth of the money supply before 1964. It was the administration of Lyndon B. Johnson, through its domestic expenditures for social reform, its increasing financial commitments to Vietnam, and its expansion of the money supply—all without a commensurate increase in the tax burden—that unleashed the heavy inflationary pressures of the decade. Meanwhile most businessmen, economists, and public officials agreed that federal budgets were indeed effective instruments for managing the country's prosperity.

By 1966 the national economy, responding to the fiscal and spending policies of the federal government, had broken every record for continuous growth. Walter Heller, chairman of the Council of Economic Advisers, began his Godkin Lectures at Harvard that year with the following boast.

> Economics has come of age in the nineteen-sixties. Two presidents have recognized and drawn on modern economics as a source of national strength and Presidential power. Their willingness to use . . . the full range of modern economic tools underlies the unbroken United States expansion since early 1961—an expansion that in the first four years created over seven million new jobs, doubled profits, increased the nation's real output by a third and closed the $50 billion gap between the actual and potential production that plagued the American economy in 1961.

The Wall Street Journal commented in December 1967: "In one sense there is an almost monotonous sameness about the country's economic record in recent years. Business has become better and better. Employment has gone up and up. American affluence, already the envy of foreign lands, has grown and grown and grown." Statistics seemed to prove the correctness of the assertion. In six years the average American's real income had jumped 25 percent; profits after taxes had increased by 71 percent. The economy had grown by $250 billion—more than the total annual output of any western European country. The nation, in short, was enjoying the biggest and longest boom in its history.

Many of the country's leading banks contributed to the boom by shifting their emphasis from asset to liability management as they extended their capacity to offer credit for business and private investment. Traditionally, liabilities in the form of deposits established the limits of a bank's lending capacity. But beginning in 1961 Citibank of New York issued negotiable interest-bearing certificates of deposit to corporations and other large investors, a practice quickly adopted by other major banks to increase their reserves. Such procedures enabled banks to engage in almost unlimited credit expansion. The Federal Reserve subjected the new certificates of deposit to interest-rate ceilings as well as traditional reserve requirements. Such restraints mattered little. With power to offer long-term loans even in the face of tight Federal Reserve monetary policies, banks were prepared to serve businessmen and consumers alike with a seemingly endless flow of credit. Bank loans underwrote the building boom of the late 1960s. So available was funding that builders borrowed huge sums for questionable condominium and resort projects. In time banks wrote off millions of dollars in losses; indeed, only the general banking prosperity saved many from collapse. The future would reveal fully the extent to which banks had extended long-term credit to doubtful risks.

American prosperity of the 1960s rolled forward on a public and private indebtedness almost beyond belief, one approaching $2.5 trillion by the end of the decade. McGraw-Hill economists provided the following breakdown: $1 trillion in corporate debt; $600 billion in mortgage debt; $500 billion in federal government debt; $200 billion in state and local government debt; and $200 billion in consumer debt. The repaying of such indebtedness was unthinkable. For the moment this caused little concern. In such booming times there was limited regard for economic discipline; a recession-free economy demanded that government, business, and consumers alike spend more than they acquired from taxes, profits, and wages. Banks, lending agencies, and merchandisers encouraged Americans to go into debt and remain there. The credit card symbolized American affluence and consumerism. Historically, the value of the free market lay less in its capacity to reward success than in its power to terminate inefficiency and bad judgment. By sustaining misadventures through additional increments of public and private credit, an irresolute government, backed by the country's banking structure, appeared to reward past mistakes by permitting their unfortunate consequences to accumulate. This it did under the assumption that the ultimate economic reckoning would never come or at least would not be tragically expensive.

INFLATION

What determined all federal fiscal policy in the 1960s was the general conviction, shared alike by economists, businessmen, and labor leaders, that the government should counter every downswing in the economy with a combination of tax reduction, public deficits, and the expansion of the money supply. Historically, such governmental efforts to create demand produced inflation when the creation of money and credit, public and private, proceeded at a rate faster than the economy produced goods, performed services, or manufactured capital in the form of savings. Price levels rose moderately until 1968, when the war in Vietnam demonstrated again the compatibility between war and inflation. Contrasted to World War II, the American involvement in Vietnam remained a small operation, but it exerted its inflationary pressure at a time when economic production had approached capacity levels. Countering pressures could have come in the form of new taxes or an American withdrawal from Southeast Asia. The President and his advisors favored neither course. Withdrawal—the acknowledgment of defeat—required a political price that they preferred to avoid. And because the Vietnam war, from its inception, was beset with internal doubts and external scorn, Washington could never arouse enough public support for the war to ask the American public to pay for it. Mounting deficits required to sustain administration policy in Indochina reached $25 billion by 1968.

These deficits, added to the Federal Reserve's decision to accelerate the growth of the money supply, increased the capacity of government, business, and ultimately much of the public to overspend. Conscious of the strong aggregate demand, many of the country's leading businesses announced major price advances. General Motors raised prices for its 1968 models by 4 percent; Chrysler and Ford responded with matching increases. The burgeoning inflation, which soon approached double-digit figures, injured those who could least afford it, especially those who existed on low incomes, those retired on fixed incomes, and those who could exercise no direct influence on their incomes. Ultimately, the price of inflation was staggering. During the postwar era the American people lost over $1 trillion in the devaluation of their insurance and bank savings. The new economics promised the nation that it could, through modern fiscal management, achieve prosperity at minimum cost. The prediction proved to be erroneous.

In some measure the persistence of the inflation defied analysis; the shortages of labor, capital, and raw materials that traditionally forced prices upward were not apparent. The inflationary pressure did not reflect economic growth or full employment. Indeed, the rate of economic growth began to decline after the mid-1960s, although the actual level of economic production continued to increase. The nation's industry, which in 1966 still operated at over 90 percent of capacity, used 87 percent of its plant capacity in 1967 and less in the following years—still high by normal standards. Farmers continued to flood the American market with grains and other produce at prices that scarcely covered the costs of production. Some economists attributed the continuing inflation to the existence of the mixed economy in which the growth-mindedness and welfare-mindedness of government combined to assure businessmen that Washington would never permit another major recession. This permitted corporations to pursue production and pricing policies without regard to future markets.

Theoretically, any reduction in employment or business expansion forces prices downward, compels businessmen to heed customer preferences and, in time, eliminates the weak and less efficient businesses—all to the benefit of the buying public. Unfortunately, the new economics in which governments dedicated themselves to the elimination of recessions through growing public and private indebtedness did not encourage adjustment at all. The flow of money and credit into the economy eliminated the need for cost curtailment or industrial efficiency. The result was increasing failure of many basic U.S. industries, such as steel and electronics, to compete with foreign competition in the American market. However inefficient the Penn Central Railroad, however unsound the management policies of Lockheed aircraft and other large businesses, Congress would attempt to save them with ample outlays of public money. Still, an economy that required massive deficits to sustain it was obviously suffering from serious maladjustments. The fiscal policies of the 1960s simply pushed the burden created by the inefficiency, waste, and overspending of business and government to a seemingly defenseless public in the form of higher prices and higher taxes.

What contributed significantly to the inflation was the nation's pricing structure. Almost every major segment of the American market came under the influence of powerful organized groups—corporations, labor unions, business associations, professional organizations of lawyers, doctors, dentists, and teachers—which protected their interests by eliminating various forms of competition. Much of the inflation resulted less from runaway demand than from rising costs, which those who controlled prices and professional charges could pass on to the public. Unions continued to secure lucrative contracts in the face of growing unemployment and managed generally to maintain wage levels that kept pace with inflation. If business had faced greater domestic price competition, it would have been far more resistant to labor demands. Even as New York City approached bankruptcy, its officials negotiated lavish agreements with the city's public service employees. These arrangements came at a time of recession, teacher surpluses, and serious restraints on the city's borrowing capacity and tax structure. Many businesses recorded mounting profits amid rising costs and declining sales. It was largely the power of organized groups to control the price of their goods and services that created the stagflation (inflation despite the stagnation of the economy) that began in the late 1960s. If the remedy for demand-pull inflation rested in more conservative federal fiscal and monetary policies, that for cost-push inflation lay in the restoration of greater competition in the private sector of the economy. To terminate the inflation with either remedy required a political and economic price that no administration seemed willing to accept; the fiscal decisions that underlay the boom served the corporations, the unions, the banks, the federal bureaus, and the legal and medical professions admirably.

For a quarter century those who controlled the American fiscal and banking structure pumped up the economy in the name of prosperity and full employment. Every administration proclaimed its purpose of moving all able-bodied people off the welfare rolls and onto the payrolls. Except for a brief period in the 1960s, unemployment hovered between 5 and 8 percent. There was no shortage of work to be done, but neither the private nor the public sector made any genuine effort to supply jobs for all Americans commensurate with their skills and expectations. The enunciated goal of full employment remained secondary to the more fundamental goal of prosperity for business and the well-employed. Some economists argued against full employment under the assumption that the only alternative to mass unemployment was double-digit inflation.

Actually, at issue was the manner in which government spent its money—whether on expensive bureaucracies, loans to industries, and lucrative defense contracts, or on programs designed to put more people to work (which could actually cost far less). With the huge sums that doctors, lawyers, engineers, government and business executives, corporations, and military officers extracted from public resources, the federal government could have made impressive inroads on the nation's unemployment. Because of the high wages and salaries shared by those employed in the defense industries, the Bureau of Labor Statistics estimated that an equal amount spent on public works projects would create twice as many jobs. Congressional studies predicted that a public service program would employ no less than four and possibly ten times as many people as would a tax cut of equal size. Tax rebates benefited those with jobs; they offered nothing to the unemployed. At the same time they fueled inflation and eliminated the funds for public works that could add thousands to the ranks of the gainfully employed.

THE STRATIFIED SOCIETY

Economic growth reserved its special benefits for the very rich.

What remained unchanged in America's mixed economy was not its institutional framework, but its structure of privilege. The United States had its class system, not rigid, but pervasive enough. Children of the working class tended to remain in the working class; professional people tended to produce professionals. Upward mobility occurred often enough to keep the assumption of broad opportunity alive, but it was still largely a myth. The relationship of mind and talent to social and economic status remained elusive. At the top of the major horizontal stratifications within American society were the rich and superrich, who comprised a national elite. Forty years of increased government intervention, high taxes, and social legislation had effected little change in the percentage of Americans who received high incomes. In the 1960s, 200,000 American families, less than half of 1 percent, enjoyed annual incomes of $100,000 or more. Those with annual incomes of more than $50,000 numbered only 1 percent of the population. Indeed, an income of $30,000 a year placed a family in the top 5 percent. Thus the truly affluent comprised no more than a thin veneer at the top of the country's social structure.

These income statistics did not reveal the true concentration of wealth in the United States; those with high incomes were not necessarily rich. What was concentrated was the *ownership* of wealth. Two largely interrelated groups comprised the economic aristocracy: those who owned substantial quantities of real estate and corporate stock, and those who held the commanding positions in the business world. American capitalism had always rewarded these groups generously. A Federal Reserve Board study of 1963 revealed that the top fifth of all families owned almost 80 percent of all private wealth; the bottom 25 percent possessed almost none. But that top fifth received only 40 percent of the total national income. In 1962 the Federal Reserve noted that an estimated 200,-000 families possessed net assets of $500,000 or more. These households together held 32 percent of all investment assets, most of it in land, corporate stock, and a variety of tax-exempt securities. Wealthy Americans—those with assets of $1 million or more—numbered approximately 90,000, or one family in every 625. In 1969 the Internal Revenue Service reported that those with more than $5 million numbered about 16,000. Somewhat over 60 families owned $150 million or more; among these were 12 women who together controlled $2.5 billion. Several Americans, such as Jean Paul Getty, John MacArthur, Haroldson Lafayette Hunt, Daniel Ludwig, the Rockefeller brothers, and the Mellons, reputedly held assets in excess of $1 billion. Apologists regarded even the management of such fortunes a major social contribution.

The largest fortunes in America were old, but the prosperous postwar decades created thousands of new millionaires. Most visible among the postwar rich were the stars of entertainment, including performers in drama, music, and the professional sports. Business fortunes, old and new, commonly grew over a lifetime, but many resulted from the exploitation of some special market advantage that permitted a quick profit. Despite the high salaries that some firms paid their executives, the postwar fortunes resulted largely from self-employment. Unlike many of the earlier millionaires who generally built their fortunes on railroad, mining, or industrial empires, the latter-day rich created their fortunes largely through financial manipulation and speculation. Only those who discovered the necessary tax loopholes managed to retain enough of their incomes to acquire large holdings. Thus the surest path to riches lay in the building up of equities in prosperous business or real estate operations, thereby accumulating wealth in the form of capital gains, which were subject to lower taxes. Because the distinguishing mark of great wealth lay in property and possessions, not income, its existence required laws that permitted the rich to pass their fortunes, largely intact, to succeeding generations. Established fortunes were often too large and diversified to be seriously affected by business cycles or governmental policies. Many rested on a strong foundation of real estate. The Merchandise Mart in Chicago, worth an estimated $75 million, dominated the Kennedy holdings. What would terminate the great concentrations of wealth was not heavy taxes on income, but direct assaults on wealth itself.

That such assaults never occurred simply measured the success of the rich in protecting their class and corporate interests. "The rich, the plain fact is," concluded Ferdinand Lundberg in *The Rich and the Super-Rich* (1968), "confront the rest of society as a solid, semi-corporate phalanx, buttressed by law and public policy. By law they hold their positions legitimately and hence can feel complete rectitude." Propertied Americans were traditionally sensitive to federal taxing policies. In general they opposed expenditures designed to increase the comfort and convenience of the broad public. They were far more generous toward military expenditures, because such expenditures contributed to the nation's security and industrial growth and lacked any social intent. Because of their ownership and control of the prime elements in the economy, those with wealth moved to block any new arrangement that might affect members of their class adversely. Large inheritances mobilized the energies necessary to defend them; otherwise they had a depressing effect on achievement. The personal triumphs of the rich were limited largely to corporate management, law, and politics. Some inheritors of great wealth made their marks as judges and lawyers; larger numbers won elective offices or received high-level federal appointments. Few gained any acclaim as scientists, scholars, editors, writers, or performers.

America's middle class was divided. The upper middle group comprised largely the professionals—doctors, dentists, lawyers, architects, and engineers; the academic forces concentrated in the cities and university communities; executives of small and medium-sized corporations; and members of the upper echelons of bureaucracy. The major achievements in letters, science, and design flowed largely from this group. Upper-middle-class families enjoyed satisfactory incomes and established social positions. Within the upper middle class, status was determined less by automobiles, furnishings, and gadgets—which were available to most through installment purchases—than by the houses in which people lived and by education, clothing, and positions in the nation's job hierarchy. This group, mostly because of its mobility, was often intensely competitive in its social relationships.

For many white-collar Americans, especially those who held the multitudinous executive and office positions in banking, commerce, and service, the pressures to conform in dress, housing, and even ideas became irresistible. C. Wright Mills, in his *White Collar: The American Middle Classes* (1951), noted the decline of individualism among middle-class Americans. Much of the change in middle-class society resulted from what David Riesman described in his book, *The Lonely Crowd: A Study of the Changing American Character* (1950), as the shift from inner-directed to other-directed behavior. The typical nineteenth-century American, inner-directed and the product of family indoctrination, believed that anyone who built a better mousetrap need not be concerned with cultivating good relations with others. But in the modern city environment, where friends and associates became more important than family, what mattered for the ambitious was getting along with others. Success was often measured by popularity, not by achievement. Morale became more essential than morality, and morality was a measure of group behavior. The real concern for much of the urban middle class was not the possession of automobiles, adequate houses, and healthful diets—which could be assumed—but the right experience that wine, good food, and automobiles could bring. Of major importance were the human relationships involved in business and social activity—how to get along in the personality market, in business, in the bureaucracy, or on the cocktail circuit. The new social ethic emphasized not competition, but membership in a group as the source of creativity and satisfaction. The goal of work was no longer accumulation, but the enjoyment of the good life. Indeed, advertising and lending agencies encouraged middle-class Americans to enjoy their pleasure and comfort on the installment plan.

Generally distinguishable from the affluent society of business executives and professionals was the lower middle class, usually less well educated, holding positions often not unlike those of the upper middle class, but lower on the scale of income and prestige. Former Under Secretary of Housing and Urban Development, Robert C. Wood, described the typical member of the lower middle class in the late 1960s.

He is a white employed male . . . earning between $5,000 and $10,000. He works regularly, steadily, dependably, wearing a blue collar or white collar. Yet the frontiers of his career expectations have been fixed since he reached the age of thirty-five, when he found that he had too many obligations, too much family, and too few skills to match opportunities with aspirations. . . . The working American lives in the gray area fringes of a central city or in a close-in or very far-out cheaper suburban subdivision of a large metropolitan area. He is likely to own a home and a car, especially as his income begins to rise. Of those earning between $6,000 and $7,500, 70 percent own their own homes and 94 per cent drive their own cars. 94 per cent have no education beyond high school and 43 per cent have only completed the eighth grade.

These low-income and middle-income workers, numbering 23 million families, were conscious of the economic and social pressures on their security and well-being. They consumed much that did them no good; they often worked at jobs they detested. Still, those who shared lower-middle-class incomes (and these included the successful working class) were not homogeneous. What separated blue-collar from white-collar labor was not income, but differences in values, attitudes, life-styles and employment. Blue-collar workers with middle-class incomes did not necessarily adopt middle-class tastes and manners. If their physical surroundings were often similar, their social patterns were generally for more traditional. Blue-collar workers usually led uncomplicated lives, their demands limited to job security, unrestricted access to their places of employment, and simple amenities such as television and time with friends at the neighborhood bar. Generally less well educated than their white-collar counterparts, they more often ignored the world of books and ideas. What separated the two groups even more was the contrasting nature of their employment. Unlike blue-collar workers who produced goods, those with white collars dispensed services. More than white-collar workers, those with blue collars were troubled by fears of unemployment, the declining value of hard work, their limited prospects for advancement, the superior social status of white-collar employees and intellectuals, and the boredom of their work. Entrusting their welfare to unions, the blue-collar elite gladly traded their independence and even a portion of their self-respect for security and material comforts. White-collar employees joined unions, sometimes very effective ones, but with less enthusiasm and convictions of necessity. White-collar and blue-collar laborers often had little in common except their incomes.

What added to the blue-collar blues was the modern assembly line. One young Ford employee explained why he would trade his assembly-line job for almost anything else: "I work on the left grille. Left grille. That's all. Day in and day out. I been working on Ford left grilles for six years. I don't miss a day 'cause I got four kids and I need the money. Left grille. I can do it with my eyes shut. Sometimes I do do it with my eyes shut. Sometimes I just fall asleep working." The assembly line could be relentless, monotonous, and insatiable in its demands. But its levels of production were often astonishing—almost one automobile per minute at Ford's River Rouge plant. Whatever its impact on production, the constant repetition of one simple task could create immense frustration. Such frustration on the assembly line often endangered the efficiency and standards of mass production. Mass layoffs from time to time merely increased the fury. Workers rebelled occasionally with absenteeism, sabotage, and strikes. One paint department employee described how Ford assembly-line workers expressed their hatred of the endless pressure.

> Sabotage against the cars themselves is common. As a matter of course, we used to force the trunks closed in a way that ensured the cars couldn't be painted properly. But most sabotage takes place in the Trim department, where dashboards, mirrors, inside panels, windows and extras are installed. Because so many items are installed in this section, it is difficult to trace the saboteur. Every day, mirrors are smashed and quarter panels are ripped. The art lies in sabotaging in a way that is not immediately discovered. As work is done further down the line, it becomes progressively more difficult to repair the original problem. Another form of sabotage is to ignore work. There is a legendary Trim worker whose job is to install six screws. He never puts in more than four.

Ultimately, what kept such employees coming back was the realization that large-scale industrial operations increased both incomes and job security, especially after the triumph of industrial unionism.

At the bottom end of blue-collar America were the millions of laborers who inhabited the sprawling low-income areas of the large cities. Twice as many whites as nonwhites resided in the low-income neighborhoods of the inner cities. Typical of whitetown inhabitants, often ethnic in origin, were laborers who, in the 1960s, earned minimum wages as factory workers, truck drivers, and clerks. Most lived closer to poverty than to affluence. Their real problem was not unemployment as much as underemployment, with as many as 60 percent of those employed earning less than enough for a decent standard of living. Ethnic neighborhoods suffered from deterioration in abandoned houses, run-down schools and playgrounds, and uncollected trash. Yet houses, often old and small, comprised for their owners their most prized possessions. Only a step or two above most blacks on the economic ladder, these urban whites faced the perenial dangers of unemployment, economic decline, and displacement. Federal urban programs that poured money into black neighborhoods were a constant demonstration of ethnic powerlessness. Earlier welfare gains had created a coalition that included working-class ethnic groups, blacks, and middle-class liberals. The civil rights revolution and the gradual dispersion of working-class blacks into former white neighborhoods shattered that coalition by threatening the stability of white ethnic society. Ethnic districts in many cities braced themselves perennially against the invasion of lower-income blacks. In this black-ethnic conflict lay the major tension in the changing urban culture.

Not all such low-income white urban areas were ethnic. For example, Cleveland's Near West Side, populated by refugees from Appalachia, was almost entirely Anglo-Saxon. Chicago's hard-pressed Marquette Park neighborhood on the city's south side was a more representative melting pot of Irish, Poles, Germans, Italians, plus a large concentration of Lithuanians—all trying to hold their own on the encroaching edge of a large, poverty-stricken black community. Equally typical of a declining urban neighborhood was Philadelphia's Kensington. Its population was white and almost entirely ethnic in composition. Peter Binzen, in his *Whitetown USA*, described Kensington in these terms.

> Kensington is a community in crisis. In many ways it looks, thinks, and acts like many of the Negro ghettos festering in American cities. Its educational, political, social, and economic problems are almost as great as those found in the black slums. It, too, has failed to solve these problems, and failure has made it sullen, surly, and suspicious. . . . Kensington's air is polluted, its streets and sidewalks are filthy, its juvenile crime rate is rising, its industry is languishing. No more than a handful of new houses have been built there in the last third of a century. Its schools are among the oldest in the city, industry is moving out.

Still, neither Philadelphia nor Washington did much to save Kensington. Generally hardworking and conservative, the inhabitants of such whitetowns across the country viewed with equal distrust the blacks who threatened them and the establishment that ignored them.

Most Americans shared in the country's economic growth. Their occupational advancement, no less than their job security, exceeded their expectations. Still, despite the widespread economic gains, the average wages of American workers never reached the cost of a "low" standard of living for a model family of four, as calculated each year by the Bureau of Labor Statistics. It was the multiple incomes of most families that permitted them to reach a minimum or somewhat higher standard. For the unemployed and underemployed the boom of the 1960s brought neither psychic nor tangible gains. It scarcely touched the country's hard-core poor; it did not change the life of the average slum dweller. About 30 million Americans still lived below what officials term the poverty line, defined during the 1960s as an income of approximately $3000 a year for a nonfarm family of four. An even larger number of urban inhabitants, most of them blacks and ethnics, had incomes of between $3500 and $5000 a year—above the poverty line but insufficient to provide a comfortable level of existence. These millions brought the number of deprived in American society to more than a third of the total population. To these low-income and unemployed citizens, business and government together seemed incapable of promoting the general welfare or resolving the multitudinous challenges that emerged from the growth of technology, complexity, and urbanization.

Chapter VI

The Troubled Nation

POVERTY IN AMERICA

The perennial prosperity of the 1960s that rolled millions of American families into the middle class carried an estimated third of the nation's poor above the poverty line. At the beginning of the decade there were 39.5 million people in the United States defined officially as poor; 10 years later that number had dwindled to 25 million, still more than 5 million families and 10 percent of the population. As inflation pushed the poverty line up to $5500 for a nonfarm family of four by the mid 1970s, the number of Americans living in official poverty again tended to increase. The escape from poverty was far easier for some than for others. Whites progressed faster than blacks. As late as 1969, black families had a median income of only $6000 compared to almost $10,000 for white families. Whereas three-fourths of the poor had been white in 1959, only two-thirds of the poor were white in 1970. Blacks, too, had gained, but in 1970 a third of all blacks in the country remained poor.

Whether poverty's victims lived in the rural South or in the urban slums, their presence in a nation of plenty was a disturbing anachronism. However, poverty, if an anachronism, had its reasons. American society demanded a measure of ability, preparation, and determination from those on whom it bestowed some economic success. Within the nation, unfortunately, were many men and women who, because of health, education, environment, mental deficiency, race, or other factors, could not compete satisfactorily in the economic life of the country. Both the hill regions of the South and the urban slums had so completely deprived many of their inhabitants of useful skills, energy, education, and incentive that few found it possible to break the stranglehold of the past on their hopes and expectations. Too often the existence of opulence and opportunity elsewhere created resentment instead of a meaningful urge for self-improvement. Without jobs, preferably steady ones, the poor would never escape their privation. Prosperity alone, the 1960s proved, could not create the needed employment.

Among the nation's citizens who existed at the fringes of national life were the 16 million rural poor, concentrated overwhelmingly in the broad strip of the Appalachian Mountains that stretched from southern New York to central Alabama. Other centers of rural poverty existed in Mississippi, Arkansas, Louisiana, Tennessee, and Florida. Outside the South the troubled states were Minnesota, Wisconsin, Oklahoma, and California, with its large contingent of migrant workers. In November 1960 Edward R. Murrow introduced the nation to its migrant farmers of the rural South in a CBS documentary entitled "Harvest of Shame." Here were Americans with annual incomes of $900 and only one in a thousand with a high school education. Here were families living in rat-infested hovels under the shadow of nearby stables costing a half-million dollars. Most of the people living in rural poverty received no federal aid. They were too poor and widely dispersed to be politically effective. Amid crumbling schools and roads, the exhaustion of soils and coal reserves, and the unavailability of credit, the plight of both subsistence and migrant farmers rendered progress exceedingly elusive. Some chose to escape to the cities but, without adequate education and skills, such migrants had little chance to meet the urban competition for jobs.

Much of the urban and suburban population rode the crest of the prosperity in the 1960s, but those who inhabited the crowded, decaying areas of the inner cities lived in a permanent depression with little or no relief. Ultimately the problems of unemployment and poverty centered in the large black slums of the cities, where the issue of race reinforced and perpetuated the gaping divisions in American society. Blacks who migrated from the rural South soon discovered that the Northern urban ghetto was not the promised land. Every large city had its black communities, such as Harlem in New York, Watts in Los Angeles, and Hough in Cleveland. These areas existed without exception somewhere in the heart of the central cities. Not all the urban poor lived in slums, since the lower-income white neighborhoods often battled the encroachments of urban decay with some success. Those who lived in the slums, therefore, were overwhelmingly black and young. Sixty percent of these concentrations of humanity were under 21. The challenge posed by these young blacks was immediate and urgent; under the surface, always ready to erupt, was a latent violence created by generations of economic deprivation and social stagnation.

Black America presented three distinct classes with little unity among them. Postwar prosperity had created a new black middle class. Blacks who had access to college educations, and those who enjoyed success in sports, entertainment, and business, had no difficulty in gaining the bottom, middle, or upper rungs of the middle class as teachers and professionals. These people readily entered the better neighborhoods and white society. In doing so, they consigned the central cities to persons embedded in poverty and unlikely to escape. It was not strange that white and black writers alike attacked them for allegedly deserting the black community. Working-class blacks especially resented the more successful, for these regularly-employed inhabitants of the ghettos carried a special burden. They knew that the normal expectations of success were not open to them; they lacked the education and training required for genuine advancement. For them there could be no escape from the slums. Foreseeing no achievement for themselves, they envied the progress of others. They drove taxis, ran elevators, and lived quiet, meager lives. Often they worked long hours to earn $75 a week, ending each weary day in fear of some new calamity. What troubled working-class blacks was the knowledge that other ghetto blacks, who did not work, lived as well or better than they on welfare, by hustling, or by pushing drugs.

If working-class blacks could scarcely identify with the middle class, they abhorred the underclass. This third class of blacks, blocked by hopelessness from any vision of the future, lived each day by its wits, exploiting everybody and everything. Men unable to support their families often abused their wives and children or simply deserted them. Such economic failure drove the women onto welfare or into prostitution and the children into the culture of the streets. Without any expectation of an adequate income to maintain a reasonable standard of family life, the unemployed and partially employed often turned to lives of promiscuity, irresponsibility and, ultimately, violence. For many such blacks, life was a series of arrests and disasters. Police sweeps and indeterminate sentences were no answer; there were always other young blacks with no respect for the law waiting to take up the slack. Going to jail was no mark of failure. "You are looked up to," observed black writer Claude Brown, "if you are a successful hustler, you have a big Cadillac and you have always got three hundred dollars in your pocket, you are taking numbers, you are selling drugs, you are a stickup artist, you are anything. . . . " Those supposedly rehabilitated could not survive the old environmental pressures when they returned. Crime flowed from poverty and the absence of shared values that alone could hold communities together; any crisis or blackout could set off a spree of looting and destruction. Job discrimination, concluded black writer Orde Coombs, had broken the resistence of blacks to continued adversity. "The refusal to honor a black man's work—to let him know that the smell of his sweat led to just recompense, that his hands were his survival, and his sinews his passport to success," he wrote, "has led to the degradation, the hostility and lethargy now threatening to engulf us."

Those who made their way out of the slums generally did so by acquiring more schooling or vocational training than others. Yet the availability of schools alone could not break the pattern of economic and social failure. Most slum dwellers did not have access to an adequate education. In part the problem was money; in part, the absence of order. The per capita expenditure for schools in the crowded big cities was no more than half the amount expended in the wealthy suburbs. Evan Hunter, in *The Blackboard Jungle* (1955), condemned slum education. "This is the garbage can of the educational system," he wrote. " . . . Our job is to sit on the lid of the garbage can and see that none of the filth blows into the streets." During the two decades that followed, the level of inner-city education did not improve. Many teachers in such urban schools were able and dedicated, but the low level of student motivation hampered their efforts and reduced much of the teaching endeavor to the futile search for attention. The low state of discipline and performance indicated that the problem ultimately was far deeper than the quality of education that the cities offered. Those who gained little from school, and thus condemned themselves to a life of poverty, were more often than not from broken homes and lacked the presence of a male breadwinner whom they might emulate. It was the inability of most adult urban blacks to earn an adequate livelihood that deprived them of their normal role as the center of family authority and leadership. From this pervading cycle of failure even youths of genuine promise could not readily escape.

Two other minorities—Spanish-speaking Americans and American Indians—suffered from poverty and discrimination no less than did the blacks. By the 1960s almost 10 million residents of the United States claimed Mexican, Cuban, Puerto Rican, or other Latin backgrounds. The Puerto Ricans, numbering about 750,000, lived largely in New York. Although scarcely 8 percent of the city's population, they accounted for one-third of all welfare recipients. About 6 million Mexican-Americans resided in five Southwestern states—California, Arizona, New Mexico, Texas, and Colorado—where they numbered 12 percent of the population. Among them unemployment ranged from 8 to 13 percent, twice the national average. Many struggled for an existence as migrant workers, living in poverty, filth, and disease. Whether they lived in urban or rural areas, they faced the disadvantages imposed by differences in race, culture, and language. The absence of Mexican language and culture in the schools sustained the cycle of underachievement. Few Mexican-American children completed high school; almost none entered college.

Mexican-American leaders adopted the term "Chicano" to assert their cultural identity. Preaching a form of ethnic nationalism, they set out to develop among Mexican-Americans a sense of community and pride in their cultural heritage. Determined to maintain their cultural distinction, they demanded bilingual instruction in the public schools. To vindicate their economic and political rights, the Chicanos turned to collective action. César Chávez achieved national recognition when he organized the National Farm Workers Association in 1962 and thereafter conducted a series of successful strikes and boycotts to improve wages for Chicanos working in the vineyards and vegetable fields of California. In New Mexico, Reies López Tijerina organized a movement among Mexican-Americans to recover an estimated 5.5 million acres of private and communal lands taken from Mexican-Americans following the American acquisition of New Mexico in 1848. Other political movements addressed the specific economic and educational needs of Mexican-Americans residing in Colorado and Texas. If cultural nationalism created a needed sense of community among Mexican-Americans, it did little to bring this minority into the mainstream of American life.

For American Indians the barriers to full membership in the country's economic and social structure were even less surmountable. Indian unemployment was the highest in the United States, exceeding 50 percent on some reservations. Half the nation's Indian population lived on $3000 a year or less. The Navajos of Arizona, living in tarpaper shacks or one-room hogans scattered over the desert, endured hardships beyond the imagination of most Americans. The Interior Department's Bureau of Indian Affairs (BIA) employed masses of bureaucrats who contributed little to the welfare of the country's special wards. Living under the guardianship of the federal government, Indians enjoyed few rights exercised by other Americans. Repeatedly the Interior Department leased reservation lands to corporations who reaped the profits of logging, mining, or ranching. By the 1970s, 300,000 Indians had deserted the reservations for the cities; there they still faced discrimination and unemployment. To recover ancestral lands, improve the economic life of Indians, and perpetuate the Indian culture, militants organized the American Indian Movement (AIM) to focus criticism on national policies and reservation officials alike. In October 1972 members of AIM occupied the Bureau of Indian Affairs building in Washington, eventually leaving with cartons of documents highly damaging to the agency. Then, from March until May 1973, AIM occupied the hamlet of Wounded Knee on the

Oglala Pine Ridge reservation of South Dakota to protest the alleged corruption in the Indian government of Pine Ridge. Behind the struggle lay deep rivalries within the Indian community itself and the plight of 800,000 Indians caught between a vanishing past and an unpromising future.

Two books, both published in 1962, brought the problem of poverty home to the Kennedy administration. Michael Harrington's *The Other America* pointed eloquently to the existence of poverty in the nation—a poverty, he declared, that had become invisible. So little, indeed, had the poor been able to publicize their condition that even the urban middle classes could live out their lives quite unconscious of the poverty around them. Harry Caudill's *Night Comes to the Cumberlands* exposed the widespread, but still generally unencountered, poverty of Appalachia. Actually, Kennedy's New Frontier, as an extension of the New Deal and Fair Deal, focused more on the immediate issue of unemployment than on the far more intractable problem of hard-core poverty. The President limited his recommendations to the Eighty-sixth Congress to measures for public works and highway construction, health care for the aged, federal aid to schools, public housing, and community development. The Public Works Act of 1962 appropriated $900 million for projects in high-unemployment areas, but otherwise the President sought and achieved little. The high level of prosperity sustained the traditional conservative bloc of Northern Republicans and Southern Democrats in Congress. Not until Homer Bigart published his account of the Cumberland Plateau in *The New York Times* during the autumn of 1963 did Kennedy begin preparation of a major antipoverty program, designed to redirect the lives of several million families with incomes of less than $3000 a year. Whether Kennedy could have extracted enough support from Congress to launch a war against poverty was doubtful.

THE STRUGGLE FOR CIVIL RIGHTS

Racism compounded the problem of poverty and widespread economic immobility for the country's 20 million blacks. These victims of a pervading social prejudice, with far deeper American roots than most white citizens, could not compete with the more recent immigrants for satisfactory employment, housing, or education. Black leaders, encouraged by the limited civil rights gains of the war years, and by the emphasis on freedom in the burgeoning conflict between the United States and Russia, launched a massive assault on the country's political and social injustice during the Truman years. Truman and other Democratic leaders joined the appeal to the nation's conscience, but Southern resistance to change eliminated action in the political realm. Thus civil rights for blacks, beginning with education, became a matter for the courts. At issue in postwar America was still the "separate but equal" doctrine, established by *Plessy* v. *Ferguson* (1896), which comprised the legal foundation for segregation. In *Sipuel* v. *Oklahoma* (1948) the Supreme Court ordered the state of Oklahoma to provide a qualified woman applicant with an equal legal education in a state institution. Two years later the Supreme Court handed down two decisions that demolished the principle of "separate but equal." In *Sweatt* v. *Painter* the court ordered the University of Texas to accept Herman Sweatt as a law student because no other state institution offered equal facilities. In *McLaurin* v. *Oklahoma State Regents* the Court ordered the University of Oklahoma's school of education to accept Professor G. W. McLaurin as a graduate student without imposing its customary provisions for classroom segregation.

These cases were merely a prelude to the landmark decision of May 1954—*Brown* v. *Board Of Education of Topeka*—which pointedly eliminated the separate but equal doctrine as a deep social injustice. Behind the decision were the efforts of black lawyers, led by Thurgood Marshall, to overthrow *Plessy* v. *Ferguson* and thus uproot every remaining legal basis of segregation. Chief Justice Warren declared that segregation creates "a sense of inferiority [and] affects the motivation of a child to learn." The unanimous court concluded that "in the field of public education the doctrine of 'separate but equal' has no place. Separate educational facilities are inherently unequal." In May 1955 the Court, recognizing the problem of immediate compliance with its decision, asked only that segregated communities establish some timetable for desegregation.

Some regions of the upper South prepared for desegregation

immediately, but in the lower South communities simply ignored the federal decrees. Among Democratic elders in the Senate the reaction was angry; Congress had upheld white supremacy through the years by perpetuating the principle that civil rights were local matters. Senator James Eastland of Mississippi declared that the South would not "abide by or obey [the Court's] legislative decision." Senator Harry Byrd of Virginia set out to nullify the Court's action. "If we can organize the Southern States for massive resistance to this order," he proclaimed, "I think that in time the rest of the country will realize that racial integration is not going to be acceptable to the South." If Virginia surrendered, he warned, the rest of the South would go down. On March 12, 1956, 101 Southern congressmen signed a Southern Manifesto for resistance to school integration. Prince Edward County, Virginia, countered the Court's ruling by abolishing its public schools and establishing a private system of education. Despite Southern opposition, Congress passed the Civil Rights Act of 1957. This law created a Commission on Civil Rights with authority to investigate violations of the rights of all citizens and to report such violations to the President. It also established a Civil Rights Division within the Department of Justice with the special power to prosecute anyone accused of violating the civil rights of others.

Another, more pervasive, struggle for black equality began in December 1955, when Mrs. Rosa L. Parks, a black seamstress in a Montgomery, Alabama, department store, refused to give up her seat in a crowded Montgomery bus. She was arrested and jailed. Formerly, divisions within the ranks of the blacks had rendered such defiance of the white community ineffective. But in this racial confrontation over an old Jim Crow law, Montgomery's black leaders organized the Montgomery Improvement Association and chose a young, courageous black minister, Dr. Martin Luther King, Jr., as its president. King conducted a successful boycott of the bus system. One year later, when almost bankrupt from the loss of riders, the bus company lifted all racial restrictions in seating. By the time that the Supreme Court, late in 1956, had declared segregation on municipal buses unconstitutional, the movement had spread to other Southern cities. King, the son of a leading Atlanta clergyman and a graduate of Boston University's school of theology, now became the pivotal figure in the entire Southern civil rights movement. During the Montgomery crisis, he had perfected his strategy of civil disobedience through peaceful resistance. By such means he would compel the white community to recognize its racism. In 1957 King organized the Southern Christian Leadership Conference, with its headquarters in Atlanta, to urge nonviolent protest against Southern segregationist practices.

Black students, adopting King's strategy, now attacked segregation in Southern restaurants and public facilities. They resorted to sit-ins, marches, picketing, and boycotts. In February 1960, four students from the black Agricultural and Technical College at Greensboro, North Carolina, sat down at a Woolworth lunch counter reserved for whites, determined to remain until the management either served them or shut down. One of the four, Franklin McCain, recalled that some whites called them "dirty niggers," but two elderly women insisted that they should have done it 10 years earlier. So effective was the sit-in in bringing pressure on restaurant owners that the tactic spread to other regions of the South. This movement created another effective civil rights group, the Student Nonviolent Coordinating Committee (SNCC). The sit-in, added to picket lines and economic boycotts, soon brought a wide variety of private segregated businesses to terms. Still the price of success came high. Many businessmen fought back with thugs and police; some even preferred bankruptcy to concession. Then, in May 1961, black leader James Farmer, chairman of the Congress of Racial Equality (CORE), took a group of "freedom riders" by bus through Virginia, the Carolinas, Georgia, and Alabama to challenge segregation in interstate bus terminals. In Alabama they faced violence and mob reprisals, but eventually, with federal protection, they ended segregation in the Birmingham bus terminal. This technique of invading segregated facilities soon attracted widespread support among Northern sympathizers who joined the freedom rides into the South and there faced jail sentences. Separate but equal facilities gradually disappeared everywhere.

But the struggle for equal rights had scarcely begun. Despite the *Brown* decision, the South had experienced no more than token integration. Most southern communities responded to court orders but to little else. After eight years of legal desegration, less than

13,000 black children out of 2.8 million in 11 Southern states attended desegregated schools. Southern universities had continued to bar black students. When, in September 1962, black veteran James H. Meredith attempted to enroll at the University of Mississippi, he faced opposition in the governor's office. Immediately President Kennedy, backed by his brother Robert, the Attorney General, placed the full power of the federal government behind Meredith's registration. Under the compulsion of a federal court order, which carried a fine of $10,000 a day beyond an immediate deadline, Mississippi Governor Ross Barnett withdrew his opposition to Meredith's enrollment at the university. Kennedy's action broke the barriers to black enrollments at the South's leading universities.

Meanwhile black protests and demonstrations across the South continued to face strong retaliation from police and white citizen's groups. During April 1963, King led a massive demonstration in Birmingham, Alabama, against the city's segregationist policies. Birmingham police, led by segregationist T. Eugene "Bull" Connor, attacked the demonstrators with clubs, police dogs, and high-powered water hoses. Kennedy told a news conference: "As it is today, in many cases they [the blacks] do not have a remedy, and therefore they take to the streets. . . . " On August 28, 1963, King led a well-publicized march on Washington. There, in a more reassuring environment, over 200,000 black and white marchers gathered at the Lincoln Memorial in a giant protest against the federal government's long indifference to the plight of blacks in American society. King's stirring address created visions of a day when equality and brotherhood would triumph.

Much of the dissatisfaction over governmental inaction centered on the President. James Reston complained as early as June: "There is something wrong with his leadership on the home front. Something is missing in his speeches, his press conferences, his trips and his timing. He is not communicating his convictions effectively. . . . The President's appeal, somehow, is to the mind of the nation and not to its heart. He defines the problems of race, unemployment and education, but doesn't come to grips with them. He is a tactician but not a teacher." Shortly thereafter Kennedy confronted the civil rights issue with a powerful television address to the nation; eight days later he presented his Civil Rights bill to Congress. In July the Senate Judiciary Committee opened its hearings on the President's measure. Southern leaders fought the Kennedy proposal relentlessly. Senator Sam J. Ervin of North Carolina, after examining the bill, termed it the most "decisive measure in this area since the Reconstruction Acts of 1867. It is a drastic assault on the principles of constitutional government and the rights of individuals." The South staked its defense on state and property rights, directing its congressional strategy at the Republicans and Far Western Democrats who feared the assaults on property that genuine racial equality might bring. What supported the administration was the nation's conscience and the Fourteenth Amendment with its "equal protection" clause. Even more fundamental, those who favored the Civil Rights bill could point to statistics that demonstrated the South's success in limiting desegregation and black voting. In some Mississippi counties less than 1 percent of blacks were registered. Despite the strong opposition to his Civil Rights measure Kennedy, using the techniques of political compromise, gradually secured the necessary commitments from Republican leaders to assure its eventual passage. But in the autumn of 1963 that was not obvious.

URBAN AND ENVIRONMENTAL CHANGE

Urban change revealed a momentum of its own, creating problems that seemed to defy solution. On November 20, 1967, the population of the United States passed the 200 million mark, an increase of 50 million since 1950. The social and economic significance of this population growth was less its rapidity than its concentration in the large cities of the country. By 1970, only 5 percent of the people lived on farms; 70 percent were urban dwellers. Yet these population shifts did not reflect the full impact of urbanization. Cities engulfed entire geographical areas; great "megalopolises" arose between Washington, D.C. and Boston, along the Great Lakes, and in the environs of San Francisco and Los Angeles. The nation's most rapid urban growth occurred along the southern rim, which extended from the South Atlantic coast across the Gulf

States, through Texas, New Mexico, and Arizona, to southern California. Texas, the fulcrum of this vast region, reaped an influx of people and investment that rivaled that of California. Many leading urban centers of the Sun Belt—Houston, Dallas, and Phoenix—trebled or quadrupled in population between 1945 and 1970. Within the country's large metropolitan areas, especially those in the North, affluence produced an ever-changing pattern of development. Millions of citizens deserted the inner cities and moved to the suburbs; minority groups—largely blacks moving out of the South—replaced them.

By 1970, 37 percent of all Americans lived in suburbs, while 31 percent lived in the central cities. Suburbanites escaped the problems of the inner cities, but they encountered new frustrations that made suburban living far from idyllic. The speed of development often destroyed the suburban dream of green space, clean air, and new housing almost overnight. The suburbanites soon discovered that they had no control of that major industry—home building—which carved up the countryside, increased the population density, crowded the schools, and elevated the taxes. To urban critic Lewis Mumford the suburbs offered fewer benefits than the cities and none of the advantages of the country. "Living in the suburbs," he observed, "isn't going back to the land, it's going back to the huge lawn and the power mower." So rapid was the urban spread that some new developments of 100,000 people lacked a daily newspaper, a hotel, or a bus system. These subdivisions were merely areas of residence, forcing their inhabitants to rely on automobiles for work, shopping, and recreation.

Actually, the cities were in serious trouble before the flight to the suburbs began. As centers of culture and administration, of opportunity and excitement, the cities beckoned the ambitious. Urban areas remained the nation's greatest producers of wealth and profit. But if the free market could bring business, labor, and buyers into a profitable relationship, it could not achieve a minimum level of efficiency, comfort, and safety for the vast concentrations of population that inhabited the major cities. In time the cities succumbed to the decades of neglect. "The crisis of our cities," wrote Ada Louise Huxtable of *The New York Times*, "can be stated in very simple terms: they are becoming unsupportably hideous." Efforts at reconstruction faced formidable odds; the processes of erosion were too widespread and pervading to bend readily to established programs. Milwaukee mayor Henry Maier observed in the 1960s, "As long as you are moving in terms of acres instead of square miles, you don't have a chance to arrest blight." In deep financial trouble after midcentury, the major cities relied on state and federal programs to combat their monetary and physical disabilities. Congestion rendered urban services, transportation, schooling, police protection, and welfare prohibitive in cost. By 1975 New York City hovered on the precipice of bankruptcy.

Housing—the chief victim of inner-city poverty—remained the most conspicuous evidence of urban deterioration. Where marginal housing became an economic liability and owners stopped all further investment, the processes of abandonment and deterioration quickly set in. Every large city had zones that succumbed to the steady shift of building after building from full occupancy, to partial occupancy, and then to no occupancy at all. Gangs and junkies moved in and ripped out everything that had a market—mostly plumbing. "I seen exterminators dump poison in these buildings to get shed of the rats," explained a New York slum resident, "and the junkies come long right behind with shopping bags and pick it up and sell it." Abandoned buildings gave any neighborhood a bombed-out appearance. One writer described the East New York of the late 1960s:

> The vacant houses . . . , many in the Model Cities tract, are now burned-out, vandalized, shattered, filled with old shoes, smashed furniture, forgotten dogs and a sour effluvium of neglect and despair. . . . Windows and doors are sealed with tin or cinderblocks or left open and broken. Scores of buildings have had the tin coverings or the metal gates which uselessly guard empty stores ripped away and the interiors ransacked, gutted and heaped with rank debris. The sidewalks and streets are littered with garbage, wind-whipped newspapers and rotting mattresses. A smashed telephone booth lies on its side in the middle of the sidewalk, the phone coin box ripped out. Broken glass is always being crunched underfoot. . . . An automobile hulk smolders at the corner. A little girl swings from the end of a thick rusty wire which dangles from the second-story fire escape of an empty brick building.

Stewart Alsop observed in *Newsweek* in February 1972, that New York's South Bronx was dying as if from some lethal disease.

"Drive down almost any street," he wrote, "and you see apartment houses that have just been abandoned—you can always tell by the broken windows. Others are sagging wrecks and some have been bulldozed to the ground. In fact, the South Bronx looks a lot like London after the blitz." More than 2000 square blocks—80,000 housing units—of the South Bronx surrendered to the process of abandonment, dislocating more than 250,000 people. For those who remained the median income reached only $5,500 by 1970.

Harlem, like other black urban communities across the country, offered scenes of degradation that reflected its poverty and the encroachment of abandoned buildings. One bar owner exclaimed bitterly: "Anyone with half an eye can see that Harlem is dying. Ain't nobody around anymore. All those who could, have moved. Only ones left is those who can't go nowhere. Everywhere you look you see boarded-up buildings. People gone. And those left don't drink whisky. They on drugs." Harlem's famous Savoy Ballroom and other popular clubs that once catered to great musicians and big spenders were gone, victims of the changing urban scene. Every street had its abandoned apartment complexes, monuments to the rapacity of landlords, generally white, who exacted what they could from their tenants until decay rendered the buildings uninhabitable.

No other country would tolerate such systematic decay. But, as Jane Jacobs, Martin Anderson, and others observed, federal urban renewal was not necessarily the answer, because such projects were sterile, regimented, and dull. Continuing poverty, moreover, subjected them to rapid decay. Far better, they argued, would be the rebuilding of old neighborhoods, preserving their diversity, self-sufficiency, and sense of direction. Through such processes, urban cores could comprise self-contained neighborhoods with many of the attributes of smaller towns. Congress on occasion denied federal funds for new construction in an effort to encourage the rehabilitation of existing neighborhoods. Unfortunately, the areas of cities that needed the most help were precisely those least able to help themselves. Perhaps the inner cities had little chance of recovery as long as the wrong people lived in them. Those large urban areas in need of change teemed with people who could not find work, whereas the high-income middle class that inhabited the towering office buildings refused to live in the cities, thus denying them civic leadership and the necessary economic base.

Urban congestion took its toll in crime and insecurity. In New York, wrote Roger Wilkins, "one can witness as advanced a case of societal breakdown and dehumanization as is to be found in America." Actually, the crime and alienation that flowed from intense competition, poverty, disappointment, and social stratification pervaded all large urban environments. What level of reconstruction could render the cities safe for their habitants was no longer clear. Lawlessness surged through urban America, making fear a fact of life for city and suburban dwellers alike. Racial tension kept the cities anxious, even explosive. A Gallup poll of 1973 revealed that one person in three living in any big inner-city area had been mugged, robbed, burgled, or vandalized during the previous year. Similarly, one in four suburban residents had suffered from a serious crime. Many urban dwellers moved about freely, denying or ignoring danger, but fear affected the general behavior—the hiring of taxis, the barracading of houses and apartments, the refusal to venture alone into parks or quiet streets at night. Unless the nation awakened to the urban crisis, warned the 1969 report of the Commission on the Causes and Prevention of Violence, the central business districts would be deserted at night except for police patrols. Residential neighborhoods, it predicted, would become more and more unsafe; slums would become places of terror. Despite all the federal efforts at law enforcement, crime in the United States during 1973 and 1974 soared to new records. The residents of cities with 500,000 and over, in a national poll of July 1975, named crime by far the country's major problem. Crime had become America's greatest growth industry.

Uncontrolled industrial expansion demanded its price in a damaged national environment. Much of the country's natural beauty suffered from the encroachments of highways, land developers, and the urban sprawl. Land use, generally planless, resulted in staggering waste and destruction that only a rich country would accept. Land development emerged as a major industry, creating more millionaires after World War II than any other form of business investment. Population growth, early marriages and early retirements, and the interest of the affluent in new suburbs placed immense pressure on land use. Urban growth swallowed up 1 million acres a year, 100,000 in California alone. Highways and airports absorbed additional millions. Strip-mining cut scars in the landscape at the rate of 153,000 acres annually. In many areas, the harvesting of timber exceeded reforestation. Bulldozers carved up the countryside, creating problems of erosion and polluting the lakes and streams with mud and debris. One noted environmentalist termed this assault on the land "grand larceny against the future." Environmentalists saw no answer except restrictive policies on land use or heavy government land purchases.

Society created an avalanche of solid waste that threatened to bury it. Piles of junked automobiles, refrigerators, washing machines, and television sets multiplied in profusion. With no curtailment of trash production in sight, cities were rapidly running out of burial space. Some cities, large and small, would face acute crises before the end of the 1970s. Americans, thriving on technology, discarded approximately 350 million tons of trash a year. Officials predicted a doubling of that tonnage within 20 years. This waste included 60 million tons of paper and paper products. Discarded packaging alone weighed 25 million tons a year. The disposal of this waste cost the nation about $4.5 billion annually. Much of the waste in paper, glass, steel, and aluminum could be recycled, but consumers and producers alike resisted the cost and inconvenience.

Industrial pollution comprised another assault on the environment, more dangerous because more deadly. Smog in one form or another could be found in most regions of the United States. At times it blanketed Los Angeles and major cities along the Atlantic Coast. Automobile exhaust was the major offender, with some 94.6 million tons a year. American factories shared in the creation of another 142 million tons of smoke and fumes each year. Electric power plants alone emitted some 75 million tons of pollutants into the air. Arizona's copper industries made a significant contribution to the air pollution of the Southwest. In 1969, forest service surveys indicated that smog had injured 161,000 acres of conifers in Southern California, including 46,000 acres of pine trees in the San

Bernadino Forest. Scientists warned that the wastes entering the air through the burning of fossil fuels were greater than the earth's atmosphere could absorb.

Every city of 500,000 or more dumped at least 50 million gallons of sewage a year into the nation's streams, rivers, and lakes. Scarcely a river system in America had not been polluted; some had become a national disgrace. Off Manhattan Island 40 years of dumping had created a heavily polluted area of ocean covering 20 square miles. Pollution had destroyed most of Lake Erie's waterlife; only their greater depths permitted the other Great Lakes to survive longer. According to the public health service, 18 million fish died of pollution in 1969. Leakage from offshore oilwells or tankers sullied large areas of ocean; gummed up wharves and beaches; killed fish and wildlife; and contaminated oysters, scallops, and soft-shell clams. Environmentalists argued against the Alaskan pipeline, warning of ecological damage from construction, the possible rupturing of the pipe where the line was submerged, and the danger of spills in transferring the oil to tankers. The Department of the Interior ultimately approved the line, although it admitted that some of the dangers still existed.

Basic decisions that polluted the nation's rivers and streams, contaminated its air, and clogged its city streets were not made by government; they were made by free individuals, operating in a free market in pursuit of private interests. The environmental problems that clouded the future represented the accumulated decisions of people who found those decisions profitable or who assumed that they could escape the ultimate price of the resulting decay or reconstruction. The price of a cleaner environment would come high— massive public expenditures, increased federal authority, and infringements on profits and property rights. In the absence of clear precedents, environmentalists could hardly foresee the actual costs of environmental reconstruction. To salvage Lake Erie, some experts feared, would require $20 billion; the bill for a general environmental cleanup, they predicted, would approximate $300 billion. Some officials doubted that the United States had the financial resources necessary to remake the environment. The American people were paying a fearful price for their carelessness, but most citizens were too caught up in the momentum of unlimited growth

to tempt either national leaders or the national parties to claim a
new consensus on matters of environmental control.

BIG GOVERNMENT: THE PRICE OF COMPLEXITY

Washington accepted the obligation to protect the public and
business alike from the undesirable externalities of a complicated
industrial and economic system. That protective effort created a
growing federal superstructure of regulatory agencies with their
reports, inspections, hearings, civil and criminal proceedings, suits
and countersuits, court orders, and fines. The federal government
did not grow by accident. At every step along the way it responded
to the demands of organized groups that could not protect their
interests in the free market, or to the visions of popular leaders who
sought a more perfect society. Whatever its contributions to the
nation's welfare, the growing bureaucracy enmeshed the lives of
Americans in an increasingly fine net of complex and burdensome
regulations. Every restraint was for some a needless imposition, for
others a procedural safeguard. The added costs of government
inflicted the public with an ever-heavier burden of taxation. To
defend the public from those who wielded dominant power in the
nation's highly complex industrial economy, the government
moved so steadily and quietly into the body of American life that
its full impact was hardly discernable.

Measured by the increases in the gross national product, the
expansion of government was not spectacular. In 1952 governmental revenues were 29.7 percent of the GNP. Thereafter, until the
mid-1960s, federal expenditures increased somewhat more rapidly
than the total economy. The number of employees in the executive
branch of the federal government leveled quickly at somewhat
below three million. After midcentury, however, congressional
staffs grew 15 times as rapidly as the country's population. By 1975,
16,000 congressional employees cost the federal government $328
million a year. Some Senators had empires with 50 or more employees. The larger staffs helped members of Congress define and
defend their positions; what their expertise contributed to congressional action was often dubious. From independence to 1962—a

span of 186 years—the federal budget moved up gradually to $100 billion. But it reached $200 billion nine years later; it passed $300 billion by 1975. In 1977 it would exceed $460 billion. The growth in the federal budget would surpass $300 billion during the 1970s. Clearly federal expenditures were out of control. The government expanded as if there were no limits on its taxing and borrowing powers. The American people had lost their influence over not only what taxes they would pay, but also how their tax dollars would be spent.

Perhaps the most startling changes occurred not in the size of government but in the nature of the expenditures. In 1952 federal outlays for domestic uses totaled $13.4 billion. During the succeeding two decades, they multiplied 10 times. As late as 1952, 81 percent of all federal spending went for defense, international relations, post office, and other traditional expenditures. More often thereafter health, welfare, and other forms of social service encroached on the federal budget. The demand for additional government services was insatiable. In 1964 the food stamp program served 400,000 people at a total cost of $35 million; by 1977 the program served 19 million people at a cost of $5.7 billion. By the 1970s half the federal budget provided for transfer payments— payments for which the government required nothing. Many feared that federal social programs were spinning out of control. For millions of Americans the growth of governmental activity had created a welfare state.

Because of its growth, the federal government maintained a mixed and often unclear relationship to the public and its needs. Federal employees were seldom subject to direct public control; in some respects their private concerns had little relationship to those of the public. Well organized and conscious of their interests, they commanded almost unassailable powers to protect themselves in matters of income, fringe benefits, and retirement pay. Against their organized power the public had little defense. Congress, which voted the federal budget, did not exert much restraint. It voted pay raises and special retirement programs for federal employees that generally outstripped the benefits which accrued to white-collar and professional employees elsewhere in the economy. Not even the White House fully commanded the federal bureaucracy and at times dealt with it as a separate division of the government. Thus the bureaucracy, under few constraints, became a self-sustaining industry, with sources of power that coalesced around the benefits it disbursed in contracts, jobs, subsidies, and services.

Conservative politicians and economic analysts questioned the federal government's power, its inefficiency, and its alleged abuses. Government programs were so formless and regulations so varied that few could master them. What made rules complex and endless was the hope that they would, when properly framed, cover every contingency and thus eliminate the need for bureaucratic judgment. So cumbersome and noncommunicative did government become that officials often could not secure needed information from other departments or agencies. Even the White House staff was so large and compartmentalized that some portions worked in isolation from others. It was not strange that programs and guidelines failed to coincide. Conflicting regulations so often victimized public and private institutions, such as hospitals, that they could scarcely function at all. Much of the effort appeared wasteful because it was mounted at endless expense against apparently intractable social problems. Some programs with promise suffered from underfunding. Some agencies struggled under the load of huge backlogs of applications or complaints. Despite the multiplicity of bureaus, the self-assigned tasks of government remained unfulfilled. Whatever its cost, the federal government could not provide an adequate national health service, improved public transportation, or a clean environment. Americans complained that Washington returned few benefits to the nation's citizens when measured by its vast expenditures.

Regulatory agencies established to defend the public interests against major industries and carriers did not necessarily serve the public at all. Too often the efforts to regulate American business eliminated, instead of enforced, competition and thereby increased the costs of products and services, encouraged inefficiency, and stifled creativity. As Lewis A. Engman, chairman of the Federal Trade Commission expressed it: "The fact of the matter is that most regulated industries have become federal protectorates living in the cozy world of cost-plus, safely protected from the ugly specters of competition, efficiency, and innovation." Much of the regulation was wasteful, compelling corporations to engage in circuitous practices to maintain some semblance of fairness in their relations with other companies and with the public. Many of the most restrictive federal regulations were instituted to serve some economic constituency, either through special funding or through the removal of competition. Where legal restrictions on business might infringe on profits, federal bureaus often refused to enforce established schedules. Occasionally programs lost their reason for existence. Yet bureaucrats and the beneficiaries of such programs together usually wielded sufficient influence to sustain them.

Thus business and government did not necessarily exist in an adversary relationship. If corporations steadily opposed the intrusion of government into their affairs, they wished only that nothing should diminish their economic power or their capacity to achieve adequate profits. When businesses believed their interests threatened by forces beyond their control, they were the first to demand that the government intrude. Through tariffs they used state power to remove foreign competition; when in financial difficulties, they sought government subsidies and credit or a wide variety of special financial or tax benefits, such as depletion allowances. The objection of businessmen was not to the federal exercise of economic power per se, but the fear that it might be used destructively or unnecessarily. Indeed, for many businesses the federal budget was a source, not of restraint, but of largesse. Government, whatever its size and regulatory powers, served the business interests of the community in countless ways. Those with access to governmental bureaucracies and agencies—contractors, promoters, and salesmen —often reaped untold rewards at public expense. What contributed to such close and often profitable business-government relationships was the readiness of many public officials to move into and out of top executive positions in business.

That balance between government and business, which supposedly would protect the interests of society, actually served the interests of power far more effectively. The danger to free society lay not only in private and corporate wealth or in the power of government, but in the concentrated power of both working together to create a vast, impersonal, mechanized, and computerized bureaucracy that dominated the nation's life. At issue for those who believed that impersonal forces threatened society was not the elimination of all bureaucracies, but the justification of their role and power. For many Americans the hierarchical control of society was neither essential nor morally justifiable; the agencies of power, both public and private, had grown too large to serve the public interest. The federal bureaucracy seemed too remote, unapproachable, and self-serving to satisfy the needs of individual citizens. Indeed, at times the public required protection from, rather than by, the government in the form of special safeguards against favoritism, corruption, and waste. Inasmuch as big government resulted from the accumulated cries of those unable to defend their interests without help, there was no easy escape from its costs and interpositions. Until the American people themselves, whether as citizens or as members of organized groups, were prepared to behave with the restraints required for the operation of a just and orderly society, the federal bureaucracy would continue to expand. The growth of governmental power in all its forms rested on the continuing conviction that government alone could protect society from individual and group injustices.

THE PROBLEM OF CHOICE

Industrial and governmental growth offered jobs, opportunities, profits, and comforts. To that extent it served the interests of most Americans admirably. That it leveled exorbitant social and economic costs seems equally apparent. But perceptions of these costs and the means to control them varied. As long as the unwanted consequences of growth did not impinge directly on the lives of most citizens, they would remain abstractions of no immediate concern. Many Americans—perhaps the overwhelming majority—accepted the need for some new directions in American life, but they assumed that changes limited enough to demand little of the nation could still be effective. Conservative economists, business leaders, and much of the public favored policies and incentives that would expand the limits of production and consumption, convinced that the free market, responding to public preferences, would exert the necessary restraints on corporate behavior and the uses of technology. Not even the control of pollution and energy lay outside the normal operation of the free market, they argued; pollution was not the result of growth, but of a system of incentives that encouraged industries to pollute the biosphere, the rivers, and the lakes. Society had never levied any charges on industry for the use of scarce resources or the damage that it did. The answer to pollution, therefore, lay not in restrictions on growth, but in the imposition of the necessary charges against industrial abuses. Industries forced to pay for their misuse of the environment would soon discover the means to clean up what they had done.

What troubled many who favored continued growth was the notion that unhampered economic and industrial expansion would proceed on a straight line and thus produce the horrors of over-population and environmental exploitation portrayed in many projections. That growth did not always enhance the quality of life, they agreed, was no argument against growth. Economic growth, one British economist explained, "provides mankind with more choice, and this greater scope for choice can be used wisely or badly; for man's happiness, or for his spiritual and physical destruction. The real issue is not whether one should have growth or not; it is how to use the choice that growth provides for good rather than for evil." Society, he believed, would make the necessary adjustments in its modes of behavior and use of resources to avoid any social or economic catastrophe. For those who believed that society's productive capacity, if raised, could create a better life for most people, values less materialistic were not necessarily more humane than those of an expanding industrial order. America's middle-class citizens, some argued, cherished their comforts; to reduce them would create frustration and tension and not a reduction in wants. Nongrowth, moreover, would comprise such a sharp break from existing habits and procedures, such a profound discontinuity in the nation's historical experience, such a discouraging impediment to ambition and employment, that no one could predict its full impact on the country's institutions. Proponents of growth warned that the end of economic expansion would result in the almost total regulation of life as public authority determined the use of goods in short supply. Such restraints on private decisions would demand obedience to government quite beyond that contemplated in a democratic society.

For the optimists technology itself possessed the power to eliminate most physical challenges to the nation's well-being. Scientist Philip Handler, speaking at the University of Virginia, identified science and technology with an improving future. "By what means," he asked, "shall we make a better tomorrow? I know of none but the wise application of yet more technology rooted in science already available and that to be developed in the years to come, but examining carefully all conceivable consequences of each new technology before its introduction into society. Those who scoff offer no alternatives." To lose faith in science and technology was to lose faith in the country and its capacity for ingenuity and inventiveness. Certainly countless citizens were tantalized by thoughts of interminable new inventions and gadgets for advancing individual comfort and efficiency. Whatever damage technology had done to American society, other technology could undo. Social scientist Peter Drucker argued that environmental renovation would require new technology as extensive as that which created the initial destruction. "If there is no expansion of output equal to the additional cost of cleaning up the environment," he warned, "the cost burden will—indeed, must—be met by cutting the funds available for education, health care, or the inner city, thus depriving the poor."

Finally, economic expansionists argued, scarcity, not abundance, governed the lives of most Americans; thus growth alone could satisfy the economic needs of all. With all of its wealth and prosperity the United States had been very good to only a few million of its citizens—professionals, executives, and businessmen. The average working man of the United States was far from affluent; he knew, moreover, what he would buy with additional income. And as Peter Passell and Leonard Ross observed, "The only way he has to get those things is through growth. The economic pie is not big enough to go around, no matter how we choose to slice it. A reasonable growth rate, however, could easily double the average American's income in the next 25 years." Without economic growth any general improvement in the lot of the poor and lower-income groups would require a corresponding loss of income and status elsewhere in American society.

Whether the nation's democratic and economic structure could withstand the strain of greater economic redistribution was not certain. The relationship of economic choice to the quality of political freedom is never clear. Current economic choices available to affluent Americans in styles of life and modes of travel resulted less from the Bill of Rights than from the country's amazing productivity. Many insisted that the options afforded by affluence were essential to the free market economy and could not be restricted without endangering the entire economic and political order. Still, if the prodigious economic expansion of the postwar era, with federal deficits soaring eventually to over $50 billion a year, could scarcely touch the disadvantaged millions who comprised the nation's poor, it was not clear what level of economic growth and government spending would do so. The Vietnamese had far less trouble in involving the United States in their concerns than did the unseen poor of America.

Environmentalists argued that the country had already entered an ecological crisis that demanded a government responsive to the challenges of scarcity and a new creed that most Americans ultimately could share. Some writers wondered how the free market could resolve questions of pollution and ecological catastrophe, of resource and energy depletion, when supply and demand were geared to the gratification of immediate wants. Reduced growth might reduce industrial jobs, but some economists pointed to areas where national needs could command energies and resources no longer required in other economic production. Many tasks in environmental recovery would be labor intensive—the rehabilitation of forests, the restoration of the soil, the reclaiming of polluted bodies of water. The rebuilding of the American railway system would require an incalculable human effort. The roadbeds had deteriorated so badly, one writer observed, that freight cars became derailed while standing still. It was not clear how the country could eliminate unemployment unless industry created more workplaces, by turning from capital-intensive to labor-intensive production with its possibilities for greater work satisfaction. Such employment would always be less harmful to the environment than that which relied on heavy technology. Not all Americans were convinced that technology had created a better, more humane, and satisfactory civilization; any advanced technological society becomes more and more vulnerable to accident and sabotage. Nor were they confident that a free-flowing technology would undo the damage of the past without creating additional problems. They questioned the basic assumption that science and technology, pure and applied, paid for themselves in economic advance. "The tech-fixation," wrote one critic, "is a kind of cultural lag. It cannot long endure."

Consumption and waste seemed wedded to the endless exploitation of cheap fuel and raw materials. Cheap oil was the foundation of the modern consumer economy. During the 1950s, and again in the following decade, the world consumed more oil than it had consumed in all history before 1950. What created the energy problem was simply the exponential growth of demand against a limited supply of an essential commodity. Rising prices might restrain the use of scarce resources and redouble the efforts of investors, scientists, and businessmen to find cheaper substitutes. Such mitigating factors could postpone the need for limited growth; they could not eliminate it. However great the production incentives, they would never enable production to increase as rapidly as demand; ultimately they would collide with the exhaustion of available resources. Infinite growth in a finite environment is an impossibility. Some experts predicted that the oil would be gone in 50 years. What technological miracle would substitute for the massive reliance on oil was not clear. The known supplies of uranium would generate the nation's electricity for scarcely another half century. Plutonium breeder reactors could provide energy for centuries, but Washington officials regarded them too dangerous for public use, mostly because plutonium reprocessing creates fuel that can be used in nuclear weapons. Because of its unavailability many hours each day, solar power appeared ill-suited for the generation of electricity. Coal remained a major source of energy, but its use as a replacement for oil and nuclear power would require enormous levels of production. Even in the 1970s there was no sure answer to the energy problem which did not begin with the need for restricted consumption.

For its critics consumerism had become an end in itself, with industry making things that people consumed in prodigious quantities under the pressure of advertising and the availability, through credit, of next month's income. Inflation measured the extent to which people lived beyond their means. Inflationary pressures from overconsumption were so powerful that not even recession and high unemployment could counter them effectively. It was not strange that many Americans were troubled less by the underconsumption of the poor than by the overindulgence of the affluent. The United States, with a mere 6 percent of the world's population, consumed one-third of the world's energy. At established growth rates, the country's energy needs would double in the 1970s. Some experts estimated that 50 percent of the fuel consumed in the United States could be saved by greater efficiency.

Such exploitation of the earth's ecosystem, warned Barry Commoner in *The Closing Circle* (1971), would cause it to collapse. This ecosystem comprised the network of biological processes between living things and their environment that sustains all forms of life on the planet. Eventually, Commoner believed, the limitations of air, water, land, energy, and resources on the earth's surface would demand a no-growth condition. For environmentalist Robert Cahn, humanity's capacity to exploit the planet had brought it into collision with the limits of nature. "The nation," he wrote, "had overdrawn its bank account in self-sustaining national elements: air, water, soil, and living space." Columnist William V. Shannon warned in *The New York Times* of September 29, 1974: "The biosphere has inviolable limits. Technology can disrupt nature but it cannot transcend it. The need everywhere is for products that are biodegradable and for prophecies that respect nature's intricate balances. [Men must] learn to live within nature's constraints or die. Nature knows nothing of trade-offs." The essential question confronting the nation was whether it could achieve some mastery over its technological and environmental challenges; the power to regulate one's own affairs is the foundation of all freedom.

Many found the simpler life, occasioned by economic and energy constraints, quite acceptable. Countless Americans, at least in opinion polls, questioned the morality of the country's heavy consumption of energy, raw materials, and food. Some writers hoped that a collapse of the land boom would compel developers and speculators to unload their tracts and terminate the urban sprawl. Others lauded the reduced projections for new automobiles and the movement toward smaller, lighter models. Many of the young, having made a conscious choice to limit their expenditures and uses of energy, discarded their automobiles and took up bicycling and walking. Henry Ford II believed that the slowing down during the recession of 1974-1975 was not all bad. "I think we were going high, wide, and handsome, just begging for a break," he declared. "[W]e got the break . . . and a lot of people suffered. We were just outliving our means. . . . " It was time, he believed, that both individuals and governments cut back and live within their incomes. James Reston of *The New York Times* doubted that further shortages of gasoline and the loss of other baggage of a consumer economy would be injurious to the nation. What Americans needed was more shortages: "We need to cut down, slow up, stay home, run around the block, eat vegetable soup, call up old friends and read a book once in a while. Americans [he concluded] have always been able to handle austerity and even adversity. Prosperity's what's been doing us in." This new creed assumed that growth and technology were subject to social control, and that human experience based on restrained tastes could be rewarding.

Chapter VII

The Rise and Fall of the Great Society

TRANSITION: FROM KENNEDY TO JOHNSON

John F. Kennedy's tragic assassination in Dallas, Texas, on November 22, 1963, transformed the inadequacies of his presidency into a vision of unfulfilled promise. After his death, his admirers asked the country to judge him not by his accomplishments, but by his good intentions. Briefly the effort succeeded; the Dallas tragedy created an instant cult that made Kennedy appear different in death from what he had been in life. Even more than Eisenhower, Kennedy possessed personal attributes—high intelligence, ideal appearance, and genuine human concerns—that, for a time, permitted his image to transcend his performance. His public style, graceful and relaxed, scarcely concealed his determination to place his imprint on the nation's history. As President, Kennedy turned Washington into a hive of activity to serve his New Frontier, a program to resolve the problems of peace and war, of ignorance and prejudice, of poverty and surplus. He flooded Congress with messages that outlined an ambitious program ranging from aid to depressed areas to expanded health insurance. Surrounded by vigorous and attractive people, Kennedy and his charming wife, Jacqueline, converted the White House into a center of unprecedented gaiety. Unfortunately for Kennedy, effective leadership required more than energy and style. The contrast between the

Kennedy image and the Kennedy record was apparent long before his death; fading memories would not erase it. Even his popularity had dropped by October 1963 to 57 percent—high but nothing compared to the eulogies that followed his assassination.

In some measure the impediments to a higher level of public performance in Kennedy's Washington lay in the administration itself. Despite its outward brilliance, the Kennedy leadership seemed to lack innovation. Moreover, for most Americans, the times did not call for significant economic or social change. Kennedy's eloquent speeches and noble appeals failed to penetrate the public mind; thus they had little effect on the country's emotions. His spirited exertions to move the nation were never quite convincing. Not even the Democratic majorities on Capitol Hill would endorse his program. Kennedy's war on poverty and racial inequality was scarcely a skirmish. But the young President, despite his limited legislative achievements, gave Washington a rebirth of vitality and made it more than ever before the center of world attention. The uncontrollable emotions unleashed across the globe by his death, often among those who had never really approved of his leadership, attested to the hope that he carried for an improving future. It was the high expectation that many shared that brought the world's leading statesmen to Washington for his funeral.

In almost every respect, personal and political, Lyndon B. Johnson stood in sharp contrast to his predecessor. Unlike Kennedy's easy ascent up the American ladder of success, Johnson's had been long and trying. Kennedy represented the Northeast and the Ivy League; Johnson's roots lay in the grasslands of southwest Texas, where he was born in 1908 near Johnson City. As a high school student in the 1920s, he experienced the pressures of rural poverty. He worked his way through Southwest Texas State Teachers College. After teaching briefly at Houston High School, he moved to Washington as secretary to Texas Congressman Richard M. Kleberg. During the early New Deal, he won acclaim as director of the National Youth Administration in Texas. In 1937 he entered the House of Representatives and remained there until 1948, when he won the Democratic nomination to the Senate in an extremely close primary election. His victory in November came easily enough. In the Senate he moved up so rapidly that he became Minority Leader in 1953 and, after the Democratic triumph of 1954, Majority Leader and perhaps the most commanding figure in the Senate. Despite his remarkable legislative success, Johnson never attained the urbane self-assurance of Kennedy. Even as Vice-President after 1961 his demeanor remained rural, his Texas twang contrasting markedly with Kennedy's Boston accent and graceful diction.

Johnson soon demonstrated that his less subtle personal qualities were far more effective in the political arena than was Kennedy's bookish wisdom. As Senate leader Johnson had seldom prepared long, formal speeches, and, with Kennedy's death, most of the former president's talented speech writers drifted out of Washington. Unable as well to match Kennedy's dexterity in handling the televised press conference, Johnson returned to the more personal methods on which he had relied in the Senate. As Majority Leader he often demonstrated a strange ability to mesmerize small groups. Columnists Rowland Evans and Robert Novak once described Johnson's technique in applying pressure on a reluctant Senator: "He moved in close, his face a scant millimeter from his target, his eyes widening and narrowing, his eyebrows rising and falling. From his pockets poured clippings, memos, statistics. Mimicry, humor, and the genius of analogy made the Treatment an almost hypnotic experience and rendered the target stunned and helpless." Johnson understood the importance of consensus, seeking it with his favorite motto, from Isaiah, "Come now, let us reason together." Through reasoning, coaxing, compromising, flattering, and arm-twisting, he set out to win where Kennedy had failed—in his relations with Congress.

Johnson entered the White House with an enormous reservoir of congressional respect and goodwill. Southern senators who had kept Kennedy's proposals off the floor were deeply committed to the new President's success. On November 27, 1963, Johnson reminded Congress: "For 32 years, Capitol Hill has been my home. I have shared many moments of pride with you, pride in the ability of the Congress of the United States to act, to meet any crisis, to distill from our differences strong programs of national action."

Johnson outlined his program in his first State of the Union message in January 1964. After promising some reduction in federal expenditures, he came to the heart of the country's troubles—poverty and civil rights. "This Administration, today, here and now," he said, "declares unconditional war on poverty in America. . . . The richest nation on earth can afford to win it." His program would be aimed at that fifth of American families that the New Deal had neglected, those whose incomes were too low to meet their basic needs. Its weapons would include better schools, better houses, better training and job opportunities. Next, the President urged passage of Kennedy's Civil Rights bill. "Today," he warned, "Americans of all races stand side by side in Berlin and Viet Nam. . . . Surely they can work and eat and travel side by side in their own country." Johnson's congressional critics termed the speech a campaign document, albeit a brilliant one. Suddenly the times seemed ripe for action.

That year the President inaugurated his war on poverty with the passage of the landmark $750 million Economic Opportunity Act. Despite vigorous Republican opposition, the measure passed the Senate on July 23 and the House two weeks later. The new law provided for work experience and training programs in conservation camps and in many towns and cities, for community action programs to combat poverty, and for a domestic peace corps known as the Volunteers in Service to America (VISTA). It included the Head Start program for preschool children and the Upward Bound program for college students. Congressman Wilbur Mills of Arkansas, chairman of the House Ways and Means Committee, managed to sidetrack the President's request for Medicare, a basic health plan for the aged under Social Security. Nor did the House approve the President's $1 billion request for Appalachia.

But the key congressional battle of 1964 was fought over civil rights. Kennedy's untimely death broke much of the congressional resistance to a strong civil rights measure. The Civil Rights bill passed through the House without difficulty in February by a vote of 290 to 130. In the Senate it faced a 75-day Southern filibuster. Throughout those weeks White House efforts concentrated on Senate Minority Leader Everett M. Dirksen of Illinois; without his support, the measure would never receive the necessary Republican votes. Finally, in a crucial move taken on June 10, the Senate adopted a cloture motion, 71 to 29. Thereafter the Senate accepted several minor amendments, but refused to weaken the measure. The Civil Rights Act of 1964, which the Senate adopted on June 19 by a vote of 73 to 27 and the House accepted immediately in its amended form, was directed more at Southern segregation than at Northern discrimination. The law terminated all legal discrimination by race in hotels, restaurants, theaters; in unions and employment; and in voter registration. It authorized the Attorney General to institute suits in behalf of aggrieved persons in desegregation or discrimination cases and permitted federal agencies to halt funds for projects that tolerated racially discriminating employment practices.

Johnson moved from his legislative triumphs to an automatic first-ballot Democratic nomination at his party's Atlantic City convention in August 1964. For the vice-presidency Johnson chose the popular Senator Hubert H. Humphrey of Minnesota. Moderate Republicans sensed that their party's front-runner, Senator Barry Goldwater of Arizona, whose pre-New Deal political philosophy emphasized individualism and states' rights, had no chance at the polls. Governor Nelson Rockefeller challenged Goldwater momentarily by taking the Oregon primary, but Goldwater regained his earlier momentum to defeat Rockefeller in the more crucial California primary in June. Republican leaders, such as Richard Nixon and Governor George Romney of Michigan, refused to lead a stop-Goldwater movement. Finally, in June, Governor William Scranton of Pennsylvania announced his candidacy; this brought Henry Cabot Lodge back from his Vietnam ambassadorship to aid the Scranton effort. But Goldwater had already captured the big-state delegations; Dirksen assured the Senator's nomination by delivering Illinois' 58 votes to him. In San Francisco Goldwater captured an easy first-ballot nomination and selected conservative Congressman William E. Miller of New York as his running mate. But Goldwater's rejection of all compromise in the convention platform's phraseology or on the vice-presidential nomination sent many Republican moderates into Democratic ranks.

Assured an easy victory in November, Johnson joined Goldwater in avoiding the real issues confronting American society. This tactic produced the dullest campaign in a generation. James Reston observed a month before the voting: "It is startling to compare the quality of the speeches delivered in this campaign even with the speeches of the Kennedy-Nixon campaign. And when they are compared with the Stevenson speeches of 1952 the contrast is almost ludicrous. . . . [I]t is difficult to point to a single distinguished speech by either President Johnson or Senator Goldwater since the battle started over a month ago." The Johnson-Humphrey triumph in November fulfilled the predictions of the opinion pools. The Democratic ticket won 486 electoral votes, losing only five Deep South states and Arizona, with their 52 electoral votes, to the Republicans. The Democrats gained 38 seats in the House and two in the Senate. The Democratic sweep assured Johnson a working majority in the new Congress.

THE GREAT SOCIETY: JOHNSON'S PROGRAM FOR THE NATION

Backed by his own and his party's overwhelming triumph, Lyndon Johnson appeared so politically dominant when the 89th Congress convened in January 1965 that he had merely to specify what he wanted to move the nation toward the "Great Society" that he had sketched out during his 1964 campaign. In the House the Democratic majority of 155 included many new liberals who had ridden the crest of the Democratic landslide. In the Senate the Democratic major of 36 seemed equally sufficient to assure future legislative triumphs. "If the President decides that it would be nice to have a coast-to-coast tunnel," suggested Richard H. Rovere in *The New Yorker,* "he need only call in some engineers and lawyers to put the scheme in order, advise Congress of his wishes, and begin letting contracts." The President set the tone of his new administration in his State of the Union message of January 1965. "We're only at the beginning of the road to the Great Society," he said. "Ahead now is a summit where freedom from the wants of the body can help fulfill the needs of the spirit." The goals that he outlined included the beautification of America, the elimination of urban blight and air and water pollution, medical care for the aged, aid for education, an intensified war against poverty, and a voting rights bill for blacks. Critics feared that the President possessed no sense of limits, that he was setting forth a dream, not a program, that would endanger any realistic assessment of the challenges before the country.

Johnson's continuing assault on racial inequality received a special impetus from the civil rights crisis that occurred in Selma, Alabama, in the early spring of 1965. To dramatize the need for an effective voting rights law, Martin Luther King, in January, inaugurated a series of protest demonstrations in Selma where the black majority had only 325 registered voters and the white minority almost 10,000. Elsewhere in the South some localities had no enfranchised blacks at all. The Selma demonstrations produced a number of violent clashes and culminated, from March 21 to 25, in a widely publicized civil rights march from Selma to Montgomery. Governor George C. Wallace denied permission for the march; those who defied his order faced clubs and tear gas. Only when the President federalized the Alabama National Guard did the marchers reach Montgomery in relative safety. The violence and repression at Selma provoked a national reaction and convinced the President that the country required a strong voting rights bill. The Voting Rights Act, which passed Congress that year, eliminated discriminatory literacy tests and anticipated federal lawsuits that would soon terminate state poll taxes. It provided for federal registrars in the South to facilitate black voter registration. It instituted major penalties for any interference with an individual's voting rights. For the first time in the nation's history, a federal law assured the eventual democratization of Southern politics. To emphasize the new trend, the President appointed the noted black lawyer, Thurgood Marshall, to the Supreme Court, and named another black, Robert C. Weaver, as head of the new Department of Housing and Urban Affairs.

Johnson extended his Great Society program into the areas of education and health. To skirt the traditional church-state and states' rights impediments to direct federal intervention in education, the President's measure emphasized aid to individual students rather than to schools. This enabled the administration to achieve a $1.3 billion general education bill in April 1965. The Elementary and Secondary Education Act granted federal aid to children of the poor whether they attended public or private schools. The Higher Education Act of 1965 extended federal aid to colleges and universities and provided scholarships and low-interest loans for students. Thereafter Congress poured billions of dollars each year into the American educational system, both to improve libraries and facilities and to encourage citizens to avail themselves of the country's educational opportunities. Also in 1965 Congress passed the $6.5 billion Medical Care Act to provide health care services for persons 65 or older. Medicare offered the elderly two months of low-priced hospital, nursing home, and home care. This compulsory plan came under the Social Security system. A voluntary supplementary plan, financed by premiums and general revenues, provided allowances for other medical costs such as doctors' charges. Medicaid, another feature of the program, offered funds to the states to help them extend medical aid to the poor.

Johnson's renewed war on poverty included the $1.1 billion Appalachian Regional Development Act. This law provided for highway construction, health centers, and economic development in an 11-state area. The Public Works and Economic Development Act extended this economic development program to other depressed areas of the country. Additional financing permitted the Office of Economic Opportunity to expand its community action and youth programs. The new program for the cities included the Housing and Urban Development Act of 1965, which established the Department of Housing and Urban Affairs and provided money for area planning. Johnson's mammoth housing measure appropriated billions not only for new units, but also for rent supplements to low-income families. The law provided as well for community health and recreation centers. The $1.2 billion Model Cities program authorized funds for slum clearance and the development of model communities. That year Congress passed laws to provide public transportation, highway beautification, clean water and air, and environmental protection. The Truth in Lending Act compelled lenders and creditors to disclose to their customers the actual interest rates they were levying. Such legislative triumphs demonstrated both the concerns of Congress and the energy and persuasiveness of the President. By October 1965, Congress had passed a dozen major laws, making it the most productive session since Roosevelt's second New Deal of 1935. With some accuracy Johnson declared that the first session of the 89th Congress "will be recorded as the greatest session in the history of our nation."

Johnson's Great Society was a tag for a major expansion of the functions of the federal government. It reflected a renewed acceptance of responsibility by government—the greatest since New Deal days—for the direction and quality of the nation's life. Differing from the New Deal, the Great Society program was concerned not with the general performance of the economy and those it normally served, but with the problems and the people that previous labor and reform legislation had overlooked. Johnson's measures focused especially on the urban environment and the nation's hard-core poverty. How high that sense of national obligation would soar in coming years few in 1965 dared to predict. During the second session of the 89th Congress the Great Society moved forward, but now at considerably reduced speed. What slowed the forward thrust of the Johnson program was clear enough. Whatever the nation's wealth, it was limited. Congress balked at much of the President's poverty program and approved most of what remained with inadequate funds.

Perhaps some retrenchment was laudable. Mike Mansfield, Senate Majority Leader, warned in September 1965 that the advances of the previous eight months rendered their repetition unlikely and perhaps even undesirable. Better, he argued, to improve the legislation already in existence. Democratic setbacks in 1966 reduced the President's Democratic majority in the House by 47 seats and pushed its membership to the right. Eventually Congress continued the poverty program for two additional years with appropriations of approximately $2 billion per year. In general, 1966 was not a good year for the poor; Congress disappointed the expectations of many. "The walls of the ghettos are not going to topple overnight," editorialized *The New York Times,* "nor is it possible to wipe out the heritage of generations of social, economic and educational deprivation by the stroke of a Presidential pen. The war against poverty is a long-range undertaking. It requires staying power as well as a sense of urgency." Still, the President's overall record, comprising no less than 40 major laws, had been impressive.

Meanwhile the civil rights movement, whose demands were not excessively expensive, lost its impetus in Congress. The reason was not hard to find. As long as congressional action was aimed at desegregation in the South, it had the full support of Northern senators and representatives. But the last milestone in Southern reconstruction was the Voting Rights Act of 1965. Thereafter the measures before Congress aimed at the establishment of equal economic opportunity for blacks. Slums, housing, unemployment, delinquency, and rioting were now the central issues, and all of these came home to the North. Suddenly civil rights enthusiasm from New York to Chicago began to disintegrate. Nowhere in the North was there any overwhelming sentiment for open housing. Responding to such attitudes, Congress refused to approve Johnson's 1966 civil rights bill with its provision for open housing. Trade unions had little interest in black membership. Members of Congress could not agree on the best means of guaranteeing security in the large cities. Where there had been fervor for civil rights before 1966, there was now disinterest. Previous acts of Congress no longer enjoyed much sympathy. The officials charged with the enforcement of civil rights legislation complained that they did not have the appropriations and administrative backing necessary to carry out their tasks.

THE CONTINUING STRUGGLE FOR EQUALITY

What characterized the poverty and civil rights programs of the Kennedy-Johnson years was the perennial gap between promise and achievement. The efforts of the 1960s stirred hope but, in the disenchantment that followed, many officials and analysts concluded that the government had tried too much and ultimately lacked the wisdom and resources to eliminate even the country's most glaring human disabilities. Perhaps the major reasons for the Great Society's failures lay in the effort itself. In reality the Congress, in its attempt to confront the country's human degradation, had not paid much or sought much. In no sense was the Democratic program radical; nowhere did it seek any redistribution of wealth or income. The entire war on poverty of the Johnson years cost the nation considerably less than 1 percent of the GNP. Such expenditures could pay the salaries of federal officials, create a number of new jobs, and build some highways and public structures. They could not do more. For the poor the little that Congress spent produced no measurable results at all. The major beneficiaries were doctors, pharmacists, nursing home operators, construction companies, real estate speculators, consulting firms, landlords, and bureaucrats. The country's basic human problems became more rather than less apparent with the passage of time.

For the tenant farmers of the Deep South the antipoverty program contributed little. The federal subsidy program for cotton managed to save the plantations but not the field hands, who faced the competition of new technology and warehouses jammed with surplus cotton. Federal efforts added almost nothing to the incomes and security of the country's migrant farm workers. Ten federal agencies with 100 programs led the assault on Appalachia's poverty. Still, the billions spent on the region effected no fundamental economic change. There were new roads and airfields, more dams, but what the expenditures contributed to the alleviation of Appalachia's problems was doubtful. The Kentucky journalist, Allen Trout, observed the impact of federal money and officials at close range. "This conglomeration," he wrote in October 1967, "came upon us like a mass of jelly the size of Mt. Everest. It has swept over towns, people, rivers, knobs and institutions. Everything in its path has been covered with jelly. But after it passes, nothing has changed. The mountains are the same." Beyond the range of the new expressways were the same tarpaper shacks with stripped carcasses of abandoned automobiles rusting in cluttered yards. In one four-county area of Kentucky, 40 percent of all families had incomes of less than $1000 per year. There were no new jobs except those created by the bureaucracy itself. "Who's winning the war on poverty?" asked one federal official in Kentucky. He supplied his own answer: "The local Establishment—the middle class. . . . All we're doing for the poor is making the poverty more bearable."

Urban America responded no more effectively to the federal war on poverty than did the rural areas; here the failure was more conspicuous and potentially more disastrous. Despite the millions spent, Washington had really attempted little. Most of the federal effort did not distinguish between the central cities and the suburbs; it assumed that what was good for one was also good for the other. Much of the urban expenditure—for highways, airports, and water and sewage systems—brought far greater benefits to the middle-class suburbs than to the congested tenement districts of the cities. Mayor Hugh Addonizio of Newark criticized the official tendency to identify the suburbs with the inner cities. "Among the cruelest of myths," he said, "are those which say that America is an urban nation; that middle class America has an interest in saving the cities. . . . In fact, we are a suburban nation, and will be more so in the future. Only fools and professional suburbanites who play with words consider the suburban rings around a city to be urban." If the residents of the fashionable suburbs around the major cities had regarded the human problems of urban America within the range of their interests, Addonizio concluded, they would have revealed far greater concern over them.

Officially, the prosperity of the 1960s had made inroads among the city's unskilled poor. Nonwhite unemployment among men over 20 dropped from 10 percent in 1960 to 6 percent in 1965. Among nonwhite youths, unemployment declined from 25 percent to 20 percent. Somehow these figures clouded the fact that the urban poor continued to fall behind the rest of the country. Purchasing power for black families increased only $120 a year between 1960 and 1965; that for white families increased $220. Half of the blacks were employed as menial laborers, janitors, porters, and busboys. Studies of several major black areas in the 1960s revealed a sizable hidden unemployment among men, young and old, who had simply stopped looking for work. Across the nation only three-fourths of black men were in the labor force. In Watts of Los Angeles unemployment in both 1960 and 1965 remained at 13 percent. But during that period large numbers dropped out of the labor force. In 1965 only 58 percent claimed membership. One study of Chicago's poverty areas indicated an unemployment rate of 37.6 percent, a full 10 points higher than federal estimates. Again, the answer lay in the refusal of many to seek jobs. Many black slum dwellers knew little about or had much interest in American middle-class values. With the movement of the whites into the suburbs, the postwar generation of urban blacks had less contact with white society than had any generation in the nation's history. White institutions that touched them, such as integrated schools, often had little influence on black cultural patterns, overwhelmingly the result of poverty. Integrated schools too often convinced blacks that they had no chance in the race for a better life. Welfare agencies encouraged irresponsibility by perpetuating the black matriarchal society. Often the policy seemed bent on keeping young blacks from encroaching on the lives of the white population.

Nothing demonstrated more forcefully the alienation of the black community from the rules, standards, and expectations of American society than the urban riots of the mid-1960s. What had been only a smoldering resentment and hopelessness suddenly erupted during August 1965 into urban violence. For six days blacks rampaged through the streets of Watts on Los Angeles' south side, destroying 200 buildings and damaging 600 others by burning and looting. That riot resulted in 34 deaths, over 1000 injuries, almost 4000 arrests, and $140 million in property damage. The following summer brought major outbreaks in Los Angeles, San Francisco, Chicago, and New York. All of these riots were merely prelude to what occurred in 1967. In July terror struck Newark's Central Ward where 200,000 nonwhites lived in a teeming, squalid slum. Here the federal government had spent $26 million of its antipoverty funds. When the riot ended, 26 had died and 1200 suffered injuries.

That same month a police arrest in Detroit's west side black ghetto set off a week of domestic violence and destruction without parallel since the Civil War. Eventually 14,000 paratroopers, guardsmen, and state and local police, using tanks and machine guns, brought the sniping and destruction to an end. The riot caused 38 deaths, 2000 injuries, and 3200 arrests. Property damage reached a half billion dollars. Yet Detroit had received $200 million in federal aid; officials had regarded the city a model in urban renewal. Between 1965 and 1967 riots struck 76 cities, killing 12 policemen and 118 civilians. What characterized these riots was the absence of racism. They were formless, violent protests. The outbursts, observed *The Washington Post* with considerable accuracy, were "not revolutionary or homicidal, but purposeless and suicidal. In these peculiar riots the mob has never marched out of the slums. . . . There has never been a manifesto, or a list of stated grievances; the people who explain articulately the reasons for the riots are rarely the rioters."

Leadership of the angry young blacks had passed into the hands of "black power" advocates. Stokely Carmichael emerged in the mid-1960s as black power's leading spokesman. This Trinidad-born black—intelligent, articulate, and determined—graduated from Howard University to assume the leadership of the Student Nonviolent Coordinating Committee. For Carmichael American blacks could never overcome the problem of poverty and blackness as long as they accepted white leadership. Since American society was built on power and power was in the hands of whites, the blacks would achieve their goal of equality only by building a position of strength. Thus, for such militants the answer lay in black power. With its emphasis on separatism and revolt, black power was the ultimate expression of black alienation. The most radical advocates of civil rights anticipated salvation only in the destruction of American society.

National reaction to the riots revealed deep divisions in both the black and the white communities. Black moderates such as Martin Luther King warned that black nationalism was doomed to failure. A June 1968 CBS survey indicated that 25 percent of all blacks favored some militant, if not extreme, course of action, but that the majority still sought integration and full rights of citizenship through peaceful progress. Similarly, a white racist minority still opposed integration in all of its forms, but the majority of whites favored integration and an open society; they still anticipated equality and justice in the country's racial relationships. National leaders were equally divided. Some members of Congress argued that the answer to black militancy lay in stronger national antiriot forces. President Johnson's special Advisory Commission on Civil Disorders, headed by Governor Otto Kerner of Illinois, submitted its report in late February 1968. The commission recommended a sweeping program to alleviate social ills. "It is time," ran the report, "to adopt strategies for action that will produce quick and visible programs. It is time to make good the promises of American democracy to all citizens. . . . " The nation, it warned, was moving toward two societies, one black and one white, separate and unequal. The consequences of that separation no one would escape. Either the country would break the tragic pattern of failure for the economically dispossessed, or the police would spend the future chasing black youths down streets and alleys of the large cities while National Guardsmen gained their diversion by protecting the cities from ultimate chaos and destruction. Without jobs to tie them down, observed black leader Roy Wilkins at Charlottesville, Virginia, black youths "have nothing to do except throw rocks."

Martin Luther King responded to the crisis in early 1968 by proclaiming a positive and hopeful creed for the nation: 'To end poverty, to extricate prejudice, to free a tormented conscience, to make a tomorrow of justice, fair play and creativity, all these are worthy of the American ideal. . . . We can write another luminous moral chapter in American history. All of us are on trial in this troubled hour, but time still permits us to meet the future with a clear conscience." Yet it was only in the aftermath of King's assassination in Memphis on April 4, 1968 and the widespread rioting that it produced that Congress passed the President's Open Housing Act, with its promise of general open housing by 1970. At the level of law the civil rights acts of the Johnson years had achieved equality of treatment for blacks in most areas of American society. However, the facts of economic life, no less than the lingering racism in the country, denied most blacks any equality at all. Perhaps a majority of Americans still opposed open housing. James Reston decried the country's slow response to the perennial search for equality. "The nation is appalled by the murder of Martin Luther King," he said, "but it is not appalled by the condition of his people. It grieves for the man, but not for his cause. This is the curse and tragedy of America."

During the 1960s the struggle for equal rights encompassed those women who regarded their sex as another oppressed element in American society. Middle-class housewives and college women rebelled at the thought that their chief contribution to a male-dominated society lay in their sex. Betty Friedan's *The Feminine Mystique* (1963) gave the women's liberation movement its basic assumptions and direction by dwelling on the problem that had no name—the dissatisfaction and emptiness that many women felt in their roles as housewives and mothers. In some women, Friedan discovered, the resultant feeling of failure produced despondency and boredom, a loss of personality, and a need for meaningful employment. To Friedan women's requirements were obvious. "The only way for a woman, as for a man, to find herself, to know herself as a person," she wrote, "is by creative work of her own. There is no other way. But a job, any job, is not the answer. . . . Women who do not look for jobs equal to their actual capacity, who do not let themselves develop the lifetime interests and goals which require serious education and training, . . . are walking, almost as surely as the ones who stay inside the housewife trap, to a nonexistent future. If a job is to be the way out of the trap for a woman, it must be a job that she can take seriously as part of a life plan, work in which she can grow as part of society."

The militants who sought a more promising and rewarding role for women condemned three factors that bound women to their unequal status: male supremacy in most areas of economic, political, and professional life; the economic and psychological exploitation of women embodied in marriage; and the job and pay discrimination women faced in their employment. Income statistics, especially for executives, revealed the pervading disparity in both employment and rewards for men and women. Not even Supreme Court decisions that proclaimed equal pay for essentially equal work could overcome the traditional disadvantages that faced women in American economic life. In 1966 Friedan and her associates formed the National Organization for Women (NOW). NOW sponsored the Equal Rights Amendment (ERA); this faced the strenuous opposition of women who either were satisfied with their domestic roles or had no desire to compromise the special privileges and courtesies that they received as women, both in society and in business. To encourage greater female participation in politics, the women's movement formed the National Women's Political Caucus in 1972. Gloria Steinem's *Ms* became the movement's leading periodical.

UNCHANGING POLICIES FOR A CHANGING WORLD

Long before 1960 the Soviet-American confrontation had ceased to dominate world politics. Containment had granted Europe a period of recovery and encouraged its leading states to reassert their independent roles in international life. Both London and Paris consistently defied American preferences on a broad spectrum of global questions. Earlier assumptions of a monolithic communism, centering in the Kremlin, had never been very accurate. The Hungarian revolt, the defections of Yugoslavia and Albania, and the dissident movements in Poland and Czechoslovakia demonstrated that Soviet authority extended into Europe only as far as the reach of Soviet tanks. Elsewhere the Kremlin still controlled some parties out of power, but wherever Communists had attained positions of authority, as in China and North Vietnam, they tolerated no external direction. National sentiment commanded the outlook and purposes of Communist no less than capitalist countries. Long before the 1960s, the evidence pouring out of Moscow and Peking dramatized the growing rift between the two Communist-led powers over a variety of historic and ideological issues. The split did not necessarily weaken either Russia or China militarily, but it created for each a new antagonist and thereby reduced the freedom of both to challenge Western interests. In restructuring a multipolar world of immense diversity, time had diminished the influence of Washington and Moscow alike.

Such profound changes on the international scene suggested the need for new, more flexible American policies toward Europe and Asia. Still, both the Kennedy and the Johnson administrations accepted the assumptions and postures of the Truman and Eisenhower years with almost no attempt at reexamination. Kennedy surrounded himself with men who believed, as he did, that only through uncompromising toughness could the United States deal effectively with the Communist states; that the Moscow-Peking axis, if not monolithic, remained united on essentials and therefore dangerous to the non-Communist world; and that a powerful United States carried the burden for peace and stability everywhere. For Secretary of State, Kennedy selected Dean Rusk over Chester Bowles, Adlai Stevenson, and J. William Fulbright, three party intellectuals who had been critical of past decisions, especially those relating to Asia. Contrasted to Dulles, Rusk, a former Rhodes Scholar, appeared urbane and self-effacing. However, his many public statements in defense of Truman's anti-Communist policies in Asia expressed attitudes and assumptions that varied little from those of Dulles. Robert McNamara, as Secretary of Defense, entered the administration as an expert on statistical analysis. To McNamara, formerly president of the Ford Motor Company, everything of importance could be quantified. When a White House assistant once questioned McNamara's judgment, the Secretary retorted, "Where is your data? Give me something I can put in the computer. Don't give me your poetry."

That spirit of toughness pervaded the Kennedy administration. In foreign policy, no less than in football and politics, Kennedy was out to win. The new President used his inaugural to read a warning to the country's global antagonists: "Let every nation know that we shall pay any price, bear any burden, meet any hardship, support any friend, oppose any foe to assure the survival and the success of liberty." For Kennedy and those around him Munich had demonstrated the high price of softness. "[A]ggressive conduct, if allowed to go unchecked and unchallenged," he said, "ultimately leads to war." Supported by his White House advisers, McGeorge Bundy and Walt W. Rostow, Kennedy welcomed every confrontation with the conviction that he could not lose. Early in his administration he explained his desire for a meeting with Soviet leader Nikita Khrushchev: "I have to show him that we can be as tough as he is. . . . I'll have to sit down with him, and let him see who he's dealing with." Kennedy's failure in the CIA-inspired Bay of Pigs venture of April 1961 merely reaffirmed his commitment to toughness. "Let the record show that our restraint is not inexhaustible," he declared as he recommitted the nation to a continuing struggle against communism in every corner of the globe.

Two factors had circumscribed the Soviet-American conflict during the Truman-Eisenhower era: the absence of vital interests in conflict, and the fear of nuclear extinction. But both administrations, in emphasizing the deterrent effect of nuclear weapons, had placed U.S. security on the altar of American power. Unfortunately, the external gains of power—whether economic or military

—can be measured only in the diminution of the challenges that prompted its creation. Inasmuch as the Soviet danger never lent itself to tested, precise definition, the changes wrought in Europe by the first dozen years of containment conveyed convictions of increasing security only to the Americans who had always regarded the USSR as fundamentally a status quo power, at least in its postwar relationship to Europe. But for Americans—many of them in high places—who identified U.S. security with the uprooting of both Communist power and Communist intent, Europe's burgeoning stability was not a measure of Western security at all. Kremlin ideology and behavior sustained their conviction that peaceful coexistence remained a global struggle by means other than war. Senator Barry Goldwater's perennial demand for total victory in the Cold War reflected such an assessment of the Soviet threat. In his inaugural Kennedy warned: "We dare not tempt them [the Russians] with weakness. For only when our arms are sufficient can we be certain beyond doubt that they will never be employed."

During his first year in office Kennedy faced a series of crisis situations that revealed the continuing clash of purpose between the United States and the Kremlin. Early in his administration Kennedy announced his intention "to explore promptly all possible areas of cooperation with the Soviet Union." Indeed, in June the President journeyed to Vienna to exchange views with Soviet Premier Khrushchev. For Kennedy the experience was not reassuring. Khrushchev warned him that unless the Western powers accepted the conversion of West Berlin into a free city, the USSR would assign control of the access routes to East Germany. Kennedy reminded the Soviet leader that the West had gained its role in West Berlin by international agreement and intended to remain. Kennedy's report to the nation, on June 6, reflected a mood of desperation. "I will tell you now," he declared, "that it was a very sober two days. . . . We have wholly different views of right and wrong, of what is an internal affair and what is aggression. And above all, we have wholly different concepts of where the world is and where it is going." That Kennedy would not challenge established attitudes toward the Soviet hegemony in Eastern Europe seemed apparent when the new President, in July, proclaimed "Captive Nations Week" and urged the American people to recommit them-

selves to the support of the just aspirations of all suppressed popula-
tions. Kennedy reconfirmed the American goal of German reunification.

As the German and West Berlin issues dragged on, unsettled,
the President inaugurated a major crisis when, on the evening of
October 22, 1962, he went before the TV cameras to inform the
American people that U.S. surveillance had discovered Soviet missile bases in Cuba. For months the movement of Russian technicians
and military personnel into Cuba had produced a growing concern
in Congress and warnings that the USSR was constructing offensive
missile bases on the island. When surveillance confirmed those
suppositions, the President and his advisers debated a series of
alternative responses. Some officials advocated immediate, drastic
action—either bombing or an invasion. The President decided on
a more moderate course, but conveyed it to the world with a tough
public statement. He proclaimed "a strict quarantine of all offensive
military equipment under shipment to Cuba." If the Soviets did not
withdraw their missiles, he warned, the United States would take
further action. Any missile launched from Cuba against a hemispheric target would bring immediate retaliation against the Soviet
Union.

Kennedy challenged Khrushchev from a position of almost
total geographical and strategic advantage, but he chose to do so
publicly rather than through a private communication. His chief
concerns, Kennedy admitted later, were national prestige and the
possible political consequences of inaction or failure. Undoubtedly
he detected as well the opportunity to destroy any misconceptions
created by the Bay of Pigs fiasco. He explained to British Prime
Minister Harold Macmillan: "What is essential at this moment of
highest test is that Khrushchev should discover that if he is counting
on weakness or irresolution he has miscalculated." The Soviets,
unfortunately, extracted the wrong lesson from their humiliation.
Recognizing Russia's nuclear inferiority in the Cuban confrontation, they now set off the greatest weapons race in history. Perhaps
Kennedy, his advisers, and the press had exaggerated the danger
of war. No rational Soviet leadership would have sacrificed Moscow for Russia's minimal interests in Havana. The crisis passed

when Krushchev agreed to dismantle the Cuban missile bases and Kennedy lifted the blockade, assuring the Cubans that there would be no invasion.

For Kennedy Western security required a stronger trans-Atlantic partnership. His Grand Design for Europe aimed at greater Atlantic unity as the foundation of a stronger and more effective alliance. On Independence Day, 1962, the President declared in Philadelphia: "We do not regard a strong and united Europe as a rival, but a partner. . . . I will say here and now on this Day of Independence, that the United States will be ready for a declaration of interdependence, that we will be prepared to discuss with a United Europe the ways and means of forming a concrete Atlantic partnership." Kennedy avoided the details, but he favored a western Europe, including Britain, united in the Common Market, moving toward political federation, and joining the United States in trade agreements to spur the economic development of the entire non-Communist world. For Europe's military strategy Kennedy favored stronger conventional forces to increase NATO's defense options. He asked, at the same time, that the European allies contribute more heavily to their security. Second, Kennedy reminded Europeans that the American commitment to their defense included, if necessary, the employment of nuclear weapons; western Europe, therefore, did not require an independent nuclear capability.

European leaders rejected both weapons proposals. Having experienced a long period of peace, they feared that any reliance on conventional forces might suggest to the Kremlin that they were prepared to fight another conventional war. Conventional forces, they argued, would merely destroy the credibility of the nuclear deterrent. However, they wondered how far they could entrust their future to a nuclear arsenal over which they had no control. Kennedy met Europe's growing insistence that it share any future nuclear decision by accepting the principle of a Multilateral Defense Force (MLF) of nuclear armed naval vessels manned by mixed NATO crews. Unfortunately, MLF resolved no issue before the alliance. Any arrangement that increased European—especially German—control of nuclear weapons would endanger western

European interests quite as much as those of the USSR. If, on the other hand, the multilateral force perpetuated purely U.S. control of allied nuclear weapons, it served no purpose whatever.

Charles de Gaulle demolished Kennedy's Grand Design in January 1963, when he announced that France would reject both Bristish membership in the Common Market and French participation in any multilateral nuclear force. He repeated his determination to build an adequate French nuclear capability. He did not question the nuclear power of the United States, only its reliability, because the United States was no longer invulnerable to attack. "Nobody in America," he said, "can say where, when, how, and to what extent American nuclear armament would be used to defend Europe." Nothing less than strategic weapons in the hands of those willing to use them, he said, could effectively deter aggression. For that reason continental Europe required a nuclear defense structure of its own. Kennedy moved to reassure Europe that the American commitment to its defense was firm by traveling to West Germany, the Irish Republic, Italy, and the United Kingdom during June 1963. He told the German people at Bonn: "Your safety is our safety, your liberty is our liberty, and any attack on your soil is an attack on our own." He condemned de Gaulle for his effort to separate Europe from America and thereby weaken the alliance. Upon his return to Washington, Kennedy announced that the United States, Britain, and Russia would shortly discuss the question of a nuclear test ban treaty. After brief negotiations, the three powers, on July 25, concluded a treaty that banned all nuclear tests except those conducted underground. Congress approved the agreement in September by a vote of 81 to 19.

What troubled NATO additionally was its perennial failure to establish any clear relationship between its power and the objectives that it pursued. Western officials had never defined their diplomatic objectives in achievable terms. The Soviet control of East-Central Europe perpetuated an uncompromising mood within the alliance and bound it to the extreme demands of each member state. George F. Kennan noted the problem in an interview that appeared in the November 19, 1963 issue of *Look*. "This coalition," he complained, "is incapable of agreeing on any negotiated solutions except unconditional capitulation and the satisfaction of the maximum demands of each of our allies. It is easier for a coalition to agree to ask for everything but the kitchen sink, rather than take a real negotiating position. This worries me because there is not going to be any capitulation. Our adversaries are not weak. If we cannot find any negotiating position, the Cold War will continue, and the dangers will not decrease." Keeping West Germany a satisfied member of the alliance took a heavy toll of Western diplomacy. Whereas the West remained committed to German unification and the revision of the Oder-Neisse line, it could never devise any policy in support of such objectives. Indeed, so enormous was the gap between purpose and interest that it never tried. Lyndon Johnson, as President, adopted the Kennedy foreign policy team and with it the revisionist purposes of U.S. policy in Europe.

Both Kennedy and Johnson were even less inclined toward innovation in their policy toward China. Rusk, taking the lead in defending established attitudes toward Peking, denied in July 1961 that the prospects of a Sino-Soviet break could serve as the basis of a new policy. "I think," he declared, "there is solid evidence of some tension between Moscow and Peiping, but I would use a little caution in trying to estimate the width of such gap as might be developing between them. . . . [H]ere are two great systems of power which are united in general in certain doctrinal framework and which together have certain common interests vis-a-vis the rest of the world." As late as April 1963, Rusk warned the country in an NBC interview to be "careful about taking premature comfort from arguments within the Communist world as to how best to bury us." Harriman that year likewise limited the Sino-Soviet quarrel to methods, not intentions. "Both Moscow and Peiping," he said, "are determined that communism shall sweep the world, but there is a deep difference between them concerning the methods to be employed."

Meanwhile, Kennedy and Johnson viewed China as a danger to the small countries of Asia. This assumption of Chinese aggressiveness underwrote their perennial refusal to recognize the mainland regime or to compromise the official American attachment to the exiled Nationalist regime on Formosa. Ambassador Adlai Stevenson, in his argument before the United Nations in December 1961, established the Kennedy rationale for prolonging the fight against recognition. It would be wrong, he said, to give "implicit blessing to an aggressive and bloody war against those Chinese who are still free in Taiwan." All nations, added Stevenson, were aware of the high standards of conduct and the contributions of the Republic of China to the principles and successes of the United Nations. "The notion of expelling the Republic of China," he declared, "is thus absurd and unthinkable." Arthur Goldberg, Johnson's ambassador to the United Nations, sustained that conclusion four years later. "The admission of Peiping," he warned in November 1965, "would bring into our midst a force determined to destroy the orderly and progressive world which the United Nations has been helping to build over the past 20 years." No longer did nonrecognition carry the promise of liberation as it did during the Eisenhower years. The Democratic administrations acknowledged both the strength and the permanence of the mainland government, albeit with a perennial tone of regret.

During 1965 the Dominican crisis put the American tendency to identify left-wing revolutions with Soviet expansion to the test. Behind the uprising was a movement to return Juan Bosch, the exiled former president, to power. Following their revolt of April 24, the rebels faced determined opposition from a right-wing, counterrevolutionary junta. As the fighting in Santo Domingo reduced the capital to chaos, President Johnson landed Marines and naval personnel because, he informed the nation, "American lives are in danger [and authorities there] are no longer able to guarantee their safety." Actually, Washington's interventionist motives ran much deeper. Thomas C. Mann, the administration's chief adviser on Latin American affairs, argued that the rebel group was Communist-dominated; only its defeat, he warned, would prevent another Soviet encroachment in the Caribbean. Responding to this fear, the President, on May 2, announced that the United States, through its intervention and that of the Organization of American States, was attempting to "prevent another Communist state in this hemisphere." Privately Washington backed the narrow-based military junta. Soon it became clear, however, that U.S. policy was a massive infringement on the principle of self-determination and had no chance of success. Thereupon Washington, with the support of the OAS, negotiated an agreement for a provisional government. That government arranged an election that Bosch entered and lost. This procedure permitted the President to escape his self-imposed dilemma. But in Vietnam the U.S. commitment to the Saigon regime, however narrow its base of support, was too deep to permit a similar escape through compromise.

QUAGMIRE: THE WAR IN VIETNAM

The assumptions of global danger that underwrote the nation's Cold War policies of containment and military preparedness culminated logically in Vietnam. After mid-century the country's foreign policy establishment had defined the enemy in Asia as an aggressive international communism whose adherents—including Ho Chi Minh—received their marching orders from the Kremlin. It was not strange, therefore, that U.S. officials had difficulty in distinguishing China from Russia, or from Korea and Vietnam. There was only one enemy. To guard the country against it, American policymakers sought above all to preserve the credibility of U.S. power by making it clear that this country would use its vast arsenal of weapons to ensure the success of non-Communist objectives in any Cold War confrontation. Vietnam became central to that intent because successive administrations made it so; they converted that country into the symbolic dike that would either contain the expansion of Communist power everywhere or, if broken, permit it to spread over South and Southeast Asia and far beyond.

Washington officials spared no words in establishing Vietnam's importance. Kennedy in 1956 called Vietnam "the cornerstone of the Free World in Southeast Asia." Eisenhower, in April 1959, stressed the military importance of the region in similar terms. "Strategically," he said, "South Viet-Nam's capture by the Communists would bring their power several hundred miles into a hitherto free region. The remaining countries of Southeast Asia would be menaced by a great flanking movement. . . . The loss of South Vietnam would set in motion a crumbling process that could, as it progressed, have grave consequences for us and for freedom." Shortly thereafter Vice-President Lyndon Johnson added his warning. "If we don't stop the Reds in South Vietnam, tomorrow they will be in Hawaii, and the next week they will be in San Francisco."

Such phraseology invariably left unexplained the processes whereby the fall of South Vietnam would actually endanger the rest of Southeast Asia and much of the surrounding world. Yet the doom that such statements predicted rendered Washington powerless to reexamine its commitments to South Vietnam's defense; at the same time, the lack of demonstrable American interests in Southeast Asia would, in the long run, deny it the means required for victory even over the limited power and human resources of North Vietnam.

Unmindful of the pitfalls in any Vietnam encounter, President Kennedy and his advisers moved quickly to recommit the nation to the preservation of the Saigon regime from its Communist-led enemies who, by 1961, threatened its very existence. Leaders who prided themselves on their toughness would not avoid any perceived challenge in Asia to the security and prestige of the United States. From the beginning the Kennedy foreign policy managers assumed that available military technology and expertise would enable them to destroy Ho Chi Minh's guerrillas with surgical precision. The Green Berets, Kennedy's highly trained elite counterinsurgency forces, would, as advisers to the Army of South Vietnam, teach the enemy some well-merited lessons in jungle warfare. Rostow, in March 1961, referred to the Green Berets as "our unexploited counter-guerrilla assets." The Vietcong, however courageous and resilient, would have even less chance against "smart" bombs, electronic detectors, chemical defoliants, the latest aircraft, and weaponry of astonishing accuracy and firepower. Perhaps General Curtis E. LeMay's observation that "Communism could best be handled from a height of 50,000 feet" exemplified the administration's faith in its superior technology.

If Kennedy's men were committed to victory in Vietnam, they shied away from a major U.S. involvement in Southeast Asia. Korea remained a vivid memory; a war in the jungles of Vietnam would be even less popular. Determined to skirt a hard decision between noninvolvement and war, Kennedy committed the nation to Saigon's success, but with increments of military and economic aid sufficient only to sustain the administration's options, not large enough to require broad national approval. During 1962 the President increased the military aid to South Vietnam from 4000 Americans advisers in January to 10,000 by October, while McNamara assured the country that the administration had no policy for introducing combat forces into Southeast Asia. Halfway measures would not bring success, but they would buy time and avoid defeat by keeping the war in progress. Meanwhile the administration would conceal the war's costs from the public, avoid thereby an enervating domestic debate, and await some miraculous display of good fortune. Thus the United States drifted into the war, fought it, and left it without the benefit of a national decision. It is not strange that the involvement ended in disaster; it could hardly have been otherwise.

In November 1963 Johnson inherited Kennedy's program of gradual escalation in Vietnam. Encouraged by military reports from Saigon, the new President reaffirmed the country's commitment to victory. "I am not going to be the President," he assured the nation, "who saw Southeast Asia go the way China went." During the succeeding months Washington remained officially confident. On March 8, 1964, McNamara arrived in Saigon on his fourth mission to that country since May 1962. On his return to the United States he repeated his former predictions: 'In the entire week, I did not talk to a single responsible official who was unable to agree that, if the proper effort is made, the war can be won." On March 26, Ambassador Henry Cabot Lodge argued that the sure defeat of the Vietcong rendered any compromise with Hanoi unnecessary. Three weeks later Secretary Rusk, on a tour of South Vietnam, assured a group of villagers, "We are comrades in your struggle. Some day that regime in Hanoi will disappear and you and your brothers in the north will be able to join in a free and democratic Vietnam." In May McNamara expressed his conviction that the major portion of the U.S. military task in Southeast Asia would be completed in 1965.

The illusion of easy success had ceased to guide American action. As Saigon's fortunes continued to disintegrate throughout 1964, the President contemplated an expanded American role in Vietnam. His choice of General Maxwell Taylor as ambassador to Saigon in June seemed to affirm his determination to reverse the course of the war with larger increments of American power. Taylor had long advocated a direct American military involvement in the struggle. During August 1964, following an alleged North Vietnamese attack on American naval vessels in the Gulf of Tonkin, Congress, at the President's request, adopted a resolution that seemed to commit it to any future action required for victory in Southeast Asia. The resolution declared that the United States was "prepared, as the President determines, to take all necessary steps, including the use of armed forces, to assist any protocol state of the Southeast Asia Collective Defense Treaty requesting assistance in defense of its freedom." At the end of 1964, the administration had 23,000 troops in Vietnam.

Already the President had moved carriers into the South China Sea and awaited the proper occasion for launching an air war against North Vietnam. That occasion came on February 7, 1965, when a Vietcong attack on Pleiku, an outpost in the Central Highlands, killed eight Americans. The bombing, Washington assumed, would undermine enemy morale, halt the infiltration from the North, and encourage resistance in the South. Victory would be cheap and swift; official White House dogma predicted Hanoi's move to the negotiating table in six weeks, at most ten. When the bombing proved to be ineffective, Johnson ordered American forces in South Vietnam to enter the fighting and announced in July that he would shortly consign 125,000 American soldiers to Vietnam. By 1966 the number exceeded 200,000; at the end of 1967 it approached 600,000. Hanoi responded with a commensurate escalation of its own. The contest for Vietnam had become a war without end.

What compelled the Johnson administration to escalate the American involvement in Southeast Asia was not the unanticipated resistance of the North Vietnamese, but its refusal to modify its established goals in the face of that resistance. The continuing assumption that victory was both necessary and achievable at limited cost closed all options and unleashed a momentum toward a larger and larger war. For Johnson there would be no diminution of the American effort. If this nation was driven from the field in Vietnam, ran his warning of July 1965, no foreign country would ever again trust the promises of the United States. Thereafter such predictions of disaster ran through official statements like a torrent. In his noted memorandum of January 17, 1966, Assistant Secretary of Defense John T. McNaughton argued that the United States, despite its entrapment in an escalating stalemate, remain in Vietnam to preserve its *reputation* as a guarantor and thereby sustain its effectiveness elsewhere. That year President Johnson informed a Japanese visitor, "If I tear up that treaty with Vietnam I tear up the one I have with you and 42 others. . . . If I go bankrupt in one place, I go bankrupt all over." Similarly, General Taylor opposed the abandonment of South Vietnam by asserting that the United States would pay dearly for its defeat in terms "of [its] worldwide position of leadership, of the political stability of Southeast Asia, and of the credibility of our pledges to friends and allies." Vietnam carried the final burden for establishing America's capacity to manage change peacefully and effectively everywhere.

What magnified the need for victory was the conviction that power serves the cause of peace far better than does diplomacy. Negotiations with aggressors, recent history seemed to demonstrate, merely encouraged further aggression. Thus, not compromise but power attached to inflexible purpose appeared the best guarantee of a stable and peaceful international order. Second, many officials argued that power of the magnitude possessed by the United States, if properly employed, should be effective in preventing war with a minimum of risk. As Admiral William F. Halsey once advised. "Touch a thistle timidly and it pricks you; grasp it boldly and its spines crumble." American power would serve the world's interest in peace most assuredly, not in its capacity to annihilate enemies, but in its alleged capacity to prevent the unwanted use of force. For Dulles after the Korean truce of July 1953, the threat of massive retaliation would eliminate the necessity of fighting additional minor wars. As late as 1964 national spokesmen such as Rostow insisted that America's capacity to respond to any aggression with superior force, up to and including nuclear war, had eliminated the danger of war in Southeast Asia.

It was left for Ho Chi Minh to expose the hollowness of the nuclear deterrent in Asia and compel the Johnson administration, if it would sustain the country's global posture, to establish the credibility of America's conventional power. To achieve this purpose, the Johnson administration rejected every argument for compromise in Vietnam. What mattered after 1965 was not the justice of the American cause, but the reassertion of an image, by word and action, that would convince the world that the United States remained "the mightiest power on earth." Challenged openly by Hanoi, American policy of maintaining world stability without fighting additional wars required the constant reaffirmation of the national will. "To leave Vietnam to its fate," ran President Johnson's warning of February 1965, "would shake the confidence . . . in the value of the American commitment, the value of America's word. The result would be increased unrest and instability, and ever wider war." Secretary of State Rusk assured Senators in January 1966, "The integrity of our commitments is absolutely essential to the preservation of peace right around the globe. . . . We know from painful experience that aggression feeds on aggression."

Ultimately, the dual effort to terrify the enemy and sustain American support for established policies failed. Whatever the intellectual burden the war carried for global stability, victory in Vietnam proved elusive. Fighting jungle opponents, often unrecognizable, striking everywhere and nowhere, limited the effectiveness of American ground action, eliminated the possibility of exerting constant pressure along distinctive battle lines, and reduced the war to simple search and destroy operations. The absence of good strategic targets minimized the influence of what became the most massive air war in history. No reasonable level of destructiveness could overcome the enemy's superior interests in victory. What Vietnam demonstrated was the fact that even a country as powerful as the United States can perform effectively with military power only within the range of its clearly understood interests. United States officials used arguments in profusion to convert Indochina into a vital American concern; the effort failed. The danger, never demonstrable, took its form from words that some believed and others rejected. The result was failure in Asia and a thoroughly divided populace at home. Congress itself created no problem. Its majorities abdicated to the foreign policy managers on Vietnam quite as much as they did on matters of national defense. In neither case did they care to contemplate the price of failure. Even as the war in Southeast Asia escalated to a cost of roughly $25 billion a year, its defenders still emerged triumphant in Congress. Time after time they won the contest for additional appropriation hands down.

ANTIWAR PROTEST AND THE STUDENT REVOLT

Criticism of the Vietnam war kept pace with the administration's efforts to escalate both its costs and its importance. The unleashing of such vast quantities of destructiveness against a jungle people 10,000 miles distant on the mainland of Asia wounded the moral sensibilities of millions of Americans and gradually embittered much of the nation as had no previous foreign experience in its history. President Johnson's decision to Americanize the war in the spring and summer of 1965 produced the first organized opposition—the "teach-ins" that began at the University of Michigan in March and spread rapidly from campus to campus and finally to Washington in August. Casting doubt on the war's necessity, many who appeared at the teach-ins warned that the conflict would ultimately turn into a military and moral disaster. To counter the teach-ins, the State Department sent teams of Foreign Service officers to the campuses to argue the administration's case; their profound inability to answer the questions of their concerned listeners contributed little to the credibility of American policy.

Soon the antiwar crusade moved from the campuses to Congress and the media. A small group of congressional critics—Wayne Morse of Oregon, Ernest Gruening of Alaska, Gaylord Nelson of Wisconsin, George McGovern of South Dakota, and Mike Mansfield of Montana—had long questioned the growing American involvement in Southeast Asia. With the escalation of 1965, that group expanded rapidly. In January 1966 J. William Fulbright, chairman of the Senate Foreign Relations Committee, conducted televised hearings on the Vietnam conflict. Within a year the leading foreign policy commentators on the television networks had turned against the war, as did distinguished retired generals such as Matthew Ridgway and James Gavin. Civil rights leaders, including Martin Luther King, joined the ranks of the war critics, convinced that the war, fought more and more by those who could find no refuge from the draft, demanded a disproportionately high involvement of blacks and other minorities. It was equally clear by 1967 that war appropriations were starving the President's Great Society programs for the poor. Late in March, King declared in Chicago: "In truth, the hopes of the Great Society have been overcome by the fears and frustrations of Vietnam. The pursuit of this widened war has narrowed domestic welfare programs, making the poor, white and Negro, bear the heaviest burdens both at the front and at home." In April King led 100,000 protestors in an antiwar march through New York City.

Comparatively few of these war critics were pacifists; most would have agreed readily that the nation had the right to kill those who threatened its welfare or existence. The domino theory and its variations had defined the enemies of Saigon as dangerous to the security of all Asia and thus of the United States. Those who challenged the American military escalation in Vietnam, on the other hand, argued that the struggle for Vietnam was largely an indigenous contest to be resolved by the Vietnamese people themselves. Such argumentation reduced the American effort to an illegitimate and unnecessary intervention in the internal affairs of another nation, and an overcommitment of national manpower and resources in an area where U.S. interests were secondary at best. The critics demanded decisions that varied from the cessation of the bombing of North Vietnam to the withdrawal of American forces to enclaves for the purpose of reducing casualties; from the imposition of a coalition government on Saigon that would include all elements involved in that country's struggle for power to, finally, a complete withdrawal of all U.S. forces from Vietnam, whatever its effect on that region's political future.

Eventually some antiwar critics proclaimed open defiance of national policy. Philip Berrigan, a priest and war veteran, joined by his brother, Daniel, destroyed draft records in Baltimore and Catonsville, Maryland. Antiwar offices throughout the country openly advised potential draftees how to avoid military service. Entire communities of draft resisters and deserters from the armed forces sprang up in Canada and western Europe. Such widespread, determined opposition to the war eventually affected the administration itself. By November 1967, both HEW Secretary John W. Gardner and Defense Secretary Robert McNamara had left the administration because of their dissent from Vietnam policy. When these two national leaders, soon joined by Dean Acheson, Averell Harriman, and Clark Clifford, turned against the war, they served notice that, for the first time in a generation, the nation's foreign policy elite had divided irreparably. The momentum of war in Southeast Asia had carried American policy beyond the point where its established constituency, including the New York Council on Foreign Relations, cared to defend it. Eventually the entire cabinet, with the possible exception of Dean Rusk, regarded the escalation a mistake, although most refused to resign on principle. At a time of great national crisis, James Reston complained, they "gave to the President the loyalty they owed to the country."

That students remained in the vanguard of dissent reflected both the nature of the times and the quality of the country's intellectual life. If the rebellion of youth is eternal, the protests of the 1960s had particular relevance for American politics and society. Previous generations had expressed the ideals of freedom, justice, and equal opportunity without examining the inapplicability of such ideals to millions of their fellow citizens. For many sensitive college-aged youths, the crisis-laden 1960s destroyed the fatalistic optimism that had undermined the concern of their elders; events demonstrated that the country had not responded well to the challenges of the cities, to the quest for civil rights, to the inequalities of economic and educational opportunity, or to the growing infringements on the aesthetic quality of national life. An examination of the past revealed that neither the policies nor the leaders of the country had always been wise. At times, it seemed, the nation had escaped disaster only because of its unique margins of safety, its excess of power and resources. Too often its human problems had simply been lost in the long stretches of landscape. That many past failures had passed as successes measured the dearth of analytical capacity among those who should have known better. For countless students of the 1960s the standards of public life reflected neither high morality nor even moderate intellectuality. Such notions, crashing against the policies and the institutions created by previous generations, set off the student revolt.

Writers and columnists soon identified the central object of student criticism as the so-called establishment. Student critics concluded that changes came slowly if at all simply because the country's institutions had become too large, too cumbersome, too dedicated to established policies and attitudes, to respond to the intellectual and physical challenges that confronted them. In their growing distrust of all decision making, students rejected the manipulated settlement. Tom Wicker defined the common denominator in the student movement in his *The New York Times* column of June 9, 1968: "A whole new generation—the children of affluence—has taken up the cause of the black and the poor, not so much out of class feeling or shared experience, perhaps, as from recognition of a common enemy—the Establishment. It is the Establishment—the elders, the politicians, the military-industrial complex, the Administration, the press, the university trustees, the landlords, the system—that represses the blacks, exploits the poor, stultifies the student, vulgarizes American life. And it is the Establishment, of course, that wages the war in Vietnam. . . . "

Animosity toward the establishment soon brought students into conflict with university administrators. They complained of the computerization and mass production that dehumanized the university experience, of the disinterested instruction of professors too busy in travel and research, of their inability to participate in decisions that affected the quality of their educative experience. Disturbances that shook the campuses began at the University of California's Berkeley campus in 1964 and culminated later in the decade with the riots at Columbia, Cornell, Stanford, Chicago, Wisconsin, and many other leading institutions. Students assaulted the universities mostly because other institutions, far more responsible for policies they deplored, were beyond their reach.

After the mid-1960s Vietnam became symbolic of everything wrong with American society. It created a merger between the antiwar and the civil rights movements, since the demands of war seemed to rule out further progress on human rights. Vietnam accounted for the unprecedented scale of campus activity across the nation. Yet despite the millions of written and spoken words of protest that emanated from the campuses, there was never a genuine confrontation with government. Walter Lippmann noted this when he wrote: "They [officials in government] announce, they proclaim, they declare, they exhort, they appeal, and they argue. But they do not unbend and tell the story, and say what they did, and what they think about it, and how they feel about it. Thus the atmosphere is secretive and standoffish, which certainly does not warm the heart in time of trouble." This explained why much of the dissent became unrestrained, why it produced riots, disorders, and the breakup of public meatings. For some students the sense of moral outrage, added to the unresponsiveness of government, destroyed all limits to their intolerance of official views and their defiant public behavior. Long before the end of 1967, national leaders were unwelcome at many of the country's leading colleges and universities. Radicals attacked the ROTC programs and all university connections with the country's defense effort.

However pervading the challenges of the 1960s, student reaction was never monolithic. The majority of students continued to be more concerned with preparation for remunerative employment, with football, fraternities, dating, and automobiles than with reforming the universities or American society. But the unresolved issues of the decade drove a tiny minority into open rebellion. Many of these students and nonstudents rejected orderly processes, majority rule, and the traditions of free and orderly discussion. They talked openly of the overthrow of established institutions. Their leading philosopher was Herbert Marcuse, who argued in his *One Dimensional Man* (1964) that social salvation would come not from the welfare state, but from the outsiders, the exploited and oppressed. To these he assigned the right to use violence if legal means proved inadequate. Often the radical student movement became identified with the Students for a Democratic Society (SDS), founded in 1962 and claiming by 1968 a membership of several thousand. The trend toward radicalism culminated in the Youth International Party (Yippies), a semiserious political movement led by Abbie Hoffman and Jerry Rubin that advocated drugs and violence. The media coverage that the radicals received failed to distinguish between them and the vast center of the student spectrum, which was neither disinterested nor violent. American campuses had tens of thousands of students who were not in the streets, but who were deeply concerned over national ills and policies that they regarded as unintelligent, if not immoral. These students were troubled over the war in Vietnam and the plight of the blacks and the poor in American society. They were the true adherents of the New Politics.

Some youths, disillusioned by the conformity, the fundamental contradictions, and the double standards of American life, dropped out of college and society completely to form the counterculture of the 1960s. The "beatniks" of the previous decade had set the style with their long hair, beads, old clothes, and sandals. Their dissent from the smugness of the 1950s found expression in Allen Ginsberg's *Howl* (1955) and Jack Kerouac's *On the Road* (1957). The larger youth defection of the 1960s—the hippie movement—perpetuated the sharp break from established social norms, with its beards and beads, shaggy hair and unkempt attire, street theaters and dashikis, astrology and other forms of mysticism. To emphasize their separation from straight society, many of the counterculture turned to drugs. Large numbers of hippies gathered in places such as the Haight-Ashbury district of San Francisco and New York's East Village, although in time some deserted their urban environments to establish communes in the countryside, especially in remote areas of the Southwest. Those who inhabited the communes attempted to practice the ideals of noncompetitiveness, gentleness, and nonviolence, sharing responsibility, property, love, and children. To sustain their simple, often squalid, existence, members raised gardens, secured outside employment, or contributed money received from home. In time the hippie movement disintegrated as its adherents, amid declining economic opportunity, again retreated to the protection of home, work, and education. Whatever their immediate concerns, those who joined the counterculture shared an intense disdain for the Vietnam war.

Unable to win the war, yet unwilling to lose or compromise it, Washington could come to terms with neither its domestic nor its Vietnamese opponents. The longer the war continued, the more pervading and illegal were the actions undertaken in the name of winning it. The rise of the so-called imperial presidency, with its unprecedented claims to executive primacy in all external matters, resulted not from intent, but from the realization that only such concentrated power could sustain the American involvement in Southeast Asia. Impelled by the self-inflicted dilemma of fighting an enervating war against a dogged and elusive enemy without the support of a national decision, the troubled government sometimes behaved as if its domestic detractors, not the Vietnamese guerrillas, were the central cause of its embarrassment. President Johnson and his advisers accused their opponents of giving encouragement to the enemy; at the same time they promised the ultimate success of the American effort. Ellsworth Bunker, the U.S. ambassador in Saigon after March 1967, took up the defense of national policy. On a reporting trip to Washington he assured the country that the allies were achieving steady progress in the war. Vice-President Humphrey, upon his return from the western Pacific, announced that U.S. policy assured success on all fronts. General William Westmoreland, commanding general in Vietnam, reported to Congress that U.S. forces had "reached the important point where the end begins to come into view. . . . " This optimism mounted until January 1968, when adviser Walt W. Rostow informed newsmen in his White House office that captured documents revealed an enemy on the verge of collapse. Even he spoke, his staff relayed the news that the Vietcong had unleashed the Tet Offensive, the most destructive enemy attack of the war. The effect on Washington was profound.

FULL BOIL; THE ELECTION OF 1968

So firm was Johnson's command on the Democratic party that his renomination and reelection in 1968 seemed assured. He entered the campaign determined to stand firm on Vietnam, poverty, and civil rights, and thus forestall any defections to the more hawkish Republicans. His efforts again would focus on the chief elements in the established Democratic coalition—the solid South, labor leaders, bureaucrats, and city bosses. If Hanoi demonstrated its good intentions, he declared in his State of the Union message of January 1968, he would reduce the bombing of North Vietnam. He would not, he added, change the goals of American policy— that of proving the credibility of U.S. power to dispose of any and all unwanted aggression. But, as the costs of the war mounted through 1967 without guaranteeing any commensurate success in Asia, Democratic critics in Congress demanded an interparty debate on the Vietnam issue to prepare the Democratic party for the forthcoming campaign. Such a debate, charged Senator Eugene McCarthy of Minnesota in October 1967, was preferable to the pretense that the party was united. During November McCarthy assured that debate when he announced his candidacy for the Democratic presidential nomination.

McCarthy, supported by a group of effective political amateurs and his own remarkable gift for political expression, countered the assault of Johnson's managers so adroitly in the March New Hampshire primary that he gained 42.5 percent of the Democratic vote, compared to the President's 49.5. Clearly the anti-Vietnam sentiment had moved beyond the students and the intellectuals. Within days, Robert Kennedy entered the Democratic race as an active candidate. His formal announcement clarified his program: "I run to seek new policies—policies to end the bloodshed in Vietnam and in our cities, policies to close the gaps between black and white, rich and poor, young and old, in this country and around the world." President Johnson's campaign now crumbled. The Tet Offensive of early 1968 against the cities of South Vietnam was scarcely a Vietcong triumph, but its momentary successes stalled the President's carefully sustained illusion of victory and sent his popularity into sharp decline. It was clear that McCarthy would win the Wisconsin primary in April; even more threatening to the President was a Gallup Poll of early March that rated Kennedy of equal strength with him among Democrats and independents. On the evening of March 31 Johnson informed a dismayed public that under no circumstance would he campaign further for the presidency. He preferred, he said, to curtail the divisiveness in the country by withdrawing from the race and to focus on the problem of ending the war in Vietnam. To facilitate negotiations with Hanoi, the President proclaimed a partial bombing halt.

Late in April President Johnson announced the forthcoming talks in Paris, with Averell Harriman acting as chief U.S. negotiator. Even as Washington officials heralded the coming exchange as a breakthrough for peace, their mood was not compromising. Some argued that the military situation in Vietnam was so favorable that the United States could be demanding. Saigon was equally adamant, warning that any political settlement would endanger its existence. South Vietnam's Foreign Minister, Tran Van Do, declared on April 12: "I feel no qualms [about the future] as long as the fighting continues, [but] I look forward to negotiations with serious misgivings." South Vietnam President Nguyen Van Thieu reminded Washington that he opposed either a political settlement or an American withdrawal from Vietnam. In response to the conditions imposed by Saigon, Harriman announced that any agreement would guarantee South Vietnam a government of its own choice. Meanwhile Hanoi, under its principle of self determination, warned that it would accept nothing less than the demise of the Saigon regime—a regime held in power by the military might of the United States. Xuan Thuy, the North Vietnamese negotiator, informed newsmen in Paris that he would avoid negotiations until the United States halted all bombing of North Vietnam. Even then he promised no deescalation of Hanoi's military effort in exchange for a bombing moratorium. The Paris talks assured no settlement of the Indochinese conflict at all.

Early in April McCarthy won an expected victory in Wisconsin with 57 percent of the Democratic votes, but it was already evident that Kennedy, backed by the family millions and much of the party's literary talent, would dominate the remaining primaries. McCarthy's low-keyed, intellectual campaign, emphasizing the Vietnam issue almost to the exclusion of all others, appealed to the educated, upper-class minority of the cities. Kennedy aimed his campaign at those whom McCarthy avoided—the blacks, the ethnics, the lower middle classes. Kennedy swept the Indiana and Nebraska primaries, whereas McCarthy captured heavily middle-class Oregon. In their final confrontation—the California primary of early June—Kennedy again emerged victorious. That night, in a kitchen corridor of the Ambassador Hotel in Los Angeles, he became the victim of another assassination.

Before McCarthy could regain his earlier momentum, he faced the telling opposition of Vice-President Humphrey, who had announced his candidacy on April 27 at the Shoreham Hotel in Washington. From the outset Humphrey enjoyed the full backing of the Democratic organization. Avoiding all primaries and public appearances, he captured enough state Democratic conventions to assure an easy first-ballot victory at the forthcoming national Democratic convention in Chicago. Meanwhile McCarthy's open and unambiguous attacks on the Vietnam war attracted large and enthusiastic crowds. In St. Louis he faced 10,000 applauding followers. One night in July he addressed over 35,000 in Boston's Fenway Park.

McCarthy's challenge to Vietnam brought a stream of students into his campaign. "When the public called out for moral responsibility in the young," he told one youthful audience, "one should not be surprised if we raise moral objections to this war."

At Chicago in August the Democratic machine quickly demonstrated its power to control the convention, write a platform, and nominate its favorite candidate; it did not demonstrate any power to command the nation or even a party majority. Never before in American history did a party in open convention repudiate its national leadership so completely. So low had Johnson's popularity fallen among rank and file Democrats that he dared not attend the national convention. Yet his personal decline in no way diminished his control of the delegates, who gave Humphrey an overwhelming nomination on the first ballot. Senator Edmund Muskie of Maine joined the Democratic ticket as the vice-presidential nominee. McCarthy's anticipated failure to control the platform and the balloting brought thousands of antiwar demonstrators to Chicago. There, along Michigan Boulevard, the young, largely under Yippie leadership, faced soldiers and police in the most massive and bitter confrontation of the decade. Shortly after midnight following the first day of the convention, the police began to probe the line of pro-McCarthy demonstrators. "Then they charged," Abe Peck, editor of Chicago's underground newspaper, *The Seed*, recalled. "The helmeted wave flowed across the park, lofting tear gas and smoke bombs and waving night sticks over their heads. . . . They had no use for the 'peace-creep dope-smoking faggots,' and they told us so with the scream that said it all. 'Kill! Kill! Kill!' " While millions of distraught viewers witnessed the carnage on television, the Democratic party, since 1936 the overwhelming majority party of the United States, slowly tore itself to shreds. Refusing to endorse Humphrey, students quietly retreated from the political scene.

Long before those August days the election year promised success to the Republican party. Richard M Nixon entered the campaign early and, by 1968, emerged as the Republican front-runner. Following his defeat for the California governorship in 1962, he had moved to New York as a partner in a highly prestigious law firm. Determined to rebuild his political fences, he campaigned loyally for Goldwater in 1964. Again leaving his plush New York law offices two years later, he campaigned hard and successfully for Republican congressional candidates. The New Hampshire primary revealed the "new Nixon," relaxed, confident, and gracious, reminding his audiences that he had been vice-president in an administration that had kept the country at peace for eight years. Facing only the disintegrating competition of Governor George Romney of Michigan, Nixon took the New Hampshire primary and then moved on to easy victories in Wisconsin, Indiana, Nebraska, and Oregon. Nixon conceded California to its favorite son, Governor Ronald Reagan. He then proceeded to consolidate his delegate strength in the nonprimary states. At the Miami convention in August, he faced a last-minute effort of Governor Nelson Rockefeller of New York, who had conducted an expensive media campaign. Nixon's strong Southern support quashed a Reagan bid from the right; some minor concessions to Rockefeller in the platform terminated the assault from the party moderates. Thereafter Nixon smashed through to an easy first-ballot nomination. To placate Republican conservatives, Nixon chose Governor Spiro T. Agnew of Maryland for the vice-presidential nomination.

Backed by the most expensive and elaborate campaign in the nation's history, Nixon set out to exploit his unique advantages. His formula was simple; he had merely to dramatize the nation's decline at home and abroad under Democratic administrations. *The Speech,* honed to perfection after the New Hampshire primary, Nixon repeated across the country with few variations. "I say and you say," he began, "that when the strongest nation in the world can be tied down in a war in Vietnam for four years with no end in sight; when the nation with the greatest respect for law is torn apart by unprecedented lawlessness; when the richest country in the world can't manage its own economy; . . . and when the president of the United States of America for the first time in history cannot travel . . . to any major city in the country without fear of a hostile demonstration, then it's time for a new leadership for the American people . . . " As the crowd roared its approval, Nixon would add quickly, "And that's what you are going to have." He promised peace in Vietnam with policies that he never revealed. Avoiding the divisive issues before the country, he focused his campaigning on the forgotten white Americans—those who worked hard but seemed to make few gains against inflation and taxes. Some Republicans complained that Nixon's speeches avoided the needs of too many Americans, that they aggravated the divisions in American society by stressing the interests of the affluent.

During September Humphrey had the support of hard-core Democrats and few others. Democratic leaders warned him that he would never win the antiwar Democrats until he deserted the administration's stand on the war. Gradually acceding to such pressures, Humphrey seemed to outline a new policy at Salt Lake City on September 30. "As President," he said, "I would stop the bombing of the North as an acceptable risk for peace. . . . " Again he demanded that Hanoi restore the demilitarized zone; he ignored the National Liberation Front, political arm of the Vietcong, altogether. His promise of self-determination for South Vietnam was scarcely a repudiation of either the Kennedy-Johnson policies or the Democratic platform. Still, Humphrey's limited concessions gradually brought antiwar Democrats, less the students, back into the party fold. At the same time his aggressive campaigning in the cities aroused traditional Democratic loyalties, especially among the urban blacks.

What complicated the Humphrey-Nixon race was George C. Wallace's third-party movement. Four years earlier the former Alabama governor had entered the race with a states' rights platform, but withdrew with Goldwater's nomination. In February 1968, however, he promised the American people that he would give them a genuine choice in November. Wallace's program emphasized property rights and freedom of local and individual decision, both endangered, he declared repeatedly in speeches, press conferences, and broadcasts, by the federal bureaucracy. People, not bureaucrats, had the right to determine where their children would go to school or to whom they would sell their houses. As late as September Wallace's appeal to the lower middle class appeared so pervading that some predicted that he might capture a third of the Northern Democratic urban vote. Thereafter his campaign began to disintegrate. His choice of Air Force general Curtis E. LeMay as his vice-presidential candidate was not helpful, because the general had once suggested that Vietnam be bombed back to the Stone

Age. During October angry whites and blacks attended his rallies, interrupted his speeches, and often terminated his oratorical efforts with their noise and shoving. Even many who came to listen no longer applauded. The Wallace appeal, simple and divisive, was wearing thin.

On October 31, perhaps in an effort to improve Humphrey's chances, President Johnson announced that new developments—which he failed to explain—permitted him to halt the bombing of North Vietnam. This move, designed to promote negotiations in Paris, proved to be ineffective. The Saigon regime opposed a diplomatic confrontation with South Vietnam's National Liberation Front, representing the Vietcong, so completely that until December it refused to send a spokesman to Paris. When Vice-President Nguyen Cao Ky, leading the Saigon delegation, arrived in Paris, he announced that he would reject any compromise on procedure or protocol. Again the President, bound by the demands of his South Vietnamese allies, failed to bring the war any nearer a solution. Yet no longer did he care to justify the war, because it had undermined all his legislative triumphs—the Great Society and the measures for civil rights. All that remained to sustain him was his conviction that by fighting in Vietnam he had prevented World War III. It was far better, he later confided to Doris Kearns Goodwin, to lose 50,000 men in Vietnam than to fight and lose another world war.

Eventually Humphrey reforged the old Democratic coalition with enough success to overcome and almost erase Nixon's early advantage. Throughout October the polls recorded the steady decline of Nixon's lead as he continued to avoid the issues. A Harris Poll of October 10 gave Nixon a narrow five point lead over Humphrey. Early in November Gallup declared the popular vote a toss-up between Nixon and Humphrey, with Nixon still holding a clear majority in the electoral college. These final predictions proved to be accurate. Humphrey captured much of the Northeast, and added Maryland, West Virginia, Michigan, Minnesota, Texas, Washington, and Hawaii, with approximately 43 percent of the popular vote. Wallace took five Southern states, with 14 percent of the total, while Nixon, often with narrow margins, gained the remaining states, again with 43 percent of the popular vote. Indeed,

Nixon's final margin over Humphrey was 310,000 out of more than 70 million votes cast. Nixon's conservative campaigning held the important border South, but it alienated the discontented of the cities. Congress remained safely Democratic. The country's leading Vietnam critics—J. William Fulbright, George McGovern, Frank Church of Idaho, Harold Hughes of Iowa, and Abraham Ribicoff of Connecticut—won reelection to the Senate with ease.

In November 1968 the country approached the final year of a tumultuous decade on a note of irony. Seldom before in American history had so many citizens questioned the values and suppositions of national policies or laid bare so thoroughly the mistaken assumptions and purposes of a major involvement abroad. Yet, in the end, the American people elected to the presidency a conservative Republican who promised no change at all. Throughout the decade those who controlled the major agencies of power—the banks, corporations, universities, Congress, and the federal bureaucracy—made few concessions to the changing times. The establishment managed to protect what mattered with token responses to the manifold challenges of the critics; it survived the revolt of the 1960s intact. Still, it was not clear on what rational basis those who determined the decisions of business and government could continue to make claims to moral leadership. They could not run the economy without serious distortion and a certain level of favoritism and exploitation that endangered the welfare of millions. They could not deliver goods and services commensurate with the prices and the taxes that they imposed on a largely powerless citizenry. They could not instill in much of the middle class or the working classes a sense of trust. They could not provide much justice for the poor; they failed to curb the profound alienation of urban blacks from the main currents of American life. The persistence of the country's human degradation and the partiality of its governing structure gave those who wielded power no greater obligation than to prove to themselves and to others that the nation's historic economic and political system could yet serve the needs of a democratic people intelligently, fairly, and equitably.

Chapter VIII

The 1970s: A Crisis in Leadership

RICHARD NIXON AND THE POLITICS OF DIVISION

Richard M. Nixon, basking in his November triumph, assured Americans that his administration would seek an end to the country's domestic divisions. Actually, candidate Nixon had directed his campaign at Republican and Democratic conservative strongholds that had opposed the protests and the rioting of the 1960s. He had neither sought nor gained the allegiance of the blacks, the poor, the alienated, or the professionals and intellectuals—the true proponents of the New Politics—who had responded positively to the troublesome issues of the decade and supported Eugene McCarthy in 1968. Where the nation's discontent and alienation were most deeply rooted, Nixon's support was almost nonexistent; in such areas the policies that he advocated promised no rewards at all. Instead of seeking political reconciliation, therefore, he would, as President, continue to build Republican strength by directing the country's fears and resentments against those activists and Democratic liberals who allegedly had promoted the defiance of law and order. For Nixon's supporters the price of alienating further the disaffected in American life was not excessive. "It is time," argued Vice-President Spiro T. Agnew, "for the preponderant majority, the responsible citizens of this country, to assert their rights. . . .

If, in challenging, we polarize the American people, I say it is time for a positive polarization."

In outlook the Nixon cabinet—mostly bankers, corporation lawyers, and millionaire businessmen—was representative of the large, forgotten middle class that had placed the new President in the White House. For Secretary of State, Nixon chose William P. Rogers, an urbane New York lawyer who had served the Eisenhower administration as Attorney General. Melvin R. Laird, former Wisconsin Congressman, entered the cabinet as Secretary of Defense. Nixon assigned the other posts to men equally competent and similarly disinclined to challenge his leadership. Nixon determined early to concentrate decision making in the White House where he could work in seclusion with a small circle of speech writers and personal advisers. To protect himself from unwanted intruders, Nixon installed H. R. Haldeman and John Ehrlichman as White House Chief-of-Staff and Chief Domestic Coordinator, respectively. These two UCLA business school graduates had served the President effectively as advance men in his 1960 campaign and again as political managers in 1968. With Nixon's approval, Haldeman and Erlichman erected an almost impenetrable wall around the President's office to keep out all whom Nixon wanted to avoid. Attorney General John Mitchell—Nixon's former New York law partner, campaign manager, and trusted adviser—enjoyed free access to the President. Two others permitted to break through the wall were Daniel P. Moynihan, former Harvard professor who joined the administration as Presidential Assistant for Urban Affairs, and Henry Kissinger, a noted Harvard scholar who entered the Nixon staff as Presidential Assistant for National Security Affairs. Kissinger soon transformed the National Security Council into the central coordinating agency for the nation's foreign policies.

Nixon faced the task of avoiding the Great Society issues that he opposed without permitting members of Congress to exploit them politically. What gave Nixon some advantage in his struggle to control national policy was the country's conservative mood. Keeping his opponents divided with exquisite timing and effective argumentation, Nixon managed to dominate the Democratically controlled Congress. He won his first major triumph with the passage of his antiballistic missile program. Former Secretary of Defense Robert McNamara had responded to Pentagon pressure for an ABM system in 1967 by advocating a "thin" defense directed against a possible attack from China and limited in cost to $6 billion. Johnson's ABM system, called "Sentinel," was designed to protect the cities against a nuclear attack. Nixon, once in power, adopted ABM, but favored a new "Safeguard" system to protect not the cities, but the country's landbased missile sites. Despite widespread opposition among congressmen, editors, and scientists who argued that the system guaranteed little effective defense, the President carried Safeguard through the Senate by a narrow 51 to 49 vote during the summer of 1969. Nixon's strenuous legislative effort tied up the Senate for five months and antagonized several Republican leaders who voted for Safeguard only because of party loyalty.

Even on social and economic issues, those traditionally the private preserve of the Democratic party, the President kept his congressional opponents off balance. He preempted the welfare issue by introducing his own wide-sweeping Family Assistance Program during the summer of 1969. The bill provided for federal cash payments of $1600, plus food stamps valued at $820, to a family of four on relief. The Philadelphia plan, which established quotas for black workers on federal construction projects, permitted the President to make an effective gesture toward blacks. Then, in his State of the Union message on January 22, 1970, Nixon preempted the more and more popular environmental issue. "The great question of the '70s," he said, "is shall we . . . begin to make reparations for the damage we have done to our air, to our land and to our water? . . . Clean air, clean water, open space, these should once again be the birthright of every American. If we act now, they can be . . . ." That Nixon had little intention of investing more than words in combating pollution appeared manifest, but the President's words alone were sufficient to deflate the cause of congressional Democrats who had invested considerable time and effort in the campaign for a better environment. When Congress returned in January 1970, it faced a strenuous election year without any promising issues. The President had appropriated all of them —Vietnam, pollution, inflation, crime control, and welfare. "Every direction we turn," declared a leading Senate Democrat, "we have been preempted." Democratic strategists admitted that in Nixon they faced the nation's most consummate politician since FDR.

Nixon's administrative organization assured high performance, but whether the policies that flowed from the White House would meet the requirements of the times depended less on administrative organization than on the political and intellectual commitments of the President. Early in his presidency Nixon listed his two domestic priorities—reduced crime and violence, and lowered taxes and inflation. During its first year in office, the administration achieved little for law and order in the nation's cities. Then, in July 1970, Congress approved Nixon's District of Columbia Crime Bill. Opponents of the measure charged that its provisions for preventive detention, mandatory prison terms, wiretap authorization, and "no-knock" privileges for policemen under certain circumstances were repressive, if not unconstitutional. Blacks in Washington viewed the law as fundamentally an antiblack measure. On October 15, 1970, Nixon signed the long-awaited organized crime bill, asserting that the new law at last gave the Justice Department the needed tools for attacking crime. The bill's controversial provisions accounted for the long and bitter debate that delayed its passage through Congress. The measure permitted a judge to add 25 years to the sentence of a dangerous criminal, limited immunities under the Fifth Amendment, permitted trial judges instead of defendants to inspect logs of illegal eavesdropping to see if any overheard conversations were used against the defendant, and allowed federal grand juries to issue reports against public officials. In these two measures Congress enacted most of the administration's basic requirements for effective law enforcement, leaving for future consideration laws on pornography, marijuana, and gambling.

Nixon set out to control inflation without paying the normal price of unemployment. From the beginning he deserted the guideposts of the preceding Democratic administrations. In his first press conference he declared emphatically, "I do not go along with the suggestion that inflation can be effectively controlled by exhorting labor and management and industry to follow certain guidelines." Assuming that inflation could be managed better through the nation's banking structure, Nixon and his economic advisers emphasized the need for restrictions on the money supply. These devices had the immediate effect of tightening credit and raising interest rates to record levels. By curtailing sales and investment, Nixon hoped to stop inflation without spreading unemployment. However, the administration was reluctant to pursue any available course of action consistently enough to curtail inflation or unemployment effectively. Expenditures for ABM, space exploration, and the war in Southeast Asia assured huge federal deficits that strengthened employment but fed the inflation. The antiinflationary efforts of government, never sufficient to overcome the deficits and suppress price increases, slowed the nation's business activity. Unemployment in October 1970 reached the highest level in six years. Administration spokesmen attributed the rising unemployment to reductions in the armed services, the continuing inflation to long-standing pressures that they could not control. AFL CIO president George Meany attacked the Nixon tight-money policies in September 1970 for serving the special interests of banks and big corporations. Those with money to lend, he complained, were earning record profits.

Ultimately Nixon could not avoid the pressures of environmentalists for stronger legislation. Student activists who had taken up the environmental issue, joined by professional environmentalists, designated April 22, 1970 as Earth Day. Antipollution, unlike the more radical causes, had the sympathy of university and public officials. Earth Day involved millions of people in teach-ins, seminars, and cleanups in hundreds of communities across the country. These activities led to no immediate action, but that year the evidences of deterioration became more dramatic as the country read about massive oil spills, mercury pollution of rivers and lakes, and the air pollution crisis of July, which blanketed the East Coast with smog. In April President Nixon signed the Water Quality Improvement Act, which increased the penalties for oil spills. Then, in December 1970, Congress consolidated the scattered programs for controlling water, air, solid wastes, pesticides, and radiation into the Environmental Protection Agency (EPA). Backed by an accumulating body of regulations, the EPA set out to protect the nation's air and water against the assaults of the country's major industrial polluters.

With the approach of the critical 1970 election, Nixon prepared to put his carefully calculated "Southern Strategy" into operation. This strategy was designed to add significant numbers of Southern whites and conservative Middle Americans to Republican ranks. To sustain his special appeal in the South, the President needed to avoid responsibility for the mounting federal pressures on the Southern schools. When segregated Southern school districts faced a September 1969 cutoff of federal funds, Nixon ordered a postponement of over 30 court-ordered desegregation programs in Mississippi. In October the Supreme Court, in the unanimous decision of *Alexander* v. *Holmes,* ordered the immediate integration of the Mississippi schools. For the rapid integration that followed, Southern segregationists could not hold Nixon responsible. Nixon's strategy elsewhere assumed that the young, the blacks, the poor, and even middle-class intellectuals who embraced the New Politics comprised only a small minority of the nation's electorate. The conviction that minority issues would lose rather than gain votes led Kevin P. Phillips, in *The Emerging Republican Majority* (1969), to conclude that 1968 marked the end of the liberal, New Deal era of American politics. Phillips insisted that political power centered in the suburbs, the American heartland, and the "Sunbelt"—the postwar boom areas of Florida, Texas, Arizona, and southern California. Middle Americans who commanded the new areas of political power, ran Phillips' argument, had rejected the complex, costly, socially oriented issues associated with the liberal establishment. Those who failed to understand the prevailing conservative mood would win no offices.

Nixon's immediate challenge lay in separating the Democratic party's liberal, antiwar leadership—the spokesmen of the New Politics—from the elements everywhere that comprised the older Roosevelt coalition. To Vice-President Agnew fell the specific responsibility to pin the issues of violence and permissiveness on the Democratic party, thus driving its more conservative elements into the GOP. Agnew had established himself as an effective administration spokesman when, in the autumn of 1969, he challenged the honesty of the mass media that opposed the Nixon policies. During September 1970 he opened his alliterative war on the Democratic "vicars of vacillation," "nattering nabobs of negativism," and "hopeless, hysterical hypochondriacs of history." He raised the campaign to a conflict of philosophies between the "radiclib elite" and the rest of the nation. Such men, said Agnew, had turned their backs on hard-working, tax-paying Middle Americans. Identifying the Democratic leadership with rebellious youth, Agnew posed the alternative. Would the nation follow an elected President or a disruptive radical, militant minority? Pointing to hecklers in Saginaw, Michigan, the Vice-President said, "That's exactly what we are running against today—the tired rationales and the general permissiveness that have brought rioting to the streets and on the campuses."

In October Nixon entered the campaign as a partisan campaigner, risking his official power and prestige in a clear bid for a Republican Congress. He appealed to the nation for a vote of confidence for himself and his program. Capitalizing on a rock-throwing incident in San Jose, California, the President closed out his hard-stumping, 22-state effort on election eve with a nationally televised appeal to law and order. He called on "the great silent majority of Americans of all ages, of every political persuasion, to stand up and be counted against the appeasement of the rock throwers and the obscenity shouters in America." The effort failed. In November the Democrats lost two seats in the Senate, but gained nine in the House. They picked up 11 additional governorships. Only in the Northeast, where its strength had been ebbing, did the Republican party rebound. The President faced his worst disasters in the South where, except for Republican victories in Tennessee, the Southern Strategy lay in shambles. Only 18 out of 52 Senate and governor candidates for whom Nixon and Agnew campaigned won their elections. The President had simply misjudged the nation's mood; voters were not as conservative and complacent as his strategists assumed.

Nixon responded to the Republican setback of November 1970 with a more determined attack on stagflation. His earlier program pushed the country into a recession even as inflation became more rampant. After studying the conflicting proposals of his economic advisers, the President, in August 1971, announced a 90-day freeze on all wages and prices. The President asked Congress to increase personal income tax exemptions in a move to stimulate consumer demand. To improve foreign sales, the President suspended the traditional practice of converting dollars to gold. This move permitted the dollar to float freely on the international money market. The resulting devaluation of the dollar reduced the price of American goods abroad. The President, at the same time, imposed a 10 percent surtax on imported goods. These moves to strengthen the economy faced resistance and threats of retaliation from Japan and the nations of western Europe. Eventually Washington negotiated adjustments whereby the leading trading partners revalued their currencies while the United States resumed its purchase of gold. The net result was a devaluation of the American dollar by 12 percent, enough to assure a shift in the balance of payments toward the United States. In October Nixon terminated the 90-day freeze and instituted Phase II of his economic program, designed to hold wage increases to 5.5 percent annually and prices to an inflationary rate of 2.5 percent. These controls broke the inflationary trend for the first time since 1968 and gave the economy a spurt that carried industrial production above that of the previous year. During the early months of 1972, corporations reported record profits. For Nixon, anticipating another run for the presidency, the economic outlook was promising indeed.

THE NIXON-KISSINGER POLICIES ABROAD

Nixon, unlike his Democratic predecessors, entered office prepared to recognize and exploit the opportunities offered by the changing international environment with policies that might serve the American interest in peace and his own ambition to build a reputation as a diplomatist. Henry Kissinger, his national security adviser, explained the situation that the country faced in 1969.

> When I came into office with the Nixon Administration, we were really at the end of a period of American foreign policy in which a redesign would have been necessary to do no matter who took over. . . . First, Western Europe and Japan had regained economic vitality and some political constancy. Secondly, the simplicities of the cold war began to evaporate.
> The domestic pressures in all countries for putting an end to tension became greater and greater, and within the Communist world it was

self-evident that we were no longer confronting a monolith. . . . So our problem was how to orient America in this world and how to do it in such a way that we could avoid these oscillations between excessive moralism and excessive pragmatism, with excessive concern with power and total rejection of power, which have been fairly characteristic of American policy. This was the basic goal we set ourselves.

Kissinger's own philosophical contribution to the Nixon policies sprang from his understanding of the nineteenth century's "stable structure of peace." This structure required above all a generally accepted legitimacy. Kissinger defined that necessary legitimacy in his book on Metternich, *A World Restored.*

"Legitimacy" . . . means no more than an international agreement about the nature of workable arrangements and about the permissible aims and methods of foreign policy. It implies the acceptance of the framework of the international order by all the major powers, at least to the extent that no state is so dissatisfied that . . . it expresses its dissatisfaction in a revolutionary foreign policy. A legitimate order does not make conflicts impossible but it limits their scope . . . . Diplomacy in the classic sense, the adjustment of differences through negotiation, is possible only in "legitimate" international orders.

Kissinger's new structure of peace required a world order in which the United States and the Soviet Union no longer sought primacy, but a sharing of responsibility with other nations for taming violence and economic disruptions in a fundamentally stable world. Such an order assumed that the former Cold War competition, in which a gain for one became a loss for another, had given way to a new interdependence in which disaster for one could spell disaster for all. Any new peace structure required above all the stabilization of the Washington-Moscow relationship through the creation of ground rules, hedging against sudden actions that might upset the Soviet-American future. But, in practice, Nixon's Washington was not prepared to base its policy decisions totally on the assumption that Russia had ceased to be a revolutionary power. Thus the Nixonian ground rules were designed to assure not only the safety of American interests in a still competitive world, but also the continued primacy of the United States. As Kissinger made clear, any new relationship that established the foundations for Soviet-American cooperation did so under the imperative that

Russia not alter any situation to its advantage. Fundamentally, the Nixon-Kissinger approach to Russia attempted to internationalize the burden of maintaining world stability and resolving the challenges of interdependence without compromising any established American objectives in regions of U.S.-Soviet competition.

Behind the march to the Moscow summit of May 1972 was a half decade of accumulating conviction that the Cold War drift in a more and more fluid and restrictive world had ceased to serve the interests of either the United States or the USSR. The overriding concern of both superpowers was the avoidance of nuclear war. Beyond that was the mutual desire to curb the ruinous arms race. For Kremlin leaders improved relations with the United States would, in addition, enable them to extend their access to Western technology and American products, especially if they received ample credits and most-favored-nation status. For Washington the special inducements were equally pervading. The American defense expenditure of $1.3 trillion over a quarter century had purchased neither peace nor security; nowhere was the end of the expenditure in sight. Twenty years of Cold War tensions and financial burdens had not eliminated Russian power or the Russian hegemony from Eastern Europe. That failure had demonstrated clearly that American security and well-being did not require the restoration of the Versailles system after all. In Europe containment had won. As an end it had stabilized the continent's division with a vengeance. As a means to an end—the negotiating of a new order for Europe— it had failed simply because no Western military structure could undo the Soviet political and territorial gains that had flowed from Hitler's collapse. The external goals that had sustained the Cold War in Europe had lost their relevance.

Conscious of the profound changes occurring in the international environment, Nixon, in accepting the Republican nomination, promised the American people a new age of negotiations. As President, Nixon urged Kissinger to establish a productive relationship with Anatoly Dobrynin, the genial Soviet ambassador in Washington. Progress toward negotiation still came hard. Washington itself hesitated to drop its goal of self-determination for Eastern Europe. But, during 1970, the basic Soviet aim of increased cooperation with the United States and western Europe became apparent in Washington. Meanwhile, in September 1970, a sharp crisis in the Middle East, with Syrian forces invading Jordan with Soviet tanks, threatened another Cold War confrontation. That same month the Soviets moved submarines into Cuban waters. Columnist James Reston warned the Russians that such behavior would drive the President back to his anti-Communist prejudices. Privately Kissinger reminded Dobrynin that the Soviets were violating the Khrushchev-Kennedy understanding on Soviet nuclear bases in Cuba. Dobrynin assured the Secretary that the Soviets would honor the 1962 agreement. Thereafter the crisis quickly evaporated. In October Nixon invited Soviet Foreign Minister Andrei Gromyko to Washington to discuss the prospects for better U.S.-Soviet relations.

These limited initiatives set the stage for the remarkable gains of 1971. In March, Soviet leader Leonid Brezhnev outlined the new direction of Soviet policy before the Communist party Congress. In May the President announced that an impasse in the strategic arms limitation talks (SALT) had been broken. Then, in August, the Big Four, after months of long and tedious negotiations, reached an agreement on West Berlin. Finally, on October 12, 1971, the President announced: "In light of the recent advances in bilateral and multilateral negotiations involving the two countries, it has been agreed that a meeting [between the leaders of the United States and the Soviet Union] will take place in Moscow in the latter part of May, 1972." During the critical spring of 1972, Kissinger flew to Moscow to work out guidelines for the summit conference with Chairman Brezhnev. Much of the presummit negotiation remained highly confidential. The careful preparations were indispensable to the smoothness and efficiency of the Moscow meeting. That the United States and the USSR shared a mutuality of interest in going to the summit received reaffirmation, at least in part, in the cordiality that characterized the private and formal exchanges between Nixon and Brezhnev.

However limited the agreements signed at Moscow, the Nixon-Brezhnev meeting was a milestone in the history of postwar international relations. Negotiators had carefully delineated the agreements in advance. One included the admission that "in the nuclear age there is no alternative to . . . peaceful coexistence."

Others obligated the two nations to continue their quest for arms limitations and closer commercial, economic, scientific, technological, and cultural ties. To restrict the competition for nuclear advantage, the negotiators at Moscow signed two nuclear arms pacts, one limiting defensive missiles to two locations, the other freezing offensive weapons to current levels for five years. Behind these nuclear agreements lay months of intricate and often disruptive negotiations between Soviet and American weapons experts. The Moscow formula imposed no restraints on the qualitative improvement of existing weapons. Secretary of Defense Laird made it clear that expenditures for missile development would not be curtailed. The nuclear accords recognized the status of the USSR as a coequal superpower. Upon his return to Washington, Nixon admonished Congress: "We can seize this moment . . . or let it slip away. Together, therefore, let us seize the moment so that our children and the world's children live free of the fears and free of the hatreds that have been the lot of mankind through the centuries."

Nixon's reversal of U.S. policy toward China was equally significant and even more dramatic. Before he entered the White House, Nixon had concluded that the faltering American effort to isolate 700 million people diplomatically and economically served no national purpose. He understood that the United States and China shared many historic interests and that two decades of animosity had been a tragic, perhaps avoidable, aberration. In 1969 the Nixon administration, working largely through President Yahya Khan of Pakistan, moved to establish better communication between Washington and Peking. However, the United States could not normalize its relations with China before China was prepared to identify its interests in Asia and elsewhere with that normalization. Long before the 1970s, the Sino-Soviet split had demonstrated the price of isolation. When, in October 1970, Yahya Khan carried Nixon's overture to Peking, the Chinese responded: "We welcome the proposal from Washington for face-to-face discussions. We would be glad to receive a high-level person for this purpose, to discuss withdrawal of American forces from Taiwan."

When Nixon received the invitation, he acknowledged only the welcome, not the purpose. Shortly thereafter Yahya Khan informed Peking of Nixon's favorable response. Finally, on July 15,

1971, Nixon announced to the press that several days earlier Kissinger had held private talks with Prime Minister Chou En-lai in Peking. The premier, he said, had invited the President to visit China at some appropriate time before May 1972. Nixon's new approach to China culminated in his trip to Peking in February 1972. Minutely prepared, the venture became one of the greatest media events of all time. The private exchanges settled few issues but, in acknowledging the legitimacy of the Peking government (which four previous administrations refused to do), Nixon admitted that the older attitudes and intentions toward mainland China, defended with such flamboyant phraseology, never made much sense. Why the President's new diplomacy enjoyed the almost universal approval of the American people William Pfaff explained in *The New Yorker* of June 3, 1972. "It reversed," wrote Pfaff, "an American China policy that under a succession of previous Administrations had delivered blows, bluster, and grand denunciations in the name of democracy and liberty. That way of conducting ourselves before the world . . . had become so corrupt in recent years, so sterile and thick with hypocrisy, that the country was ready for some Metternichian realism. . . . " During 1973 the United States established a permanent liaison office in Peking.

Throughout his campaign for the White House Nixon had promised an end to direct American military involvement in Southeast Asia. Still, in January 1969, Saigon and Hanoi gave the Nixon administration little room to maneuver. Saigon hoped to end the fighting with minimum changes in the political structure of South Vietnam; its negotiators in Paris denied that the peace conference had any right to discuss South Vietnam's political future at all. But Hanoi and the National Liberation Front (NFL), having pursued nothing for 15 years except the destruction of the Saigon regime, insisted that a political settlement precede any withdrawal of military forces. The insurgency's power to influence the political future of South Vietnam lay in its military effectiveness, not in its capacity to win an election. If Saigon's permanent independence required the destruction of its enemies, the Nixon administration would accept that goal, but with the hope that other means might make the cost more palatable. In Vietnamization—the training and equipping of South Vietnamese combat forces capable of replacing

American troops—Nixon quickly discovered an acceptable Vietnam policy, because it promised both victory and the de-Americanization of the war. During June Nixon announced a 25,000-man American troop withdrawal, but repeated his intention to limit such force reductions in accordance with South Vietnam's success in assuming the military burden.

Critics predicted that Vietnamization would never succeed. Throughout the autumn the antiwar movement centered on the campuses, where student activists prepared for the nationwide moratorium of October 15. Hundreds of rallies that day comprised the largest demonstration of antiwar sentiment during four years of war. Student leaders, facing determined opposition in the White House, now planned the giant mobilization on Washington, set for November 15. Nixon met the student challenge with an effective television speech on election eve, November 3. The nation, he said, had two choices if it would end the war—either "a precipitate withdrawal of all Americans from Vietnam without regard to the effects," or a "search for a just peace through a negotiated settlement if possible, or through continued implementation of our plan for Vietnamization if necessary. . . . " The President quickly disposed of the first alternative by warning that failure in Vietnam would lead to worldwide disaster. Vietnamization, on the other hand, would bring the war to a successful conclusion whether the negotiations in Paris succeeded or not. By posing two alternatives, one promising victory and peace, the other presaging humiliation and disaster, the President aroused the overwhelming support of the silent majority. But he managed to skirt the alternatives posed by the war's critics—a modification of the Saigon regime or a war without foreseeable end. On November 15 more than 250,000 antiwar demonstrators converged on Washington to march, sing, and listen; thereafter they had nowhere to go, for the President had effectively blocked their appeal to Middle America.

Suddenly, in early May 1970, Nixon unleashed a new assault on the nation's conscience when he ordered American forces into Cambodia to terminate the infiltration of North Vietnamese men and supplies into that country. The action, he said, was essential to protect Vietnamization and demonstrate American power and will. "If we fail to meet this challenge," he warned, "all other nations will be on notice that despite its overwhelming power the United States, when a real crisis comes, will be found wanting." The reaction was violent. In a confrontation at Kent State University, National Guardsmen killed four demonstrators and wounded nine others. Within days over 400 campuses across the country were in turmoil, beset by strikes, closings, building seizures, and bombings. On May 8 protestors streamed into Washington for the largest demonstration since the November 15 mobilization. Militarily, the Cambodian venture was a success; U.S. forces uncovered and destroyed vast quantities of North Vietnamese supplies. But the invasion turned Cambodia into a permanent battleground and broadened the scope of the war.

Nixon assured the nation that the new demonstration of will would produce more satisfactory negotiations with Hanoi. To open his new peace offensive, the President dispatched the noted American diplomat, David K. E. Bruce, to Paris. Unfortunately, successful negotiations required a new formula more than a new negotiator. Nixon's insistence on a cease-fire in place, with Saigon remaining in control of all political negotiations, eliminated every possibility of a settlement. Faced with endless resistance, Washington sustained the war by shifting the burden of American involvement from the ground to the air. The heavy bombing of 1971 permitted extensive troop withdrawals and a sharp decline in American casualties. But the official claims for Vietnamization could not prevent the massive and violent confrontations of April and May in Washington; eventually the government arrested and detained over 12,000 antiwar protesters. In June 1971 the administration faced another crisis when Daniel Ellsberg, former Pentagon official, leaked the Pentagon Papers—a massive study of Vietnam policy from 1945 until 1968—to *The New York Times* and *The Washington Post*. The administration quickly secured a court ruling to prevent the publication of any material that the government regarded vital to the national security. The *Times* and the *Post* carried their case to the Supreme Court and there won a critical 6 to 3 decision. The Nixon White House now prepared to strike at its enemies through a new investigative unit known as "the plumbers." The first target was Daniel Ellsberg.

Backed by prosperity and scheduled visits to Peking and Mos-

cow, Nixon's standing before the country in 1972 seemed uncontestable. The President had even eliminated Vietnam as a
troublesome political issue; the bombing had enabled him to
reduce American forces in Vietnam to less than 200,000—a decrease of almost 400,000 since the Johnson years. Still, several
Democrats were prepared to challenge his reelection. Senators Hubert Humphrey and Edmund Muskie, the party's nominees of
1968, shared presidential ambitions with Senators Henry Jackson
of Washington and George McGovern of South Dakota, Governor
George Wallace of Alabama, and Mayor John V. Lindsay of New
York. Because of his long and vigorous opposition to the Vietnam
war and general identification with the New Politics, McGovern
loomed as the special beneficiary of the Democratic reforms of
1970, which guaranteed women, blacks, and young voters delegate
representation roughly proportional to their numbers in the general population. Muskie, the front-runner in January and February,
performed badly in the early New Hampshire and Florida primaries, losing the lead to McGovern, who scored well in New Hampshire and moved on to victory in Wisconsin. The Wisconsin
primary damaged the prospects of Humphrey and Muskie and
prompted Lindsay to leave the race. After McGovern's victory in
Massachusetts, Muskie also withdrew. Wallace swept the Florida
primary and showed surprising strength in the big industrial states
of the North until an attempted assassination left him paralyzed
below the waist. McGovern faced his final preconvention challenge
from Humprhey in the California primary. Humphrey ridiculed
McGovern's defense and welfare programs, but could not prevent
another McGovern victory.

In July McGovern arrived at the Democratic convention in
Miami with an almost uncontestable lead. There he faced a determined "Stop McGovern" movement but, in the final showdown,
emerged victorious on the first ballot. Yet his nomination predicted
tragedy; in no way did it conform to the preferences of the vast
majority of Democrats, much less of the American electorate.
McGovern received fewer votes in the primaries than did Humphrey and scarcely more than Wallace. He captured the conventions, including the one at Miami, with the votes of the young, the
blacks, and the women. Many influential Democratic politicians and

labor leaders refused to endorse the nomination. What further damaged McGovern's chances was his choice of Senator Thomas Eagleton of Missouri for the vice-presidency. Shortly after the convention, newspapers reported that Eagleton had received psychiatric care on three different occasions in the 1960s. Eventually McGovern, admitting bad judgment, dropped Eagleton from the ticket and replaced him with Sargent Shriver, former head of the Peace Corps.

For Nixon the Republican national convention at Miami Beach in mid-August was a coronation. Thoroughly united, the Republican party had purged itself of all who maintained some compassion for losers and represented only those who wanted protection of their economic and social status. The convention awarded Nixon a first-ballot nomination by a vote of 1347 to 1, then ratified his chosen running mate, Spiro T. Agnew. Nixon had never dominated American politics as he did at the convention, where every detail was calculated to produce the desired pro-Nixon effect. Yet, with victory assured, Nixon delivered an acceptance speech so bitterly partisan that James Reston termed it "a jumble of distortions, misleading halftruths, and downright lies." By the end of August polls gave Nixon a 2 to 1 lead over McGovern, while the powerful Committee for the Re-election of the President (CRP) collected an estimated $40 million to finance the campaign. Throughout September the President remained quietly behind the scenes, permitting members of the administration to carry the Republican campaign across the nation. Even when Nixon ventured forth in October, McGovern could not move him beyond the motorcades, the fund-raising dinners, or the evening news shows. Newsmen who covered the Nixon campaign could discover no way to break through the shield erected around the President and his views. The press no more than McGovern could drive the President into any discussion of the nation's problems. The reason was clear. The unconcerned majority of the American people, Nixon understood correctly, desired no recital of the issues, much less a national debate.

The Republican party still experienced one potential embarrassment. In September a federal grand jury indicted two former White House aides—E. Howard Hunt and G. Gordon Liddy—plus five accomplices, on eight counts of stealing documents and bugging the Democratic headquarters at Washington's Watergate complex on June 17. Never before in the nation's history had White House aides been indicted for crime. The President and the Attorney General denied that anyone then employed in the administration was involved in the Watergate affair, but the fact that the accused had access to funds collected by the Nixon campaign organization continued to implicate the administration. Gradually it appeared from an accumulation of evidence that the Watergate raid was only part of an elaborate Republican attempt at disruption and sabotage to spread confusion throughout the Democratic campaign effort. This activity, it seemed, had extended to forging letters, seizing confidential files, disrupting schedules, and seeking information on the private lives of Democratic campaign workers. For some writers this evidence of wrongdoing was deeply alarming. Columnist Stewart Alsop (scarcely anti-Nixon) termed the Watergate affair the scariest event to occur in Washington since the days of Joseph McCarthy. *The Washington Post* editorialized on October 29 that the sabotage comprised "a sinister operation without precedent in the history of this nation." But every McGovern effort to capitalize on the Watergate affair proved ineffective, simply because most Americans favored the President and opposed any move to implicate him in wrongdoing.

Nixon's victory in November was as overwhelming as the polls predicted. His popular vote topped 60 percent; his 49 states (he lost only Massachusetts and the District of Columbia) gave him a strong 521 to 17 advantage in the electoral college. He carried New York City, the first Republican nominee to do so since Calvin Coolidge in 1924. He splintered the old New Deal coalition, breaking completely the traditional Democratic hold on the South. In the cities he gained half the blue-collar vote, the base of Democratic power since the 1930s. However, Nixon's victory was deceptive and assured few if any permanent gains for the Republican party. That only 55 percent of the American people bothered to vote demonstrated the President's failure to arouse any general enthusiasm. Nixon acquired much of the Wallace vote, but only because McGovern's New Politics had no appeal among low-income whites. The Republicans gained 12 seats in the House; they lost two in the Senate. But the President, having triumphed over-whelmingly even if his party did not, could look forward to four years of uncontested leadership.

WATERGATE AND THE NIXON RESIGNATION

For the Nixon administration—and for Americans generally—the Republican triumph of 1972 buried the Watergate issue beyond resurrection. *The Washington Post* reporters Carl Bernstein and Bob Woodward had disclosed CRP's secret funds, its eaves-dropping and bugging, its efforts at political espionage, but White House denials of wrongdoing sustained the public's disinterest. On January 8, 1973, Judge John J. Sirica of the U.S. District Court in Washington opened the trial of the "Watergate Seven." Soon five of the defendants, including former White House employee E. Howard Hunt, pleaded guilty to conspiracy, burglary, eavesdrop-ping, and bugging. Late in January the jury found the other two defendants—G. Gordon Liddy and James W. McCord, Jr.—guilty on all counts. To Judge Sirica the trial's failure to implicate the White House or the President's reelection committee suggested the presence of a massive cover-up. Already it was known that Jeb Stuart Magruder, deputy director of CRP, had instructed Liddy to establish a political intelligence operation, and that Hugh W. Sloan, Jr., a CRP finance officer, had turned over large sums of money to Liddy. Sloan still denied that he or any CRP official knew that Liddy had planned the Watergate break-in.

Sirica delayed the sentencing in the hope that one of the de-fendants would talk. Finally, in late March, Sirica announced that McCord, in a letter of March 19, had informed him that Nixon officials had brought pressure on all under trial to plead guilty and remain silent, that some defendants and witnesses had committed perjury at the trial, and that others, not identified, had been in-volved in the Watergate affair. McCord then informed Sam J. Er-vin, Jr. of North Carolina, chairman of the Senate's Watergate Committee, that former Attorney General John Mitchell, White House counsel John Dean III, White House staffer Charles Colson, and Magruder had either approved or personally knew of the

CRP's political espionage operations. Magruder and Dean—the latter convinced that the administration had designated him as the scapegoat in the coverup—implicated themselves as well as Mitchell and the President's two top White House aides, Haldeman and Ehrlichman.

As the Watergate disclosures began to mount Nixon, on April 17, admitted publicly for the first time that the scandal might reach into the White House. He declared that Dean had first informed him of a cover-up in March 21. Then, on April 30, in a major televison address, Nixon accepted full responsibility for the Watergate affair, but denied any personal involvement in either the break-in or the cover-up. Dean, he charged, had masterminded the cover-up and had kept him in the dark. When he discovered the facts, he said, he had ordered his own probe. There would be, he assured the nation, "no whitewash in the White House." The President accepted the resignations of Haldeman, Ehrlichman, Attorney General Richard Kleindienst, and Dean. He replaced Kleindienst with Elliot L. Richardson. Strangely, the President refused to condemn those around him whose alleged activities now endangered his presidency. He called Haldeman and Ehrlichman "two of the finest public servants it has been my privilege to know." For Nixon the escape from Watergate remained a matter of effective public relations.

In May the government lost its case against Daniel Ellsberg for his release of the Pentagon Papers. Late in April, Judge W. Matthew Byrne, who presided at the trial, announced that two members of the White House investigative unit—Hunt and Liddy—had managed the break-in of the office of Ellsberg's California psychiatrist, Dr. Lewis J. Fielding, during September 1971. On May 11 Judge Byrne declared a mistrial, thus freeing Ellsberg and his codefendant, Anthony Russo. To defend the White House against the accusation of improper conduct Nixon, on May 22, released a 4000-word statement to the press that explained that national security had demanded the establishment of the special intelligence unit and the authorized wiretapping. Those who conducted illegal activities without his knowledge, he said, may have "felt justified in engaging in specific activities that I would have disapproved had they been brought to my attention." Nixon insisted that the country distinguish matters of national security, which involved him, from Watergate.

That same month Ervin's Select Senate Committee opened its televised Watergate hearings. Through the following summer the committee heard a long succession of witnesses who revealed that CRP had been involved in burglary, bugging, spying, and a variety of "dirty tricks" to undermine the Democratic campaign of 1972. Nixon's own case rested on his often stated argument that he was innocent of the cover-up. Magruder's key testimony in June implicated CRP and the White House in the cover-up that began, he said, "that Saturday when we realized there was a break-in." Subsequent testimony revealed the pattern of payments to buy the silence of the Watergate burglars. Dean challenged the President's defense directly when he charged that the President knew of the cover-up almost from the beginning. Not until March 1973, when the President faced a Senate investigation, recalled Dean, did Nixon become concerned over Watergate. Dean declared that the President discussed clemency for the Watergate Seven and even a payment of $1 million to buy their silence. The testimony of McCord, Ehrlichman, Haldeman, and Mitchell failed to contradict Dean's accusations. But these men refused to implicate the President and thus prevented the Ervin committee from breaking the Watergate case.

For Nixon there was no escape; in July Alexander Butterfield, a former White House operations man, revealed that a secret White House electronics system had recorded all the office and telephone conversations of the President after its installation in the spring of 1971. To prepare the Justice Department's legal case against White House officials accused of wrongdoing, Attorney General Richardson had appointed Harvard law professor Archibald Cox. Cox immediately demanded nine tapes as necessary evidence for his staff. Claiming executive privilege, Nixon refused to release the tapes. Cox and the President's lawyers argued the validity of the subpoena before Judge Sirica's court; by October Cox had obtained two court rulings that upheld his right to the tapes. Nixon offered a compromise. When Cox rejected it, Nixon ordered him fired. Richardson and his deputy, William D. Ruckelshaus, refused to carry out the order and resigned. It was left for Robert Bork, the newly appointed Solicitor General, to remove Cox in the so-called "Saturday night massacre." Early in November Nixon named Leon Jaworski, a prominent Texas lawyer, as Watergate prosecutor.

Meanwhile disaster struck the Nixon administration from another direction. In August 1973, a federal grand jury in Baltimore began to investigate allegations that Vice-President Agnew, when governor of Maryland, had accepted kickbacks from contractors and businessmen. These charges raised questions of criminality and tax evasion. Agnew proclaimed his innocence as rumors of an eventual indictment spread through the capital. Finally, in October, amid denials of wrongdoing, the Vice-President resigned, accepting a $10,000 fine, a suspended sentence, and immunity from further criminal prosecution. Agnew's resignation, added to Cox' dismissal, brought a flood of telegrams into Washington demanding the President's impeachment. Nixon quickly turned over the subpoenaed tapes, but this action merely spurred demands for his removal. Almost two dozen House resolutions called for impeachment. The House Judiciary Committee began to prepare its case for impeachment; in December it appointed John M. Doar, a Republican lawyer who had served in the Justice Department under Robert Kennedy, to direct its investigation of charges against the President. Nixon struck back with Operaton Candor, in which he argued his case before appreciative audiences away from Washington. Again the effort faltered when the President admitted that one key White House tape had an 18-minute gap that experts later attributed to deliberate erasure. On December 6 Congressman Gerald R. Ford of Michigan became the new Vice-President of the United States. Both houses of Congress had approved the President's choice overwhelmingly. In a final gesture of Operation Candor the President released a massive financial statement to answer mounting allegations of irregularities in his personal finances. Gallup polls indicated a sharp drop in the President's support to 27 percent.

Despite Nixon's continued claims to innocence, the accumulating evidence of White House wrongdoing undermined the foundations of his presidency. Late in February 1974, the second Watergate grand jury, impaneled in April 1973, indicted seven White House officials on charges of covering up the Watergate burglary by destroying evidence, lying to investigators, buying silence, and offering clemency. Among the accused were Haldeman, Ehrlichman, Mitchell, and Colson. The jury not only delivered to Judge Sirica evidence of the President's role in the cover-up, but also revealed that it had, by a vote of 19 to 0, named Nixon an unindicted coconspirator in the cover-up. At the same time concurrent reports of the Internal Revenue Service and the special congressional investigative unit found the President some $432,000 shy in back taxes and interest for his four years in the White House. Shortly thereafter a House report indicated that federal expenditures on the President's San Clemente and Key Biscayne houses had reached $17.1 million. Even the White House admitted that over $200,000 went into home improvements.

Nixon continued to assure the nation that Jaworski had all the information he needed to conclude the Watergate investigation. But in April the Judiciary Committee voted unanimously to subpoena tapes of 42 presidential conversations. Nixon responded on April 30 by announcing on national television that he was delivering to the committee—and making available to the American people—transcripts of 31 of the 42 tapes, totaling 1200 pages. He hoped that this action would encourage his supporters, divide his critics, and shake the bipartisan unity of the Judiciary Committee. The gamble almost worked. Only by a narrow 20 to 18 vote did the committee remind the President that he had not complied with the committee's request. The transcripts did not implicate the President in the Watergate cover-up, but they revealed that the President had made no effort to stop the payments of hush money or examine the cover-up itself. It was equally clear that the President had encouraged his associates to keep information from the grand jury. In one segment Nixon, on March 22, 1973, told Mitchell, "I want you to stonewall it, plead the Fifth Amendment, cover up or anything else." Not once did the President condemn his associates for defying what should have been the standards of conduct in his administration. Even with the deletions of unprintable language, the document was massively self-incriminating. Eric Sevareid of CBS termed it "a moral indictment without known precedent in the story of American government." Even Republican leaders expressed public dismay over the quality of White House leadership. James D. St. Clair, who headed the President's legal staff, rested his defense on the claim that Nixon had acted only as an interested spectator. Nixon used every occasion to warn the country that the Watergate investigation endangered the presidency itself.

During July, St. Clair threatened to take Judge Sirica's ruling —which ordered the White House to turn over 64 tapes—to the Court of Appeals. Jaworski countered by moving the question directly to the Supreme Court. Later that month the Court, by a vote of 8 to 0, declared that the President could withhold no tapes that contained evidence required for a criminal trial. Recently appointed Justice William H. Rehnquist removed himself from the case because of his previous association with Attorney General Mitchell. Nixon promptly complied with the decision. What troubled the Judiciary Committee, meanwhile, was the search for the proper grounds for impeachment. In February the committee staff released a report, replete with English precedents, that named dereliction of public duty and abuse of presidential power, as well as criminality, indictable offenses. St. Clair argued that the President could be impeached only for serious criminal acts committed in his official capacity. Clearly the President's future rested on the extent of agreement among congressmen that obstruction of justice, misuse of power, and failure to prevent illegal actions by others were indeed impeachable offenses. The committee's decision in July to base its impeachment charges on a broad definition of impeachable offenses provoked outrage in the White House. Vice-President Ford observed that the anti-Nixon Democrats were using impeachment to reverse the national decision of 1972.

Subsequent White House efforts to hold House Republicans in line failed. Late in July in Judiciary Committee, in televised debate, voted its first article of impeachment, charging the President with obstruction of justice. Six Republicans joined 21 Democrats to create a 27 to 11 majority. Then, by a vote of 28 to 10, the Committee charged the President with misuse of power. A third article charged the President with disobeying House subpoenas. Even as the President looked to his friends in the Senate, his position collapsed. On August 5 he released transcripts of three June 23, 1972 conversations with Haldeman that revealed that he had used the CIA to stall an FBI investigation of Watergate. This terminated Nixon's two-year claim to innocence. The 10 Republican stalwarts on the House Judiciary Committee, joined by top House and Senate Republicans, now defected. On the evening of August 8, as his Senate minority evaporated, the President announced his resignation before a national television audience. "I have felt it was my duty," he said, " . . . to make every possible effort to complete the term of office to which you elected me. In the past few days . . . it has become evident to me that I no longer have a strong enough political base in the Congress to justify continuing that effort. . . . With the disappearance of that base, I now believe that the constitutional purpose has been served. . . . I shall resign the Presidency." On the following morning he delivered his one-sentence statement of resignation to the Secretary of State.

THE FORD PRESIDENCY

On August 9, at noon, Gerald R. Ford took the oath of office in the East Room of the White House. In the brief address that followed, he said: "I am acutely aware that you have not elected me as your President by your ballots. So I ask you to confirm me as your President with your prayers. . . . [O]ur long national nightmare is over. Our Constitution works. Our great republic is a government of laws and not of men." For the departing Nixon he added, "May our former President who brought peace to millions, find it for himself." What troubled many Washington observers was not the new President's promise of openness and candor; it was the Ford record itself. Throughout his 25 years in the House, Gerald Ford had consistently voted a narrow Republican line. His thousands of House votes revealed a persistent skepticism toward government action, devotion to military interests, hostility toward social protest, disinterest in civil rights, and approval of the war in Southeast Asia. "Forget the voting record," he admonished one critic. "The voting record reflects Grand Rapids." Yet, even as Vice-President, Ford had busied himself with political campaigning, not preparation for national leadership. Possessing neither the knowledge nor the desire to manage national affairs, he hoped as President to decentralize the decision-making process, moving power from the White House to the cabinet-level agencies. But, believing that the country wanted continuity and stability, Ford kept the Nixon staff only to find himself surrounded by councils and staffers who dominated his administration. Senators soon discovered that Ford was as inaccessible to their complaints as Nixon had been.

Ford's eventual choice for the vice-presidency—Governor Nelson A. Rockefeller of New York—was generally popular. For the first time in the nation's history both the President and the Vice-President had gained office without a national election. Ford's next major decision proved to be far more divisive. On Sunday, September 8, he announced that he had decided to grant former President Nixon a full pardon, both to heal the wounds of a troubled nation and to spare the former President and his family further suffering and public humiliation. Nixon, in accepting the pardon, admitted that he had made mistakes but denied that he was guilty of wrongdoing. Many were outraged over the President's action; some accused Ford of carrying out a secret deal. Others believed that the President had acted too soon—that the country had a right to know more about Nixon's role in Watergate. One critic lauded the expression of mercy, but recalled that "mercy without justice is favoritism." Ford's approval of Nixon's $850,000 request for the transition produced additional recriminations. By late September the President's rating in the Polls had dropped over 20 points from the 71 percent approval rating of August.

Ford inherited a declining economy troubled by double-digit inflation. During the first half of 1974, consumer prices rose at an annual rate of 12 percent to create the worst inflationary record in the country's peacetime history. Behind the inflation were major increases in federal spending, the rapid increase in world oil prices, a long drought and its effect on farm prices, and the final abandonment, in April 1974, of the Nixon controls on prices and wages. Production losses failed to offset the inflationary pressures. In September President Ford arranged a series of sessions with experts on food, agriculture, business, health, welfare, banking, housing, transportation, and economics. These sessions, designed to bring together leading spokesmen for a variety of approaches to the country's economic problems, culminated in an economic summit conference in Washington. Fiscalists—largely old-line liberals—

placed their emphasis on government spending and taxes to create jobs and purchasing power. Monetarists, led by Professor Milton Friedman of the University of Chicago, advocated the management of prices and business expansion through control of the money supply. Both approaches recognized the power of the federal government to manipulate the economy. Both groups focused on the overall forces moving the economy; both avoided the more precise factors that influenced prices and unemployment, such as price-fixing and the divergence in income among Americans. In Kansas City in October the President urged the American people to curtail inflation by ending waste and spending less—as if the decisions of government and the country's major institutions contributed nothing to the problem. Clearly the summit recommendations had added up to very little. *The Wall Street Journal* described Ford's first 100 days as "a makeshift team in search of a theme."

By early 1975 a crisis mood had overwhelmed the country. Joblessness had passed 7 percent, with predictions that by summer unemployment would be higher than at any time since the Great Depression. Experts predicted the biggest year for bankruptcies on record. The shock waves from the decline in automobile production, creating a 20 percent unemployment rate in the industry itself, reached hundreds of firms that held contracts with the major automobile manufacturers. Unfortunately, no recommendation could protect the interests of Americans equally. The President's chief economic advisers, Alan Greenspan, chairman of the Council of Economic Advisers, and Treasury Secretary William E. Simon, favored budget reductions and restraint of the money supply to control inflation. But a number of leading Democratic economists, concerned less with inflation than the state of the economy, prepared an alternative program for House Democrats that emphasized the need to increase purchasing power among low- and middle-income groups. Economist Arthur M. Okum advocated a body of tax incentives to encourage wage and price restraints.

Ultimately the President opted to fight the recession with a revival of the nation's purchasing power. He recommended an immediate rebate on 1974 taxes of $12 billion to individuals plus a $4 billion tax credit to encourage business construction and the purchase of new equipment. To reduce both the import of foreign oil and American oil consumption, the President recommended a higher tariff on overseas petroleum. The energy levies, he said, would underwrite an additional $16.5 billion reduction in federal taxes. The federal deficit for 1975 reached $35 billion; that for 1976 would approach $75 billion. Economists predicted that the President's program to cure the recession would unleash new inflationary pressures on the economy. Actually, the federal stimulants of 1975 halted the economy's downward course without increasing inflation. The government-inspired recovery brought benefits to business and labor. It scarcely touched the perennial stagflation. Unemployment continued at between 7 and 7.5 percent.

During the Ford presidency, the Vietnam war reached the dead end that critics had predicted for a decade. Saigon's final demise began with Nixon's cease-fire agreement of January 1973. This agreement, for which Secretary Kissinger received the Nobel Peace Prize, terminated the American phase of the ground war by providing for the return of all American prisoners in exchange for the withdrawal of all U.S. military personnel in 60 days. The cease-fire left the struggle where the Americans had found it 12 years earlier. Nothing that the United States had done in expending over $150 billion in Vietnam had diminished the goals of either the North or the South Vietnamese, who again faced each other in a conflict that knew no political or territorial bounds. As the open struggle for Cambodia continued into the spring of 1973, Nixon attempted to impose a cease-fire there by launching a massive air war in that country. In May a Gallup Poll revealed that 60 percent of the American people opposed the Cambodian bombing and that over 75 percent believed that the President should seek congressional approval before carrying out additional military action in Southeast Asia. Soon thereafter congressional majorities defied the administration's claims to primacy in all military matters by attaching, to more and more essential appropriation bills, riders phrased to restrict the use of federal funds in Cambodia. In July the administration capitulated. The House and Senate agreed to the President's proposal of a cutoff on August 15. That day the American struggle in Southeast Asia came to an end, sealing the fate of Cambodia.

As the Vietnam struggle continued without a direct American presence, the administration insisted that the United States was bound morally and politically to support Saigon with ample quantities of economic and military aid. Throughout the spring of 1975 the inexorable disasters in South Vietnam created a profound moral and intellectual crisis in Washington. Administration officials battled Congress into March and April for $722 million in military aid to save the South Vietnamese regime. What concerned the administration, however, was less the future of Saigon than the need to assure the world that the final tragedy of Indochina would not be the fault of the United States. In April the North Vietnamese closed in on Saigon while American officials struggled to avoid a decision. For so long had they suppressed intelligence that they could not accept the pervading evidences of doom. At the end they could save neither the tens of thousands of Vietnamese on the U.S. payroll, the billions of dollars in American equipment, nor the secret files left behind in the rush to the helicopters. Ambassador Graham Martin's final escape from the embassy roof symbolized the 12-year disaster. The administration still assumed no responsibility for what it and previous administrations had done. Kissinger simply assigned the problem to future historians. If the American people would demand no explanation of a disastrous policy at the moment of its collapse, they would not do so thereafter. For them Vietnam no longer mattered.

Many Republicans who acclaimed Ford for his decency and success in restoring some dignity to the presidential office did not regard him competent to win the 1976 election or to run the country for another four years. Still, no Republican moderate cared to challenge the President for the party's nomination. Ford's committed opposition came from the right in the person of former Governor Ronald Reagan of California; moderates understood clearly that a three-way contest would take more votes from the President than from Reagan. Ford, facing only Reagan, won his first five primaries. He lost to Reagan in North Carolina, but captured New York and Wisconsin. Then Reagon won overwhelmingly in Texas and moved on to victories in Indiana, Georgia, and Alabama. Ford quickly evened the race by taking Michigan. Despite additional losses, Ford managed to retain a narrow lead as Republicans prepared for their nominating convention in Kansas City. Anticipating a close ballot, the Reagan forces demanded that the President announce his choice for the vice-presidency before the voting began, just as Reagan had done in naming Senator Richard Schweiker of Pennsylvania. Ford objected and carried the convention on the issue, 1180 to 1069. This show of strength presaged Ford's first-ballot nomination by the narrowest margin of any Republican convention since 1912. Ford chose Senator Robert Dole of Kansas as his running mate.

Democrats again faced a Republican incumbent. But among those prepared to contest his reelections were Senators Birch Bayh of Indiana, Lloyd Bentsen of Texas, Henry Jackson of Washington, and Hubert Humphrey of Minnesota, former senator Fred Harris of Oklahoma, Congressman Morris Udall of Arizona, Governors Milton Shapp of Pennsylvania and George C. Wallace of Alabama, and the former governor of Georgia, Jimmy Carter. With his victory in the New Hampshire primary in March, Carter quickly established himself as the Democratic front-runner. Thereafter, in a series of primaries, he edged out Wallace, Jackson, and Udall, his strongest competitors. Latecomer Senator Frank Church of Idaho defeated Carter in Nebraska; Governor Jerry Brown of California, another late entry, took the Maryland Democratic primary. But further Carter victories in May and June prompted Wallace to retire from the race. Then, in mid-June, Mayor Richard Daley of Chicago, a powerful voice in the Democratic establishment, announced for Carter, as did Church, Udall, and Brown. New York's endorsement in July assured Carter a first-ballot nomination. In his acceptance speech Carter, a relative unknown, could declare that the American people were searching for new voices, new ideas, new leaders. For the vice-presidency he selected the popular Senator Walter Mondale of Minnesota.

Jimmy Carter's nomination was perhaps the most successful bootstrap operation in American political history. Unlike his predecessors, he was not the protégé of a party or an individual of influence. Carter had followed his graduation from the U.S. Naval Academy in 1947 with six years of active naval service. Returning to Georgia, he gradually converted his peanut farm at Plains into a sizable agribusiness. In 1962 he won a narrow election to the Georgia senate. He failed in his try for the governorship in 1966, but won easily four years later. Unknown outside Georgia, Carter began his uphill battle for the presidency in 1974, supported only by his family and a few Georgia friends. By 1976 he had begun to win where it mattered—in the media. He answered everyman's question; he smiled into everyman's camera. But few people knew him. Columnists agreed that Carter waged a brilliant primary campaign, but they could not agree on what the candidate said. Carter presented himself as an outsider, a fellow-suffering citizen who opposed the costs and inefficiencies of big government. "I have been accused of being an outsider," ran Carter's basic appeal. "I plead guilty. Unfortunately, the vast majority of Americans are also outsiders. We are not going to get changes by simply shifting around the same groups of insiders, the same tired old rhetoric, the same unkept promises. . . . The insiders have had their chances, and they have not delivered. Their time has run out." So tirelessly did Carter campaign against Washington that he compelled Ford to do the same. But when Carter moved from questions of honesty and public concern to the substantive issues confronting the nation, he invariably promised the unachievable—control of inflation and unemployment with a balanced budget and a host of new federal programs. In November he remained a puzzle, even to his supporters.

Ford countered Carter's appeal for new leadership by citing the achievements of his administration. But the final run for the presidency produced no new ideas, no ideological conflicts. Unable to recommend solutions for the problems that troubled most citizens—inflation, unemployment, taxes, and big government—both candidates simply avoided them. Even the three televised confrontations between Ford and Carter, and the one between Mondale and Dole, made no impact on the country's thought and revealed surprisingly little about the candidates. Troubled by a campaign that most Americans could not take seriously, 15 percent of potential voters remained undecided until a few days before the election. The results were close. Carter, capturing 50.4 percent of all votes cast, triumphed with a margin of 2 percent in an election that brought only 53 percent of eligible voters to the polls. The country had rejected an incumbent president for the first time in 44 years. Eventually Carter received 297 electoral votes to the President's 241. Carter scored heavily in the South, carrying all of the former

Confederate states except Virginia. In addition, he carried key
states such as New York, Massachusetts, Pennsylvania, Minnesota,
and Wisconsin. Except for Texas, he lost the entire West. Carter
carried 23 states and the District of Columbia, compared to 27 for
Ford. The Democratic majority in the Senate remained firm at 61;
changes in the House were insignificant. With both liberals and
conservatives going down in defeat, the congressional elections,
like the presidential vote itself, revealed no trend in public sentiment.

JIMMY CARTER: THE POLITICS OF RETREAT

President-elect Carter perceived long before inauguration day
in January 1977 that he had promised more than his administration
could attain. In his inaugural address he set forth no new dreams,
no redemptive schemes, but only a pledge to uphold the country's
values. During his campaign, the new President had demonstrated
a tough political shrewdness and an unusual capacity to manipulate
symbols. Again, on Inauguration Day, his walk down Pennsylvania
Avenue with his family offered symbolic reaffirmation of his promise to represent the American masses in Washington. The public
responded with an almost universal expression of warmth and
goodwill. But Carter soon discovered that even his minor campaign
promises were too divisive to arouse any general approval and too
contradictory to serve as a guide for strategy. His first official act
—to pardon the Vietnam draft dodgers—infuriated veterans and
families of the dead who believed that the President had gone too
far; it displeased deserters, many of whom had made major sacrifices before they deserted, who believed that he had not gone far
enough. Carter pleased only those directly affected or not affected
at all.

Many who took Carter's anti-Washington campaign seriously
found his cabinet appointments disillusioning; they revealed a clear
symmetry with the past. Most of the top members of his administration, representing the small universe of business and public life,
knew each other well, having met in corporate boardrooms or in
federal agencies. Together they held 30 corporate directorships.

Their average income in 1976 was $211,000. Carter's cabinet "outsiders" had accumulated 70 years on the federal payroll. Six had been members of the Kennedy-Johnson administrations. One wit noted that Carter had chosen the "junior varsity" of the New Frontier and had given them starting positions. None of Carter's New Frontiersmen had objected publicly to Vietnam, although later most of them acknowledged the mistakes of the 1960s. Zbigniew Brzezinski, the new national security adviser, had been in the vanguard of Vietnam defenders. Cyrus Vance, the new Secretary of State, had shared Robert McNamara's mindset as Deputy Secretary of Defense. Harold Brown, the new Secretary of Defense, was in charge of the Vietnam bombing. Joseph A. Califano, Jr., the new Secretary of HEW, was another of McNamara's prowar enthusiasts in the Pentagon.

Large Democratic majorities in Congress did not assure Carter any easy legislative victories. The balance of power in the federal government had tipped toward Congress under Gerald Ford; it would continue to do so under Carter. Few Democratic House members owed anything to the President, just as Carter owed little to them. What enhanced the independence of many young congressmen was the conviction that they commanded talent and knowledge equal to that of the executive branch. The preoccupation of the Senate with its privileges, entitlements, and independence was far stronger than its corporate conception of its effectiveness or popularity. Senators, generally assured of reelection, shared a loyalty to place, not to programs. Their sense of self-importance, not their allegiance to party, determined their response to White House directives. Their small numbers and six-year terms rendered them uniquely susceptible to lobbyist pressure. As one labor lobbyist phrased it, "You only need ten or fifteen guys with you to tear hell out of the Senate." It was not strange that Carter began his administration by concentrating on programs, such as government reorganization, that required little of Congress and the public.

In time the Carter administration prepared a succession of proposals that recognized many of the country's most pervading challenges. Invariably these proposals exposed deep divisions within the Congress and the electorate, compelling the President either to modify them beyond recognition or to withdraw them totally from public consideration. To limit crime in the United States, Carter had promised gun control; after 18 months in office he dropped the issue completely, despite the rising number of deaths from handguns. Carter proposed a health bill designed to limit increases in hospital costs to 9 percent a year; after a long delay, Congress rejected the limitation completely. Meanwhile the President discovered that a national health program exceeded the capacity of government to command the resources or to confront the special interests of the health industry. In August 1977 the President unveiled a comprehensive welfare program to guarantee a family of four an income of $4200 a year and to create 1.4 million public service jobs at generally minimum wages. Against the complex and deeply ingrained challenges of welfare reform, the Congress could not move at all. Tax reform remained equally elusive. Having promised a war against unemployment, the President accepted, with deep reluctance, the goal of 4 percent unemployment in five years, but only if the goal would not be inflationary. Candidate Carter promised the country a balanced budget by 1980; during his first year in office he admitted that the goal was unachievable. So hesitant was the President's support for the cities and the poor that he antagonized his needed black constituents. Disturbed by this persistent record of retreat, critics questioned the administration's lack of coordination with congressional leaders. Yet the central issues in governmental performance were not technique and procedure, but the country's needs and interests.

Carter made energy the critical test of his leadership. "Our decision about energy," he informed his national television audience on the evening of April 18, 1977 "will test the character of the American people and the ability of the President and the Congress to govern this nation. This difficult effort will be the 'moral equivalent of war. . . .' " Two nights later the President placed his energy program before Congress—a surprisingly limited program that demanded little of industry or the public. The House, operating under the astute guidance of Speaker Tip O'Neill of Massachusetts, passed the measure almost intact. As the momentum slowed, the oil and gas lobbies closed in on the Senate. While Louisiana's Russell Long took up the cause of natural gas deregulation, Senate committees gutted various portions of the President's energy package. Proadministration forces deserted the struggle for the original bill and, with the President, worked for a compromise. On occasion the impatient administration turned on the consumer advocates in the Senate for delaying action. Not until May 1978 did the Senate approve a compromise measure on natural gas that would lift federal controls on the price of newly produced gas by 1985. On the President's key proposal—a tax on crude oil—Congress was still not prepared to act. The challenge to Congress and the President lay not in the immediate depletion of oil resources, but in the prospect that, by 1985, the world demand for oil, unless drastically reduced, would outstrip world production and send prices skyrocketing. That eventuality would create an international scramble for oil, strain the international trade balance structure, enhance the power of the oil-producing Arab states, stoke the inflation, and threaten the world with economic collapse. How the sprawling cities of the United States would survive such energy restraints was scarcely predictable.

What concerned Americans during the Carter presidency was the state of the economy. The astonishing rise in the GNP between 1946 and 1978 was more and more a measure of inflation. In 1946 dollars the GNP in the latter year stood at $596 billion instead of the $1,993 billion in current dollars. The 47 percent inflation of the 1970s almost wiped out the 52 percent gain in median family income. A four-member family that lived in reasonable comfort on $16,600 in 1971 required $27,500 to live equally well in 1978. Inflation in the United States, again exceeding an annual rate of 8 percent, had overtaken that of other industrial nations. The widespread invasion of women into the job market permitted some working families to maintain their living standards. For others a house, a new car, a vacation trip, or a college education for their children had become unaffordable.

The heavy demand that sustained the country's prosperity against the depressing effect of inflation required huge annual increases in the nation's public and private indebtedness. Federal spending in 1978 exceeded that of the previous year by 13 percent. With the economy at or near the top of the business cycle, the deficit reached $65 billion. The new Carter budget, unveiled in

January 1978, would push federal expenditures for fiscal 1979 to
$500 billion, with another projected deficit of $60 billion. At the
same time, the rapid expansion of the money supply between 1975
and 1977 supported almost unprecedented levels of borrowing.
The flow of credit into the economy pushed the total governmental,
business, and private indebtedness to $3 trillion. The farm debt
reached $120 billion in 1977, an increase of $17 billion over the
previous year. Some analysts feared that consumer indebtedness,
increasing at the rate of about $4 billion a month, had reached its
outer limits. The inflated economy underwrote high business
profits and distributed prosperity among those who needed it the
least. Most Americans could discover no gains in fiscal policies that
produced inflation at a faster rate than benefits in the form of
increased wages and additional employment. Early in 1978, when
the economy had experienced three years of recovery, general
unemployment stood at 7 percent. For blacks the 14.5 percent
unemployment was as high as at any time in 30 years. Almost 40
percent of teenage blacks lacked jobs, as did 14.7 percent of teenage whites. Inflationary policies designed to sustain prosperity had
done little for the nation's structural unemployment.

What helped to prolong the country's inflation amid inadequate incomes and widespread unemployment was the power of
large, special-interest groups that controlled huge shares of the
national income without returning an equal amount of productivity. The giant industries, facing little price competition and
wielding an influence over the political process that others could
not match, made little effort to perform efficiently and at minimum
cost. Hospitals, operating without cost restraints, increased their
charges after 1970 by 15 percent a year, twice the rate of prices
generally. Physicians' fees, outpacing inflation by 80 percent, gave
doctors a median income in 1978 of $63,000. Reaping large profits
from a shared market, industrialists neglected to match the performance of foreign competitors. In some industries the loss of
competitiveness was disastrous. It threatened the existence of the
nation's maritime industry; not even federal subsidies could keep
some fleets in operation. It compelled the steel industry to seek
restrictions on steel imports. Confronted with business powerful
enough to push any additional costs to the buying public, the large

unions consistently demanded and received annual wage increases of 8 percent, both to offset price increases and to share the gains in productivity. Actually annual productivity gains in the United States were the lowest among all the major industrial nations. Even as the steel industry forced restrictions on steel imports, it announced extensive wage and price increases. It was not strange that labor supported the demands of industry in its pursuit of special favors from government in the form of subsidies, appropriations, tax benefits, or import quotas. That industry and labor succeeded in pushing wages and prices upward, despite widespread economic stagnation, demonstrated their power over the market, the government, and the general public.

Government costs, reflecting the power of those who determined them, rose much more rapidly than personal income. The American people in the 1970s paid almost 40 percent of their incomes to government at all levels in the form of taxes. So powerful was the federal bureaucracy that neither Congress nor the President cared to contest its demands. Analysts estimated federal salaries at 15 to 20 percent higher than comparable salaries elsewhere in the economy. The average annual salary of government employees in Washington exceeded $20,000. President Carter, under bureaucratic pressure, deserted his earlier promise to reduce executive costs. His White House staff—the largest on record—had 50 members, many of them young, whose salaries were more than $40,000 a year. The Postal Service, one of the largest business operations in the country, had an annual budget of $17 billion, almost 1 percent of the GNP. At least 85 percent of that budget went into the payroll of some 700,000 employees whose incomes were one-third above those prevailing in private industry. Pensions of federal officials were larger than those in the private sector; these benefits, moreover, required shorter length-of-service requirements and included cost-of-living escalators. Whatever the size, efficiency, and need of the huge bureaucracy, the pressures that maintained it were enormous. Aside from services, approximately one-third of all Americans derived their personal income from some federal dispensation—Social Security, welfare payments, salaries, contracts, unemployment compensation, or other benefits. Constituents who reaped the gains of regulation were so numerous that every effort at regulatory reform faced a massive assault from businesses that feared open competition.

Throughout his first 16 months in office, President Carter refused to enter the inflation battle. Finally, in April 1978, unable to escape the issue any longer, he proposed a wage freeze for federal executives and a 5.5 percent limit on raises for federal white collar employees. He threatened to veto any bills that exceeded his budget. The President appealed to industry and labor to hold their wage and price increases below the averages of the previous two years. He assigned the task of conferring with business and labor leaders to Robert S. Strauss, his trade representative, who now became his special counselor on inflation. Even optimists doubted that voluntary controls would reduce inflation by more than half of one percentage point a year. What disturbed economic conservatives was the President's focus on business and labor. Economist Milton Friedman observed: "Only government produces inflation and only government can reduce inflation, since only government possesses a printing press (or its equivalent) on which to turn out those colored pieces of paper we call money." Tighter fiscal policies, the administration feared, might set off a recession. The persistence of inflation and unemployment, the huge federal deficits, and the failure of Congress to act on energy convinced many Americans and foreigners that the government was incompetent to discharge its public responsibilities.

THE SEARCH FOR A POST-VIETNAM ROLE

Carter, like his predecessors, attempted to escape the burdens of political decision by pursuing the easier rewards of leadership in the realm of foreign affairs. Unfortunately for Carter, the pursuit presaged few triumphs. In part, the limitations on his capacity to perform in the international realm lay at home, where the widely shared fears and ambitions that had created the "imperial presidency" of the Johnson-Nixon years no longer existed. Congress, moreover, had circumscribed the President's freedom in the external realm with a myriad of restrictions. Abroad, the limitations on presidential leadership were even more profound. That comparatively simple Cold War environment in which power was the essence of policy had evaporated years earlier. With its disappearance, the nation's authority had similarly receded. For more than a decade Washington had perpetuated the notion of effective global leadership, based on strength and the will to use it, by fighting in Vietnam. But in that struggle the American commitment to resist communism in all of its forms reached a dead end. After Saigon's fall in 1975, the United States remained the world's leading power, but now the troublesome issues that captured the headlines challenged few traditional American interests and thus defied the exertion of will. The United States had reached the stage where it could neither admit that what happened abroad was not its concern nor act effectively when it did.

Undaunted by the absence of any clear consensus regarding America's proper post-Vietnam role, Carter set out to rebuild both the country's international reputation and a foreign policy consensus at home that would restore the primacy of the White House in the realm of foreign affairs. The President hoped to construct this new consensus around two large groups that Henry Kissinger had alienated—those who objected to the former secretary's amoral realism in his attitude toward the repressive behavior of certain countries aligned with the United States, and those who believed that the former secretary had given away too much to the Russians in his quest for détente. For Carter the issue that would build public support and reestablish America's global leadership was that of human rights. The issue was ideal; it would permit him to reinstitute both a moral tone for American intentions and the occasion for admonishing the Soviet Union. It would require neither a heavy expenditure of money nor an intricate and taxing foreign policy.

Carter's human rights campaign began early. "Because we are free," he declared in his inaugural address, "we can never be indifferent to the fate of freedom elsewhere." Thereafter the human rights theme pervaded the administration's pronouncements on foreign policy. Few questioned the President's sincerity; some wondered about his humility and sense of proportion. One British critic wondered "just how many countries [the President] wanted to govern." Analysts failed to understand how the President intended to reconcile his idealistic objectives, which concerned the internal conditions in other countries, with the more conventional requirements of foreign policy. In its formulation of goals the administration carried a greater obligation to the country's political, economic, and security interests than to human rights. Whatever the repressive nature of the regimes of South Korea, the Philippines, and Iran, for example, American economic and military interests rendered all three governments too important to permit Washington the luxury of altering its established relationships with them. In his address before the University of Georgia Law School in April 1977, Secretary of State Vance recognized the limitations of any human rights policy. American objectives, he said, would of necessity be circumscribed by the conflict of commitments, by the willingness of other governments to tolerate outside investigation, by the prospects of effective action, and by the realization that violence or the withdrawal of aid could result in loss instead of gain for human rights. Such acknowledged limitations left little room for major human rights initiatives.

Some Americans warned the administration against even the appearance of an intention to link the normalization of U.S. relations with the USSR to changes in the Soviet system. Yet, during its first weeks in office, the Carter administration issued statements criticizing the governments of Russia and Czechoslovakia for harrassing and intimidating citizens who attempted to exercise their right of protest. In February 1977 Carter responded to a letter from the noted Russian dissident, Andrei Sakharov, with a well-publicized letter of his own. In March he invited another Soviet dissident, Vladimir Bukovsky, to the White House. Soviet leaders expressed anger at the President's behavior. Even Eastern European leaders accused the administration of interfering in the internal affairs of other nations. Critics reminded the State Department that statements aimed at the Soviet Union would endanger the ongoing strategic arms negotiations without achieving anything for human rights. Vance replied that the administration would divorce the issue of human rights from its efforts to reach an arms agreement with the Kremlin; each question, he assured reporters, would be discussed on its own merits. It was not clear that the Kremlin would acknowledge such a separation.

If Carter's human rights crusade, despite its general popularity, permitted few changes in the substantive performance of American policy, the President's relaxed attitude toward the countries of Asia, Africa, and Latin America encouraged several major reversals of policy. "Being confident of our own future," the President declared at Notre Dame University in May 1977, "we are now free of that inordinate fear of communism which once led us to embrace any dictator who joined us in that fear." In office Carter quickly reversed the previous administration's policies toward Vietnam; in 1977, with American approval, Vietnam entered the United Nation. Thereafter the movement toward the normalization of relations with Vietnam began to drift, as did U.S. policy generally toward East and Southeast Asia. The reasons were obvious enough. Americans hoped to avoid any further military involvements in the Far East. Moreover, they could discover no clear U.S. interests in post-Vietnam Asia. Former anti-Communist policies, which found their logical expression in military alliances and defense commitments, no longer had any discernible purpose. The ongoing war in Southeast Asia between Vietnam and Cambodia, as well as the Sino-Soviet rivalry over the outcome of that struggle, destroyed whatever illusions of Communist unity still remained. So marked was the deterioration of Sino-Vietnamese relations over Cambodia that during the spring of 1978 Vietnam began to expel its Chinese residents. Thousands arrived at the border, often wounded or beaten and usually without money or personal belongings. Peking warned Hanoi that it would "bear full responsibility for all the consequences arising from these unwarranted measures." Unable to base its Asian policies on past ideological affinities, the Carter administration had no choice but to recognize the multipolarity of Asian politics and link its future purposes to Communist and non-Communist countries alike.

What sustained the ambivalence in U.S. policies toward Asia was the still fluid nature of this country's relationship to China. Whereas congressional supporters of the Republic of China opposed any diminution of the American commitment to Taiwan's welfare and security, the Peking regime insisted that the establishment of full diplomatic relations would require the severance of all U.S. diplomatic ties with Taiwan, the abrogation of the mutual defense treaty with the Taipei government, and the withdrawal of all remaining American troops from the island. In Peking during May 1978, national security adviser Brzezinski assured Chinese leaders that the United States favored full diplomatic relations with the mainland, although it was not certain that the administration was prepared to meet Peking's conditions. Brzezinski reminded his Chinese hosts that the United States and China shared an interest in maintaining the stability of Asia. In Washington the administration announced that this country would sell airborne geological surveying equipment to China that it had withheld from the Soviet Union.

Elsewhere in the Third World the Carter administration revealed the same nonideological innovation. When Washington accompanied its annual offer of $50 million in military aid to Brazil with a report on the status of human rights in that country, the Brazilian government rejected the offer. Argentina, Uruguay, El Salvador, and Guatemala followed Brazil's lead. Under previous administrations these dictatorships, despite their known reliance on terrorism and torture, had flourished with American aid. Now, angered by Carter's outspoken human rights statements, they rejected credits totaling $74 million. The changed relationship mattered little; American military support added nothing essential either to Latin American security or to that of the United States. Meanwhile, the new President announced his intention to normalize relations with Cuba. Rejecting policies in Africa based on anti-Sovietism alone, the administration refused to counter the previous Sovet presence in Somalia or the heavy 1977 shipments of Soviet arms to Ethiopia.

Nowhere did the prospects for innovative American leadership seem more propitious than in the Middle East. Both Arabs and Israelis had grown weary of their perennial quarrel; any breakdown in the peace, Washington understood, would again threaten the flow of oil into the West and invite another Soviet-American confrontation. However, Secretary Vance discovered quickly on his trip to the Middle East in February 1977 that both Egyptian and Israeli positions remained as uncompromising as ever. Israel, its leaders warned, would never return to the boundaries that existed before the 1967 war; Egyptian officials retorted that they would not surrender "a single inch of Arab land." Egypt supported Palestinian demands for an independent Palestine state; Israel offered no more than Palestinian home rule under Israeli jurisdiction. In pursuit of victory by diplomatic means, Middle Eastern leaders streamed into Washington to denounce every suggestion of compromise. On one occasion the President confessed to White House visitors: "I doubt that any foreign negotiating effort has been attempted that is more complicated, more thankless and more frustrating." Carter's open approach to Middle Eastern diplomacy, designed to maximize this country's leadership role, captured the headlines and encouraged a series of major media events. Both Egyptian President Anwar el-Sadat and Israeli Prime Minister Menahem Begin scored well on television and in the press during visits to the United States. The effort gained little; a settlement required a genuine diplomatic confrontation between the contestants, and not the approval of Washington.

Unfortunately the feasibility—even the acceptability—of the administration's flexible posture toward Asia, Africa, Middle East, and Latin America hinged on the status of U.S.-Soviet relations. Both Carter and many of his top advisers had joined David Rockefeller's Trilateral Commission, which accused Kissinger of overemphasizing the importance of Soviet-American relations to the detriment of this country's relations with western Europe and Japan. In accordance with the Trilateral approach, Carter, during his first week in office, dispatched Vice-President Walter Mondale to western Europe and Japan to outline the new administration's foreign policy intentions. But no less than Kissinger could Carter ignore the critical importance of the USSR to American foreign policy. On matters of Russia, moreover, the new President faced a seriously divided nation. There was no agreement on whether U.S. policy toward Russia should emphasize relaxation and agreement on arms control or continued confrontation with Soviet and non-Soviet communism as a scarcely diminished threat to Western society.

Troubled by the persistent buildup of Soviet military power after 1965, a group of former generals, admirals, State Department officials, and academicians formed the Committee on the Present Danger in October 1976. The committee argued that the Soviet drive for dominance, based on unparalleled military preparations, required a higher level of American expenditure for defense. At the same time a government panel, headed by Professor Richard Pipes of Harvard University, concluded an intelligence estimate of Soviet global strategy with the warning that the Soviets based their planning on the assumption that they could win a limited nuclear war, destroying American society totally while losing no more than 20 million Russians. Critics of détente reminded the country that Russia was not merely another state, or even a classic despotism. "It has," wrote columnist George F. Will in *Newsweek,* "the implacable dynamism of a state permanently waging war on human nature, pulverizing and impoverishing civil society to satisfy militarist ravenousness."

Other Soviet watchers questioned the assumption that Russia was both confidently and aggressively contemplating war. Why, they wondered, should the Soviets assume that they would suffer less than the West in a nuclear war? G.B. Kistiakowsky, once security adviser to President Eisenhower, wrote in *The New York Times Magazine* on November 27, 1977: "It is difficult to regard these doomsday scenarios as anything more than baseless nightmares." Some observers doubted that Soviet preparedness necessarily reflected a Soviet aggressiveness. They argued that the Soviet military expenditure was designed largely to sanctify Russia's status as a global power, not to wage aggressive war. Soviet expert George F. Kennan observed that countries seldom provoked war, even when they could do so successfully, without cause. "Normally," he declared in an interview in May 1978, "people have gone to war for a purpose, and if they didn't have a purpose, they didn't do it. And I don't see the purpose, from the standpoint of the Soviet Government. It would set up disarray in Western Europe, and that would unquestionably lead to disarray in Eastern Europe as well. And that's the last thing they want."

During its first year in office the Carter administration adopted a relaxed view toward Soviet power and policy. Moderate voices in Washington emphasized the continuing search for a SALT agreement and the hopes for improved Soviet-American relations. Viewing the future with confidence, the President, in June 1977, announced his decision to abandon the continued production of the B-1 bomber, regarded by many essential for the country's long-range nuclear defense strategy. The President preferred the cruise missile as an air-to-ground delivery system. Republican leaders in Congress criticized the President for placing major reliance on sea-based missiles. General Robert J. Dixon, chief of the Air Force's Tactical Air Command, warned in April 1978 of a growing numerical gap between Soviet and American air power. Unless the President reversed the trend, he predicted that the USSR would shortly overcome the qualitative edge in American fighter forces. Meanwhile, in March, Carter stunned NATO leaders when he announced a delay in the production of the neutron bomb, a high-radiation weapon regarded especially ideal for countering massive tank assaults. West German officials, disturbed by NATO's numerical deficiency in conventional forces, had pushed the neutron bomb as a needed deterrent against a Soviet invasion. Europeans, joined by Republican and Democratic hardliners, attacked the decision as a unilateral concession to the Soviets. Defense had again become a major issue in American politics.

What exacerbated the defense issue was the concomitant charge that weakness was leading to a loss of national will. Such assumptions underlay the long, acrimonious national debate on the 1977 Panama Canal treaties before the Senate's approval in April 1978. At issue was not the control of the Canal, but the alleged decline of America's global stature. A *New Yorker* cartoon illustrated the central issue. Two men are standing at a bar, one saying to the other, "What's wrong with me? For thirty years I never gave a thought to the Panama Canal. Now I can't live without it." Some treaty opponents feared that the Panamians, once in control of the Canal, would not operate it efficiently or fairly. Others doubted that the treaties guaranteed American naval access to the waterway in time of crisis. But what above all sustained the condemnation of the treaties was the conviction that the Canal, as a remarkable engineering triumph managed successfully by the United States for over 60 years, was symbolic of American power. For that reason any effort to negotiate the Canal away by treaty under the threat of violence and sabotage was ignominious in the extreme and further evidence of the nation's deterioration as a world power.

Amid domestic ruminations about the nation's failure of nerve, the expanding Soviet-Cuban presence in Africa could only embarrass the administration and embitter U.S.-Soviet relations. During the spring of 1978, State Department officials charged Cuban leader Fidel Castro with maintaining 37,000 military personnel in 20 African countries. In March the Ethiopian army, directed by Russian generals and spearheaded by Soviet-equipped Cuban shock troops, destroyed what remained of Somalian resistance and took possession of the contested Ogaden Desert region. By May that war had entered the rebel province of Eritrea, with its long frontage on the Red Sea. Late that month Katanga rebels, who had fled to Angola during the Congo's civil war of the early 1960s, invaded Zaire's Shaba Province and massacred numerous Africans and Europeans in the rich mining town of Kolwezi. President Carter, despite Castro's repeated denials, claimed proof that Cuban forces in Angola had trained the rebels. Brzezinski, interviewed on NBC's "Meet the Press," placed responsibility for the Shaba invasion also on the Sovet Union. Such Soviet behavior, he said, was not "compatible with what was once called the code of detente." "I do not believe," he added, "that this kind of Soviet-Cuban involvement ought to be cost free." President Carter invited European leaders to share America's concern for Africa. French and Belgian paratroopers rescued the surviving whites in Kolwezi and drove the rebels back into Angola. Shortly thereafter, U.S. Air Force planes transported Moroccan occupation forces into Shaba. Washington, complained Carter, could not do more.

Finally, the President used the occasion of his Annapolis address in June to accuse Soviet leaders of waging an "aggressive struggle for political advantage" in Africa and elsewhere. His challenge was blunt. "The Soviet Union," he declared, "can choose either confrontation or cooperation. The United States is adequately prepared to meet either choice." He acknowledged that the Kremlin was negotiating in good faith on nuclear arms limitations, but charged the Soviet with gross human rights violations. After ridiculing the Soviet economy for its lack of productivity, he boasted that the United States enjoyed not only a higher national product, but also a political system admired throughout the world. Many in Washington scarcely concealed their satisfaction at the President's tough words. "We are coming out of the trough," said one high official. "Vietnam is behind us." The administration, it seemed, had finally assumed its proper post-Vietnam posture. The Soviet response was bitter. Tass, the Soviet news agency, warned the President that his tough line endangered the gains of previous years as well as the arms limitation talks. Those Americans who favored confrontation and rivalry, concluded *Pravda,* were gaining the upper hand in Washington.

Critics challenged the fears that underwrote the new toughness. They reminded the country that Britain, France, Portugal, Belgium, Italy, and Spain had abandoned their respective possessions in Africa because they found them economically unprofitable and impossible to govern. How others could succeed where the Europeans had failed was not clear. It seemed incredible that African countries that had sought independence for so long would willingly become puppets of Cuba or the Soviet Union. Most Africans could detect nothing objectionable in Soviet behavior; the Russians and Cubans had gone only where they were invited. "[L]et both sides, imperialists and dependents," advised columnist Jonathan Power, "find out for themselves what the cost is." When New York Senator Daniel Moynihan and Former Secretary Kissinger charged that the United States should not have permitted the Cubans to enter Ethiopia, *The New York Times* editorialized: "One man says threaten anything, no matter what the chances of making good on the threat. The other says never mind the particular stakes or possibilities, in geopolitics everything is tied to everything else. . . . There, we submit, walks the ghost of Vietnam. . . . Whatever the stakes on the ground, or the possibilities, for geopolitical reasons Hanoi had to be stopped. . . . To resurrect that logic against a President who seeks new techniques for applying American influence around the world is a dangerous game indeed." Far better, said the *Times,* to portray the risks and costs to Moscow. Experience suggested that the Kremlin would be no more successful than Washington had been in converting Ethiopia into a bulwark against anything.

GOVERNMENT WITHOUT CONSENSUS

What troubled American society in the 1970s was not the

absence of scientific and practical knowledge. For more than a decade the country's most prestigious newspapers and magazines had delineated the inadequacies of the nation's performance without equivocation. Democracy assumed some relationship between the combined intelligence and virtue of its citizens and the behavior of government. If the Carter presidency, like those that preceded it, failed to meet the challenges of the times, the answer, perhaps, lay less in the quality of leadership than in the possibility that the country as a whole was not convinced that the work of government required doing. But governmental processes continue whatever the knowledge or concern of the public. Legislative decisions are no demonstration of authentic popular rule. Throughout the country's history men of power and influence repeatedly gained the allegiance of congressional majorities for the most narrow of purposes. But on matters of major significance, those that demanded a potentially high price of the electorate, national policy required a broad accord known as *consensus*. In facing problems of national consequence, no government could function without it. As Congressman John B. Anderson of Illinois once observed, "Government simply can't direct a society that doesn't know where it wants to go."

Except in scattered moments of great crisis, American society has functioned in the absence of that consensus. During only two periods of this country's history did a national consensus clarify the public will on matters of broad intent. One was the American Civil War; the other was the Great Depression. John Dewey, the noted American philosopher, once observed that the American reality was not consensus or commonality, but pluralism. The American public comprised countless publics that had little in common. The fragmentation ran through the entire population, separating rich from poor, the skilled from the unskilled, the educated from the uneducated, urban dwellers from farmers, those who cherished the ideal of hard work from those without hope. The complexities of modern life merely magnified those divisions. New culture patterns and life-styles accentuated the pluralism. No less so did the demands of special interest groups, which favored their own brands of liberty, equality, and justice. At no time in the postwar era could Americans agree on the status of society. Some saw their cup half full; others saw it half empty. Some found everything the same;

The 1970s: A Crisis in Leadership 303

others perceived vast, disturbing changes in American civilization.

Not one issue before the American people—not even inflation and unemployment, which impinged directly on the public's economic well-being—created the necessary consensus on a proper national response. The challenges of the 1970s assumed too many forms, remaining for most Americans a bundle of abstractions of no immediate concern. Beyond inflation and unemployment, the threats to American society embraced matters that scarcely touched the lives of most people. The energy debate had less to do with technology, exploration, and conservation than with the protection of individual and group interests under the pressure of contemplated, not immediate, shortages. The potential price for environmental reconstruction in increased taxes, public restraints, and reduced standards of living appeared disporportionate to the capacity of the average American to tolerate social ills and a slowly diminishing environment. The interests that mattered were narrow. "I can't remember a time in Washington," observed Meg Greenfield in an April 1978, issue of *Newsweek,* "when interest-group issues and politics so dominated events. And every day the units of protest and concern seem to be subdividing into even smaller and more specialized groupings. . . . " The decline of the parties as purveyors of national issues simply reflected the pulverization of the electorate into small, competing interest groups.

Congress passed legislation in profusion, but much of it served the public only coincidentally, if at all. Issues of major importance remained almost as untouchable as the Milky Way. What divided the people and negated its effectiveness would, in no lesser measure, create confusion in government. One Democratic Congressman phrased the problem: "There is no way you're going to get a consensus in the House when you don't have a consensus in the country." Politicians, performing outside a recognizable national purpose, embraced or dodged issues in a manner best calculated to guarantee reelection. For most members of Congress the problem of winning had little relationship to the performance of Congress itself. Declared one member of the House, "I don't care what my district thinks of Congress as long as it likes me." Whatever their contributions to the nation's welfare, House and Senate members had little difficulty in maintaining the support of their constituents.

To remain in office, most public officials maintained a low profile, avoiding issues that might damage their support among leading constituents. It was the absence of public concern for national issues —or concern for only one issue—that produced disillusionment among politicians who attempted to confront the long-term challenges to American society.

Democracy suffers its first serious loss when candidates compete for power, not to achieve specific goals, but as an end in itself. People might still retain the right to choose in terms of the personal qualities of the candidates, but their choice has no meaning in terms of the substance of policies. Elections determined who held office; they did not determine the course of national policy. Thus it was not strange that many who voted cared little who won, or that half of the citizenry did not bother to vote at all. The percentage of Americans who went to the polls in presidential elections declined steadily after midcentury and, in 1976, reached the smallest proportion since 1948. Theodore White explained this attitude of resignation in the electorate: "Something in this turn of time had made Americans feel that their votes were unconnected with the control they should have over their lives. . . . 'Alienation' was the fashionable word for the vague feeling. What it meant was that . . . you had lost the right to vote on when your son should be drafted, and where he should be sent to fight. Most of the major problems that affected 'you'—from taxes to smog, from busing to war—you could not reach by voting for anyone."

In the absence of consensus to guide them, both Congress and the executive responded most acutely to those with high expectations who were organized to define and defend their policy preferences. Often national decisions emerged from compromises worked out among interest groups that appeared to have special legitimacy. Consensus became, by definition, not general agreement on national needs, but agreement among those in positions of power who established national policy with a minimum of public involvement and controversy. The ease whereby federal officials and the spokespersons of industry and labor arrived at basic decisions suggested the existence of a broad mutual interest among them. Seldom did a congressional majority choose to oppose such organized power. What underwrote the widespread public acceptance of private or corporate influences on congressional and bureaucratic decisions was the fact that the benefits, whatever their magnitude, were always specific, whereas the costs to society were distributed so widely that often they comprised no burden at all. If the chief goals of most Americans remained convenience, comfort, and tranquility, it was not strange that they preferred the prevailing tendencies in national life to costly forms of social and economic restraint. Public wrath focused on those whose policy proposals threatened daily routines or job security.

Only a sense of common purpose and urgency could counter the dominant moods of satisfaction, complacency, and hopelessness that sustained the power of organized minorities in American life. There could be no general public—for the Founding Fathers the essential element in a democratic order—without the willing submergence of the most narrow and potentially destructive personal and corporate ambitions to a broad concern for society as a whole. For Russian exile Aleksandr Solzenhitsyn, speaking at Harvard University in June 1978, the major defect in American life was the tendency of citizens to be bound only by law, not by conscience or morality. "One almost never sees voluntary self-restraint," he said. "Everybody operates at the extreme limit of the legal framework." President Carter recognized the problem when he admonished the nation: "We favor sacrifice, so long as someone else goes first. We want to abolish tax loopholes, unless it's our loophole. We denounce special interests, except for our own." But Carter as President did little to encourage self-restraint as he repeatedly compromised national purposes to satisfy constituent pressures, yielding to their claims, group by group. Countless Americans, having lost confidence in the capacity of such unpolitical conduct to deal effectively with matters of general concern, such as energy and inflation, developed "a looter's mentality" to get what they could while there was yet time. Those unable to protect their interests simply discounted the government's commitment to their welfare.

Any public effective enough to direct government toward some national goal could exist only as some politician created it. The public of the media and the pollsters was not a political body; it had neither a voice nor an institution through which it could act. "The making and remaking of a genuine public, as distinct from the phantom public of the media," wrote British journalist Henry Fairlie in *Harper's* in December 1977, "is the highest task of the politician, whether his constituency is a district or a state or the country." Political leadership alone could forge a collection of individuals with many special concerns into a civic entity that could act in behalf of public purposes. But a politician, to be effective, required some confidence in his or her leadership role, and a badly splintered public offered no assurance of adequate support. Benjamin Barber once defined the necessary role of the public in a functioning democracy: "It is no good for us to go looking for leaders; we must first rediscover citizens. It will not help to indict the faceless system if we are without common purpose that can be used to challenge facelessness and turn systems back into servants. If America is to have leaders, it will have to agree upon goals. If we wish to have leaders to follow, we will have to show them the way."

The consensus that would at least give direction to government would come either as the result of an intelligent examination of alternate courses or in the wake of catastrophe. The country's future remained uncertain; Americans, still free to exercise their judgment, would determine in large measure what triumphs and tragedies that future would bring. The struggle for adequate economic, environmental, and energy policies would ultimately test their character and cohesion. But only if sufficient numbers of citizens accepted their full democratic responsibilities would the country meet the outsized requirements of its future through collective intelligence. Democracy, welding the leaders and the led into an effective political force, would serve the nation most assuredly when it increased the wisdom and rationality of national decisions. The ultimate purpose of a free, democratic government is the creation of a superior human society.

Chapter IX

A Bibliographical Essay

One cataclysmic event shaped much of the nation's history during the long generation that followed the outbreak of the European war in 1939. That event—World War II—came at the beginning, not the end, of the period. Thus the lines of analysis in this volume flow from that war forward toward an uncertain ending, since no major war, depression, or other human or environmental disaster occurred to aid the processes of selection and refine the processes of understanding. However, the country's experience as a global power generated enough evidence to elucidate the dominant trends in its recent evolution. History moves forward in a cause and effect progression. What concerns the analyst is whether any occurrence establishes or continues a policy or trend that will reveal itself in subsequent events and decisions. The actions of one administration, especially in foreign and economic affairs, can limit or determine the choices of those that follow; it is the historian's task to segregate such decisions from the mass and to note why they might have continuing significance. Although historians generally make no effort to predict future events, sound historical scholarship should not permit some unforeseen cataclysm to reconstruct the past in any major degree. The writings on the wartime and postwar American experience vary enormously in nature and content, yet together they make clear the character and direction of the country's foreign and economic policies.

Much in the American attitude toward events in Europe and
Asia in the late 1930s was ironic. As late as 1941 a large majority
of Americans still opposed any military involvement in Europe,
where the threat to historic American interests was clear; but those
same Americans supported policies in the Far East, where U.S.
interests were vague and remote, which could lead only to war.
What mattered in regard to Europe was the shifting relationship
between the powerful pressures against involvement and the conviction of Roosevelt and others that the United States dare not, at
any price, permit England to suffer defeat. Writings on these
themes are voluminous, often superb, and generally in agreement
on broad interpretations. Among them are William L. Langer and
S. Everett Gleason, *The Challenge to Isolation, 1937-1940* (1952);
Langer and Gleason, *The Undeclared War, 1940-1941* (1953);
Wayne S. Cole, *America First: The Battle Against Intervention, 1940-
1941* (1953); Donald Drummond, *The Passing of American Neutrality, 1937-1941* (1955); and Robert A. Divine, *The Illusion of
Neutrality* (1962). The variations in this progression of books lie
more in details and emphasis than in basic disagreements over
events, decisions, and the pressures for involvement.

In the Far East, where U.S. historic interests were ill-defined
and anchored to the largely intangible promises of the Open Door
in China, the limiting factor in U.S. policy was not isolationism, but
the peculiar brand of American internationalism that rejected
change—any change—based on force. At issue in U.S. relations
with Japan after 1937 was the relationship between the denial of
Japanese rights in China and the varying Japanese reactions to the
persistent demand for capitulation. Historians have long detected
a fundamental tendency of the United States to overdemand in its
relations with Japan. Yet they disagree on American motivation.
Charles C. Tansill attributed unsubstantiated pro-Communist motives to Roosevelt's inflexibility toward Japan, but otherwise his
Back Door to War: The Roosevelt Foreign Policy, 1933-1941 (1952)
traces well the diplomatic demands that the Roosevelt administration placed on Japan. Using much of the same evidence, Herbert
Feis, in his *Road to Pearl Harbor: The Coming of the War between the
United States and Japan* (1950), attributes Roosevelt's decisions to

false assumptions and drift. Paul W. Schroeder, in *The Axis Alliance and Japanese-American Relations, 1941* (1958), accentuates what he regards the more and more moralistic demands of the United States on Japan during the crucial year of 1941. This fundamental American internationalism, based on the Wilsonian principle of peaceful change, embodied far more continuity than did the country's pre-Pearl Harbor isolationism.

World War II unleashed so much industrial and military power that it created a genuine watershed in American and world history. Historians have delineated the economic and political impact of the war on the home front. Geoffrey Perrett's *Days of Sadness, Years of Triumph: The American People, 1939-1945* (1973) offers many vignettes of wartime America, but it focuses as well on the more fundamental economic and social impact of the war on the American people. How the war affected those at home receives similar analyses in Richard R. Lingeman's *Don't You Know There's a War On? The American Home Front, 1941-1945* (1970) and Richard Polenberg's briefer *War and Society: The United States, 1941-1945* (1972). John Morton Blum's more recent *V Was for Victory: Politics and American Culture During World War II* (1976) dwells on all the major trends in American political and economic life during the war years. Blum notes the special benefits that the war brought to major corporation, the growth of the federal bureaucracy, the resultant trend toward the concentration of economic and political power in America, and the movement toward greater conservatism in the country's politics.

What continues to attract scholars to the question of Cold War origins is not only the enormous cost of that struggle to the nation, but also the suspicion that it might have been mitigated, if not avoided, by different policies in Washington. Basic to the postwar struggle was the clash between Soviet power and Western principle in Eastern Europe, where the Soviets had not only the greater interest, but also the total strategic advantage. William Hardy McNeill, in his *America, Britain, and Russia: Their Cooperation and Conflict, 1941-1946* (1953), focused on the clash between Stalin's specific goals and the effort of Roosevelt and Hull to postpone all settlements in the hope that somehow they could prevent the creation of a Soviet sphere of influence. Still, for McNeill, the wartime conflict over Eastern Europe was not irreparable; he places the beginning of the Cold War in 1947. Employing the same intellectual framework, James McGregor Burns discovers the origins of the Soviet-American conflict, as revealed in his *Roosevelt; The Soldier of Freedom* (1970), in the perennial wartime quarrel over the postwar design for Europe. Concentrating directly on the Eastern European theme in wartime, Lynn Etheridge Davis's *The Cold War Begins: Soviet American Conflict over Eastern Europe* (1974) traces in detail the conflict within the State Department, mostly between the professionals and adviser Isaiah Bowman, over the question of the recognition of Soviet interests in Eastern Europe. Robert Beitzell's valuable *The Uneasy Alliance: America, Britain, and Russia, 1941-1943* (1972) develops the second theme in Big Three conflict during the early years of the war—that largely between Britain and the United States over military strategy and the second front.

Several books on the Cold War have emphasized Washington's illusions of ultimate success in Europe, its refusal to exercise the choices available to it, the heavy financial and emotional price of the resulting policies, and their predictable failure to achieve the freedom of East-Central Europe or the unification of Germany. Norman A. Graebner's *Cold War Diplomacy, 1945-1975* (1977) centers on these themes, as does Martin F. Herz's *Beginnings of the Cold War* (1966). Frederick L. Schuman, in *The Cold War: Retrospect and Prospect* (1962), recalled that the West, after Munich, gave Hitler a free hand in Eastern Europe, which enabled him to invade Russia with ample preparation and on his own terms. The West, in abdicating its responsibilities in 1938, Schuman argues, had no right, after 20 million Russian deaths, to demand equal rights in liberated Europe seven years later. Placing his emphasis on the realities of a divided Europe, Louis J. Halle, in *The Cold War as History* (1967), eschews moral judgment and views the Soviet-American confrontation in 1945 as a tragic and unavoidable condition created by the war itself, not unlike the one that faces a scorpion and a tarantula in a bottle, each compelled to protect itself by seeking to kill the other. John Lewis Gaddis developed this moderately revisionist approach to the Cold War with infinite care and balance in his prize-winning *The United States and the Origins of the Cold War, 1941-1947* (1972).

Daniel Yergin's *Shattered Peace: The Origins of the Cold War and the National Security State* (1977) is merely the last in a long series of volumes on the origins of the Cold War that have continued to ask the same basic questions regarding Soviet and American behavior. Yergin—who, like others, studied the Cold War through Western eyes—details two contrasting theories about Russia that struggled for control of American policy. The first he defines as the Riga axioms, named after the Baltic port and former capital of Latvia, where U.S. officials gathered information on Bolshevik Russia during the years of nonrecognition and concluded that Russia was a menace to the Western world. What broke this group's influence momentarily was the Nazi invasion of Russia in June 1941, because this prompted Roosevelt, much to the dismay of some Soviet experts, to support the Russian military cause. The view of Russia that underlay the years of wartime cooperation Yergin calls the Yalta axioms—the assumption that the Soviet Union was a great power that behaved in a traditional fashion, motivated not by ideology, but by self-interest, which it hoped to satisfy through the time-honored *accoutrements* of power politics. For Yergin the Yalta axioms succumbed to the Riga axioms amid the burgeoning postwar conflicts that again enabled the traditional apprehensions of the Soviet Union to dominate official American thought. It was within the context of the Riga axioms that the Truman administration made its assumptions and formulated its hard-line policies toward the USSR.

Even as much of the historic scholarship moved toward this realist critique, the orthodox (official) views of the Cold War received their most complete and learned treatments in Dean Acheson's *Present at the Creation: My Years in the State Department* (1969), Herbert Feis's *From Trust to Terror* (1970), and Charles E. Bohlen's *Witness to History* (1973). Acheson's volume reveals the self-assurance of a man who never questioned the validity of his assumptions while he was secretary of state, who never doubted that the Soviets intended to dominate the world. Acheson had no use for those who would argue about Soviet intentions or insist that power could provoke as well as deter. It was on such questions—

not on the basic need for defense or the inexcusable character of Soviet behavior—that George F. Kennan's *Memoirs: 1925-1950* (1967) and *Memoirs, II: 1950-1963* (1972) stand in sharp contrast to Acheson's views. Kennan doubted that the Soviets threatened western Europe, much less the world, and that policies of military containment would assure the military division of Europe by provoking similar policies within the Soviet Union. Two basically sympathetic studies of Dean Acheson, but critical of Acheson's overestimation of Western power and Soviet weakness in his anticipation of an ultimate Western victory in the Cold War, are David S. McLellan's prize-winning *Dean Acheson: The State Department Years* (1976) and Gaddis Smith's *Dean Acheson* (1972).

New Left revisionist historians, a large group who wrote largely in the 1960s, challenged both the moderate critics and the orthodox defenders of American policy by asserting that the United States possessed the power necessary to prevent the Cold War. The war-battered Soviet regime, they insist, wanted only the security of a buffer of pro-Soviet states to prevent Russia's encirclement by the West. Thus the Soviets had legitimate security and economic interests in Eastern Europe. But the United States, the New Left writers argue, sought to deny the Soviets a sphere of influence in Eastern Europe because it wanted universal markets and investment opportunities. To encourage a Soviet retreat, the United States had two sources of power available to it and sought to use them both. One was the atomic bomb; the other was the nation's vast economic power. Eventually neither of these Western advantages could force a Soviet withdrawal from Eastern Europe. But it was the enunciation of American ambition in Eastern Europe, these revisionists agree, that produced a distrust in the Soviet Union and needlessly forced the termination of Soviet-American collaboration in the postwar world. Not all revisionists have accepted all of these suppositions, but they have agreed that the overdemanding that provoked the Cold War began with the United States, not with the USSR, and that its motive was economic.

The volume that above all others established this revisionist interpretation of American postwar diplomacy was William Appleman Williams' *The Tragedy of American Diplomacy* (1959). Williams developed the theme that the United States, since 1898, has pursued as its fundamental policy objective a worldwide economic open door for American trade and investment—a program designed ultimately to make the globe conform to the requirements of American capitalism. Applying this framework to the postwar world, Williams explained U.S. rejection of the Soviet sphere of influence as an effort to prevent the closing of a portion of Europe to American business. Convinced that they were dealing from strength and that pro-Western states would provide better markets for American goods, American leaders refused to recognize governments friendly to the USSR in Eastern Europe. The special power that allegedly would enable the United States to control Europe's reconstruction lay in the nation's monopoly of atomic power. That power, Williams argued, was used as much to influence Russia in Europe as to end the war in the Pacific. The strategy proved to be ineffective because Russia refused to back down. Gar Alperovitz's *Atomic Diplomacy: Hiroshima and Potsdam* (1965) added little to Williams' conclusions. By limiting his study to the critical five months between April and August 1945, however, he produced detail and documentation in an effort to substantiate the atomic thesis.

In his book, *A World Destroyed: The Atomic Bomb and the Grand Alliance* (1975), Martin J. Sherwin developed in detail a secondary theme that revisionist historians have raised regarding the atomic bomb. Sherwin wondered less about the bomb's use than about Roosevelt's wartime guardianship of the atomic program and how it affected long-term U.S.-Soviet relations. Two other mildly revisionist studies merit special attention. Lloyd C. Gardner's *Architects of Illusion* (1970), in analyzing specifically the policy contributions of a number of American leaders, shows that invariably they pursued postwar goals, sometimes economic, that they could not achieve. Thomas G. Paterson, in his *Soviet-American Confrontation: Postwar Reconstruction and the Origins of the Cold War* (1973), stresses the theme that U.S. officials made the mistake of believing that they were negotiating from strength instead of from weakness, and that U.S. interests in Eastern Europe were minimal and not worth a serious quarrel with Russia. Robert W. Tucker has written the most useful critique of the New Left historians in his *The Radical Left and American Foreign Policy* (1971). Tucker notes the variations in approach, interpretation, and emphasis among the New Left writers. Fundamentally he agrees with the more orthodox critics that the foreign policies of the United States have been those of a status quo power and thus transcend the ideology of the nation's leaders or the specific needs of the American economy. Robert James Maddox, in *The New Left and the Origins of the Cold War* (1973), is concerned less with the views of the revisionists than with the quality of their scholarship.

Undoubtedly the globalization of the Cold War rested on the assumption of a Communist monolith that rendered Communists everywhere members of a worldwide conspiracy and enemies of the Western world. Such notions of a Soviet-led danger underwrote the war in Korea, the nonrecognition of the Peking regime, the creation of a worldwide alliance system, the war in Vietnam, and the more recent pressures for involvement in Africa. One of the first major studies that explained and criticized the growing American involvement in Asia was Edwin O. Reischauer's *Wanted: An Asian Policy* (1955). Many of the themes regarding China appear in Tang Tsou's *America's Failure in China, 1941-1950* (1963), Foster R. Dulles's *American Foreign Policy Toward Communist China, 1949-1969* (1972), and Donald S. Zagoria's *The Sino-Soviet Conflict* (1962). The major work on the U.S. involvement in Korea is David Rees's *Korea: The Limited War* (1964). More general studies that criticize the globalism in American foreign policy, identifying it largely with counterrevolutionary behavior, are Richard J. Barnet's *Intervention and Revolution* (1968), Ronald Steele's *Pax Americana* (1967), Edmund Stillman and William Pfaff's *Power and Impotence* (1966), Theodore Draper, *The Abuse of Power* (1966), and J. William Fulbright's *The Arrogance of Power* (1966).

Both the dynamic quality of the Truman years and the general availability of historical materials for the Truman period have encouraged an impressive evaluation of Truman's political leadership and the events of his years in office. The first major work on his administration, thoroughly favorable, was Cabell Phillips, *The Truman Presidency: The History of a Triumphant Succession* (1966). Two, more recent, studies of great merit are Bert Cochran's *Harry Truman and the Crisis Presidency* (1973) and Robert J. Donovan's *Conflict and Crisis: The Presidency of Harry S Truman, 1945-1948* (1977).

Truman's policies toward industry, labor, agriculture, and civil rights have all been subjected to excellent analyses. The McCarthy controversy, much of which occurred during the Truman years, has produced a surprisingly large number of books. Earl Latham's *The Communist Controversy in Washington, From the New Deal to McCarthy* (1966) exposes most of the issues and personalities of the conflict, as does Alan D. Harper's *The Politics of Loyalty: The White House and the Communist Issue, 1946-1952* (1971).

Truman's leadership raises questions regarding continuity, because his presidency embodied two conflicting realities that emanated from the past: the wartime and postwar economic growth that enhanced the power of American conservatism, and the ongoing New Deal tradition that sustained a national concern for the still unresolved questions of distribution, employment, civil rights, labor, housing, and urban reform. Susan M. Hartmann, in her prizewinning study, *Truman and the 80th Congress* (1971), shows a President of liberal convictions struggling against conservative power blocs in Congress with limited success. Alonzo Hamby, in his larger and more inclusive prize-winning *Beyond the New Deal: Harry S. Truman and American Liberalism* (1973), focuses directly on Truman's generally futile struggle for American liberalism. Hamby gives high marks to Truman's effort, but concludes, as did Samuel Lubell in *The Future of American Politics* (1951), that governmental power was so evenly divided between Democrats and Republicans, liberals and conservatives, that any legislative or political gain on one front would result in a countervailing deficit elsewhere.

It makes considerable difference whether the historian views the Eisenhower years as a distinct period, dominated by a singular personality, or as an ongoing process that responded to the policies and assumptions of previous administrations and passed them on—expanded, unchanged, or modified—to those that followed. Inasmuch as none of Eisenhower's decisions led to any significant public embarrassment before he left office, the historian can assume that the realities they overlooked did no harm. Judged by the general calm of the Eisenhower years, especially when contrasted to the turbulent 1960s, the Eisenhower leadership appears laudable, even nostalgic. Eisenhower's popularity remained high to the end. Yet so wide was the gap between the ends and means of most Eisenhower policies that any administration that followed would be in trouble. In the long run the major Eisenhower foreign policies would remain meaningless or be reversed. What would hold was the nation's prosperity, the expansion of world trade and investment, and the stability of western Europe and Japan.

The first major study of the Eisenhower administration was Robert J. Donovan's *Eisenhower: The Inside Story* (1956). Donovan's volume contains much useful material; although it seldom passes judgment, it presents material that questions both the assumptions and the performance of that administration. That the administration revealed a historical Republicanism is clear from two books : Edwin L. Dale, Jr., *Conservatives in Power* (1960), and Gary W. Reichard, *The Reaffirmation of Republicanism: Eisenhower and the Eighty-Third Congress* (1975). Emmet John Hughes' *The Ordeal of Power: A Political Memoir of the Eisenhower Years* (1962) is an insider's account, highly illuminating and mildly critical of the Eisenhower leadership. Hughes gave Eisenhower little credit for consolidating the changes of the previous two decades. If the President accepted the New Deal as a political necessity, he continued to oppose many of its essentials. Hughes doubted that Eisenhower was successful in his foreign relations. The inner contradictions of his administration, Hughes argued, demanded policies that could only be negative or passive even while they promised unprecedented success. Another early study critical of Eisenhower's management of the presidential office is David A. Frier's *Conflict of Interest in the Eisenhower Administration* (1969).

It was only natural that the turmoil of the 1960s would compel a reevaluation of the Eisenhower leadership, which had managed to dispose of McCarthy, maintain the country's prosperity with a minimum of inflation, limit the growth of the federal budget and bureaucracy, avoid foreign wars and, in general, keep the nation calm. Among the first major efforts at reassessment was Herbert S. Parmet's *Eisenhower and the American Crusades* (1972). In this highly balanced, careful account of the Eisenhower years, Parmet depicts Eisenhower as a hardworking and effective president. In many respects the same judgment of the Eisenhower years appeared in Charles C. Alexander's *Holding the Line: The Eisenhower Era, 1952-*

1961 (1975). This largely factual account does not gloss over Eisenhower's lack of leadership on many important issues, such as McCarthy and civil rights. Perhaps the book's most substantial chapter is its long evaluation of American life and society during the Eisenhower years. On foreign affairs the presentation is equally balanced and straightforward, but the general neglect of analysis establishes no clear connection between the Eisenhower decisions and the ongoing challenges that confronted later American policy. On balance, Alexander concludes that the Eisenhower leadership was effective, if not totally praiseworthy. Another recent and noteworthy account of the Eisenhower leadership is Peter Lyon, *Eisenhower: Portrait of the Hero* (1974).

Studies of John Foster Dulles fall into the same categories as do those on Eisenhower. By neglecting any analysis of Dulles' words and actions and the possible liabilities they created for the external relations of the United States, books such as John Robinson Beal's *John Foster Dulles, 1888-1959* (1959) and Michael Guhin's *John Foster Dulles: A Statesman and His Times* (1972) remain largely uncritical. Guhin describes Dulles as a shrewd diplomat whose appreciation of the limits of power remained undisturbed by his ideological and moral concerns. Among the first of the critical appraisals of the Eisenhower-Dulles foreign policies was Norman A. Graebner's *The New Isolationism* (1956), which focused on the administration's effort to create the impression of more determined policy formulations than those of Truman, largely through the use of dramatic phrases. Each phrase promised greater success at less risk and cost than the Truman administration had achieved; in practice, each left U.S. policy exactly where it was. Herman Finer, in his *Dulles over Suez* (1964), contributed an exceedingly critical analysis of the secretary's actions in that episode. Equally unflattering is Townsend Hoopes' major study, *The Devil and John Foster Dulles* (1973). This book, reflecting the new evidence available in oral history interviews, is a markedly well-researched, thoughtful, and altogether honest endeavor to understand a very complicated man. Crowded with details on Dulles' life and thought, it goes far to explain both the successes and failures of a long career. Dulles, writes Hoopes, had no feel for diplomacy. In seven years as Secretary of State, he scarcely settled one major world issue. He left every challenge inherited from the Truman-Acheson years either in its established state or exacerbated by additional years of missed opportunities and vituperation.

Obviously, the domestic and foreign inheritances of the Kennedy and Johnson administrations of the 1960s were prodigious. How these Democratic administrations dealt with them is now recorded in surprising detail. On foreign policy, the Kennedy-Johnson leadership attempted to live with its inheritances and push them on to subsequent administrations, unchanged. On the domestic front the Kennedy administration accepted the general validity of past economic policies, but gave them additional force by arguing for increased levels of national indebtedness to enlarge the flow of government-stimulated purchasing power into the economy. What complicates historic judgment of the Kennedy years was the physical attractiveness of the Kennedy team, the Camelot quality of the administration, its catering to intellectuals, its apparent imaginativeness and innovation, its spirited activism, and its hope for the future. Such aspects of the Kennedy years have pervaded two impressive studies of the administration by insiders. Neither Arthur M. Schlesinger's *A Thousand Days: John F. Kennedy in the White House* (1965) nor Theodore C. Sorenson's *Kennedy* (1965) praise every Kennedy decision, but both create an altogether favorable image of the Kennedy administration. Two other insider's accounts of the Kennedy years are the generally laudatory Roger Hilsman's *To Move a Nation: The Politics and Foreign Policy in the Administration of John F. Kennedy* (1964) and Pierre Salinger's *With Kennedy* (1966).

Far more critical are Henry Fairlie's *The Kennedy Promise* (1973) and Richard J. Walton's *Cold War and Counter-Revolution: The Foreign Policy of John F. Kennedy* (1972). Walton criticizes Kennedy for the military buildup of 1961-1962 (which unleashed the momentum in military expenditures), the Bay of Pigs, the Berlin crisis of 1961, and the Cuban missile crisis of 1962 (which, Walton believes, required no naval quarantine). Kennedy, concludes Walton, retained all the assumptions about Chinese aggressiveness and falling dominoes that characterized Eisenhower's counterrevolutionary outlook and thus trapped the country in the Vietnam war and all its consequences. Kennedy's civil rights policies receive a generally favorable analysis in Carl M. Brauer's *John*

Kennedy and the Second Reconstruction (1977), while Jim F. Heath traces another Kennedy connection in *John F. Kennedy and The Business Community* (1969).

The favorable accounts of the Johnson years by insiders are Lyndon Johnson's own memoirs, *Vantage Point* (1971), and Walt W. Rostow's *The Diffusion of Power* (1972). Eric Goldman's inside account, *The Tragedy of Lyndon Johnson* (1969) is highly critical. Somewhat less so is Philip L. Geyelin's *Lyndon B. Johnson and the World* (1966). The writings on President Johnson's experience in Vietnam are as numerous as they are critical, perhaps none more so than David Halberstam's *The Best and the Brightest* (1972) and Frances Fitzgerald's *Fire in the Lake* (1972). Three general studies of the Kennedy-Johnson years, social and economic as well as political, are Tom Wicker, *JFK and LBJ: The Influence of Personality upon Politics* (1968); William L. O'Neill, *Coming Apart: An Informal History of the Sixties* (1971); and Jim F. Heath, *Decade of Disullusionment: The Kennedy-Johnson Years* (1974).

By 1978 the writings on the Nixon administration had analyzed its foreign policies in detail and had also begun the process of uncovering the sources of power and weakness in the Nixon administration. Any study of the Nixon years must begin with unique qualities of Nixon himself. Perhaps the most revealing book on Nixon is Gary Wills's *Nixon Agonistes* (1970), a study of personality and politics. A kinder evaluation is Earl Mazo and Stephen Hess, *Nixon: A Political Portrait* (1968). Nixon's own interpretation of his presidency can be found in his massive *RN: The Memoirs of Richard Nixon* (1978). A very useful study of Nixon's first term, by an insider, is William L. Safire's *Before the Fall!* (1975). The Watergate revelations can be traced in Carl Bernstein and Robert Woodward, *All the President's Men* (1974). The behavior of the Nixon administration in response to Watergate has been delineated variously by a number of participants. These insiders' accounts include Nixon's own memoirs, Jeb Stuart Magruder's *An American Life* (1974), John Dean's *Blind Ambition: The White House Years* (1976), and H. R. Haldeman's *The Ends of Power* (1978). Theodore H. White has written his perceptions of Watergate and its impact on American society in *Breach of Faith: The Fall of Richard Nixon* (1975).

Any study of the Nixon-Kissinger approaches to foreign policy might begin with Henry A. Kissinger's *American Foreign Policy: Expanded Edition* (1974). The essays in this book set forth the basic premises and purposes of the Nixon foreign policies. James Chace's *A World Elsewhere* (1973) seeks to explain the changes in direction during the early Nixon years. Contrasting Nixon's prepresidential positions with those adopted after 1969 is Lloyd C. Gardner's *The Great Nixon Turnaround* (1973). On Nixon's China policy see Robert G. Sutter's *China-Watch: Toward Sino-American Reconciliation* (1978). On Kissinger himself the growing literature includes the highly favorable Stephen R. Graubard, *Kissinger: Portrait of a Mind* (1973); the largely factual and detailed volume by Marvin Kalb and Bernard Kalb, *Kissinger* (1974); and the more critical David Landau, *Kissinger: The Uses of Power* (1972). Stanley Hoffmann's excellent volume, *Primacy or World Order: American Foreign Policy Since the Cold War* (1978), analyzes the major contradiction in the Nixon-Kissinger policies—the effort to establish a new world order based on trust and cooperation while still protecting the primacy of the United States and the established anti-Soviet positions of the Cold War.

The book list that follows is not all-inclusive; no list of moderate length could be. But it incorporates many perceptive and challenging studies that dwell on the domestic and foreign events and policies of the six administrations from Roosevelt to Nixon. The list includes books that amplify or challenge all of the themes that appear in this volume, including those of the Nixon years. There are no lists for either the Ford or the Carter administrations. The writings on the years since 1974, as they apply to domestic issues and leadership especially, are voluminous and often remarkably judicious, but they exist overwhelmingly in the form of articles.

Some Books for Further Reading

An asterisk indicates that there is a paperback edition.

THE COMING OF THE WAR

Beard, Charles A. *President Roosevelt and the Coming of the War* (1948).
Borg, Dorothy, and Shumpei Okamoto, eds. *Pearl Harbor as History: Japanese-American Relations, 1931-1941* (1973).*
Carr, E. H. *The Twenty Years' Crisis, 1919-1939* (1939).
Cole, Wayne S. *America First: The Battle Against Intervention, 1940-1941* (1953).
———. *Senator Gerald P. Nye and American Foreign Relations* (1962).
Divine, Robert A. *The Illusion of Neutrality: Franklin D. Roosevelt and the Struggle over the Arms Embargo* (1962).*
Drummond, Donald. *The Passing of American Neutrality, 1937-1941* (1955).
Feis, Herbert. *The Road to Pearl Harbor: The Coming of the War between the United States and Japan* (1950).*
Johnson, Walter. *The Battle Against Isolation* (1944).
Kimbell, Warren F. *The Most Unsordid Act: Lend-Lease, 1939-1941* (1969).
Langer, William L., and S. Everett Gleason. *The Challenge to Isolation, 1937-1940* (1952).
———. *The Underclared War, 1940-1941* (1953).
Lash, Joseph P. *Roosevelt and Churchill, 1939-1941: The Partnership That Saved the West* (1976).
Schroeder, Paul W. *The Axis Alliance and Japanese-American Relations, 1941* (1958).
Tansill, Charles C. *Back Door to War: The Roosevelt Foreign Policy, 1933-1941* (1952).
Wilson, Theodore A. *The First Summit: Roosevelt and Churchill at Placentia Bay, 1941* (1969).
Wohlstetter, Roberta. *Pearl Harbor: Warning and Decision* (1962).*

THE WAR YEARS

Ambrose, Stephen E. *Eisenhower and Berlin, 1945: The Decision to Halt at t* *Elbe* (1967).*

Beitzell, Robert. *The Uneasy Alliance: America, Britain, and Russia, 1941-19* (1972).

Blum, John Morton. *V Was For Victory: Politics and American Culture Duri* *World War II* (1976).

Buchanan, A. Russell. *The United States and World War II*, 2 vols (1962).*

Burns, James MacGregor. *Roosevelt: The Soldier of Freedom, 1940-19* (1970).

Craig, William. *The Fall of Japan* (1967).

Divine, Robert A. *Second Chance: The Triumph of Internationalism in Amer* *During World War II* (1967).*

Feis, Herbert. *The China Tangle* (1953).

————. *Churchill, Roosevelt, and Stalin: The War They Waged and the Pea* *They Sought* (1957).

Harriman, W. Averell, and Elie Abel. *Special Envoy to Churchill and Stalin, 194* *1945* (1975).

Kolko, Gabriel. *The Politics of War: The World and United States Foreign Poli* *1943-1945* (1968).

Lingeman, Richard R. *Don't You Know There's A War On? The American Hor* *Front, 1941-1945* (1970).

Loewenheim, Francis L., Harold D. Langley, and Manfred Jonas, eds. *Roosev* *and Churchill: Their Secret Wartime Correspondence* (1975).

McNeill, William H. *America, Britain, and Russia: Their Cooperation and Confl.* *1941-1946* (1953).

O'Connor, Raymond G. *Diplomacy for Victory: FDR and Unconditional Surrend* (1971).*

Perrett, Geoffrey. *Days of Sadness, Years of Triumph: The American Peop* *1939-1945* (1973).

Polenberg, Richard. *War and Society: The United States, 1941-1945* (1972)

Rose, Lisle A. *Dubious Victory: The United States and the End of World Wa* (1973).

Sherry, Michael S. *Preparing for the Next War: American Plans for Postv* *Defense, 1941-1945* (1977).

Smith, Bradley F. *Reaching Judgment at Nuremberg* (1977).

Smith, Gaddis. *American Diplomacy During the Second World War, 1941-19* (1965).*

Snell, John L. *Illusion and Necessity: The Diplomacy of Global War, 1939-19* (1963).*

land, John. *The Rising Sun: The Decline and Fall of the Japanese Empire, 1936-1945,* 2 vols. (1970).

RIGINS OF THE COLD WAR, 1941-1950

heson, Dean. *Present at the Creation: My Years in the State Department* (1969).
perovitz, Gar. *Atomic Diplomacy: Hiroshima and Potsdam* (1965).*
kes, Hadley. *Bureaucracy, the Marshall Plan, and the National Interest* (1972).
hlen, Charles E. *Witness to History* (1973).
emens, Diane Shaver. *Yalta* (1970).
vis, Lynn Etheridge. *The Cold War Begins: Soviet-American Conflict Over Eastern Europe* (1974).
is, Herbert. *Between War and Peace: The Potsdam Conference* (1960).
———. *From Trust to Terror: The Onset of the Cold War, 1945-1950* (1970).
rrell, Robert H. *George C. Marshall* (1966).
ming, D. F. *The Cold War and Its Origins, 1917-1950,* 2 vols. (1961).
ddis, John Lewis. *The United States and the Origins of the Cold War, 1941-1947* (1972).*
rdner, Lloyd C. *Architects of Illusion* (1970).*
mbel, John. *The Origins of the Marshall Plan* (1976).
rring, George C., Jr. *Aid to Russia, 1941-1946: Strategy, Politics, the Origins of the Cold War* (1973).
rz, Martin F. *Beginnings of the Cold War* (1966).
nes, Joseph Marion. *The Fifteen Weeks* (1955).*
nnan, George F. *Memoirs, 1925-1950* (1967).
lko, Joyce, and Gabriel Kolko. *The Limits of Power: The World and U.S. Foreign Policy, 1945-1954* (1972).
klick, Bruce. *American Policy and the Division of Germany: The Clash with Russia over Reparations* (1972).
pmann, Walter. *The Cold War* (1947).
Lellan, David S. *Dean Acheson: The State Department Years* (1976).
ddox, Robert James. *The New Left and the Origins of the Cold War* (1973).
rgenthau, Hans J. *In Defense of the National Interest* (1951).
hoenberger, Walter Smith. *Decision of Destiny* (1969).
erwin, Martin J. *A World Destroyed: The Atomic Bomb and the Grand Alliance* (1975).
ith, Gaddis. *Dean Acheson* (1972).
ell, John L., ed. *The Meaning of Yalta* (1956).
ker, Robert W. *The Radical Left and American Foreign Policy* (1971).*

Walker, J. Samuel. *Henry A. Wallace and American Foreign Policy* (1976).

Walton, Richard J. *Henry Wallace, Harry Truman, and the Cold War* (1976).

Westerfield, H. Bradford. *Foreign Policy and Party Politics: Pearl Harbor to Kore* (1955).

Williams, William Appleman. *The Tragedy of American Diplomacy* (1959).*

Yergin, Daniel. *Shattered Peace: The Origins of the Cold War and the Nation* *Security State* (1977).

THE COLD WAR: GENERAL STUDIES

Deutscher, Isaac. *The Great Contest: Russia and the West* (1960).

Gaddis, John Lewis. *Russia, The Soviet Union, and the United States: An Interpr* *tive History* (1978).*

Graebner, Norman A. *Cold War Diplomacy, 1945-1975* (1977).*

————, ed. *The Cold War: A Conflict of Ideology and Power* (1976).*

Halle, Louis J. *The Cold War as History* (1967).

Hoffmann, Stanley. *Gulliver's Troubles, or the Setting of American Foreign Poli* (1968).

Kennan, George F. *Memoirs, II: 1950-1963* (1972).

LaFeber, Walter. *America, Russia, and the Cold War, 1945-1975* (1976).*

Lerche, Charles O., Jr. *The Cold War and After* (1965).*

May, Ernest R. *"Lessons" of the Past: The Use and Misuse of History in Americ* *Foreign Policy* (1973).*

Schuman, Frederick L. *The Cold War: Retrospect and Prospect* (1962).

Seabury, Paul. *The Rise and Decline of the Cold War* (1967).

Shulman, Marshall D. *Beyond the Cold War* (1966).*

Spanier, John W. *American Foreign Policy Since World War II* (1971).*

Ulam, Adam B. *Expansion and Coexistence: The History of Soviet Foreign Polic* *1917-1967* (1968).

————. *The Rivals: America and Russia Since World War II* (1971).*

THE GLOBAL COLD WAR

Bachrack, Stanley D. *The Committee of One Million: "China Lobby" Politi* *1953-1971* (1977).

Barnet, Richard J. *Intervention and Revolution: America's Confrontation w* *Insurgent Movements Around the World* (1968).*

Baskir, Lawrence M., and William A. Strauss. *Chance and Circumstance: T* *Draft, the War and the Vietnam Generation* (1978).

Cooper, Chester. *The Lost Crusade* (1970).

)raper, Theodore. *Abuse of Power* (1966).*

)ulles, Foster R. *American Foreign Policy Toward Communist China, 1949-1969* (1972).

itzgerald, Frances. *Fire in the Lake* (1972).*

ulbright, J. William. *The Arrogance of Power* (1966).*

iraebner, Norman A., ed. *Nationalism and Communism in Asia: The American Response* (1977).*

ialberstam, David. *The Making of a Quagmire* (1965).*

———. *The Best and the Brightest* (1972).*

ierr, Michael. *Dispatches* (1977).

ioopes, Townsend. *The Limits of Intervention* (1969).*

1ay, Ernest R., ed. *The Truman Administration and China, 1945-1949* (1975).*

:eischauer, Edwin O. *Wanted: An Asian Policy* (1955).

:ees, David. *Korea: The Limited War* (1964).

:ose, Lisle A. *Roots of Tragedy: The United States and the Struggle for Asia, 1945-1954* (1975).

haplen, Robert. *The Lost Revolution: The U.S. in Vietnam, 1946-1966* (1966).*

heehan, Neil et al., eds. *The Pentagon Papers as Published by the New York Times* (1971).

hepp, Frank. *Decent Interval* (1978).

panier, John. *The Truman-MacArthur Controversy and the Korean War* (1959).*

iteele, Ronald. *Pax Americana* (1967).*

itillman, Edmund, and William Pfaff. *Power and Impotence* (1966).*

aylor, Telford. *Nuremburg and Vietnam* (1970).

sou, Tang. *America's Failure in China, 1941-1950* (1963).*

agoria, Donald S. *The Sino-Soviet Conflict* (1962).

HE TRUMAN ADMINISTRATION

erman, William C. *The Politics of Civil Rights in the Truman Administration* (1970).

ernstein, Barton J., and Allen J. Matusow, eds. *The Truman Administration: A Documentary History* (1966).*

ochran, Bert. *Harry Truman and the Crisis Presidency* (1973).

onovan, Robert J. *Conflict and Crisis: The Presidency of Harry S Truman, 1945-1948* (1977).

ied, Richard M. *Men Against McCarthy* (1976).

oldman, Eric F. *The Crucial Decade—And After: America, 1945-1960* (1961).*

oulden, Joseph C. *The Best Years, 1945-1950* (1976).

riffith, Robert. *The Politics of Fear: Joseph R. McCarthy and the Senate* (1971).

Griffith, Robert, and Athan Theoharis, eds. *The Specter: Original Essays on th* *Cold War and the Origins of McCarthyism* (1974).*

Hamby, Alonzo L. *Beyond the New Deal: Harry S. Truman and American Libera* *ism* (1973).

Harper, Alan D. *The Politics of Loyalty: The White House and the Communi.* *Issue, 1946-1952* (1971).

Hartman, Susan M. *Truman and the 80th Congress* (1971).

Haynes, Richard F. *The Awesome Power: Harry S. Truman as Commander* *Chief* (1973).

Latham, Earl. *The Communist Controversy in Washington, From the New Deal* *McCarthy* (1966).

Lee, R. Alton. *Truman and Taft-Hartley* (1966).

Marcus, Maeva. *Truman and the Steel Seizure Case: The Limits of Presidenti.* *Power* (1977)

Martin, John Bartlow. *Adlai Stevenson of Illinois* (1976).   Years

Matusow, Allen J. *Farm Policies and Politics in the Truman Administration* (1967

McClure, Arthur F. *The Truman Administration and the Problems of Postwa* *Labor, 1945-1948* (1969).

Parmet, Herbert S. *The Democrats: The Years After FDR* (1976).

Patterson, James T. *Mr. Republican: A Biography of Robert A. Taft* (1972).

Phillips, Cabell. *The Truman Presidency: The History of a Triumphant Successio* (1966).*

Rogin, Michael P. *The Intellectuals and McCarthy* (1967).

Rovere, Richard H. *Senator Joseph McCarthy* (1959).

Theoharis, Athan G. *The Yalta Myths: An Issue in U.S. Politics, 1945-1955* (1971

THE EISENHOWER YEARS

Albertson, Dean, ed. *Eisenhower as President* (1963).*

Aliano, Richard A. *American Defense Policy from Eisenhower to Kennedy* (1975

Alexander, Charles C. *Holding the Line: The Eisenhower Era, 1952-1961* (1975

Beal, John Robinson. *John Foster Dulles, 1888-1959* (1959).

Dale, Edwin L., Jr. *Conservatives in Power* (1960).

Donovan, Robert J. *Eisenhower: The Inside Story* (1956).

Eisenhower, Dwight D. *Mandate for Change, 1953-1956* (1963).

——. *Waging Peace* (1965).

Finer, Herman, *Dulles Over Suez* (1964).

Frier, David A. *Conflict of Interest in the Eisenhower Administration* (1969).

Graebner, Norman A. *The New Isolationism* (1956).

Guhin, Michael A. *John Foster Dulles: A Statesman and His Times* (1972).

opes, Townsend. *The Devil and John Foster Dulles* (1973).

ighes, Emmet John. *The Ordeal of Power: A Political Memoir of the Eisenhower Years* (1962).*

on, Peter. *Eisenhower: Portrait of the Hero* (1974).

eichard, Gary W. *The Reaffirmation of Republicanism: Eisenhower and the Eighty-Third Congress* (1975).

itter, Harold G. *The U.S. Economy in the 1950's* (1963).

hite, Theodore H. *The Making of the President, 1960* (1961).*

HE ECONOMY AND SOCIETY

nderson, Martin. *The Federal Bulldozer: A Critical Analysis of Urban Renewal, 1949-1962* (1964).

ckstein, Morris. *Gates of Eden: American Culture in the Sixties* (1977).

albraith, John Kenneth. *The Affluent Society* (1958).*

———. *The New Industrial State* (1967).*

azer, Nathan, ed. *Cities in Trouble* (1970).

azer, Nathan, and Daniel P. Moynihan. *Beyond the Melting Pot: The Negroes, Puerto Ricans, Jews, Italians, and Irish of New York City* (1963).

arrington, Michael. *The Other America: Poverty in the United States* (1962).*

arris, Seymour. *Economics of the Kennedy Years* (1964).

eilbroner, Robert L., in collaboration with Aaron Singer. *The Economic Transformation of America* (1977).*

———. *An Inquiry into the Human Prospect* (1974).

———. *Business Civilization in Decline* (1976).

cobs, Jane. *The Death and Life of Great American Cities* (1961).*

cobs, Paul. *Prelude to Riot: A View of Urban America from the Bottom* (1966).*

eps, Juanita M. *Women and the American Economy: A Look to the 1980s* (1976).*

kachman, Robert. *Inflation: The Permanent Problem of Boom and Bust* (1973).*

Masters, E. E. *Blue-Collar Aristocrats: Life-Styles at a Working-Class Tavern* (1975).

owry, George. *The Urban Nation, 1920-1960* (1965).*

ckard, Vance O. *The Hidden Persuaders* (1957).*

isman, David. *The Lonely Crowd: A Study of the Changing American Character* (1950).*

kin, Jeremy, and Randy Barber. *The North Will Rise Again: Pensions, Politics and Power in the 1980s* (1978).

thschild, Emma. *Paradise Lost: The Decline of the Auto-Industrial Age* (1973).*

Sale, Kirkpatrick. *Power Shift: The Rise of the Southern Rim and Its Challeng to the Eastern Establishment* (1975).

Sarratt, Reed. *The Ordeal of Desegregation: The First Decade* (1966).

Solberg, Carl. *Riding High: America in the Cold War* (1973).

Whyte, W. H. *The Organization Man* (1956).*

Wood, R. C. *Suburbia: Its People and the Politics* (1959).*

THE KENNEDY-JOHNSON YEARS

Berman, Ronald. *America in the 1960s: An Intellectual History* (1968).

Brauer, Carl M. *John Kennedy and the Second Reconstruction* (1977).

Chester, Lewis, Godfrey Hodgson, and Bruce Page. *An American Melodram* (1969).

Fairlie, Henry. *The Kennedy Promise* (1973).

Geyelin, Philip L. *Lyndon B. Johnson and the World* (1966).

Goldman, Eric F. *The Tragedy of Lyndon Johnson* (1969)

Health, Jim F. *Decade of Disillusionment: The Kennedy-Johnson Years* (1974

———. *John F. Kennedy and the Business Community* (1969).

Hilsman, Roger. *To Move a Nation: The Politics and Foreign Policy in the Admini tration of John F. Kennedy* (1964).

Johnson, Lyndon B. *Vantage Point* (1971).

McGinnis, Joe. *The Selling of the President* (1969).

O'Neill, William L. *Coming Apart: An Informal History of the Sixties* (1971).

Robert, Charles. *LBJ's Inner Circle* (1965).

Rostow, Walt W. *The Diffusion of Power* (1972).

Salinger, Pierre. *With Kennedy* (1966).

Schlesinger, Arthur M., Jr. *A Thousand Days: John F. Kennedy in the Wh House* (1965).

Sorenson, Theodore C. *Kennedy* (1965).*

Walton, Richard J. *Cold War and Counter-Revolution: The Foreign Policy of Jo F. Kennedy* (1972).

White, Theodore H. *The Making of the President, 1964* (1965).*

———. *The Making of the President, 1968* (1969).*

Wicker, Tom. *JFK and LBJ: The Influence of Personality upon Politics* (1968

NIXON AND WATERGATE

Bernstein, Carl, and Robert Woodward. *All the President's Men* (1974).

Brandon, Henry. *The Retreat of American Power* (1973).*

Chace, James. *A World Elsewhere* (1973).

Dean, John Wesley. *Blind Ambition: The White House Years* (1976).

Gardner, Lloyd C., ed. *The Great Nixon Turnaround* (1973).*

Graubard, Stephen R. *Kissinger: Portrait of a Mind* (1973).

Haldeman, H.R. *The Ends of Power* (1978).

Hoffmann, Stanley. *Primacy or World Order: American Foreign Policy Since the Cold War* (1978).

Kalb, Marvin, and Bernard Kalb. *Kissinger* (1974).

Kissinger, Henry A. *American Foreign Policy: Expanded Edition* (1974).*

Landau, David. *Kissinger: The Uses of Power* (1972).

Magruder, Jeb Stuart. *An American Life* (1974).

Mazo, Earl, and Stephen Hess. *Nixon: A Political Portrait* (1968).

Nixon, Richard M. *RN: The Memoirs of Richard Nixon* (1978).

Phillips, Kevin P. *The Emerging Republican Majority* (1969).

Safire, William L. *Before the Fall!* (1975).

Scammon, Richard M., and Ben J. Wattenberg. *The Real Majority* (1970).

Silk, Leonard. *Nixonomics* (1972).

Sutter, Robert G. *China-Watch: Toward Sino-American Reconciliation* (1978).

Szulc, Tad. *The Illusion of Peace: Foreign Policy in the Nixon Years* (1978).

White, Theodore H., *The Making of the President, 1972* (1973).*

———. *Breach of Faith: The Fall of Richard Nixon* (1975).*

Wills, Gary. *Nixon Agonistes* (1970).

Index

235-237; expansion of, under Johnson, 237-240; rationalized, 238-240; opponents of, 241-242, 244-245; defended in 1967, 246-247; sustained by Nixon's Vietnamization program, 267-269; faces antiwar movement under Nixon, 268-269; termination of, under Ford, 282-283
Villard, Oswald Garrison, 47-48
Volunteers in Service to America (VISTA), 214
Voting Rights Act of 1965, 217, 220

Wake Island, falls to Japanese, 29
Wallace, George C., 217, 252-253, 270, 284
Wallace, Henry A., 52, 68, 74, 85, 87-88
War contracts, 37, 39, 41-42
War Labor Board, 40
War on poverty, under Johnson, 214, 218-219
War Production Board, 35
Warren, Earl, 87, 136-137, 188
Warsaw, captured by Russians, 56
Warsaw Pact, formed, 121
Wartime financing, 37-38
Wartime profits, 39
Wartime prosperity, 37-42
Watergate, break-in at, 271-272; issue of, before Judge Sirica, 273; and Nixon's defense, 274-275; hearings on, 275; and collapse of Nixon's position, 275-279
Water Quality Improvement Act, 259
Watts, Los Angeles, rioting in, 183, 222-223
Wealth in America, concentration of, 172-173
Weapons race, 230
Weaver, Robert C., 217
Weeks, Sinclair, 109-110
Welch, Joseph, 117
Welles, Sumner, 17, 25
West Berlin, 91, 93, 143-144, 229
Western Europe, Soviet threat to, 69, 75-76,

92-95; recovery of, 79; stability of, 229
West Germany, birth of, 75, 91; freed to conduct own policies, 94; determines NATO's objectives in Central Europe, 233
Westmoreland, General William, 247
Wheeling, West Virginia, and McCarthy, 100
White, Theodore, 304
White, William Allen, 12, 17
White, William S., 114-115
Whitetowns, in American cities, 177-179
Wigner, Eugene P., 34-35
Wilkins, Roy, 225
Will, George F., 298
Willkie, Wendell, 51
Wilson, Charles E., of General Electric, 42
Wilson, Charles E., of General Motors, 82, 119
Wilson, Hugh R., 25
Wilson, Woodrow, 2, 5
Women's liberation movement, 225-226
Wood, Robert C., 175-176
Wood, Robert E., 13
Woodward, Bob, 273
World Bank, 78
World commerce, 155
World Court, 3, 4
Wounded Knee, and American Indian Movement, 186

Xuan Thuy, 249

Yahya Khan of Pakistan, 266
Yalta Conference, 63-65, 68
Yalu River, issue of, in Korean War, 103
Yippies, 245, 250
Youth International Party, 245
Yugoslavia, 30, 91, 227

Zaire, and Cuban issue in Africa, 300
Zhukov, General Georgi, 31
Zwicker, General Ralph, 116